Questioning

Geography

QUESTIONING GEOGRAPHY

Fundamental Debates

Edited by
Noel Castree,
Alisdair Rogers
and
Douglas Sherman

Blackwell
Publishing

BLACKWELL PUBLISHING
350 Main Street, Malden, MA 02148-5020, USA
9600 Garsington Road, Oxford OX4 2DQ, UK
550 Swanston Street, Carlton, Victoria 3053, Australia

First published 2005 by Blackwell Publishing Ltd

2   2006

Library of Congress Cataloging-in-Publication Data

Questioning geography : fundamental debates : essays on a contested discipline / edited by Noel Castree, Alisdair Rogers, and Douglas Sherman.
    p. cm.
Includes bibliographical references and index.
ISBN-13: 978-1-4051-0191-2 (hard cover : alk. paper)
ISBN-10: 1-4051-0191-1 (hard cover : alk. paper)
ISBN-13: 978-1-4051-0192-9 (pbk. : alk. paper)
ISBN-10: 1-4051-0192-X (pbk. : alk. paper) 1. Geography. I. Castree, Noel, 1968-
II. Rogers, Alisdair. III Sherman, Douglas Joel, 1949-
G62.Q84 2005
910–dc22

                    2005008544

A catalogue record for this title is available from the British Library.

Set in 10/12.5pt Palatino
by SPI Publisher Services, Pondicherry, India
Printed and bound in India
by Replika Press, Pvt. Ltd

For further information on
Blackwell Publishing, visit our website:
www.blackwellpublishing.com

Contents

List of Contributors   viii
List of Figures   x
List of Tables   xi
Acknowledgements   xii

Introduction: Questioning Geography   1
Douglas Sherman, Alisdair Rogers and Noel Castree

Part I   The 'Nature' of Geography   7

1   **Geography – Coming Apart at the Seams?**   9
    Ron Johnston

2   **A Divided Discipline?**   26
    Heather Viles

3   **What Difference Does Difference Make to Geography?**   39
    Katherine McKittrick and Linda Peake

Part II   Approaches in Geography   55

4   **Is Geography a Science?**   57
    Noel Castree

5   **What Kind of Science Is Physical Geography?**   80
    Stephan Harrison

6   **Beyond Science? Human Geography, Interpretation
    and Critique**   96
    Maureen Hickey and Vicky Lawson

Part III   Key Debates in Geography   115

7   **General/Particular**   117
    Tim Burt

8   **Process/Form**   131
    Bruce L. Rhoads

9   **Representation/Reality**   151
    Matthew Hannah

10   **Meta-Theory/Many Theories**   167
    Michael R. Curry

Part IV   The Practice of Geography   187

11   **Cartography and Visualization**   189
     Scott Orford

12   **Models, Modelling, and Geography**   206
     David Demeritt and John Wainwright

13   **Ethnography and Fieldwork**   226
     Steve Herbert, Jacqueline Gallagher and Garth Myers

14   **Counting and Measuring: Happy Valentine's Day**   241
     Danny Dorling

15   **Theory and Theorizing**   258
     Elspeth Graham

Part V   The Uses of Geography   275

16   **A Policy-Relevant Geography for Society?**   277
     Alisdair Rogers

17   **Whose Geography? Education as Politics**   294
     Noel Castree

Index   308

Contributors

Tim Burt is a Professor in the Department of Geography, Durham University, UK.

Noel Castree is a Professor in the School of Environment and Development, Manchester University, UK.

Michael Curry is an Associate Professor in the Department of Geography, UCLA, California, USA.

David Demeritt is a Senior Lecturer in the Department of Geography, King's College, University of London, UK.

Danny Dorling is a Professor in the Department of Geography, Sheffield University, UK.

Jacqueline Gallagher is a graduate student in the Department of Geography and Geology, Florida Atlantic University, USA.

Elspeth Graham is a Reader in Geography at the School of Geography and Geosciences, University of St Andrews, UK.

Matthew Hannah is a Professor in the Department of Geography, University of Vermont, USA

Stephan Harrison is a Lecturer in the Department of Geography, Exeter University, UK.

Steve Herbert is an Associate Professor in the Department of Geography, Washington University, Seattle, USA.

Maureen Hickey is a graduate student in the Department of Geography, University of Washington, Seattle, USA.

Ron Johnston is a Professor in the School of Geographical Sciences, Bristol University, UK.

Vicky Lawson is a Professor in the Department of Geography, Washington University, Seattle, USA.

Katherine McKittrick is a graduate student in the Women's Studies Program at York University, Scarborough, Canada.

Garth Myers is an Associate Professor in the Department of Geography, University of Kansas, Lawrence, KS, USA.

Scott Orford is a lecturer in the Department of City and Regional Planning, Cardiff University, UK.

Linda Peake is an Associate Professor in the Women's Studies Program, York University, Scarborough, Canada.

Bruce Rhoads is a Professor in the Department of Geography, University of Illinois, Urbana-Champagne, USA.

Alisdair Rogers is a Fellow of Keble College, Oxford University, UK.

Douglas Sherman is a Professor in the Department of Geography, Texas A & M University, College Station, Texas, USA.

Heather Viles is a Reader in the School of Geography and the Environment, Oxford University, UK.

John Wainwright is a Professor in the Department of Geography, King's College, University of London, UK.

Figures

4.1	Two routes to scientific explanation	68
7.1	The relationship between rain gauge altitude and average annual rainfall in the Northern Pennine hills, UK	121
10.1	Berry's cube	169
10.2	Geography and other academic disciplines	170
10.3	Human geography	171
11.1	Part of Dr Snow's map of deaths from cholera, Soho, 1854	191
11.2	[CARTOGRAPHY]^3 – a graphical representation of how maps are used	195
11.3	A view of the Cartographic Data Visualizer (cdv)	198
12.1	A conceptual model of the processes involved in the greenhouse effect	209

Tables

1.1   Journals with most papers published by geographers in
nominations for the RAE 2001 evaluation   15

3.1   Some examples of scales of difference   45

3.2   Some examples of scales of 'inclusions' and 'exclusions'   46

11.1   The relationships between visual variables and the
characteristics of the features to be mapped   197

Acknowledgements

We would like to thank the editorial and production teams at Blackwell publishers, Sarah Falkus, Jane Hotchkiss, Will Maddox, Justin Vaughan, Angela Cohen, Brian Johnson, Katherine Wheatley, Simon Alexander, and especially Kelvin Matthews for seeing the project home. Many thanks also to Susan Dunsmore for copy-editing and to Sara Hawker for proofing. We are grateful for the constructive comments from Rob Kitchin, an anonymous reviewer and our many colleagues. Finally, we wish to thank the contributors for their efforts and for being receptive to our sometimes demanding editorial interventions.

The editors and publisher gratefully acknowledge permission granted to reproduce copyright material in this book:

Fig. 4.1 'Two routes to scientific explanation', from David Harvey, *Explanation in Geography*, (Edward Arnold, 1969). © 1969 by David Harvey. Reprinted with permission of Edward Arnold.

Fig. 10.1 'Traditional Grouping of Dimensions', from B.J.L. Berry, *Annals of the Association of American Geographers*, (Lawrence, Kansas: Allen Press, 1964). Reprinted with permission of Blackwell Publishing.

Fig 10.2 'Geography and other academic disciplines', from O.W. Freeman and H.F. Raup, *Essentials of Geography*, (New York: McGraw-Hill Book Co., 1949).

Fig. 10.3 'Human Geography', from De Blij and Murphy, *Human Geography*, (New York: John Wiley, 2003).

Fig. 11.1   'Part of Dr Snow's map of deaths from cholera, Soho, 1854', from the Department of Epidemiology website, UCLA.

Fig. 11.2   [CARTOGRAPHY][3], from A.M. MacEachren (1994) 'Visualization in modern cartography: setting the agenda', in A.M. MacEachren and D.R.F. Taylor (eds), *Visualization in Modern Cartography*, (Oxford: Pergamon, 1994) © 1994 with permission from Elsevier.

Fig. 11.3   'A view of the Cartographic Data Visualizer' appears by kind permission of Jason Dykes, City University, London.

Every effort has been made to trace copyright holders and to obtain their permission for the use of copyright material. The publisher apologizes for any errors or omissions in the above list and would be grateful if notified of any corrections that should be incorporated in future reprints or editions of this book.

Noel Castree, Alisdair Rogers and Doug Sherman

Introduction
Questioning Geography

Douglas Sherman, Alisdair Rogers and Noel Castree

Upper-level undergraduates and postgraduates taking geography degrees are usually required to take a course unit on the history, nature and philosophy of their subject. For many undergraduates it is a unit to be endured rather than enjoyed. For many postgraduates, by contrast, it is an important part of their journey to becoming professional geographers. Whether you're reading these words because you have to or because you want to, we hope that *Questioning Geography* demonstrates why close scrutiny of our discipline's character is necessary, interesting and even, perhaps, intellectually exciting. Before we explain the book's distinctive approach to its subject matter, let us first remind you why your degree course contains a unit that requires you to consult a book like this one. There are at least two major reasons for such modules.

Most modern university degrees are modular. Students have a lot of choice about the course units they take. The degree of choice typically increases for undergraduates as they move through the successive years of their degree. For postgraduates, meanwhile, the amount of choice depends very much on the master's or doctoral programme in question. While choice is a good thing – it allows students to tailor their geographical education, among other things – it also comes with a risk.

The risk is that students will graduate with no sense of what, if anything, was 'geographical' about their higher education. It is all too easy for students to become so immersed in the specialist knowledges they encounter in different course units that they lose sight of the wood for the proverbial trees. This is the first major reason why most geography degrees have a compulsory unit on the history, nature and philosophy of geography. Without such a unit, professional geographers worry that their students will graduate with no understanding of geography as a whole as opposed to its constituent sub-fields.

The second principal justification for these kinds of units is that they are an effective way of conveying a very important truth: there is more than one way of knowing about the world and not necessarily any single correct way. What do we mean by this? Geographers are in the fortunate position of trying to explain different kinds of phenomena, everything from ecological succession to industrial location and environmental perception. It would be surprising if the assumptions we made about what counts as facts, how causes operate, whether our own values should enter our explanations and other such issues were the same for all conceivable phenomena. What's more, even accounts of the same processes, say, domestic labour by migrant workers, could look very different depending on whether one's understanding was influenced by feminism or mathematical modelling. We don't want to labour these points here, because they are raised again and again by the contributors in their chapters. What is worth remembering is that, in common, with other scholars, geographers regularly interrogate the assumptions contained in their ways of knowing. If they didn't, they'd still be operating with the intellectual tools of bygone eras.

Questioning Geography is intended to offer degree students a fresh perspective on a discipline of unusual intellectual breadth. It is hardly the first book to consider the history, nature and philosophy of geography. But it is the first to approach its subject matter in the way it does. The many rival texts now available seem to us to be split into three rather unsatisfactory kinds. First, there are those that explore geography's development through time, tracing the succession of major 'paradigms' since Western geography was founded as a university subject in the late nineteenth century. Second, most books on the nature, history and philosophy of geography focus on human geography alone. Finally, several of these books discuss geography by way of a survey of its several sub-fields. In the first case the problem is that some of geography's intellectual vitality is lost, as students feel they have to memorize those 'isms' and 'ologies' that have supposedly succeeded each other over time. In the second case the problem (obviously) is that half the discipline is ignored. In the third case the risk is that the broader issues cross-cutting sub-disciplines are not apparent to student readers.

In light of this, *Questioning Geography* tries to do something different. Its starting point is the undeniable fact that geography is a *contested* discipline. Students often think that academic subjects are rather civilized, even dull, places where harmony prevails. The reality is that they are hotbeds of disagreement and dissent. Geography's present and past are a testimony to this fact. For all its internal diversity (both within and between human and physical geography), it remains animated by several fundamental issues that impinge on many areas of the discipline and that cannot be resolved in any straightforward way. These issues concern everything from what geography's subject matter should be to how topically broad it is to its wider social role. These are issues that concern geographers of all stripes (human and physical) and can be articulated as a set of key questions. These questions force all geographers to confront fundamental problems with the discipline as currently organized and practised. They also make us consider possible and probable actions to change geography for the better. Above all, the debates that have congealed around these questions over the years speak to geography's self-reflexive character and intellectual dynamism. Sometimes heated, these debates cut to the heart of what geography is (or should be) about, how it studies the world, and what geographical knowledge is to be used for.

The book's title refers, then, not so much to the questions geographers ask about the world they study as to the questions they ask about the constitution of their discipline. The title is both a statement of fact and an invitation to student readers. As the chapters show, geography has been and remains a discipline prepared to ask tough questions about itself. Accordingly, we want students to feel confident that they can question geography once they know the kinds of questions that are worth asking and the kinds of considered (but rarely consensual) answers that professional geographers have provided.

Each chapter seeks to address a key issue about the way the discipline of geography is organized and practised. In most cases the issue is announced in the title as a question. The chapters do not need to be read sequentially since there is not a consistent 'message' that runs through the book. As editors, we felt it necessary to let contributors offer their own informed discussion of the issues they were asked to discuss. Consequently, each chapter does not in any way offer a 'correct' answer to, or resolution of, the question posed or issue discussed. Rather, contributors were asked to identify the key points of debate, the principal contributions to the debate and their own specific viewpoint on the matter at hand. In this way, we hope, student readers will appreciate that there is no right or wrong answer to the questions posed by contributors. Instead, there are only contests among geographers vying to take geography in the directions that seem to them to be fruitful, whether the issues are philosophical, theoretical, methodological or practical (i.e. the uses of geographical knowledge in society).

Whether you are an undergraduate or a graduate student, we hope that *Questioning Geography* will persuade you that an examination of how geography is organized as a discipline amounts to more than indulgent navel gazing or dull introspection. The book, we hope, conveys some of the key tensions that make geography what it is: an exciting discipline that offers distinctive perspectives on the world yet which progresses (if 'progress' is the word) through self-criticism and honest recognition of its shortcomings. After reading some, or all, of this book, degree-level geographers should understand why the philosophy, history and practice of geography are more than merely 'academic' matters that concern their professors alone.

Though the chapters can be read in any order, we have grouped them into five parts according to broad thematic overlaps. 'The "Nature" of Geography' (Part I), as the scare-quotes suggest, contains chapters that explore how the discipline of geography has been defined and the reasons why it does or does not possess a coherent identity. Ron Johnston, Heather Viles, Katherine McKittrick and Linda Peake, in their respective chapters, together explore some of the fundamental fault-lines that make geography's identity, relative to other subjects, a contested one and they examine whether and how that identity can be changed.

Part II, 'Approaches in Geography', examines the different ways in which geographers have chosen to 'do geography'. Noel Castree's Chapter 4 discusses the venerable issue of whether geography can be considered a 'scientific' field of study. Stephan Harrison, in Chapter 5, discusses this issue in relation to physical geography, where the appellation 'science' still informs the self-understanding of practitioners (unlike human geography where the term 'science' is sometimes treated with a good deal of suspicion). Finally, in Chapter 6, Maureen Hickey and Vicky Lawson discuss the 'post-scientific' approaches increasingly common in human geography but they do so, subversively, by redefining what the still-prized label 'science' means.

In Part III, 'Key Debates in Geography', some fundamental philosophical issues that span both human and physical geography are examined. These issues cut to the heart of both what geographers study and how. Tim Burt, in Chapter 7, considers whether geographers study unique configurations of things or more general phenomena common to many situations. Bruce Rhoads, then, in Chapter 8, examines whether geographers examine visible forms in the landscape, the processes producing them or both. Following this, in Chapter 9, Matthew Hannah debates the hoary question of whether geographers' knowledge is a reflection of an outer reality or else a construction forged by geographers themselves. This relates to the final chapter of this part, by Michael Curry, which looks at the issue of whether multiple perspectives on geographical reality are somehow preferable to those that claim to 'unlock' the world's truths with some sort of single master key.

The book's penultimate part is entitled 'The Practice of Geography'. The chapters in it consider key issues surrounding some of the 'tools of the geographical trade'. These tools are not so much methods of investigating geographical reality, as broad categories of investigative practice. These include cartography and visualization (discussed by Scott Orford in Chapter 11), modelling and prediction (discussed by David Demeritt and John Wainwright in Chapter 12), fieldwork (discussed by Steve Herbert, Jacqueline Gallagher and Garth Myers in Chapter 13), counting and measuring (discussed by Danny Dorling in Chapter 14) and theorizing (discussed by Elspeth Graham in Chapter 15). In each case, the contributors examine the debates on the tools in question.

Finally, the short concluding part discusses 'The Uses of Geography'. In Chapter 16, Alisdair Rogers rehearses the debates over geography's ir/relevance to the formation and implementation of policy measures that improve the human and environmental worlds. Following this, in the final chapter, Noel Castree poses the broader question of who has the right to determine what geography is and should be. He focuses particularly on teaching and in so doing brings the issues home to student readers taking geography degrees. Even though this is the final chapter in the book, we could equally well have started with it and some readers might find that it makes sense to read it first.

Readers should be warned, however, that there is, inevitably, an element of recapitulation throughout the book since the chapters do not have to read in order or as a whole. Each contributor thus assumes little or no prior knowledge, meaning that material dealt with in a certain way in one chapter recurs in other contexts in other chapters. Readers can skip some of this recapitulatory material if they feel confident that have already picked up the necessary information elsewhere in the book.

As editors, we are sure that *Questioning Geography* conveys something of the richness, dynamism and dissent that characterize contemporary geography. Where so many texts on the nature, history and practice of geography end up as rather dry discussions of the discipline's 'nature', we hope here to convey its vitality to student readers. By organizing the book around key questions and issues, our intention is to add bite to students' understanding of the discipline whose future many of them will help make as teachers and researchers.

The 'Nature' of Geography

Geography – Coming Apart at the Seams?

Ron Johnston

Rather than police the margins of the discipline, let's stretch them. Geography is an open, vibrant and exciting place to be.

(Adam Tickell; *RGS Newsletter*, December 2002)

For most outsiders, an encounter with the discipline of geography may suggest that it studies everything, from global environmental change at one extreme to the minutiae of body-space at the other. It spans the physical, environmental and social sciences, and reaches into the humanities too. Nor might it look much like geography as they understand the term and as it is promoted in other contexts. Closer inspection – a list of the modules on offer in most degree programmes, say – may further suggest a lack of coherence around either core themes or methods. Geographers study and write about a lot of different subjects sometimes with few apparent links between many of them. So, is there a specific discipline of geography or does it comprise a group of loosely related specialists?: is whatever once might have held together dissolving so that geography is now coming apart at the seams?

To address that question, this chapter explores the current diversity of geography and what, if anything, holds its practitioners together in an identifiable discipline.[1] Until fairly recently – certainly within my own academic career, now some 40 years long – geographers did proclaim themselves as having a distinctive perspective and substantive focus. During those decades, however, the perspective has fragmented and the focus has virtually disappeared. Having traced those changes, the chapter finishes by asking whether that matters, whether by its very current existence and structure geography performs a valuable role within universities and their wider society. Is a core (an agreed set of basic concepts) necessary, or is a vibrant periphery without an apparent core viable – both intellectually and politically? Do geographers have to agree on a disciplinary mission statement in order to sustain their separate identity (the political project) as well as their academic coherence (the intellectual project)?

'Twas Ever Thus? Geography as a Series of Sub-disciplinary Communities

Has geography always been fragmented and incoherent? Not in its early decades, when those who created the discipline – many not trained as geographers themselves – sought to give it a clear rationale and coherence. The language of that coherence still characterizes much geographic writing, but more as rhetoric than reality.

Geography emerged as an academic discipline in the late nineteenth and early twentieth centuries as a subject bridging the physical and social sciences by studying the interactions between people and their environments. Demand for university courses came from a number of directions: some geographic subject matter was seen as desirable for students of geology and of economics, for example, and teachers were appointed to the relevant university departments. But the main demand, especially in Europe, came from the need for trained geography school teachers. Geography was seen as an important component of an education that promoted citizenship through national and self-awareness: people learned about themselves through contrasts with others. Knowledge of other lands was also used to promote notions of Western superiority, especially when it was linked to imperialism. (On the history of the discipline in several countries, see the essays in Johnston and Claval, 1984, and Dunbar, 2001.)

When established in universities, therefore, geography was promoted as an integrating discipline, bringing together scientific understanding of the natural environment with studies of the use of that resource, as illustrated by patterns of land use and settlement. The core concept which demonstrated this integration was the region, an area of relative uniformity according to selected phenomena: the earth's surface comprised a mosaic of regions, areas with separate physical and human characteristics (at a variety of scales) and the geographer's task was to define and account for that regional pattern.

To produce regional definitions and descriptions geographers drew material from other disciplines. Increasingly, they became interested in that subject matter and started to study some of those topics as ends in themselves. Geography was then divided into two main long-recognized types of study: systematic geography, which investigated individual aspects of the earth's mosaic, such as climate and land use; and regional geography, which drew the various systematic studies together. The latter remained the core geographical concern according to many of the discipline's leaders: every geographer was expected to specialize on (and teach about) a particular region and the systematic studies were seen as secondary, as means to the end rather than as ends in themselves.

This view of the discipline was explicit in *American Geography: Inventory and Prospect*, a volume edited by Preston James and Clarence Jones in the mid-1950s which provided a grand summary of the state of the discipline (James and Jones, 1954). Although each chapter addressed a different systematic component of geography, the editors were certain that the true nature of the discipline was based on the unifying features of the regional concept and cartographic analysis. Some 40 years after this book, a further overview of American geography also contained chapters on systematic sub-disciplines in physical and human geography that again predominated (Gaile and Wilmott, 1989). This time, however, editors could provide neither a concise definition nor a clear synoptic view of the discipline. To them, Geography 'was not bounded' around a core, but held together by an integrative perspective.

Diversity and divergence had replaced disciplinary cohesion around a core focus over the preceding decades, despite attempts to promote unity through the concepts of place, space and environment. Human geographers had increasingly shifted their attention to the social sciences and humanities while physical geographers had built stronger links with environmental scientists – a 'schism [that] undermines the ability of geographers to meaningfully contribute to our understanding of nature–society interactions' (ibid.: xxxi). Meanwhile, 'geographers continue to ply their trade abroad and to attempt regional syntheses, albeit in diminished numbers' (ibid.: xl). But the region as the core concept had been subject to violent attacks from which it had failed to recover (for a review, see Johnston, 1997), and the search for alternative synthetic cores (as in Abler et al., 1992) had failed to either convince or deliver.

Academic Disciplines and Communities

Geography now comprises a wide range of systematic studies which have one or more of environment, place and space as their foundational concepts (or organizing themes) but whose external links to other disciplines are sometimes at least as strong as their ties with other fields within their home discipline. As Heather Viles suggests in Chapter 2, the split between physical and human geography has widened in recent years, as physical geographers ally themselves increasingly with other environmental scientists and participate in large projects aimed at eluci- dating past, present and future environments through mathematical modelling and laboratory analyses of physical, chemical and biological processes allied to large collaborative data-collection programmes. Human geographers, meanwhile, have explored a variety of approaches within the social sciences and the humanities, employing a range of epistemologies, ontologies and methodologies which apparently have little in common with each other, let alone with those deployed by physical geographers. The discipline is divided into two very substantial, but separate, sub-disciplines, each of which is further subdivided into a number of separate fields. Many of these seem to operate quasi- independently within the holding companies provided by university departments of geography.

Appreciation of the nature of research within these sub-disciplines and their subsidiary fields can be approached by visualizing the discipline as a hierarchy of communities of practitioners. All academic activity takes place within established paradigms, blueprints which define what is undertaken through general agreement regarding both accepted know- ledge – that accepted as (at least provisional) understandings and ex- planations of particular subject matter – and methods of extending that knowledge. Individuals join academic disciplines via socialization into those paradigms, through undergraduate and postgraduate training dur- ing which they learn about the accepted knowledge (the 'facts', or prob- lems that have been solved) and the ways of advancing knowledge (methods for tackling unresolved problems). When they have joined the community – having served an apprenticeship and been accepted into it as somebody who will contribute to further advancement of knowledge – they undertake their own research, which is published and adds to the store of knowledge on which future generations draw.

These communities of scholars are hierarchically arranged. At the top is the discipline with which individuals have affiliated, and with which they both identify and are identified by others: most work in a university department of geography and their training involved gaining a degree in geography. Within that large community, however, they will specialize, having decided at some point in their training – almost certainly before they became a postgraduate – to be either a physical or a human geog- rapher and, within each, to associate with a specialist sub-discipline, such as geomorphology or economic geography. That will not have been the end of the choices, however: within their chosen sub-discipline they have elected for a particular field of activity – the study of manufacturing or service industries within economic geography, perhaps – and a mode of addressing problems within it. In that area of work there will probably be only a relatively small group of others addressing related problems, a community of cognate researchers (perhaps spread widely over space) interested in what the others are doing, in reading their research findings and sharing their own with them.

These small communities of researchers have been likened to villages by Clifford Geertz (1983). For many (even most) geographers, their intra-village research links may extend well beyond the formal boundaries of their academic discipline, and their interactions may be as much (if not more) with scholars affiliated with other disciplines as with their own: most geographers who emphasize space and place in the study of elections, for example, interact more with political scientists, sociologists and statisticians than with geographers working in other specialist fields. Many individual geographers belong to a number of overlapping research communities, participating in a wide range of conferences and other meetings and both reading and contributing to a broad conspectus of research literature. Some operate contemporaneously in more than one community; others move communities as their interests change. The communities themselves may wax and wane as interest in their work grows or declines. And there are continuing inter-community as well as intra-community debates over the best ways forward, on what should be accepted as useful knowledge and how research should be undertaken.

All disciplines are divided into such communities and sub-communities: geography is by no means peculiar in this regard. Where geography is distinct, perhaps, is in the breadth of its subject matter and the range of very different communities co-existing under the disciplinary umbrella. In part, this reflects its origins as a discipline whose subject matter embraced the natural and human environments and their interactions, and whose core concerns – space, place and environment – can be applied to a plethora of subject matter, all also studied in one or more other disciplines. The potential range of cross-disciplinary contacts for geographers is large and recent decades have seen an increasing number of them being realized, while links with their own disciplinary peers have weakened: for many geographers, the focus of their intellectual projects is outside the formal discipline of geography as constituted in the universities, but their political projects – their recruitment of students to sustain their activities – remain centred on departments of geography.

Contemporary Fragmentation within Geography

The advancement of both science itself and individual careers within disciplinary communities involves the conduct and reporting of research. Knowledge production is a shared activity: by publishing their findings (and their critiques of others' work) researchers contribute to the validation and extension of knowledge. The chosen media for publication – perhaps after less formal discussions in group meetings, seminars and conference sessions – are predominantly academic journals. Some of them – especially those published by the learned societies that promote disciplines as wholes – are relatively general, attracting papers from a range of specialisms within the discipline and relaying them to wider audiences. But most journals are specialized, aimed at workers within, at best, a few communities only: to reach the potential audience for their findings, researchers publish in journals that those with shared interests regularly consult. Communities have their own journals, so that the discipline's contemporary fragmentation is readily appreciated through investigating its journals.

A clear difference between human and physical geography is the general location of the journals they contribute to. Many of those favoured by human geographers contain geography in the title, for example, *Economic Geography*, *Political Geography*, or the *Journal of Transport Geography*: in most, the majority of papers are written by geographers, defined as those currently affiliated to a university department of geography. This does not mean that human geographers do not publish in inter-disciplinary journals, or in those dedicated largely to other disciplines – though examples of the latter are relatively rare, save in some specialized areas. But it does mean that human geography is to a considerable extent a relatively closed set of fields and associated communities. This is much less so with physical geography. Few of the journals they regularly contribute to are identified as geography journals, although a number are edited by physical geographers. Unlike their human geographer colleagues, physical geographers are much more likely to publish in inter-disciplinary science journals (many more of them American in origin), where their contributions form only a minority of the contents.

This difference between human and physical geography is further illustrated by Table 1.1, which lists the 23 most-cited journals by members of geography departments in the UK 2001 Research Assessment Exercise (RAE). This exercise is used to rate all departments on a seven-point scale for the allocation of unhypothecated government research funding.[2] All

Table 1.1 Journals with most papers published by geographers in nominations for the RAE 2001 evaluation.

Journal	Number of citations
Environment and Planning A	141
Transactions, Institute of British Geographers	102
*Earth Surface Processes and Landforms	97
*Hydrological Processes	90
*Quaternary Science Reviews	60
Environment and Planning D: Society and Space	59
*Journal of Quaternary Science	57
*Geomorphology	57
*International Journal of Remote Sensing	51
*Holocene	50
Journal of Historical Geography	49
Regional Studies	46
Area	44
Urban Studies	41
Geoforum	41
Political Geography	38
Applied Geography	34
*Progress in Physical Geography	33
*Journal of Hydrology	33
Geographical Journal	32
Progress in Human Geography	28
Annals of the Association of American Geographers	24
Economic Geography	20

Journals with a* preceding their title are identified here as nominated almost exclusively by physical geographers.

individuals identified as members of a department's research staff have to identify four publications which illustrate their best work in the preceding five years. Most of the items submitted by geographers (91 per cent) were journal articles, with a total of 3870 listed (for further details, see Johnston, 2003a.) The journals that were only cited by physical geographers are indicated by an *: very few of them published in the other journals – including the general geography journals (*Transactions of the Institute of British Geographers, Annals of the Association of American Geographers* and *Geoforum*).

Of the journals cited by physical geographers only one, *Progress in Physical Geography*, is an explicitly geographical journal, although only

67 per cent of the papers that it published in 2001 were authored by geographers (as defined above) as were 60 per cent in 2002. *Earth Surface Processes* was established by an Institute of British Geographers Study Group – the British Geomorphological Research Group – but again geographers authored only 67 per cent of its papers in 2001 (Volume 26). Both journals are in effect multi-disciplinary. The other six are explicitly so, and are journals in which papers from geographers form a minority.

Physical geographers, then, are putting their best work in journals outside their own discipline, sub-discipline or even field, aiming at audiences of topical specialists within the environmental sciences among whom physical geographers are a minority only. Human geographers, on the other hand, are placing much more of their best material in geography journals, whether those serving the discipline as a whole (within which human geography predominates), those aimed relatively widely within the sub-discipline of human geography (such as the *Environment and Planning* journals), or those aimed at a specific topical field only (such as *Journal of Historical Geography* and *Political Geography*).

Geography is divided into two separate sub-disciplines – human and physical – each of which is fragmented into a number of distinct fields. Each of those fields operates to a considerable extent as a separate academic community with its own norms, practices and debates; only occasionally do they come together in wider discussions beyond the initial training stages. In addition, physical and human geographers interact beyond their disciplinary boundaries in somewhat different ways. Thus it might be concluded that the academic discipline of geography is little more than a holding company for researchers who operate in quasi-independent communities, some of which are populated mainly by outsiders.

Why Fragment and with What Consequences?

The reasons for fragmentation within all academic disciplines are relatively straightforward to discern – and geography is by no means different in being divided into separate intellectual communities. The volume of knowledge is expanding, much more rapidly than the number of academics – in part because of the pressures for productivity and in part because of the major technological and other advances which have not only made some (especially technical) practices much easier but also facilitated questions being addressed that were previously unanswerable. It is impossible for individuals to assimilate that volume of knowledge – or even become generally acquainted with it, as were the polymaths of old: today, they must specialize in just a section of knowledge if they are to keep on top of the amount published annually. Furthermore, in many fields within the sub-disciplines the amount of technical knowledge needed for state-of-the-art research calls for substantial periods of training: even then, in many cases no one individual can master it all (or have the needed technology available) so working in groups with a specialized division of labour becomes the norm. As a consequence, some become specialists in fields that are much wider than geography. This has especially been the case in the past 30 years with both remote sensing and GIS, technologies that facilitate many advances in geographic research, in which geographers have played leading roles in developing applications and for which geography departments provide much of the basic training for potential users. Both fields have their own learned societies, journals and conferences in which geographers are a prominent minority, with many of them identifying themselves professionally with those specialist fields rather than with geography, in whose university departments they work: their intellectual projects spread well beyond their political milieux.

Such reasons for fragmentation are common to virtually all disciplines, certainly in the sciences. There is, however, a further reason for fragmentation within human geography, which it shares with other social sciences though not the environmental sciences. In the latter, there is general agreement regarding the nature of science as knowledge production: they share a world-view which privileges observation and measurement, and defines additions to knowledge as statements regarding how the world works that can be validated and replicated by comparable experimentation. Although that world-view, with its associated epistemology and ontology, is shared by some human geographers, others of their colleagues reject it. For them, there is no 'reality' independent of the observers: their science involves studying, appreciating (but rarely explaining and never predicting), and relating the actions of knowing subjects. They deploy separate epistemologies and ontologies from those applied by both physical geographers as well as some human geographers – according to Sheppard (1995), the latter are divided into 'spatial analysts' and 'social theorists' – and, in general, study particular subject matter: cultural geography, for example, is predominantly the preserve of 'social theorists' in Sheppard's terms.

For these additional reasons, geography appears to be an even more fragmented discipline than many others, despite many claims that it has three basic concepts at its core – space, place and environment – and remains one of the few disciplines that provides such a wide range of teaching and initial professional training across the sciences and social sciences. But, it is frequently claimed, there is no core, no integrating foundational concept with the disappearance of the region from that position – and of the map as the predominant geographical 'tool'. Certainly there are attempts at integration: many physical geographers, for example, combine with others in building models of environmental systems, of especial value in assessing contemporary changes and their likely impacts. And the boundaries between fields are porous, at least for some workers. But the overall impression remains: geography is an umbrella organization with a lot of separate components having relatively little in common with regard to their research agenda, even though they form the parts of generally offered degree programmes.

What are the consequences of this fragmentation? One major associated problem is a lack of appreciation outside the discipline as to what geographers do, an issue perhaps more problematic for them than for those in some other disciplines (history or physics, say) because of the general association of geography with a particular subject matter that is now, at best, only on the margins of the academic discipline's concerns. As noted earlier, in the 1950s two terms were key to geographers' definitions of their subject matter and their approach – the region and the map. Although region is still commonly used by geographers, defining and accounting for regions are no longer the dominant activities: knowing what is where may be central to vernacular understandings of geography, but such background information is sometimes of only marginal relevance to fields within the academic discipline. Maps, too, have been marginalized: there is little training in map construction and use in geography degree programmes, and many pieces of geographical writing see no need for cartographic illustration. Map-making skills have moved from the field and drawing-board to the laboratory and keyboard, involving members of a separate profession using remotely-sensed imagery, geographical positioning systems and computers. So too have the production of maps to display patterns of interest to geographers: standard computer packages provide geographers with illustrative material without any deployment of pen and ink. (On the contemporary use of maps in geography – especially human geography – see Dorling, 1998; Martin, 2000; Wheeler, 1998.)

Political and intellectual projects

Given the absence of a core to the discipline and a definition that can embrace the great variety of activities now undertaken under geography's academic umbrella, two potential, interlinked, problems arise. The first concerns political projects, and the second intellectual projects.

Regarding political projects, few academic disciplines can feel entirely secure within the rapidly changing map of knowledge: there is always the fear that their approaches will be rendered obsolete by developments elsewhere, that their utility (however defined) will recede, and that the demand for student places on undergraduate degrees and postgraduate programmes will decline. The discipline has to be seen – and must therefore portray itself – as 'relevant': the knowledge it produces must add value to the society that pays for it, and students must see the potential (for their careers as well as their roles as citizens) to be derived from obtaining qualifications in it. Geographers, like the members of all other disciplinary communities, must defend their territory and promote their importance.

Such a political project needs an associated intellectual project – or at least it probably has a better chance of success if it has one. To some extent, the existence of geography as an academic discipline with a presence in many universities is a self-sustaining enterprise – as long as students are enrolling, and then getting jobs (whatever the occupations and their relevance to having studied geography), the political project may be relatively unimportant. But complacency is rarely sensible. The discipline has to retain an appearance of vitality and relevance. How does it do that? How does it present an intellectual project that will sustain its political goals?

The answer to this varies from context to context, and can be briefly illustrated by three cases from different countries. In the United Kingdom, geography has been a strong discipline in the country's secondary (high) schools for over a century, with large numbers of students studying it among their subjects in the public examinations that precede university entrance. For much of the twentieth century, university geography departments could readily fill their places with students who were well grounded in the discipline (as it was practised then), many of whom went back to the schools as geography teachers after graduation (see Johnston, 2003b). The flow of students remains fairly strong in the early twenty-first century, although few graduates now become schoolteachers. But several departments have experienced recruiting difficulties recently and some have been closed. The political project to defend geography in the universities involves defending its presence in the schools. Without such a defence, the discipline may wither in the universities: fewer students means less income and decreased viability for geography departments (Cooke, 2002). This is the situation that has evolved over recent decades in Australia, where few independent departments of geography are now to be found in the universities. Instead, geography has been merged into multi-disciplinary programmes, from which its name may be absent, and a small number of geographers are left with a difficult political task (Holmes, 2002).

If the political project faces no major problems regarding viability, an associated intellectual project may be less crucial. The flowering of so many quasi-independent fields within British geography departments in recent years (especially within human geography) may have been substantially facilitated by the ease of attracting students: academic geographers could follow their research agenda wherever they led them, irrespective of the impact on the discipline's coherence, because there were students ready to follow the lead. But where that is not the case, an intellectual project is necessary.

This has certainly been the situation in the United States where, in contrast to the British experience, geography has been weak in the country's high schools and is absent from a majority of the country's universities. Very few students have any experience of geography beyond basic classes in primary schools, and therefore do not proceed to university intending to read for a degree in the discipline. University geography departments thus have to attract students through the quality and perceived value of their courses. While the region was at the core of the discipline's scholarship, this was most commonly done by departments offering introductory courses in world regional geography, hoping to convince at least some of the takers to opt for more courses in systematic subjects, and perhaps proceed to graduate school for a full training in the discipline. More recently, the focus of the attractive force has changed. As Hill and LaPrairie (1989: 26) put it:

> Americans, consummate pragmatists, will judge geography by what it proves it can do to help them improve their lives and their worlds, as they define them. Significant research will be the major criterion of status in academe. Teaching quality will count with students at all levels.

Increasingly, those high-quality courses are being offered in technical fields – notably Geographical Information Science – which offer skills in high demand in the labour market: students come to geography because getting those skills brings labour market advantages, and surveys in the mid-1990s showed that increasingly departments of geography are hiring individuals who can teach them (NAS-NRC, 1997). At the same time, geography is being promoted as a research discipline that deploys those skills in a wide variety of arenas, including studies of environmental processes and society–nature interactions, plus 'homeland security' (Cutter et al., 2003).

The existence of a political project – defending and advancing the interests of university departments of geography, and thus of geographers – thus stimulates thoughts about an intellectual project as a foundation for the political lobbying: geography needs to prove its relevance in certain arenas. The chosen intellectual project may not be supported by all, of course: there are contests over the technical focus currently deployed in the United States, for example, and the consequent down-playing of other activities, notably those involving 'social theorist' human geographers (Johnston, 2000).

Conclusion: Does Fragmentation Matter?

Contemporary academic disciplines are necessarily fragmented into spe-cialist sub-disciplines and fields: without it, scientific progress would be substantially hindered. Fragmentation can create problems, however, since it can readily stimulate centrifugal forces that are much stronger than any countering centripetal forces. Individual academics – in our case, geographers – are drawn to work in small communities, many of which are relatively isolated from other communities within their discip-line, and indeed may have more contacts without than within their parent discipline. When this happens, disciplinary cohesion declines. Individuals identify with it because it was the focus of their training and provides them with a career, but their scholarly interests mean they have more in common with people having other identifications than with members of their own discipline as defined in the academic division of labour.

Whether such fragmentation and centrifugal change are detrimental to a discipline, and whether this is a particular problem for geography and geographers, are moot points. For three physical geographers, such frag-mentation within geomorphology has resulted in a very significant change in the nature of work in their field (Smith et al., 2002). The shift from denudation chronologies to process-related studies initiated in the 1960s was intended to provide a sounder basis for appreciating long-term landscape change. Instead, there has been what they term a 'diaspora' as various groups of physical geographers have 'become more closely allied with other professions and increasingly distanced from the mainstream' (ibid.: 414). Indeed, in their view the mainstream is drying up: work deploying process studies as the basis to landscape appreciation has resulted in 'researchers certain that they know the answers, but possibly ignorant of the questions' since they invariably start with the processes they wish to understand rather than the landscape changes they wish to explain. For them:

> If geomorphologists ignore their central role in the study and understand-
> ing of landscape, there is the danger that for all their short-term appeal, our
> new clothes might turn out to resemble those of the emperor. Moreover, as
> we discard our traditional garments, others are quickly coming behind,
> trying them on and finding that they fit quite well! (ibid.: 414)

Clearly, to them, a discipline – or sub-discipline – has to have a central purpose that distinguishes it from others, which for geomorphology should be the explanation of landscape change. Without that central purpose, fragmentation into specialist sub-communities is likely to lead to, at best, inter-disciplinary competition and, at worst, disciplinary decay: no core means, ultimately, no future because no distinctiveness.

At present, therefore, geography is considerably fragmented. It is a discipline that embraces a wide range of disparate intellectual projects which, whatever their separate value, do not apparently cohere around key disciplinary concepts and goals. One of geographers' long-established concepts, the region, has sometimes been defined as a whole that is greater than the sum of its parts, an organic unity that reflects the interacting diversity within places. The region may well have been a useful metaphor for geography itself for some time: it isn't now.

Geography as a fragmented academic discipline lacks a coherent intel-lectual project. Rather, it is a congeries of disparate projects that share a dwelling but not a home. Furthermore, geography as an academic dis-cipline bears little resemblance to geography as recognized subject matter outside the universities. If the former discipline is healthy and vibrant, this may not be a problematic situation. But if it is under threat, then it needs a political project to defend it – which may call for an intellectual project which rejects some of the fragmentation and seeks to impose and imbue a common purpose.

But should that common purpose mean a coherent core and adherence to a dominant disciplinary project that is more constraining than enab-ling? Should geographers, as Clayton (1985) advised, restrict their range of activity – 'do less to do anything better'? Should such retrenchment, as Smith et al. (2002) argue, refocus on certain traditional concerns – defined as much as anything by the spatial scale of their investigations? Or should they, as Tickell suggests in the epigram to this chapter, continue to let as many flowers bloom as seeds are fertilized, to continue pressing against (even beyond) the sub-disciplinary research frontiers in order to advance knowledge? For the discipline as a whole, if Clayton's advice were followed, this could be the prelude not only to interminable and unproductive debates about what is and isn't geography (thereby potentially limiting academic freedom) but also to disciplinary stagnation. For individuals, specialization is clearly absolutely necessary, and each university department will undoubtedly have to decide to concentrate its human, technical and other resources in order to reap their potential, but within those parameters Tickell's advice is surely the most sensible: researchers should develop skills and pursue research interests that they perceive as best for the advancement of knowledge, and which are recognized as such within wider intellectual communities. If topics like landscape change are ignored by geographers, then if they are important enough scholars will return to and reinvigorate them (and will it matter whether they are geographers?).

Will accepting this path mean the absence of a disciplinary core? Yes, certainly sometimes, and perhaps for most of the time. Some think that the current absence of a clearly defined, commonly agreed core is unfortunate with regard to geography's political project (for example, Martin, 2002). And yet there will always be elements of a distinctive core. To deploy another geographical metaphor, the practice of geography, like any other discipline, can be likened to a major river. All of the water it carries to the sea comes from defined catchments; in its middle reaches, the separate streams combine in a single channel; and in its lower reaches braiding is common, as different segments pursue their own course, occasionally recombining. For geography, the catchments are the origins of their students, the middle-reach channels are the undergraduate and postgraduate programmes within which new geographers are socialized into the discipline; and the lower-reach braiding reflects the specialist sub-disciplines and fields into which researchers migrate – occasionally recombining with those from other channels as their interests converge (for a time at least). Those braided channels form the contemporary intellectual project that continually renews the vitality of the degree programmes (a form of reverse flow unknown to hydrologists?!). The political project for geographers involves sustaining the health of the entire river basin.

ESSAY QUESTIONS AND FURTHER READING

1   Is fragmentation into specialized sub-disciplines a necessary consequence of geography's expansion in recent decades? Stimulating material for use in answering this question can be found in Clayton (1985), Gregory et al.

(2002), Dear (1988), Thrift and Walling (2000) and Thrift (2002). These authors address the issue from the perspectives of both physical and human geography. You might also reflect upon the organization of the course in your own department.

2   Is the future of geography its demise as a separate academic discipline? The same sources are relevant to this question. You could also follow the debate initiated by Thrift (2002) in a series of papers in the journal *Geoforum*.

NOTES

1   The original (pre-edited) version of this chapter contained illustrative material and quotations to sustain the arguments developed therein. Copies of that original can be obtained from the author at the School of Geographical Sciences, University of Bristol, UK.

2   An eighth point (6*) was added in 2003, without any further evaluation and three of the top-graded departments (5*) in 2001 were promoted to this new level.

REFERENCES

Abler, R.F., Marcus, M.G. and Olson, J.M. (eds) (1992) *Geography's Inner Worlds.* Rutgers University Press, New Brunswick, NJ.

Buttimer, A. (1993) *Geography and the Human Spirit.* Johns Hopkins University Press, Baltimore, MD.

Clayton, K.M. (1985) The state of geography. *Transactions of the Institute of British Geographers* NS **10**, 5–16.

Cooke, R.U. (2002) Presidential address. *The Geographical Journal* **168**, 260–263.

Cutter, S.E., Richardson, D.B. and Wilbanks, T.J. (eds) (2003) *The Geographical Dimensions of Terrorism.* Routledge, London.

Dear, M. (1988) The postmodern challenge: reconstructing human geography. *Transactions of the Institute of British Geographers* NS **13**, 262–274.

Dorling, D. (1998) Human cartography: when is it good to map? *Environment and Planning A* **30**, 277–289.

Dunbar, G.S. (ed.) (2001) *Geography: Discipline, Profession and Subject since 1870.* Kluwer, Dordrecht.

Gaile, G.L. and Willmott, C.J. (1989) Introduction: the field of geography. In Gaile, G.L. and Willmott, C.J. (eds) *Geography in America.* Bobbs Merrill, Columbus, OH, pp. xxiv–xliv.

Geertz, C. (1983) *Local Knowledge: Further Essays in Interpretive Anthropology.* Basic Books, New York.

Gregory, K.J., Gurnell, A.M. and Petts, G.E. (2002) Restructuring physical geography. *Transactions of the Institute of British Geographers* NS **27**, 136–154.

Hill, A.D. and LaPrairie, L.A. (1989) Geography in American education. In Gaile, G.L. and Willmott, C.J. (eds) *Geography in America*. Bobbs Merrill, Columbus, OH, pp. 1–26.

Holmes, J.H. (2002) Geography's emerging cross-disciplinary links: process, causes, outcomes and challenges. *Australian Geographical Studies* **40**, 2–20.

James, P.E. and Jones, C.F. (eds) (1954) *American Geography: Inventory and Prospect*. Syracuse University Press, Syracuse, NY.

Johnston, R.J. (1997) *Geography and Geographers: Anglo-American Human Geography since 1945*. Arnold, London.

Johnston, R.J. (2000) Intellectual respectability and disciplinary transformation? *Environment and Planning A* **32**, 971–990.

Johnston, R.J. (2003a) Geography: a different sort of discipline? *Transactions of the Institute of British Geographers* NS **28**, 133–141.

Johnston, R.J. (2003b) The institutionalisation of geography as an academic discipline. In Johnston, R.J. and Williams, M. (eds) *A Century of British Geography*. Oxford University Press for the British Academy, Oxford, pp. 45–90.

Johnston, R.J. and Claval, P. (eds) (1984) *Geography since the Second World War: An International Survey*. Croom Helm, London.

Martin, R.L. (2000). In memory of maps. *Transactions of the Institute of British Geographers* NS **25**, 3–6.

Martin, R.L. (2002) Geography and *Transactions*: some valedictory reflections. *Transactions of the Institute of British Geographers* NS **27**, 387–390.

NAS-NRC (1997) *Rediscovering Geography: New Relevance for Science and Society*. National Research Council, Washington, DC.

Sheppard, E.S. (1995) Dissenting from spatial analysis. *Urban Geography* **16**, 283–303.

Smith, B.J., Warke, P.A. and Whalley, W.B. (2002) Landscape development, collective amnesia and the need for integration in geomorphological research. *Area* **33**, 409–418.

Thrift, N. (2002) The future of geography. *Geoforum* **33**, 291–299.

Thrift, N. and Walling, D. (2000) Geography in the UK, 1996–2000. *Geographical Journal* **166**, 96–124.

Wheeler, J.O. (1998) Mappophobia in geography? 1980–1996. *Urban Geography* **19**, 1–5.

Whittlesey, D.F. (1954) The regional concept and the regional method. In James, P.E. and Jones, C.F. (eds) *American Geography: Inventory and Prospect*. Syracuse University Press, Syracuse, NY, pp. 19–69.

A Divided Discipline?

Heather Viles

'Physical geographers are from Mars, Human geographers are from Venus'. Discuss.[1]

Geography is in an unusual position. Along with a few other subjects such as psychology and archaeology, it straddles the divide between the physical (or natural) sciences and the social sciences. This position can be seen as, on the one hand, geography's unique and vital strength and, on the other, a grave impediment or problem for the subject. Many geographers over many years have argued that the bridging role of geography is an essential and important one, and that human and physical geographers should unite in trying to achieve a more successful, more useful synthetic study of natural and human relations on the earth. The quotation with which I start this chapter is a modification of the title of a popular book *Men Are from Mars, Women Are from Venus* (Gray, 1992). It presents a caricature of the alternative view of many other geographers, i.e. that human and physical geographers are worlds apart, and unable to provide any meaningful dialogue across the divide. In this chapter I aim to examine the nature, causes and consequences of the division of geography into two potentially incompatible components, and to investigate to what extent such a division can and should be overcome.

The divide between the arts and the sciences has long been recognized, debated and analysed. In 1959 C.P. Snow wrote a polemical essay entitled 'The Two Cultures' in which he bemoaned the increasing gulf between scientists and what he called 'literary intellectuals' within Britain. Arts-based academics, in Snow's analysis, are unwilling and unable to comprehend recent scientific advances, and scientists are dismissive of the soft and imprecise research undertaken in the humanities. Following Snow's work, there have been discussions about how real such a gulf is, how it might be bridged and, indeed, to what extent it needs to be. For example, the differences between the sciences and the arts (broadly defined to encompass all 'non-science' modes of understanding) were hyped up during the so-called 'Science Wars' of the 1990s. In books, articles and in the pages of newspapers, 'hard' scientists traded blows with sociologists of science, post-structuralists, feminists and post-colonial scholars among others. These critics argued that conventional models and practices of science commonly ignore some crucial questions about what knowledge is important, how it is produced and who is involved in producing it (Ziman, 2000; Sardar and Van Loon, 2002). For their part, the hard scientists challenged what they regarded as the irresponsibility of questioning the power of reason and the sanctity of scientific claims in the face of real-world problems such as HIV/AIDS or global warming. Skirmishes across the divide have led to important debates about the social accountability of science. More recently, Tony Becher and Paul Trowler in their book *Academic Tribes and Territories* (2001) have made a more sophisticated analysis of the differences be-tween academics of all types. They identify the development of distinct-ive academic cultures associated with different academic communities (tribes) who deal with very different academic ideas (territories). In their analysis, academic studies can be categorized on hard/soft and pure/applied axes, leading to a more nuanced series of distinctions than the bipolar arts/sciences divide presented by Snow. The tribes stake out their territories on the landscape of knowledge, with some being more open and diffuse, while others are close-knit and closed. Becher and Trowler believe that understanding the differences between diverse approaches to knowledge should go some way towards bridging the gaps.

Because physical geographers are scientists who largely study natural phenomena, and human geographers generally study human communi-ties, geography as a whole spreads over the divide between the sciences and the arts, in terms of both subject matter and approaches to study (or in Becher and Trowler's terms, tribes and territories). Is this good for the discipline as a whole or not? Is the gulf between the two sides getting wider? It might seem quite difficult to understand why these questions are so important to geographers that they have been regularly debated in the pages of geographical journals for many years, but they matter for a range of reasons. First, in the eyes of many geographers, the relationship between people and the environment, humans and nature is the funda-mental focus for geography as a subject. Thus, if physical and human geography are really incompatible and unable to communicate, then the 'heart' of geography is under attack. Second, there are challenges to geography as a discipline in terms of funding and recruitment of staff and students. Divisions between the two major parts of the discipline can be seen as a source of weakness, making such threats more acute.

The third reason why it matters may seem less important at first. Physical and human geographers have a shared heritage in terms of their disciplinary history, which many would be sad to see come to an end. Looking at some of the famous early works in geography, such as Mary Somerville's book *Physical Geography* (written in 1848), it is clear that, for many nineteenth-century geographers, physical geography provided a major foundation for human geography. The discipline's founders, the likes of Friedrich Ratzel, W.M. Davis, Paul Vidal de la Blache and Halford Mackinder, all regarded the unity of geography as essential. Many of the concepts used by geographers in the past to provide some shape or structure to the discipline, such as regions, landscape, and systems presented a clear vision of how human and physical components were interlinked. In academic circles, as in other walks of life and their institutions, such traditions and communities matter even if they cannot always be defended on grounds of utility and practicality.

How Divided are Physical and Human Geography?

The degree to which human and physical geography is divided, and the extent to which any such division has waxed or waned cannot be established in any straightforward way. The academic discipline of geography is both diverse and dynamic, and everyone (whether viewing the subject from within or without) will have a subtly different perspective on what the relationship looks like. Geography has its own geography, by which I mean that it takes on very different forms, and has different challenges, in different countries. What we might say about geography in the UK may have very little relevance to geography in the USA or China or the Czech Republic, even in today's highly interconnected world. For example, in the Netherlands there has always been a clear demarcation between physical and human geography worlds, with separate chairs and two versions of their national geography journal. Similarly, the Swedish journal *Geografiska Annaler* has long had two series: one covering human geography and one dealing with physical geography.

Bearing such points in mind, there is plenty of evidence to support the claim that there is increasing tension or division between physical and human geographers. Some of it is expressed in print (see, for example, Gober, 2000; Thrift, 2002), but much of it takes the form of anecdotes, conversations in conference halls, clashes in departmental committees etc. But is the divide between the scientific and social science/humanities components of geography really ever-widening? At this point it is worth pausing to consider how much these 'signs of increasing tension' and 'clashes' are real and deep-seated. What evidence is used to back up these claims? Why are geographers publishing such statements? We might be able to make a plausible case that there are actually many signs of increasing conciliation between physical and human geography, focusing in detail on human–environment relations (Turner, 2002). The point is that it is by no means clear that geography is irredeemably divided, and that students should be alert to the evidence people use and their motives for making statements about the future of the subject.

However great the division, its causes and/or symptoms include the different philosophical and methodological positions often adopted by the two sides, the sometimes radically different subject matter, and the division of many courses and even departments. For understandable reasons, the philosophies and methodologies appropriate to studying the natural world may differ from those relevant to the lives and minds of human beings. While laws and causation seem applicable to the former, motives, intentions, beliefs and values are less easily explained in natural science terms. One might reasonably ask different kinds of questions about coasts and tufa than about domestic workers or landscape paintings. Although many epistemologies have been shared, such as positivism and realism, these differences have often been easy to caricature. At worst, physical geographers are depicted as naïve positivists who expect reality to fit their models and can only deal with things that can be measured and counted. By the same token, human geographers can be stereotyped as other-worldly Marxists or postmodernists who spend endless time worrying about philosophical issues without ever doing anything real. At worst (or best depending on how you look at it) physical geography papers are rife with technical jargon and a barrage of quantitative information and analyses. Conversely, at worst, or best, human geography papers descend into a convoluted psychobabble replete with the current buzzwords and phrases, arcane references and so many long words that the authors' spell-checkers must burn out. What is often not fully appreciated, is that these differences in approach and language arise from the different sorts of questions with which we engage as geographers.

Looking at subject matter, we might argue that there is virtually no common ground between, for example, research on self-organized behaviour in meandering river channels and that on the socio-spatial boundaries of orthodox Jewish communities, articles on which both appeared in an issue of the *Transactions of the Institute of British Geographers* (see Hooke, 2003; Valins, 2003). As Nick Clifford puts it in a commentary on the future of geography:

> Who but the geographers would seriously attempt to sustain a dialogue, let alone a working relationship, between researchers into cosmogenic nuclides and the commodity chain of cut flowers? Yet try we do, and, if this is not to look increasingly foolhardy, it must, then be turned into some kind of virtue. (2002: 433)

However, looking more deeply at these pairs of topics (meandering rivers and orthodox Jewish communities; cosmogenic nuclides and cut flowers), it is probably true that there are some common underpinnings – they all deal with space and time, place and context in some shape or form, for example. They might all be analysed through maps, or based on evidence gained from work in the field. So, what appear to be randomly diverse topics may share some things. The key point, however, is that the differences between them (in terms of techniques used, types of research needed, intellectual context) can often appear very real and very large.

Divergent subject matter and approaches in physical and human geography are perhaps also reflected where scholars choose to publish. As both Rob Ferguson (2003) and Ron Johnston (2003) point out, human and physical geographers have very different publication strategies. By analysing recent work by UK geographers, Johnston shows that physical geographers tend to publish more in wide-ranging, inter-disciplinary journals whereas human geographers characteristically publish their work in core geography journals. This might imply that physical geographers are more outward-looking, keen to engage with other cognate disciplines, while human geographers are more inward-looking. An alternative interpretation could be that human geographers have more of a sense of community than physical geographers, who are split up into climatologists, biogeographers etc. Are we different tribes whose different territories have shaped our culture in radically different ways? Becher and Trowler (2001) make a useful distinction between what they term 'urban' and 'rural' research specialisms. These terms are applied to describe the fundamental nature of the research problems under study in particular areas. 'Urban' research is characterized by a high people-to-problem ratio, much competition and a rapid, heavily used information network. It leads to many, often multi-authored, outputs in terms of articles. In contrast, 'rural' research areas have a relatively low number of people involved in a theme, often clustered around particular issues, and frequently engaged in long-term issues, with lower frequency of publication. The book or monograph is the pinnacle of this kind of research, which takes longer to gestate. Some parts of both physical and human geography conform to the urban research model, others fit more accurately into the rural model.

All these differences between human and physical geography, perceived or real, are acted out in and reinforced by, the structure of degree courses and the layout of departments. Many geography courses in the UK, for example, encourage rapid specialization in order to produce a BA (human geography) stream and a BSc (physical geography) stream. In some universities physical and human geography staff occupy different buildings, or are otherwise spatially segregated within a single building. Some departments, for example, at Macquarie University (in Sydney, Australia) have gone further and are now split into two autonomous units: the Department of Physical Geography and the Department of Human Geography. Recent restructuring of several British universities has also led to mergers, closures and moves of several geography departments, usually into the life or natural sciences faculties.

Not all academic geographers by any means agree with the diagnosis presented above of physical and human geography as diverging in comparison with some 'golden age' of togetherness. As Ron Johnston points out in Chapter 1, geography is just as much characterized today by distinctions within human geography as it is by any simple division between human and physical geography. Most academic subjects as they grow become more diverse, with new areas opening up often on the fringes of other subjects, as is apparent from looking at the rise of biochemistry, nanotechnology and molecular biophysics. As Becher and Trowler (2001) note, academic tribes are increasingly becoming organized into smaller specialist groups within overarching disciplines. Physical geographers, for example, are increasingly differentiated into geomorphologists, biogeographers, and Quaternary scientists (among others), while further subdivision can be made into, for example, cosmogenic dating, glaciology and disturbance ecology specialisms. At the same time however, Gregory et al. (2002) note signs that there is a restructuring of physical geography occurring with Quaternary, fluvial and climatic studies growing especially strong and developing into a more holistic physical geography.

Getting Back Together or Splitting Up?

Let us assume that human and physical geography are in some way divided. If so, there would appear to be at least three ways forward: integration (or perhaps re-integration); splitting up; or some kind of uneasy co-existence.

What are the arguments in favour of re-uniting the two halves of geography, how might this best be achieved and are there any signs of this happening? Three types of argument for re-unification have been presented in recent literature. The heritage argument claims that as geography has always been united, therefore it should stay so. It refers back to the foundational texts of the great American geographers W.M. Davis and Carl Sauer, the 'father' of French geography, Paul Vidal de la Blache, and many others to establish tradition. The related holistic argument indicates that geography simply *is* the study of human–environment relations, and that the two component parts cannot be separated (Stoddart, 1987). The pragmatic argument stresses that physical and human geography would be too small and weak as individual disciplines to survive in a harsh, under-funded academic climate (Gregory et al., 2002).

So, how might a re-integration of human and physical geography, perhaps building on the strengths of today's human–environment relations work, be achieved? Many geographers have contributed to this debate, but the main types of approaches they have put forward can be categorized as focusing on shared subject matter, methodology, philosophical standpoints or big questions. Looking first at shared subject matter, there are many areas in which human and physical geographers from different specialisms within geography work on a range of similar topics from different perspectives. Topics of interest include land degradation and societal change in South America and Africa (see, for example, Endfield and O'Hara, 1999; Dougill et al., 1999), geography and global environmental change (as outlined neatly by Liverman, 1999), water resource conflicts (Swyngedouw, 1999), wildlife conservation and issues such as biodiversity prospecting and genetic engineering.

Natural hazards, resources, environmental history and environmental management are all topics which can be approached from either the human or physical side, although there remain reasonable questions of what exactly is added. Some discussions on the challenges awaiting such work are presented in a series of papers on African Environments in the December 2003 issue of *Area*, authored by historians, human geographers, ecologists and economists.

The possibility that physical and human geographers could share methods and techniques has been debated for a long time, and many connections have been proposed. Modelling, fieldwork, cartography and data analysis are all methods which have the potential to be shared by many human and physical geographers. Taking the case of GIS, for example, presentation and analysis of spatially referenced data could provide a powerful way of understanding a whole host of geographical topics, from cut flower commodity chains to geomorphic surfaces dated with cosmogenic nuclides (Openshaw, 1991). All that is required is suitable data and a reasonable grasp of computer technology – oh, and of course, an appreciation that something might be gained from the exercise. In reality, such a bridging methodology would work best only if there was a shared vision of which forms of knowledge creation were valid. Many of the arguments raised in the Science Wars make this quite a difficult task.

Another potential way of bringing together physical and human geographers in useful discussion and interchange of ideas (perhaps a different form of integration) is through consideration of potential bridging ideas or themes. For example, Doreen Massey (1999) shows how both physical and human geographers have wrestled with issues of space and time. She illustrates how useful insights might come from jointly considering these issues. Other points of commonality are issues of scale and hierarchies, and the increasing use of dynamic (rather than equilibrium) ideas and metaphors in both physical and human geography. Such a vision of integration encourages mutual respect, discussion and debate, while maintaining separate research foci and methods. Slightly different approaches have recently been proposed by Rhoads (1999) and Urban and Rhoads (2003) who suggest that human and physical geographers should get involved in re-examining the Cartesian dualism between humans and nature, in an effort to unravel the complexity of human–biophysical relations. Keith Richards (2003) presents yet another prescription for integrating physical and human geography, this time through ethical considerations.

There is also a case for the two parts of geography to go their separate ways. Peter Worsley (1979) made an early plea for British geomorphology to leave geography and, since then, there have been several calls for a decisive split between physical and human geography. There are currently two forces encouraging separation. First, it can be argued that both physical and human geographers might be taken more seriously if they were aligned more closely with researchers in closely allied subjects. In the highly competitive academic world, strength comes at least partly from outsiders' perceptions of the value of one's research and the term 'geography' is not viewed strongly by many natural scientists (could the same be said of other social scientists?). Physical geography already faces this dilemma. Much ecology and biogeography research, for example, is carried out by biologists. Biogeographers and ecologists currently working in geography departments may realize significant advantages to working in plant science or biology departments. Similarly, climatologists might benefit from working in atmospheric physics departments, and geomorphologists and Quaternary scientists in earth science departments. Might historical geographers thrive better in history faculties, or urban and social geographers benefit from closer alliance with urban planning and sociology? Another option might be to redesign 'academic space' to form new centres focusing on inter-disciplinary problems.

A second reason why physical and human geography might split is if the tensions between science and social science methodology, philosophy and subject matter become too great to be either shoe-horned together in an effort to re-integrate the two, or to co-exist reasonably happily as at present. If, for example, physical geographers such as glaciologists or Quaternary scientists bring in big research grants and require substantial research infrastructure (laboratories, post-doctoral staff, computing suites, etc.), they might outgrow the rest of the department. Put bluntly, there's competition for floorspace! Some human geographers, especially those engaged in work greatly separated from, or critical of, science, may feel increasingly uncomfortable shackled to physical geographers pursuing the natural science research model. Mildly co-existing tribes might become polarized onto opposite sides of the 'Science Wars' and find little benefit in remaining together.

Or Letting Things Develop Naturally?

If geography is 'in a bit of state' with divisions between human and physical geographers, why can't it just continue like this? Is there any real evidence for geography being seriously threatened by division? Although many authors have written about tensions, schisms and differences, we may ask whether they are actually affecting the progress of research and teaching. Or are they just an excuse for the 'chattering classes' in academic geography to knock off a quick journal article?

Is there anything to be said for trying to maintain a continued state of 'uneasy co-existence'? I suggest that there are four main reasons why such co-existence might be worth preserving. First, it works. Although human and physical geographers may not publish in the same journals, and although we have many differences and do not share very much, geography hasn't blown apart. Two tribes can perhaps cover similar academic territories without threatening each other, but also without necessarily competing. Something about our uneasy alliance must be working. We can effectively devise, and share teaching for, meaningful geography undergraduate courses which remain popular. Second, to use an ecological analogy, diversity may be just as healthy for an academic discipline as it has often been seen to be for an ecosystem. Perhaps geomorphologists occupy the same sort of niche in academic geography as earthworms do in a temperate grassland – although no doubt most geomorphologists would rather be referred to as a top carnivore rather than a worm. We could argue that, even if limited, the scope for intellectual cross-fertilization of ideas between different parts of the discipline is useful – we physical geographers may occasionally get some really good insights into particular scientific problems by talking to a human geographer, but are not under pressure to do so all the time. This allows all of us to engage in creative collaboration with others in chemistry, physics or biology departments, for example. Collaboration between economists, geomorphologists and ecologists might be just as able to tackle important issues of human–environment relations in multi-disciplinary projects, as a group of physical and human geographers. New ideas generally arise from the juxtaposition of quite different concepts and assumptions, whether it's in advertising or academia.

Keeping physical and human geography in bland co-existence may be the easiest alternative, but it is only likely to work if we can keep a creative and healthy tension and diversity. It might, curiously, enable more work to be done on human–environment relations by geographers working as part of multi-disciplinary teams, without trying to claim that geography somehow 'owns' that territory.

Whether the subject becomes re-integrated or whether the divide widens, the forces encouraging increasing divergence between physical and human geography research may combine to provoke a major re-assessment of the status of geography as a university discipline today. This may be very timely at the start of the twenty-first century when academic disciplines largely defined in the nineteenth century may require reassessment in order to facilitate the best, most useful research. If, as Becher and Trowler believe, specialisms are in many ways the fundamental unit of academic grouping, then it may be that combinations of specialist fields from within geography and outside could form the basis of new, developing tribes moving onto fertile new academic territories.

Geographers could be at the forefront of attempts to set up new interdisciplinary research and teaching units focused on areas of the world, big issues or methodologies.

Where Next?

Gazing into the crystal ball for insights into tomorrow's world is always a dangerous game, and I do not want to make any predictions about the future of geography. There is no reason why all of the above future scenarios (re-integration, co-existence, splitting up) cannot occur at different times in different places. I doubt very much that there is one, unitary future of geography, just as there has been no single history of geography. Conflicts and debates between physical and human geography are only one part of the overall picture of what geography is like today. The issues and tensions they reveal are, however, of great importance to all of us. What is happening in geography needs to be set within the context of real debates over science in an age of global uncertainty, informed by an understanding of the differences between the spectrum of academic tribes and territories as outlined by Becher and Trowler (2001). As responsible scholars and scientists we should always ask ourselves is our research worth doing, do we have the skills to do it, and can we attract the funding to pay for it and ensure its continuation in the future. We need to keep open dialogues between all geographers and other scientists – natural and social – with whom we have common interests. Understanding the dynamics that have influenced our discipline in the past and continue to do so can help us to shape the future of our academic tribes in the face of a changing world, crammed full of geographical problems which need addressing. Whether we are from Venus or Mars matters less than whether we understand ourselves, where we are coming from and what we are trying to do.

ESSAY QUESTIONS AND FURTHER READING

1   Does the viability of Geography as a discipline depend upon the closer integration of physical and human geography? As well as reading Clifford (2002), Gober (2000), Johnston (2003), Stoddart (1987), Thrift (2002) and Urban and Rhoads (2003), you should reflect on those parts of the course that you have personally done to date. Consider the question from the perspectives of both research and teaching. You could use examples from the special issue on African Environments in the December 2003 issue of *Area*.

2 In what ways do the practices and theories of Physical and Human Geography differ? Becher and Trowler (2001) distinguish between 'urban' and 'rural' modes of research, which might be a good place to start. But even if you cannot get hold of this book, you will find answers in Ferguson (2003), Johnston (2003), Worsley (1979), and more indication of common ground in Massey (1999) and Openshaw (1991). Read two of the case studies in the references closely to try to work out how the authors go about things differently. Consider also the possibility that differences within the two sub-disciplines are as great as those between them.

NOTE

1 Question in an undergraduate Geography final examination paper, University of Oxford (1999).

REFERENCES

Becher, T. and Trowler, P.R. (2001) *Academic Tribes and Territories*, 2nd edn. Society for Research into Higher Education and the Open University Press, Buckingham.

Clifford, N.J. (2002) The future of Geography: when the whole is less than the sum of its parts. *Geoforum* **33**, 431–436.

Dougill, A.J., Thomas, D.S.G. and Heathwaite, A.L. (1999) Environmental change in the Kalahari: integrated land degradation studies for nonequilibrium dryland environments. *Annals of the Association of American Geographers* **89**, 420–442.

Endfield, G.H. and O'Hara, S.L. (1999) Degradation, drought and dissent: an environmental history of colonial Michoacan, west Central Mexico. *Annals of the Association of American Geographers* **89**, 402–419.

Ferguson, R.I. (2003) Publication practices in physical and human geography: a comment on Nigel Thrift's 'The future of geography'. *Geoforum* **34**, 9–11.

Gober, P. (2000) Presidential address: in search of synthesis. *Annals of the Association of American Geographers* **90**, 1–11.

Gray, J. (1992) *Men Are from Mars, Women Are from Venus*. HarperCollins, New York.

Gregory, K.J., Gurnell, A.M. and Petts, G.E. (2002) Restructuring physical geography. *Transactions, Institute of British Geographers* NS **27**, 136–154.

Hooke, J.M. (2003) River meander behaviour and instability: a framework for analysis. *Transactions, Institute of British Geographers* NS **28**, 238–253.

Johnston, R.J. (2003) Geography: a different sort of discipline? *Transactions, Institute of British Geographers* NS **28**, 133–141.

Liverman, D.M. (1999) Geography and the global environment. *Annals of the Association of American Geographers* **89**, 107–120.

Mackinder, H. (1887) On the scope and method of geography. *Proceedings of the Royal Geographical Society* **9**, 141–160.

Massey, D. (1999) Space–time, 'science' and the relationship between physical geography and human geography. *Transactions, Institute of British Geographers* NS **24**, 261–276.

Openshaw, S. (1991) A view on the GIS crisis in geography, or, using GIS to put Humpty Dumpty back together again. *Environment and Planning A* **23**, 621–628.

Rhoads, B.L. (1999) Beyond pragmatism: the value of philosophical discourse for physical geography. *Annals of the Association of American Geographers* **89**, 760–771.

Richards, K. (2003) Ethical grounds for an integrated geography. In Trudgill, S.T. and Roy, A. (eds) *Contemporary Meanings in Physical Geography*. Arnold, London, pp. 233–258.

Sardar, Z. and Van Loon, B. (2002) *Introducing Science*. Icon, Cambridge.

Somerville, M. (1848) *Physical Geography*. John Murray, London.

Stoddart, D.R. (1987) To claim the high ground: geography for the end of the century. *Transactions, Institute of British Geographers* NS **12**, 327–326.

Swyngedouw, E. (1999) Modernity and hybridity: nature, Regeneracionismo, and the production of the Spanish waterscape, 1890–1930. *Annals of the Association of American Geographers* **89**, 443–465.

Thrift, N. (2002) The future of geography. *Geoforum* **33**, 291–298.

Turner, B.L. (2002) Response to Thrift's 'The future of geography'. *Geoforum* **33**, 427–429.

Urban, M. and Rhoads, B. (2003) Conceptions of nature: implications for an integrated geography. In Trudgill, S.T. and Roy, A. (eds) *Contemporary Meanings in Physical Geography*. Arnold, London, pp. 211–232.

Valins, O. (2003) Stubborn identities and the construction of socio-spatial boundaries: ultra-orthodox Jews living in contemporary Britain. *Transactions, Institute of British Geographers* NS **28**, 158–175.

Worsley, P. (1979) Whither geomorphology? *Area* **11**, 97–101.

Ziman, J. (2000) *Real Science: What It Is, and What It Means*. Cambridge University Press, Cambridge.

What Difference Does Difference Make to Geography?

Katherine McKittrick and Linda Peake

Ron Johnston in Chapter 1 argues persuasively that the discipline of Geography no longer has any recognized core but rather is characterized by its 'diversity and divergence' in the sense that its sub-disciplines are running off in all directions, creating communities of researchers that simultaneously look inwards to their own areas of specialization while also stretching out, making contact with researchers in other disciplines. In this chapter we specifically address how this very geographically evoked understanding of 'diversity and divergence' necessitates engagement with a third 'd', that of difference (or, to be more exact, *differences* in the plural). We suggest that these contemporary trajectories, while allowing for the reproduction of sameness, have also resulted in encounters with difference(s). These encounters have increasingly caused geographers to think about how their discipline reproduces itself and how the two central concerns of Human Geography, that is space and place, are central to the production of difference. These concerns we refer to as 'geography', as distinct from the discipline, 'Geography', and which we speak of together as 'G/geography'. We should also indicate that our interests in this chapter lie specifically in Human Geography.

In order to delineate how sites of G/geographic inclusion and exclusion can be understood we start this chapter with a brief outline of 'difference'. We then go on to address difference in Geography (the discipline) and difference in geography (space and place): that is, the ways the Anglo-American tradition of Geography has traditionally included Western white men and excluded women, non-white communities, and non-Western geographical subjects; and the material and conceptual spatialization of difference. This is followed by a discussion pointing to two key concepts geographers have used in order to think through difference and exclusion: nature–culture and the body. We conclude briefly with alternative geographies and imagining G/geography and difference in more just ways.

What is Difference and Why Study Difference?

There are several ways to approach the concept of difference. While geographers and other social theorists have used divergent definitions of 'difference', we understand difference through socially produced markers (such as race, class, gender, and sexuality) *and* their attendant geographies (colonial geographies, post-colonial geographies, patriarchal geographies, feminist geographies, white geographies, non-white geographies, cross-cultural geographies, and so on). The relationship between these markers and their geographies is a dialectical one: one constitutes the other with neither being understood outside the context of the other. Difference, then, signals diverse geographies and geographic experiences; it implies that 'the social relations of spaces are experienced differently, and variously interpreted by those holding different positions' (Massey, 1994: 3). Hence, difference always implies difference-in-place. Moreover, the concept of difference also signals the ways in which non-dominant identities are *socially constructed as different from* dominant identities. Thus, rationality has been centred on the figure of the white, heterosexual and patriarchal Western man with all others deemed to be 'outside' this orienting figure. To put it another way, social markers such as race and gender are visible social constructs which mark differences (between whites and non-whites and men and women, for example); these differences are spatially organized and therefore not only visible through the scale of the body, but also through material geographies – different people hold different geographic positions (in the home, the workplace, the city, or the suburbs for example). Difference-in-place, then, allows us to examine 'the hierarchical and unequal relationships among different groups' (Scott, 1988: 179). It also gives insight into the ways in which the geographic positions of non-dominant groups challenge geographic hierarchies. For example, how we come to know difference through geography is framed by geographic projects such as imperialism and capitalism. These projects signal how broad geographic patterns (such as spatial and economic expansion) shape our world according to profit, displacement and power. Yet difference also signals critical emancipatory knowledges (such as feminism, post-colonialism, and anti-racism) and experiential knowledges, such as the geographies which we all live in the everyday world, which unsettle broad geographic projects such as imperialism and capitalism. In other words, 'different' bodies are not only assigned 'different' geographies, they are also actively experiencing and producing space.

One further point is worthy of note in relation to difference-in-place. Not only do various people occupy place in various ways – across time and space – but control over the production of space gives powerful groups the ability to produce difference as well as the right to be in space. Ghettos, under-funded women's shelters, sprawling suburbs, over-polluted regions, gated communities, under-developed and over-developed nations, homeless hostels, and native land claims, are just some examples of how geography and geographic knowledge are, locally and globally, tied to practices of spatial unevenness. What these spatial formations reveal is the ways in which geography is mapped according to race, class, and gender-specific interests. They also reveal that geographic knowledge – how we 'know' and 'understand' the external world – is inevitably tied to spatial formations and hierarchies.

We are not asserting, however, that formations of race, class, gender, and so on are spatially rendered in the *same ways* over time and space but, rather, that geographic expression is extremely variable. David Delaney contends that axes of power can combine in multitudinous ways 'to produce the richly textured, highly variegated, and power laden spatialities of everyday life' (2002: 7). He claims that what is important about these spatialities is how the division of continuous territory into 'insides' and 'outsides' facilitates the categorization of groups into 'us v. them'. He states that racialized, gendered and classed identities '[are] what [they are] and [do what they do] precisely because of how [they are] given spatial expression' (ibid.: 7). In other words, these spatialities are not simply *reflections* of axes of power, rather, they are *constitutive* of them. It follows that it is insufficient to simply recognize difference; we need to ask how and where difference is produced, and as we address in the following sections of this chapter, for what purposes and whose interests? We start by addressing difference in relation to the discipline of Geography itself.

Coming to Know Geography through Difference

Historians of Anglo-American Geography have only recently addressed the exclusion of subordinated groups from the discipline. It took nearly a century of study before questions were asked about the exclusion of these groups, both as practitioners of the discipline and as subjects of study. It was the tumultuous late 1960s – the Vietnam War protests, strikes and student uprisings throughout Western Europe – that created a dissatisfaction among certain groups of geographers with the seemingly apolitical nature of their discipline. But we would argue the discipline has always been political. The way in which a discipline develops over time – what kinds of questions it asks and of whom, what is considered 'knowable', and how we can know things – is saturated with politics. Thus, the kind of Geography that develops depends on who geographers are. In other words, the practitioners of a discipline are not coincidental to the dominant forms of knowledge that are produced in the discipline. The problem was (and is) not only that middle-class white men were numerically dominant in departments of Geography in Britain and North America in the twentieth century but also that they held sway over the status quo. It was hardly surprising that knowledge production was pervaded by a particular kind of 'masculinism', one that valued objectivity and rationality above everything else and which assumed that this knowledge was free of values and spoke directly to all people in all places (see Rose, 1993). But as the work of Donna Haraway (1991) and other social theorists has since shown, the knowledge produced by white middle-class males is as partial and situated as the knowledge produced by any other group.

The continuing dominance of this masculinist form of knowledge production meant that the interests of these practitioners were served by studying people like themselves and not others. This resulted in the dismissal of class-based studies until the early 1970s; the exclusion of the study of women and women's activities until the mid-1970s; the disregarding of sexualities until the late 1980s; and the neglect of non-humans until the late 1990s. The exclusion of non-dominant groups/species was and is not simply a dilemma of Geography. Second-wave feminism and feminist studies, Native studies, black studies, queer studies, and studies of civil rights and multiculturalism illustrate that several academic disciplines (and political agendas) were not adequately addressing diverse and different histories and lives. For example, with the collapse of socialism in the USSR and Eastern Europe, the issue of class fell out of favour in many academic analyses in the late 1980s although it re-emerged in the late 1990s (see Haylett, 2001, for example). And until the 1990s the last sustained discourse on white identity by geographers took place between 1890 and 1930, coinciding with the peak and then decline of the British Empire (Bonnett, 1997).

Indeed, it is impossible to recognize the spaces of exclusion that exist within Anglo-American Geography – its hidden geographies – without an understanding of its origins in the nineteenth century in relation to European economic dominance and to practices of empire building. Geography was utilized as a tool to document and facilitate the building of empires and the mapping of colonial expansion. The work of Felix Driver (2001), for example, outlines how the practice of British Geography in this period explicitly reproduced masculinist and white European ways of knowing. But attempts to open up these ways of knowing only appeared from the 1970s onwards. The general silence around what one might term 'meta-narratives' of whiteness, heterosexuality, masculinity and middle-classness made these axes of power appear normative or natural, suggesting that they could not be questioned. But, in opening them up to inspection, geographers have begun to unearth the legacy of domination within Anglo-American Geography and its attendant ideologies of patriarchy, sexism, homophobia, racism, disablism and anthropomorphism.

Notwithstanding these efforts, and despite the fact that a number of geographers are already challenging the demographic makeup of the discipline, the legacy of patriarchal whiteness is still very influential.[1] David Delaney recently, and wryly, noted that Geography 'is nearly as white an enterprise as Country and Western music, professional golf, or the Supreme Court of the United States' (2002: 11). And while he is referring to Geography in the United States where over 90 per cent of Geography department members are white (Puildo, 2002), these comments could equally apply to departments in Britain, Canada, New Zealand, Australia and in Europe (ask yourself, how many of the lecturers and professors in your department are white, compared to the population at large where you live?).

Coming to Know Difference through Geography

The legacies of whiteness and masculinity within the discipline of Geography can undermine what Donna Haraway (1991) calls 'situated knowledges'. We argued earlier that Haraway's contention, that knowledge is local, specific and embodied, encapsulates an important way in which difference can be understood. That is, space and place are intimately connected to race, gender, class, sexuality and other axes of power; all geographic knowledges are situated, and location matters. Situated knowledges create a conceptual and material space through which non-dominant geographies can be articulated and theorized. Difference, it could be said, can be located within and around situated knowledges.

So, what is considered different in geographic terrains and why? How does the landscape perpetuate or democratize difference? Why does difference matter so much to spatial organization? Do difference and situated knowledges unsettle conventional geographic patterns? That geographic organization is also an organization of difference is probably most obvious in colonial projects, which segregate and hierarchically 'manage' non-white populations for economic and geographic profit. But difference in geography is also produced in other ways. For example, home may be a place in which different people occupy different areas and perform different tasks according to age or gender (and this differs, of course, from home to home, region to region). Who cleans homes? Is a clean home a gendered space, a racial space? How are local, regional, national and global spaces differentiated according to social markers? What we are trying to stress is that the particularity of 'identity' and 'self' (*who* is different) implies some sort of *spatial* difference – be it race, sexuality, gender, body, dress, community, nation, citizenship, or status: socio-cultural markers make a geographic difference, and vice versa.

Difference reflects both oppressed/oppressor relations, and the complex situated knowledges that challenge these relations. Geographic difference is layered. It is a spatial expression of geographic problems (such as the 'other' who is segregated, incarcerated, profiled) and it is a spatial opportunity to express political, social, and economic possibilities. Racial segregation, for example, is a spatial expression of difference – it separates communities, perpetuates uneven economies, and geographically marks the landscape.[2] But geographies of segregation also invoke varying responses to cycles of domination: migration, music, graffiti, art, community gatherings, literature, protests, violence, and celebrations all reconfigure the meanings of places.

The tensions between difference and geography point to the ways in which, despite progressive resistances to social and geographic domination, the spatial organization of the world is still hierarchical. This hierarchy is, moreover, naturalized; it emphasizes and hides particular processes which profit from what Ruth Wilson Gilmore calls 'the displacement of difference' (2002: 16). That is, geographic hierarchies – different scales of power and knowledge which can be seen in cities, on streets, in homes, on bodies, across nations – continually privilege white, heterosexual, and patriarchal patterns so that different bodies are shaped by the world around them in favourable or adverse (or both) ways. As demonstrated in Table 3.1, the scales of the body, the home, the nation, and the globe are interwoven with broad geographic projects of domination. These include imperialism, globalization, transatlantic slavery and the 'carving up' and colonization of Africa, processes of 'white flight' and of 'no go' zones in cities. These dominant geographies contain within them experiential geographies and critiques, that is, those spaces and places where the 'dailyness' of difference is lived (gendered workplaces, heterosexualized homes, buildings only accessible to the able-bodied, and so on) and resisted (through, for example, narratives of displacement, difference, race/racism).

Table 3.1 illustrates that the geographies and knowledges that have developed from legacies of difference have been repeated and recycled in particular ways at multiple scales and yet are inevitably intertwined. Different forms of domination and of experience produce variegated flows which shape complex geographic subjects and spaces. Table 3.2

Table 3.1   Some examples of scales of difference.

	Body	Home	Nation	Globe
Geographies of domination	Racialization and racism, heterosexism	Domestic violence, domestic labour	Colonization and genocide, uneven distribution of national resources, systems of apartheid	Imperialism, globalization, re-distribution of natural resources and of people
Experiential geographies	Bodily geographies of difference such as queer bodies, transgendered bodies	Geographies of fear; geographies of fleeing or of staying put	Geographies of diaspora and of migration; critiques of the nation and of belonging	Geographies of fair trade and of refugees; anti-globalization activism
Some useful theoretical concepts	Body, scale, embodiment, race, gender and sexuality as social constructs, naturalization	Sex-gender systems, patriarchy, scale, home–work, value, social reproduction	Nation, citizenship, nation-state, colonialism, scale, geographical expansion	Scale, globalization, capitalism, global-capital, time–space compression

Table 3.2 Some examples of scales of 'inclusions' and 'exclusions'.

	Home	Neighbourhood	Nation	Globe
Spaces of assimilation and/or exclusion	Master bedrooms, den	Suburbs, ethnic neighbourhoods, gated communities, golf courses	Public spaces, e.g. parks, shopping malls, airports, national borders	Common markets, trading blocs
Spaces of containment/ internment/ exile	Homeless shelters, homelessness	Ghettos, ethnic neighbourhoods	Concentration camps, prisons, reserves, refugee camps	Systems of apartheid
Spaces of objectification	Women in the home being viewed solely as housewives	Youth hanging out in shopping malls and street corners being labelled as idle and/or delinquent	Immigrants and/or refugees being portrayed as a drain on national welfare	Third World women stereotyped as victims of development processes

outlines some of the ways we can imagine how spaces – of assimilation, exclusion and containment, for example – can be rendered at different spatial scales and how any geographic site can act to include and/or exclude at the same time. Shopping malls, for example, can be places where one can encounter many others, but as privately owned places, anyone deemed undesirable can be removed and denied re-entry. Similarly, suburbs can be seen as the natural preserve of certain ethnic groups – whites and non-whites – serving to include some and exclude others.

Geographic difference is both the profitable spatialization of non-dominant groups and critical/resistant responses to this spatialization; this two-way process indicates that the difference 'difference(s)' make to geography is not only about mapping unjust spaces and places of subordination, but is also an indicator of the ways in which geography, as an analytical tool and an experiential process, makes available a place of resistance. We turn to nature–culture and the body in order to show how difference(s) have been taken up in the discipline of Geography and to illustrate that difference(s) have advanced important challenges to how we can and do imagine Geography and geography.

Geographic Responses to Difference: Nature–Culture and the Body

Some of the key concepts geographers have raised in order to think through difference include nature–culture, human species, uneven development, the body, the psyche, and race, gender and sexuality as social constructs. In this section we address the ways geographers have drawn attention to one particular aspect of difference, namely, its visibility. Difference is *placed*, in part, because difference is visible. So being able to see difference, through social markers (race, gender, class, for example) speaks to historical and contemporary practices of racial, sexual, and economic domination.[3] Visible differences, although having different meanings to different social groups, have been used by dominant groups to structure geographic organization, i.e., uneven social relationships are spatialized according to social markers. We briefly explore two key modalities – hybridity and corporeality – for thinking through visible differences in relation to the concepts of nature/culture and the body.

The nature–culture divide has long been a preoccupation with geographers, most commonly with individual geographers studying just one side or the other. A number of critical geographers have, however, pointed out that this separation is impossible; both humans and non-humans are now recognized as active agents (although not necessarily intentionally or consciously) in the making of geographies. From initial Marxist concerns with the 'production of nature' through interest in the worlds of animals and animal geographies, to more recent work on the interaction between nature and culture, geographers have turned their attention to the necessity of a 'relational resituation of the human' (Matless, 1996: 381).[4] David Harvey (2000: 208), for example, discusses the notion of 'species being': he states that we 'are sensory beings in a metabolic relation to the world around us', thereby viewing human nature in relative or hybrid terms and recognizing the need to take into account more than human differences. Thinking about species-difference, as bound to human relations and social systems, reconfigures the work of Human Geography. Casting the analytical net wider, to include the question of 'species being' rather than simply humans dominating the so-called 'natural' production of space, makes it clear that human beings are not outside of nature (ibid.: 218).

The nature–culture divide, and the debate on it, also signals the body – the feminine, the masculine, the rational, the irrational, 'good' flesh, 'bad' flesh, the natural body, the cultural body. There is now a vast amount of work on the body and it is not easy to categorize, but two major camps may be discerned: those who prioritize the body as a discursive construction versus those who start with the 'real' body, seeing the body as more than representation. Geographers did not focus on the body until the 1990s, however. Before then, Geographers were preoccupied with the distinction between sex and gender, arguing that the former was a matter of biology but that gender was a social construction that varies over space. This early focus on gender at the expense of the body can be explained by the pervasiveness of masculinist rationality as a form of knowledge that is divorced from emotions and the body and the attendant mapping of the mind–body dualism onto masculinities and femininities. However, a number of geographers have increasingly turned their attention to the body (see Longhurst, 1997, for an overview). An interest in the corporeal – the flesh – and of thinking through the body has developed alongside an understanding that the body is not only the primary site of identity but also the place, the site, of the individual. Indeed, it is bodily practices that enable us to become subjects. The feminist scholar, Judith Butler (1990) has argued that woman and men learn to perform their gendered identities in bodily ways that are so routinized and habitual that they appear totally natural. Thus, Butler argues that identity is not fixed but performed. Embodiment – the ways in which identity, corporeal markers, and the self simultaneously exist and articulate themselves – is an important geographic process; bodies that are differentially racialized, sexualized, nationalized (and so on) perform their identities differently. Moreover, as Neil Smith has argued, the body does not 'stand alone,' unitary and untouched. Rather, community, regional, national, and global processes are inscribed onto it (1993: 87–119). The site of corporeality, the flesh and the self, thus performs 'expected' or 'habitual' tasks (such as keeping certain kinds of dress or displays of affection in their 'appropriate' places) while they are also continually expressing different geo-political conditions (such as poverty, violence, pleasure, commodification, and racism).

We end this section with an illustrative human geography drawn from the Caribbean scholar Edouard Glissant. The passage in Box 3.1 addresses how the physical landscape is a site through which Glissant can politicize difference and humanness. The landscape itself, he writes, 'unfolds,' and reveals hidden geographies such as those of the maroons – escaped slaves – locations of retreat, sites of indentured labour, and resistance/strikes. Nature-culture coalesce; tree roots, the North, the mountain and the leaves, are underwritten by a non-white, and violent, human bodily history which has seeped into the land. This selection,

Box 3.1 Nature, Culture, Bodies, Race: Edouard Glissant's *Caribbean Discourse*

Throughout his book, *Caribbean Discourse* (1989), Edouard Glissant, uses the natural landscape to explore non-white identities and philosophies in the Caribbean. The passage below is an example of how nature, culture, racialization, bodies and difference, and history, together, frame Glissant's concerns and delineate his interest in a spatial politics of being.

> [The landscape] is a concentrated whole that offers an intelligible dimension. At the same time, the threshold of heat blocked by rain; deeper yet, those fissures that become visible when the landscape unfolds. In the north of the country, the knotted mass of somber greens which the roads still do not penetrate. The maroons found refuge there...The root of vine and its violet flower. The dense network of ferns. The primordial mud, impenetrable and primal. Under the acomas that disappear from view, the stuffy erect mahogany trees supported by blue beaches on a human scale. The North and the mountains are one. There were dumped those peoples from India who were part of nineteenth century trade and whom we call Coolies, in Guadeloupe, Malabars. Today, the flat fields of pineapple cut arid grooves in this aloof and remote world. Yet this prickly flatness is dominated by the shadow of the great forests. The strikers of the Lorrain district, coolies and blacks, all Martinican, were trapped there in 1976: *they turned over with their machetes the field of leaves soaked in blood.* (1989: 10)

then, uses the physical landscape, non-white cultural histories and bodies, and the human and non-human to signal species connections.

Just Geographies

We have argued that dominant geographic patterns, while uneven and hierarchical, also contain alternative geographic locations, imaginations, and knowledges. These alternative geographies are predicated on difference and the spatialization of non-dominant groups; alternative geographies are points of struggle which highlight the tension between dominant geographies and difference. Thus, imaginary geographies which do not neatly align themselves with conventional geographies, knowledges which reconfigure established geographical meanings, and resistant political locations, all suggest that difference is indicative of alternative geographies and geographic struggles. Of course, these dissenting practices do not obliterate the unevenness of spatial hierarchies. But they do suggest that spatial experiences, of the dominating and the dominated, are neither distinct and separate, nor wholly stable, indecipherable or unchangeable.

Those identities, places and geographic arrangements which crisscross and subvert the 'natural' geographic hierarchy – 'other' scales of power and knowledge, narratives of displacement, difference – are unseen and/or deemed outside the 'natural' order of geography. Articulating difference, writing and living geographies which are not replicating spatial hierarchies, is, however, a way through which more just, or repoliticized geographies can be imagined. This can be seen in David Harvey's (2000) re-imagination of local–global geographic organization (Box 3.2), where boundaries and connections are supposed to dissolve and re-emerge in a new way, 'natural' spatial hierarchies are not immovable, geographic knowledge is in no way bound to natural spatial hierarchies; Harvey makes available a different 'place' for difference in geography, one which is predicated on geographic-species mutuality and fluid boundaries.

We end by asking, is there an orthodoxy being produced from the somewhat variegated and burgeoning body of work about difference? Does it give rise to hope and to hopeful, more just geographies? Clyde Woods argues that his experience of the ravages that have been experienced by African-American communities in the United States have led him:

> [to] seriously question a social science literature that is, for the most part, seemingly incapable of hearing the cries emanating from the soul of this nation. The same tools that symbolize hope in the hands of the surgeon symbolize necrophilia in the hands of the coroner. Have we become academic coroners? Have the tools of theory, method instruction, and social responsibility become so rusted that they can only be used for autopsies? Does our research in any way reflect the experiences, viewpoints and needs of the residents of these dying communities? (2002: 63).

Similarly, Neil Smith (1996) wrote a tongue-in-cheek editorial for the journal *Society and Space* about the nature of sleep. It was a metaphorical

---

Box 3.2   An Alternative Spatiality: David Harvey's 'Edilia'

One example of a different imagining of the organization of space is given in an appendix to David Harvey's book *Spaces of Hope* (2000) in which he describes a utopian future he calls 'Edilia'. In this future people do not live in families but in 'hearths', that is groups of 20–30 adults and children, ten or so of which group together to form 'neighbourhoods'. Approximately 20 neighbourhoods combine together to form an 'edilia' (of about 60,000 people). About 20 to 50 edilias come together to form the largest contiguous political unit, called a 'regiona' (of at most three million people). This is also a bioregion that aims to be as self-sufficient as possible for its inhabitants. This spatialized form of organization may not seem to be very different from what already exists in a number of places and at a number of scales but Harvey radically departs from current forms of organization in that regionas combine to form 'nationa', which are not spatially contiguous but combine regiona in temperate, tropical, sub-tropical and sub-arctic parts of the world, brought together for the purposes of trade and barter. Moreover, nationa are not permanent features of the geopolitical map. They are expected to periodically dissolve and reform.

---

cri de cœur that so many geographers appear to be sleeping, i.e., are indifferent to a world characterized by profound injustices and material inequalities. David Harvey (2000: 254), however, argues that our ability to create new geographies (and inevitably having to do so constrained by geographical conditions that are not of our own choosing) is hampered or enabled by three aspects of our intellectual engagements:

1   where we can see geography from;
2   how far we can see; and
3   where we can learn geography from

Building on feminist concerns with 'situated knowledges' and going beyond the visibility of difference, Harvey highlights the necessity of recognizing alternative ways of thinking and dreaming about our futures, in ways that consciously desire difference.

Conclusion

We hope we have shown that G/geography invokes both openings and closures when we investigate difference. G/geography is an analytical and material site through which the particularities of social difference can be perpetuated, exposed, and challenged. Recognizing difference(s) asks that processes of geographic placement and displacement be understood not simply for what they are or where they are, but also for the ways the rules and regulations that result in geographic 'placing' reveal how we know and organize the world we live in – and how we might come to know and organize this world differently. More clearly, geographies of difference ask how we are differently *implicated* in the production of space, and how geography shapes our present life. This means that we must think through how we participate in processes of exclusion, the displacement of difference, and socio-spatial order, within and outside the academy. This is not an easy task; indeed, geography is difficult. It is difficult because it is a site of desire. We are rewarded for different forms of capitalist geographic ownership, we succeed (particularly in over-developed nations) when we own space, place, and 'things'; we are rewarded when we control space, provide spatial order, exude spatial authority, follow maps. And we are punished when we act 'out of place', or are simply deemed 'out of place'. Hence we argue for a confrontation with the geographic desire to profitably displace difference but also for a recognition of the ways in which we perpetuate this desire through recycling body-codes, nature–culture divisions, race, and geographic differentiation which is predicated on visible (racialized, sexualized, classed) bodily differences.

ESSAY QUESTIONS AND FURTHER READING

1   How are visible body differences such as gender, race, class, and sexuality, spatialized in your home, community and beyond? To answer this question, see Neil Smith's (1993) discussion of the impact of homelessness and difference upon various spatial scales in New York City; see also Haylett (2001) and Woods (2002) for analyses of the ways in which white and non-white racial codes are spatialized.
2   To what extent has human geography, as a discipline, acknowledged 'differences? Most of the sources for this chapter are relevant, but see in particular the books by Don Mitchell (2000), Gillian Rose (1993) and Sarah Whatmore (2002), and articles by Gilmore (2002), and Pulido (2002)

NOTES

1   See, for example, articles in the special edition of *The Professional Geographer* (2002), vol. 54, no. 1, devoted to studies on race and racism.

2   Don Mitchell, for example, points to the geographical project that spatializes difference *vis-à-vis* the racialization of both whiteness and blackness: 'the aim has been – and is – in white racist societies to create and maintain a world in which whites have near total freedom of movement precisely because blacks do not. The "travel" of whites is predicated on the sequestration of blacks' (2000: 257). What Mitchell allows us to see is the ease with which whiteness, and white identities, through a constant process of distancing, can displace, and hold in place, non-white communities and their geographies. The principal geographies of whiteness they point to include freedom, the creation of the world, and movement; the 'natural' exclusion is of blackness. See Peake and Ray (2001) and McKittrick (2002) for examples relating to the Canadian context.

3   Implicit in visible differences (such as race) are practices which dismiss and/or erase the histories and voices of non-dominant groups. The flip side of what might be called racial-sexual hypervisibility, then, is invisibility, disavowal, and silence. See Trinh (1989).

4   See, for example, the special issue of *Society and Space* (1995), edited by Jennifer Wolch and Jody Emel, and Sarah Whatmore's book *Hybrid Geographies* (2002).

REFERENCES

Bonnet, A. (1997) Geography, 'race' and whiteness: invisible traditions and current challenges. *Area* **29**, 193–199.

Butler, J. (1990) *Gender Trouble*. Routledge, London.

Delaney, D. (2002) The space that race makes. *The Professional Geographer* **54**, 6–14.

Driver, F. (2001) *Geography Militant: Cultures of Exploration and Empire*. Blackwell, Oxford.

Gilmore, R.W. (2002) Fatal couplings of power and difference: notes on racism and geography. *The Professional Geographer* **54**, 15–24.

Glissant, E. (1989) *Caribbean Discourse: Selected Essays*, trans. M.M. Dash. University Press of Virginia, Charlottesville, VA.

Haraway, D.J. (1991) *Simians, Cyborgs and Women: The Reinvention of Nature*. Routledge, New York and London.

Harvey, D. (2000) *Spaces of Hope*. Blackwell, Oxford.

Haylett, C. (2001) Illegitimate subjects? Abject whites, neoliberal modernization, and middle-class multiculturalism. *Environment and Planning D: Society and Space* **19**, 351–370.

Longhurst, R. (1997) (Dis)embodied geographies. *Progress in Human Geography* **21**, 486–501.

Massey, D. (1994) *Space, Place, and Gender*. University of Minnesota Press, Minneapolis.

Matless, D. (1996) New material? Work in cultural and social geography, 1995. *Progress in Human Geography* **20**, 379–391.

McKittrick, K. (2002) 'Their blood is there and you can't throw it out': honouring Black Canadian geographies. *Topia* **7** (Spring), 27–37.

Mitchell, D. (2000) *Cultural Geography: A Critical Introduction*. Blackwell, Oxford and Malden, MA.

Peake, L. and Kobayashi, A. (2002) Anti-racist policies and practices for geography at the millennium. *The Professional Geographer* **54**, 50–61.

Peake, L. and Ray, B. (2001) Racialising the Canadian landscape: whiteness, uneven geographies, and social justice. *The Canadian Geographer* **45**, 180–186.

Pulido, L. (2002) Reflexions on a white discipline. *The Professional Geographer* **54**, 42–49.

Rose, G. (1993) *Feminism and Geography: The Limits of Geographical Knowledge*. Polity Press, Cambridge.

Scott, J.W. (1988) *Gender and the Politics of History*. Columbia University Press, New York.

Smith, N. (1993) Homeless/global: scaling places. In Bird, J., Curtis, B., Putnam, T., Robinson, G., and Tickner, L. (eds) *Mapping Futures: Local Cultures, Global Change*. Routledge, New York and London, pp. 87–119.

Smith, N. (1996) Rethinking sleep. *Environment and Planning D: Society and Space* **14**, 505–506.

Trinh, M. (1989) *Woman, Native, Other*. Indiana University Press, Bloomington, IN.

Whatmore, S. (2002) *Hybrid Geographies*. Sage, London.

Wolch, J. and Emel, J. (eds) (1995) Theme issue, 'Bringing the animals back in'. *Environment and Planning D: Society and Space* **13**, 631–760.

Woods, C. (2002) Life after death. *The Professional Geographer* **54**, 62–66.

Approaches in Geography

Is Geography a Science?

Noel Castree

The title of this chapter is, at first sight, both odd and untimely. Since geography was founded as a university discipline, many practitioners have insisted that it is a science. Consider the following statements that span the history of English-speaking university geography:

> geography is the science whose main function is to trace the interaction of man ... and ... his environment. (Halford Mackinder, 1887: 143)

> geography, I would argue, is a strict science. (William Bunge, 1962: x)

> geography is ... a science. (Keith Richards, 2003: 25)

These three confident declarations – made by one of academic geography's founders, a leading mid-twentieth-century human geographer and a much respected contemporary physical geographer respectively – suggest a continuous belief that geography is a scientific subject. This is why the title of this chapter may seem odd. After all, if geographers have declared geography a 'science' for more than a century, then what is there to debate? All we need to do is to explain what science is and then present evidence that shows why these and other geographers were and are entitled to use the appellation with reference to geography – right?

In fact, things are not so simple. Only if we define science in very general terms can we say, without much fear of contradiction, that geography is a science. For example, the *Oxford English Dictionary* defines science as 'the pursuit of systematic and formulated knowledge'. This general definition implicitly distinguishes science from other forms of knowledge, such as religion, poetry or common sense. Since, for the most part, geographers conduct their research in a considered, systematic way with a view to producing relatively accurate, formulated knowledge of the world, then it is fair to call geography a science. *But* – and it is an important but – ascribing geography scientific status in these very general terms misses a host of crucial issues. As we shall see in this chapter, different geographers have used the term 'science' in a *range* of specific and substantive ways that are by no means the same. Many others have rejected the term altogether. Depending on which particular view of science we are dealing with, our answer to the question 'Is geography a science?' will vary. This doesn't mean that the question is unanswerable or that the different definitions of science are all equally applicable to geography. Our aim should be to establish *which* definitions of science (in the plural) apply (or not) to *which* parts (some or all?) of human and physical geography.

Some readers might think it a peculiar decision to even consider the question of geography's scientific status. Although many physical geographers still actively debate what kind of science their field is (as Stephan Harrison demonstrates in Chapter 5 of this volume), contemporary human geographers now tend to avoid the issue altogether (for reasons to be explained later). This is in stark contrast to the 1960s–1980s when physical *and* human geographers vigorously debated the question, though not always together. What is more, the word 'science' has become tarnished in Western societies in the past decade or so. The old, positive image of benign men in white coats has given way to an altogether darker one. Recent surveys in Britain, the United States and elsewhere reveal that the general public has become more suspicious about science and scientists. In light of these facts, why am I bothering to discuss the topic at all? Even though the practices called 'science' are not as revered as they used to be, they still, I think, serve as something of a benchmark against which other forms of inquiry are measured. As Andrew Sayer (1992: 7) put it:

> Those who want to stand apart from the ... academic game of trying to appropriate and monopolize this [often] vague but prized label for their own favoured approaches are liable to be accused of the heresy of not caring about science and, by implication, rigour and other virtues.

This is especially true in relation to research funding bodies, who often wish to be assured that geography is as rigorous a field as any others in the social and physical sciences. So even if geographers do not debate the exact scientific status of their subject as much as before, the question of science nonetheless still lurks just below the surface of the discipline.

The next section begins by explaining why geographers have wanted to appropriate or reject the label 'science'. In this section I also describe briefly the history of debates over science in geography as a scene-setter for the sections that follow. Then, I grapple with the substantive issues, covering the same ground but in more detail in three following sections. In conclusion, I argue that there is nothing intrinsically scientific about geography. Rather, the term science refers to an array of investigative practices whose positive and negative points need to be judged on a case-by-case basis. Even if it were possible to agree that geography is a science, in itself this would tell us nothing about the quality of the research conducted under this proper name.

What's in a Name? The Vicissitudes of 'Science' in Geography

It's no accident that many geographers have called the discipline a 'science' since its late nineteenth-century inception. The word is not simply an innocent description of a particular set of intellectual practices and principles. It is a highly loaded term that has been used to deliberate effect by those who are 'for' and 'against' it. The key to the word's power is that it is uniquely associated with the ideals of truth, objectivity and accuracy. As Alan Chalmers (1990: 1) put it: 'scientific knowledge is [seen as] proven knowledge'. However, there are different routes to 'proven knowledge' and different geographers have offered their preferred versions of 'science' in order to out-flank other ways of doing geography. Rhetorically, the word has thus been a useful weapon that geographers have wielded in response to pressures emanating from outside the discipline and as a means of effecting intellectual change within the discipline. The term performs 'boundary work', dividing scientific 'insiders' from supposedly lesser non-scientific 'outsiders' (Gieryn, 1983). Let me explain.

Beginnings

In most Western countries, geography did not exist as a teaching and research subject in the mid-nineteenth century. What was then called 'geography' was a hotchpotch of mostly factual information, a good deal of it the result of European ventures into Africa, Asia and the Americas. Though useful in the service of colonialism, this information was largely banal and descriptive: it amounted to an exhaustive catalogue, captured in books and maps, of soils, climate, resources, landforms, cultural practices, and the like. What is more, with the era of colonial conquest coming to an end by the late nineteenth century, geography's continued existence was by no means secure. Geography's early proselytizers – like Mackinder and A.J. Herbertson in Britain, and William Morris Davis in the USA – thus wanted to put this nascent subject on a firmer intellectual footing. They dubbed the new school and university discipline they sought to create a 'science', partly in order to align it with prestigious disciplines in the 'natural sciences' such as chemistry and geology. These were empirical subjects whose *raison d'être* was the scrupulous study of the material world so that its true workings could be revealed. The people who studied these subjects had made a succession of profound discoveries about nature's inner workings. Their reward was the admission of these subjects onto school curricula and their recognition as university disciplines at a time when Western governments were expanding their educational and research base. Geography, in seeking to emulate this success, was to find its academic niche as that science which studied two related things: namely, human–environment relationships and regional differences. Like other sciences, geographical knowledge was to be the product not of dogma, not of opinion, not of mysticism, not of theology, nor of metaphysical beliefs: instead, it was to be the objective result of careful observation (accurate description and classification) with a view to explaining how the material realities of people, environment and region came to be. As the President of the Royal Geographical Society put it, 'by applying thought to the facts . . . observed, we seek . . . for the causes of which the observed phenomena are the result, and the conclusions thus obtained constitute science' (Strachey, 1888: 149).

The first professional university geographers (working from the 1890s onwards) tended to understand the term 'science' in what we would nowadays call a vernacular fashion. That is, they operated with a non-technical and non-specific definition of science similar to the dictionary definition mentioned earlier. Use of the term was simply a means to make a broad distinction between geography and other evidence-based fields of study, on the one hand, and the arts and humanities on the other. For example, in one of the great geographical works of the mid-century, Richard Hartshorne's *The Nature of Geography* (1939), the author made frequent and casual reference to geography as a science in the sense that the knowledge the discipline produces is 'distinct from either common-sense knowledge or from artistic and intuitive knowledge' and aspires to be 'as accurate and certain as possible' (ibid.: 343). But beyond this, the book says little of substance about science, with Hartshorne even admitting at one point that he 'would gladly us[e] . . . some other term than "science" ' if one could be found.

Geography as a spatial science

The precursor to a more sustained and serious attempt to make geography a science was the Second World War. Many geographers were
drafted into the military and intelligence services and quickly found that
their knowledge and skills were found wanting. Before the war, school
and university geography – in the English-speaking countries at least –
was a rather dilettantish subject. Geographers tended to be generalists
rather than specialists. They were trained to know a bit about everything
from meteorology to transportation patterns as these things combined in
different regions. But this training was inadequate to the demands of
fighting a war where precise, in-depth analysis of accurate information
was required. As the American geographer Edward Ackerman reflected
in 1945, the war had exposed geographers as 'more-or-less amateurs in
the subject on which they published' (1945: 124), with one later commen-
tator indicting the pre-war discipline's 'bumbling amateurism and anti-
quarianism' (Gould, 1979: 140). Indeed, soon after Ackerman wrote,
Harvard University president James Conant insisted that 'geography is
not a university subject' (Livingstone, 1992: 311) and Harvard's geography programme was closed down.

The stage was set for a major shake-up in the practice of geography. And
this shake-up was undertaken in the name of making geography a 'real
science'. If the discipline was to contribute, through its research and
teaching, to the rebuilding of war-torn societies, it needed to be scientific
in more than the minimal sense claimed by Hartshorne and his predeces-
sors. This more scientific geography would embrace three related things:
namely, what is sometimes called the 'scientific world-view', a standard
investigative procedure (the so-called 'scientific method'), and a desire to
carefully measure, using statistics and other quantitative techniques, geographical phenomena. In short, geography would mimic, not just the
general ideals of the natural sciences – namely the quest for truthful
knowledge of the material world – but also the whole apparatus of beliefs
and practices that made that quest possible. Later we will see that this first
serious attempt to make geography a science fell short of many of its
ideals, at least according to its critics. But in the late 1950s and through to
the early 1970s a whole generation of human and physical geographers
became thoroughly enthralled with the idea of making geography a 'spatial science'. After germinal papers by the American geologist Arthur
Strahler (1952) and geographer Fredrick Schaefer (1953), as well as
the inspiration from studies of spatial diffusion by the Swedish
geographer Torsten Hägerstrand, a string of manifesto-like books

followed: these included William Bunge's *Theoretical Geography* (1962), two books by the young British geographers Richard Chorley and Peter Haggett (*Frontiers in Geographical Teaching* [1965] and *Models in Geography* [1967]), Haggett's *Locational Analysis in Human Geography* (1965), David Harvey's *Explanation in Geography* (1969) and, in the USA, Richard Morrill's *The Spatial Organization of Society* (1970) and Adams, Abler and Gould's *Spatial Organization* (1971). Certain geography departments rapidly became known for their scientific research in human and physical geography, notably those at the universities of Iowa, Wisconsin, Washington, Cambridge and Bristol. As PhD students graduated from these departments, they went on to spread the scientific gospel in other universities where old-style geography still prevailed. In less than a decade the result was a 'scientific and quantitative revolution' (Burton, 1963) in Anglophone geography. Some 60 years after the modern discipline's founders had first deliberately appropriated the term 'science' to describe their subject, a new generation of geographers used it in a different, more substantive way in order to persuade outside bodies (such as governments) that geography was a 'serious' and 'useful' subject, and also to effect intellectual change within the discipline.

Spatial science under attack

Yet their victory, if one can call it that, was relatively short-lived. From the early 1970s the idea that geography could be a spatial science came under attack, not only by those who were never fans in the first place but also by several of its former advocates. The criticisms were, for the most part, made by human geographers who questioned whether their side of the discipline could be a 'social science'. Chief among them was David Harvey, whose *Social Justice and the City* (1973) paved the way for Marxist geography. At the same time, figures such as David Ley, Yi-Fu Tuan and Anne Buttimer pioneered what became known as humanistic geography. It is not necessary for us to examine these two approaches here (interested readers should consult the relevant chapters in Peet, 1999). What's important is that both turned the label 'science' to their own specific ends. For Harvey and several other Marxist geographers, the problem was not that human geography couldn't be scientific but that the particular *version* of science expounded in the 1960s (sometimes called 'positivism') was deeply flawed. In other words, they argued for a different *kind* of scientific human geography to that which Harvey and his generation had advocated in the previous decade. They did so because positivism, in their view, failed to correctly explain the world it claimed to objectively analyse. What is more, it became clear by the early 1970s that many of the scientific geographers had been researching what seemed to be rather trivial topics – like the optimal location of supermarkets. In an era of the civil rights movement, the Vietnam War, the Cold War, labour unrest and student revolts, Marxists (and other so-called 'radical geographers') argued for approaches that would properly analyse the key issues of the time – such as developing world debt, environmental degradation and inner city poverty.

Yet others remained unconvinced, though equally resistant to positivism. For them *any* substantive attempt to make human geography 'scientific' was problematic from the start. Humanistic geographers argued that while scientific approaches might be appropriate for studying the material world of rivers and manufacturing industries, they were wholly inappropriate for exploring the 'lifeworlds' of sentient human beings. These geographers argued that there was a need to comprehend people's complex attachments to place and local environment. Such a comprehension came from an empathetic engagement with one's research subjects via in-depth interviews, focus groups, ethnographic immersion and other qualitative methods. What this meant was that 'science' was something of a dirty word when it came to researching the humans in human geography. Though humanistic geographers had few reservations about the vernacular definition of science, they strongly questioned whether the two substantive versions championed in the 1960s and from the early 1970s were valid approaches in human geography. They were, in effect, anti-science on the grounds that human geographers should seek to *understand* and *interpret* different people's thoughts and feelings rather than try to *explain* their actions as if they could be encompassed within some over-arching law, theory or model.

While these human geographic debates unfolded, physical geography continued to work broadly within the model of science laid down in the 1960s. This is not to say that physical geographers rigidly applied this model. On the contrary, through trial-and-error, and by engaging with new philosophical and methodological developments in the physical sciences, these geographers adapted it to the practical imperatives of researching complex and dynamic physical systems (see, for example, Haines-Young and Petch, 1986). But these modifications notwithstanding, physical geographers in the 1970s and 1980s never criticized science as deeply as some of their human geography colleagues did. Since then they have continued to modify their research practices and are still, for the most part, happy to label their field a science (witness Richards' quotation at the start of this chapter). One can speculate on why there has been a continued faith in the scientific nature of the physical half of geography. For one thing, the whole idea of science is still very much associated with the natural sciences, and physical geography, like those sciences, studies the natural world. At the same time, physical geographers have long had to compete with geologists, chemists, biologists and physicists for research funding. In order to do this effectively it has been important for these geographers to convince their rivals that their discipline is a 'proper science'. Not to label their field a science would, quite simply, give out all the wrong signals. Meanwhile, not all (perhaps only a few) human geographers today use the word science when describing their research for reasons I stated in my introduction.

In this section I have traced some of the changing ways in which the word 'science' has been appropriated and rejected by human and physical geographers. I have done so in order to show how rhetorically powerful this word has been and also to set the scene for the substantive discussion of science that will now follow. What my all-too-simple (indeed caricatured) history has shown is that geographers have, since the discipline's foundation, used the term 'science' in quite calculated ways. Though the word's meanings have changed, what has remained constant is its strategic use by geographers to respond to outside pressures and to instigate internal disciplinary change.

Geography as a Positivist Science

Let us now discuss the question of geography's scientific status in earnest, adding substance to the sketch provided above. For the term 'science' has not *just* been a rhetorical weapon used by geographers; it has also described specific ways of investigating reality. It is these ways I want now to explain in this and the next two sections before moving on to an assessment of geography's scientific credentials.

I suggested above that the first substantive attempt to make geography a science was a mid-twentieth-century affair. It was arguably inaugurated by one of Richard Hartshorne's sternest critics, Fredrick Schaefer – at least symbolically. *The Nature of Geography* defined the discipline as the study of 'areal differentiation'. For Hartshorne, geography was a synthesizing or *idiographic* discipline. Unlike the 'systematic' subjects (such as chemistry), geography looked at how multiple human and physical phenomena *came together* at the earth's surface. Hartshorne thus favoured the established idea that geography was the study of regional difference.

However, it was not attractive to all geographers. Schaefer, originally an economist, was a German *émigré* based in the geography department at the University of Iowa. In Europe he had been heavily influenced by the Vienna Circle, a group of philosophers, linguistic theorists and mathematicians dedicated to spelling out the exact nature of scientific inquiry. In 1953 Schaefer published an essay in a leading professional geography journal (the *Annals of the Association of American Geographers*) entitled 'Exceptionalism in geography'. The exceptionalism he was critical of was the idea, expressed by Harsthorne, that geography was unlike the specialist sciences because it studied *unique* phenomena (exceptions to rules). Schaefer insisted that the world is not a mosaic of specific regions with little in common. Rather, he maintained that careful observation would reveal that human and physical phenomena were organized into regular spatial patterns. This meant that geography could be a *nomothetic* or law-seeking discipline, just like many physical sciences were. Its role would be to discover the 'morphological laws' governing different geographical phenomena (e.g. river systems or people's choice of where to buy a house). Laws are regular associations, modes of behaviour or patterns that are relatively invariant and which apply to all the phenomena they describe. They can be deterministic or probabilistic. They are, in the physical sciences at least, usually valid across time and between places and regions. For Schaefer, where the natural and social sciences discover 'process laws' (like that describing the temperature–pressure relationship), geography's role would be to discover the spatial patterning of the visible phenomena those process laws lay behind (morphological laws). And, because such discovery could only proceed on the basis of meticulous observation of numerous instances of these visible phenomena, it followed that for Schaefer geographers would have to become specialists (geomorphologists, economic geographers, hydrologists, etc.) rather than the generalists that Hartshorne so admired.

The precise influence of Schaefer's paper on post-war geographers is unclear, but what is certain is that others soon followed his lead knowingly or otherwise. As a division between (and divisions within) human and physical geography began to solidify, geographers pursued the common goal of describing and explaining spatial patterns. Chorley and Haggett (1967: 20) expressed this view succinctly: 'that there is more order in the world than appears at first sight is not apparent until the order is looked for'. But was the search for geographical order via specialization the only thing that made post-war geography more 'scientific' than pre-war geography? I mentioned in the previous section that the post-war 'spatial scientists' (as they became known) were committed to the scientific world-view, the scientific method, and the use of quantitative and statistical methods – a trinity that is sometimes called positivism. So let me now explain each of these. The scientific world-view is a set of precepts or principles that define the general nature of science. It was the French philosopher, Auguste Comte, who first codified this world-view in the early nineteenth century. Comte was writing at a time when dogmatism, superstition, mysticism and royal diktat still governed much of people's worldly knowledge. For Comte, science should possess five characteristics: *le réel*, *le certitude*, *le précis*, *l'utile* and *le relative* (Habermas, 1972). The first meant that scientific knowledge was based on direct experience and observation of reality; the second meant that this observation and experience should be replicable so that all scientists could test its accuracy; *le précis* meant that all scientific statements about reality should be formally testable; *l'utile* meant that scientific knowledge should be practically useful because it was based on a correct understanding of how the material world functions; finally, *le relative* meant that scientific knowledge was unfinished, progressing by continual testing and exploration of new topics. In sum, scientific knowledge would be objective (or value-free), universal, exact, useful and ever-expanding. It would dispel illusions and liberate humankind through its commitment to the discovery of truth.

But how was this thing called science to be undertaken in practice? This is where the Vienna Circle of 'logical positivists' came in, whose work had influenced Schaefer. The Vienna Circle was (and still is) famously associated with explaining the 'proper' scientific method. Their understanding of this method was inspired, in part, by their observation of how the 'experimental' or laboratory sciences, like physics, operated. The Vienna Circle wanted the method to be common to all scientists so that different academic disciplines were distinguished not by *how* they studied but by *what* they studied. This method was based on the principle that if a statement or proposition about the world cannot be factually tested, it is meaningless and thus unscientific. The Vienna Circle called the method 'deductive-nomological' in order to distinguish it from the inductive or Baconian method (see Figure 4.1). The latter, implausibly, assumes that scientists observe the material world with no preconceptions and then make inferences based on a limited number of observations that are applied to a much wider set of similar but not observed phenomena (so-called 'extended inference'). Against this, the deductive-nomological method takes the following form. Scientists, equipped with a set of hunches, observe the portion of reality that interests them. They then form an impression of both *what* exists and *why* and *how* it comes to be the way it is. The why and how impressions (explanatory concerns) are then codified into an initial law, model or theory. I defined a law earlier. In basic terms, a model is a simplified representation of reality that aims to depict the key causal variables at work (or the 'signals in the noise'). A theory is a more sophisticated and detailed attempt to offer a rational explanation of reality and comprises a set of consistent, logical statements that would account for the existence of the 'what' (a descriptive concern). In time, models can become theories and theories laws, but this is not to imply that laws are somehow the highest form of scientific knowledge. The initial laws, models and theories that scientists devise are then used to generate empirically testable hypotheses. In turn, these hypotheses are tested by using appropriate methods to gather relevant data. These data are then analysed – again, using appropriate methods – in order to determine whether the laws, models and theories initially proposed can logically and consistently explain that data. If, after a good deal of data have been gathered and analysed, the laws, models and theories are found wanting, then they are either rejected or else modified until they are accurate. Eventually, after repeated verification (i.e. a persistent search for data that show the modified laws, models and theories to be true), the Vienna School believed one could arrive at explanations and, indeed, predictions of the following form:

$$L1, L2 \dots Ln \qquad \text{(Laws, theories and models)}$$
$$T1, T2 \dots Tn$$
$$M1, M2 \dots Mn$$
$$+$$
$$C1, C2 \dots Cn \qquad \text{(Initial conditions)}$$
$$\overline{E} \qquad \text{(Past, present or future event/s)}$$

Here, a set of empirical events can *necessarily* be described, explained and predicted from a set of well-confirmed laws, theories or models coupled with factual information about the local conditions prevailing at the site where the explanation or prediction applies. For instance, if a hydrologist has a set of general laws about soil porosity and water throughflow, plus information about the local soil type and its antecedent moisture content, s/he might be able to both explain *and* predict why and whether overland flow occurs during a particular rainstorm as opposed to sub-surface flow. Some years after the Vienna Circle disbanded, the philosopher of science, Karl Popper amended its account of the deductive-nomological approach by arguing that science is more rigorous and efficient if it is based on

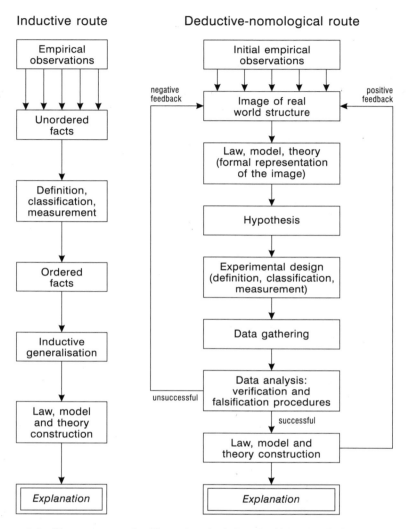

Figure. 4.1 'Two routes to scientific explanation', from David Harvey, *Explanation in Geography*, (Edward Arnold, 1969). © 1969 by Hodder Arnold.

falsification rather than verification. That is, he argued that scientists should look for evidence that *disproves* their laws, theories and models. His logic was that one refutation will lead scientists to reject or amend a proposed explanation whereas even a thousand verifications only tell us that the explanation has not failed *as yet*. Popper's 'critical rationalism' (as it has been called) was thus a speedier, more exacting route to scientific truths – though perhaps *too* exacting for most practising scientists.

So much for scientific method. I mentioned above that specific techniques of both data gathering and data analysis were a key part of this method. It would be futile trying to list all the techniques that scientists have used in their research over the years. Suffice to say that many of these techniques rest upon very precise measurement and equally precise analysis. The appeal of quantitative methods (as opposed to qualitative ones) is that they offer this kind of precision. For instance, there's a difference between observing that water boils when it gets hot and knowing that it normally boils at 100 degrees Celsius at normal atmospheric pressure.

Having discussed this scientific trinity – world-view, method and quantification – it would seem logical to examine the kind of research the spatial scientists did in the 1960s and 1970s and see whether the practice matched the ideas laid down by Comte and the Vienna Circle. In fact things are not so simple. No one, not even Schaefer, laid out a detailed template at the start of geography's 'scientific and quantitative revolution' for others to follow (in fact he died before the 1953 paper was in print). For instance, Schaefer's paper said nothing about scientific method, while it took until 1969 for someone (David Harvey) to spell out the deductive-nomological route to explanation and prediction. Meanwhile, none of the leading spatial scientists had much to say about Comte's positivist world-view – it was very much a 'hidden philosophy'. Yet, as we shall see in the next section, critics of spatial science in the 1970s and in more recent text-book treatment have given the impression that things were otherwise – that spatial scientists had a 'grand plan' and a worked-out conception of science from the very start. The reality is that they operated in a more piecemeal fashion with little formal understanding of positivist world-view or method.

In light of this, what we can say about the spatial scientists? We can't say that they all adopted every last detail of the scientific trinity outlined above. We can say, though, that these geographers tried vigorously to describe and explain a variety of spatial patterns at different scales; that they did so using formal laws, theories and models (the titles of Bunge's book and of Haggett and Chorley's second volume openly advertised the fact); that they thought of themselves as relatively objective seekers after geographical truths; and that they enthusiastically employed quantification in their research. In human geography, for example, the 1960s were the era when Christaller's central place theory, Weber's industrial location theory, Alonso and Muth's urban land use theories and Von

Thünen's agricultural land use theory (among many others) were tested and refined. Human geographers hunted for static and dynamic geographical patterns (such as urban hierarchies and the spatial diffusion of innovations respectively). And they did so using statistics (descriptive and inferential), as well as a number of other numerical measures and procedures. The question is, was this kind of research scientific? And if it wasn't, why not?

Positivism: A Poor Model for 'Scientific Geography'?

As the previous paragraph implies, the answer depends entirely on whether one operates with a *normative* or an *empirical* definition of science. The former defines science in terms of an ideal-type terms and then judges the actual conduct of scientists against the ideals. The latter is more pragmatic and can be captured thus: 'science is what people who call themselves scientists actually say and do'. Sometimes, the first definition of science is confused with the second. This was the case with the first full-blooded criticisms of spatial science in the 1970s, notably those of Gregory (1978) and Guelke (1971; 1979). Together, these authors created the impression that spatial science was explicitly positivist in both world-view and method. It is not possible to rehearse all of the above author's criticisms. I will just offer a sampling of their complaints in relation to the world-view/method/quantification trinity that supposedly underpinned that search.

First, to take one of Comte's five principles of science, Guelke and Gregory pointed out that the spatial scientists often failed to respect the first, i.e. that scientific knowledge was based on direct experience and observation of reality. For example, Bunge's *Theoretical Geography* (1962) deployed geometry as a descriptive language that might depict – albeit approximately – real spatial patterns. Yet his clean geometric lines bore little relation to the complexities of real physical and human landscapes. The elegance of geometry seemed to take precedence over what the evidence suggested was actually happening. Second, Gregory and Guelke identified problems with geographers' use of the deductive-nomological procedure. For instance, Guelke argued that no laws could be found to describe human behaviour because people do not behave in regular, law-like ways. Yet human geographers during the 1960s frequently tried to explain human geographic behaviour as examples of (or 'deviations' from) a core rationality that all people were said to possess. Gregory, meanwhile, argued that many spatial scientists' laws, theories and models were descriptive rather than explanatory. They often took the form of identifying regular associations (or correlations) among certain phenomena (e.g. high rainfall events and floods), yet without offering real explanations of whether these associations were accidental or causally connected. To add to all this, Guelke pointed out that geographers cannot usually exert experimental control over the things they wish to study. Where the laboratory sciences can isolate the variables whose causal relations are of interest, geographers must study large-scale, complex and often changeable 'open systems'. This, Guelke, maintained, can make hypothesis testing very difficult: here 'the goal of investigation becomes ... expla[ining] ... the discrepancies between theoretical constructs and reality, rather than the explanation of reality itself' (Guelke, 1971: 49). Finally, Gregory and Guelke both suggested that spatial science's obsession with measuring spatial patterns had produced a lot of precise factual information as if this was an end in itself. The impulse to measure became disconnected from the wider goals of positivist world-view and method in their view. As Holt-Jensen (1995: 829) observed in a retrospective essay, 'spatial science research developed greater refinement of description rather than explanation'. Guelke thus concluded that spatial science was saddled with the double embarrassment of having sets of untestable/simplistic laws, theories and models, on the one hand, *and* masses of confusing empirical data, on the other.

These were devastating criticisms but many geographers persisted with some or all of the elements of the positivist approach to geographical inquiry. This was not unreasonable. A central problem with criticisms such as those of Guelke and Gregory is that they measured spatial science against an ideal-type that supposedly dictated what 'real science' looked like. But this normative critique was and is problematic because it is unclear why philosophers like Comte and the Vienna Circle were entitled to dictate the nature of science to practising scientists. In any case, the Vienna Circle drew some of its inspiration from how physicists did their research, raising the question of why a mainly laboratory science should form the benchmark of scientificity for a mainly field subject like geography.

In light of this, an empirical critique of spatial science suggests itself. Such a critique looks at what spatial scientists actually *did* and evaluates their activities within the specific disciplinary context that was post-war geography. In this approach, there is no question that these researchers were not fully or properly scientists. Because they *called themselves 'scientists'* we look at the actual research conducted under this banner and evaluate it in its own right and also in relation to alternative approaches in geography advocated at that time. Again, it is not possible to do this in detail, but two illustrative points can be made. First, though Guelke and Gregory were right that spatial scientists often produced few compelling explanations of the phenomena they measured, description *per se* is often illuminating and useful. Many of the spatial associations discovered in the 1960s and 1970s were hitherto unknown and could be acted upon. For example, knowing the exact number of vehicles in rush-hour traffic in a given city day-in, day-out, is central to knowing whether it is necessary to build relief roads or to introduce extra park-and-ride schemes. *Explaining* the traffic volume–time-of-day link is, strictly, immaterial (though, of course, interesting and potentially useful). Second, in relation to the regional geography that carried on despite the Schaefer–Hartshorne debate, spatial science research certainly produced more general and precise understandings of the geographical landscape. Descriptive or not, these understandings allowed geography to gain wider social respectability and gave geographers a role in environmental management and urban and regional policy.

Post-Positivist Science and its Alternatives

There's much more that could be said about the strengths of spatial science research. Whether we adopt a normative or a descriptive stance, the criticisms made in the previous section amount to an internal evaluation of spatial science. An *internal critique* judges something according to its own standards and criteria, rather than those external to it. An *external critique*, by contrast, judges a research approach according to alternative standards and criteria. In human geography, such a critique of spatial science gathered momentum from the mid-1970s in the form of the already mentioned humanistic and Marxist approaches.

Humanistic geography took the view that the aim of research should be to understand the diverse thoughts, values and feelings of capable human actors rather than try to seek general laws, models or theories to explain (let alone predict) their behaviour. It thus rejected the term 'science' because, in human geography at least, it had become associated with simplistic, *a priori* depictions of human actors as if they shared a common rational core that controlled their locational decision-making (e.g. where to live, where to shop, where to open a new factory, etc.). For humanistic geographers, to understand people as individuals and groups, one had to dispense with the presumption that their behaviour is governed by common principles or processes. An offshoot of spatial science – so-called 'behavioural geography' (see Johnston, 2003) – had built on this presumption in order to research the mental understandings of the world that people possess. But even this more sophisticated under-standing of the humans in human geography was not complex and subtle enough for humanistic geographers. For them human geography couldn't be – or rather shouldn't attempt to be – a science because science was *simply the wrong approach to the subject matter of human geography*. That is, the humanistic geographers made both an ontological and a methodo-logical argument. The former was that people's behaviour is not subject to general logics, rules or processes and thus is not amenable to over-arching laws, models or theories. Their behaviour was seen to be more idiosyncratic and unpredictable than that. This argument was indebted to humanistic geographers' reading of the existential and phenomeno-logical philosophers, the likes of Jean-Paul Sartre and Maurice Merleau-Ponty. The latter argument was that in order to 'get inside people's heads', researchers had to give up the distance and objectivity so central to the positivist world-view. The 'hermeneutic' approach entailed 'get-ting under the skin' of the researched so that their lifeworlds could be understood from within.

Marxist geographers, while also critical of spatial science, were less certain one needed to dispense with the label science altogether. For instance, in his *Limits to Capital* (1982), David Harvey describes his analysis of the geography of capitalist accumulation as a scientific one, yet not in the positivist mould. So what was this alternative form of science? Most early Marxist geographers failed to provide an answer. Then in 1984 the British geographer-cum-sociologist Andrew Sayer, in his book *Method in Social Science*, described what a non-positivist but scientific approach to human geography research looked like. This ap-proach, called critical realism (also known as scientific or transcendental realism), is usually associated with the contemporary philosophers Roy Bhaskar and Rom Harré. Sayer was exposed to it during his years at Sussex University, where the geography department existed in an inter-disciplinary environment that encouraged the sharing of ideas across the disciplines. Critical realism is very much an empirical rather than a normative approach to describing science. It looks at what scientists do when researching the world and tries to codify it into a set of principles for researchers to follow. In Sayer's case, several Marxist researchers practised a critical realist form of research (though not all Marxists did, including Harvey) and his book explained to both them and the spatial scientists what that actually meant.

We can encapsulate critical realism in the following three points. First, like positivism, it is concerned with seeking truthful accounts of a material world of both people and things. It is 'realist' in this minimal sense. Second, unlike humanistic geography, critical realism shares the spatial scientists' presumption that social and environmental systems are ordered rather than disordered. If disorder reigned, then life on earth would be impossible since one could never rely on anything being the same or repeated over time or space. Third, critical realism challenges the idea that this order is manifest as regular associations between two or more visible phenomena. In Sayer's words: 'what causes something to happen has nothing to do with . . . the number of times it has happened . . . and hence with whether it constitutes a regularity' (1985: 162). For critical realists, the 'order' existent in social and environmental systems is not empirical (that is, visible to the eye) but virtual (that is, one must see empirical events as material expressions of real but non-empirical, invisible processes). To illustrate, Sayer (1985) takes the example of the spatial science research by David Keeble, an economic geographer. Keeble's research into the relocation of industry in Britain in the 1970s looked for factors that were spatially proximate to where firms closed down and opened up (e.g. high rates of union membership among workers might be associated with firms leaving an area). Sayer argued that while there might be a close *correlation* between these factors and rates of firm closure/opening, these correlations might be quite irrelevant to the *causes* of firm relocation. The only way to discover these causes, Sayer argued, was to undertake 'intensive research' (not extensive research like Keeble's) into each individual firm so as to ascertain the precise combination of reasons that caused it to open or close in a particular locality (for an excellent introduction to realism, see Chapter 5 of Cloke et al., 1991). Looking at lots of firms superficially and hunting for proximate factors was, in Sayer's view, to mistake 'constant conjunctions' (i.e. regular spatial patterns) for 'causal conjunctions' (the precise combination of reasons that cause an event to occur).

Critical realism inspired a new kind of 'scientific' research in human geography during the 1980s and 1990s – one less concerned with the search for geographical order than the spatial scientists had been. Somewhat later, it also inspired research in physical geography – especially geomorphology. The delay was probably due, in part, to physical geographers' aversion to abstract discussions of science and other issues when compared to their enthusiasm for 'getting their hands dirty' by 'doing geography'. Whatever the reason, critical realism was enthusiastically embraced by some physical geographers, because it allowed them to still claim the mantle of science while moving beyond the limitations of positivism. While models, theories and laws, as well as quantification and the use of a structured method of investigation, were still *de rigueur* (see Richards, 2003), critical realism allowed physical geographers to take account of the open systems nature of physical environments without giving up on the search for order in, and precise knowledge of, the non-human world. Many physical geographers have become even more pre-occupied with how to understand the seeming irregularity, contingency and 'messiness' of nature: its 'fuzzy order' if you like. Complexity theory, chaos theory and quantum mechanics have all been drawn upon to inspire new thinking about how environmental systems work (Phillips, 1999; see also Chapter 5 in this volume by Harrison). What has remained consistent, though, is physical geographers' commitment to the idea that these systems can be understood accurately and objectively – that is to say 'scientifically' – if care is taken in the classification, observation and measurement of those systems.

Beyond Science?

This chapter has been a long one, so I'll keep this penultimate section short en route to my concluding comments. At the present time, it seems to me that geography is 'beyond science' in a literal but also a figurative sense. The literal sense arguably applies to human geography. Since critical realism enjoyed its heyday, a raft of new approaches to research have been developed, many of them derived from the humanities disciplines rather than the social sciences. For instance, post-colonial theory, which is now quite influential in cultural and historical geography, has been drawn from the fields of cultural studies and English literature. This has meant a dilution in the debates over human geography's scientific status, with even critical realism – once a real force in human geography – now just one of a *pot pourri* of approaches. On top of this, the aversion of many human geographers to classifying their 'half' of the discipline as a science was arguably exacerbated by the so-called 'science wars' of the mid-1990s. Here a group of practising natural scientists fought back against what they saw as the irresponsible arguments of several sociologists and cultural critics. The latter had argued that scientists *construct* their knowledge of nature, rather than that knowledge being an accurate reflection of nature's truths (Woolgar, 1988). The scientists, understandably dismayed, insisted that science still offers the most secure route to objective understandings of the world (see Gross and Levitt, 1994; Ross,

1996). The result was a stand-off between those who maintain a faith in science's objectivity and those who believe that science is a cover for bias, power and the control of both people and nature.

Meanwhile, contemporary physical geographers are also arguably 'beyond science' but in a more figurative sense. What I mean by this is that, as per my comments at the end of the previous section, they still prefer the appellation science when describing their research. *However*, with some notable exceptions (e.g. Rhoads and Thorne, 1996), they prefer not to debate what science means too frequently, in part because they do not adhere to a single, coherent vision of what science is any longer (if they ever did). As the decades have passed, physical geographers – like other field scientists – have adapted their ontological assumptions and investigative procedures so that their conception of science is, today, arguably a pragmatic one derived from practical experience not intellectual diktat (Sherman, 1999). Rather than being handed down by philosophers of science, this conception is derived 'indigenously' on the basis of perceived good research practice within physical geography itself and other earth sciences.

Conclusion

What can we conclude from this discussion? It is clear that there is not, and never has been, a single thing called Science with a capital S that can be used as a benchmark against which to measure the research practices of geographers or anyone else. It is equally clear that geography as a whole is a 'science' only if we employ a vernacular, insubstantial, and ultimately rather trivial definition of the word. The real question, therefore, is this: what *kind* of sciences are those *parts* of human and physical geography where the term is used in a substantive sense? We have also seen that many human geographers consciously avoid using the term science to describe their research because, in their view, it is simply inappropriate as a descriptor. Finally, we have seen that physical geographers still regard their work as scientific for the most part, but do not hold to some grand conception of Science specified by either philosophers or those in other natural science disciplines. As we look to the future of Anglophone geography, it seems to me that, for those who believe in the scientificity of their research, no one definition of 'proper science' is likely to win out. Well over a century since the discipline's formation as a proper university subject, scientific geographers of different stripes perhaps agree only on the generalities, not the specifics. They agree, that is, that science is about the systematic pursuit of accurate knowledge but dispute quite how that pursuit should be conducted and to what precise ends. In the meantime, many human geographers remain wary of the 'scientific' label for either reasons of principle or pragmatism. The only thing that is clear is that the word 'science' has become rather tired through its persistent use as a term of approbation or condemnation. Yet many in geography will wish to brandish the term for years to come, if only because it still has a talismanic power over funding bodies, sections of the wider public and many students.

ESSAY QUESTIONS AND FURTHER READING

1   Was geography ever a positivist science? Guelke (1971; 1978) and Gregory (1978: Introduction and Chapter 1) offer a critical response to the question, as, to a lesser extent, does Johnston (1986: Chapter 2) for human geography. Hay (1979; 1985) and Marshall (1985) are far more positive, while Holt-Jensen (1995) and Sheppard (1995) offer balanced retrospectives.

2   If not all geographers adhere to positivist or critical realist approaches, does this mean that their research is 'unscientific'? Here the key readings are Sayer (1985; 1992: Chapter 6), Johnston (1989), Rhoads and Thorne (1996), Rhoads (1999) and Richards (1994). Note that in each case the term 'science' is implicitly or explicitly used in different ways and with different degrees of precision. In human geography several approaches to research do not routinely describe themselves as sciences – such as humanistic geography and feminist geography (see Peet, 1999: Chapters 2 and 7). Is this significant?

Maybe cite these .

REFERENCES

Abler, R., Adams, J. and Gould, P. (1971) *Spatial Organization*. Prentice Hall, Englewood Cliffs, NJ.

Ackerman, E. (1945) Geographic training, war-time research and immediate professional objectives. *Annals of the Association of American Geographers* **35**, 121–143.

Bunge, W. (1962) *Theoretical Geography*. C.W.K. Gleerup, Lund.

Burton, I. (1963) The quantitative revolution and theoretical geography. *The Canadian Geographer* **7**, 151–162.

Chalmers, A. (1990) *What Is This Thing Called Science?* Open University Press, Buckingham.

Chorley, R. and Haggett, P. (eds) (1965) *Frontiers in Geographical Teaching*. Methuen, London.

Chorley, R. and Haggett, P. (eds) (1967) *Models in Geography*. Methuen, London.

Cloke, P., Philo, C. and Sadler, D. (1991) *Approaching Human Geography*. Paul Chapman, London.

Demeritt, D. (1996) Social theory and the reconstruction of science and geography. *Transactions of the Institute of British Geographers* NS **21**, 484–503.

Gieryn, T. (1983) Boundary work and the demarcation of science from non-science. *American Sociological Review* **48**, 781–795.

Gould, P. (1979) Geography 1957–77. *Annals of the Association of American Geographers* **69**, 139–151.

Gregory, D. (1978) *Ideology, Science and Human Geography*. Hutchinson, London.

Gross, P.R. and Levitt, N. (1994) *Higher Superstition: The Academic Left and its Quarrels with Science*. Johns Hopkins University Press, Baltimore, MD.

Guelke, L. (1971) Problems of scientific explanation on geography. *Canadian Geographer* **15**, 38–53.

Guelke, L. (1978) Geography and logical positivism. In Johnston, R. and Herbert, D. (eds) *Geography and the Urban Environment*, vol. 1. Wiley, Chichester, pp. 35–61.

Habermas, J. (1972) *Knowledge and Human Interests*. Heinemann, London.

Haggett, P. (1965) *Locational Analysis in Human Geography*. Edward Arnold, London.

Haines-Young, R. and Petch, J. (1986) *Physical Geography: Its Nature and Methods*. Harper and Row, London.

Hartshorne, R. (1939) *The Nature of Geography*. Association of American Geographers, Washington, DC.

Harvey, D. (1969) *Explanation in Geography*. Edward Arnold, London.

Harvey, D. (1973) *Social Justice and the City*. Edward Arnold, London.

Harvey, D. (1982) *Limits to Capital*. Blackwell, Oxford.

Hay, A. (1979) Positivism in human geography: response to critics. In Johnston, R.J. and Herbert, D. (eds) *Geography and the Urban Environment*, vol. 2. Wiley, Chichester, pp. 1–26.

Hay, A. (1985) Scientific method in geography. In Johnston, R.J. (ed.) *The Future of Geography*. Methuen, London, pp. 129–142.

Holt-Jensen, A. (1995) Achievements of spatial science. In Douglas, I., Huggett, R. and Robinson, M. (eds) *Companion Encyclopedia of Geography*. Routledge, London, pp. 818–836.

Johnston, R.J. (1986) *Philosophy and Human Geography*. Arnold, London.

Johnston, R.J. (1989) Philosophy, ideology and geography. In Gregory, D. and Walford, R. (eds) *Horizons in Human Geography*. Macmillan, London, pp. 48–66.

Johnston, R.J. (2003) Geography and the social science tradition. In Holloway, S., Rice, S. and Valentine, G. (eds) *Key Concepts in Geography*. Sage, London, pp. 51–72.

Livingstone, D. (1992) *The Geographical Tradition*. Blackwell, Oxford.

Mackinder, H. (1887) On the scope and methods of geography. *Proceedings of the Royal Geographical Society* **9**, 141–160.

Marshall, J.U. (1985) Geography as a scientific enterprise. In Johnston, R.J. (ed.) *The Future of Geography*. Methuen, London, pp. 113–128.

Morrill, R. (1970) *The Spatial Organization of Society*. Wadsworth, Belmont, CA.

Peet, R. (1999) *Modern Geographical Thought*. Blackwell, Oxford.

Phillips, J.D. (1999) *Earth Surface Systems: Complexity, Order and Scale*. Blackwell, Malden, MA.

Rhoads, B. (1999) Beyond pragmatism: the value of philosophical discourse for physical geography. *Annals of the Association of American Geographers* **89**, 760–771.

Rhoads, C. and Thorne, B. (eds) (1996) *The Scientific Nature of Geomorphology*. Wiley, Chichester.

Richards, K. (1994) 'Real' geomorphology revisited. *Earth Surface Processes and Landforms* **19**, 273–276.

Richards, K. (2003) Geography and the physical sciences tradition. In Holloway, S., Rice, S. and Valentine, G. (eds) *Key Concepts in Geography*. Sage, London, pp. 23–50.

Ross, A. (ed.) (1996) *Science Wars*. Duke University Press, Durham, NC.

Sayer, A. (1985) Realism and geography. In R.J. Johnston (ed.) *The Future of Geography*. Methuen, London, pp. 159–173.

Sayer, A. (1992) *Method in Social Science*, 2nd edn. Routledge, London.

Schaefer, F.K. (1953) Exceptionalism in geography. *Annals of the Association of American Geographers* **43**, 226–249.

Sheppard, E. (1995) Dissenting from spatial analysis. *Urban Geography* **16**, 283–303.

Sherman, P. (1999) Methodology in geomorphology: traditions and hypocrisy. *Annals of the Association of American Geographers* **89**, 687–690.

Strachey, R. (1888) Lectures on Geography. *Proceedings of the Royal Geographical Society* **10**, 146–160.

Strahler, A. (1962) Dynamic basis of geomorphology. *Bulletin of the Geological Society of America* **63**, 923–927.

Wooldridge, S. and East, W. (1958) *The Spirit and Purpose of Geography*. Hutchinson, London.

Woolgar, S. (1988) *Science: The Very Idea*. Ellis Horwood, Tavistock.

What Kind of Science Is Physical Geography?

Stephan Harrison

For physical geographers, being scientific matters. It means that they can engage in debates with the other natural sciences; they can use their methods and their philosophies and they can share (and be driven by) their motivations. If physical geography is not regarded as a science, then its status is lessened. Establishing the scientific status of physical geography is not the end of the story, however. There is more than one kind of science or, to put it another way, there are many different ways of pursuing scientific inquiry. The aim of this chapter is to explore some of those ways, with particular reference to geomorphology. The diversity of science can be understood in two main ways. First, I present a brief history of geomorphology, showing how the leading ideas have changed over time. Second, I concentrate on some of the key debates that cross-cut different sciences today, namely, reductionism, emergence and complexity.

Before we ask what kind of science physical geography is, it is worth reminding ourselves what we might mean by the term science in the first place (see also Chapter 4 in this volume by Castree).

Science and Why it Matters

Science has been a remarkably successful set of tools to explore the workings of the world and universe. Despite those who argue that it is only one of many – equally valid – ways to establish truth, science has touched all parts of human life and provides a stable ruling paradigm whose aspirations and devices (such as objectivity), while contested, have constructed a most powerful understanding of nature. As a result, it would be difficult for an academic subject to claim objective understandings of nature if that subject weren't in some way able to call itself 'scientific'. To be a science is therefore crucial for physical geography because it embeds the discipline into a string of different scientific disciplines. These disciplines are different in important ways but have a crucial theme linking them. This is the belief that understanding and explanation of complex systems can be achieved by recourse to a set of formal, rational devices, and that the results from such an operation are testable. Upon the results of such operations is built the edifice of 'scientific knowledge'. Some see this as a pyramid with 'ultimate truth' at the apex. Since there are limits to scientific explanation, and since there may be more than one final truth, we must be aware that this pyramid metaphor reflects only one particular model of scientific progress.

A naïve view of science often assumes that it must contain a significant component of laboratory work where accurate and replicable measurements are made of a system, and where we try to verify statements or hypotheses. Replicable measurements are made when the apparatus is controlled and extraneous 'noise' is minimized. In principle, therefore, an experiment conducted in one part of the world should be exactly replicable in another. In this view we might see the 'hard' physical sciences (chemistry and physics) as living up to this ideal and we would relegate field-based subjects (such as physical geography, ecology and geology) in which replicable measurements often cannot be made, to the realm of non-science.

However, there are many different ways in which we can try to define science, and as we will see, all of them have problems. We could define science as an organized body of knowledge where objects are classified into significant types or kinds. An example might be taxonomy, the classification of plants or animals. This definition might be a necessary condition, but few would now argue that it is a sufficient condition for a science. Science also can be seen as ways in which we seek to describe, explain and maybe predict the conditions under which events in the human or natural worlds occur. This is done by the observations of repeatable patterns in which related propositions about the shape and causes of those patterns are linked in deterministic ways. Third, science can also be seen as the development of explanatory principles by which a large number of propositions help us to construct 'a logically unified body of knowledge' (Nagel, 1961: 4). Such an approach is sometimes *deductive*, where one statement may be said to follow from others as a consequence of reasoning from general theories to specific instances (see Chapters 4 and 7 in this volume for more on this topic).

The ideas of testability and falsifiability are often cited as being crucial attributes of scientific practice. A testable statement is, as the term suggests, one that can be determined to be either true or false by making observations about the world. One version of this is verifiability. Can a statement be supported by observations? But a more widely supported version – at least among philosophers of science if not its practitioners – is falsifiability. Falsifiability, according to philosopher of science, Karl Popper, is sometimes seen as the bedrock upon which science rests and the way in which science and non-science can be distinguished. It argues that the aim of scientific testing is to refute a hypothesis, not seek evidence to support it. The process of science starts when an observation is capable of contradicting an existing theory. Once this happens, the theory is open to rejection such that a new one is proposed, or the existing one modified, and the logical consequences of this new or modified theory are once more subject to empirical testing.

For some commentators, it is easier to describe what science is *not*. For some, it is not an investigative procedure to be followed mechanically and rigidly. As the philosopher of science, Ernest Nagel says, 'There are no rules of discovery and invention in science, any more than there are such rules in the arts' (1961: 12).

I hope that we can now see that there may be no inherently coherent description of all sciences. Perhaps we should be prepared to say that the consequences of the scientific endeavour have been sufficiently impressive (and, on occasion, counter-intuitive) to make the set of practices which can be described as 'science' more useful and superior to alternatives to it.

Physical Geography and its Historical Evolution

An ordered list of the sciences usually places physics at the head and subjects like psychology and ecology near the base. On what basis is this distinction made? Some would argue that the list of sciences starts with physics because of its closeness to the purity of formal logic and mathematics. Others believe that certain types of physics offer the best exemplars of the relationship between cause and effect. To understand this distinction between the sciences is to understand contemporary debates on the future direction of physical geography. We must be aware that science is a mixed set of subjects. For instance, there are important differences between subjects such as physics and ecology, which are at the opposite ends of our spectrum. The former deals with replicable measurements carried out under laboratory conditions. Here, the variables under analysis can be isolated, investigated and tested. Much of physics can be described in the language of mathematics and by the necessary truths of formal logic. Ecology, by contrast, is dominated by complexity associated with contingent conditions, multivariate system parameters and issues such as scale problems, non-linearity and emergent phenomena. Therefore, in this case, the notions of explanation and causation are not always definable and the completeness with which explanations are constructed varies. Where in this list can we locate physical geography?

We can, perhaps, define physical geography as the study of the 'natural' elements that constitute landscapes. It is concerned with landforms, soils, biological elements and the effects of climate and weather (Spedding, 2003). In many ways, geomorphology can be viewed as forming the core of physical geography. On historical grounds, we will see that geomorphology (allied to geology) played a crucial early role in constructing models of landscape evolution. Other physical geography subdivisions were given a less important role since the models were based largely upon contemporary understandings of geomorphological processes and evolution, rather than on the knowledges based upon soil science, ecology or climate. There are also practical reasons why physical geography can sometimes be seen to be synonymous with geomorphology. Most geography departments in Britain and North America will contain one or more geomorphologists in their complement of physical geography academic staff; many will also contain hydrologists. However, relatively few will contain soil scientists, biogeographers or climatologists. Not all physical geographers would now agree with the centrality accorded to geomorphology. But for our purposes it is a useful introduction to some of the key debates in science, since it shares certain of the characteristics of both physics and ecology outlined above.

One way to grasp the different meanings of science is by examining how a discipline has changed over time. Geomorphology has changed from a pre-scientific (and purely descriptive) subject, to a historical science (concerned with evolutionary change), and then to a science based upon detailed descriptions of processes using the laws of Newtonian mechanics.

Geomorphological understandings of landscapes have played a crucial role in testing the veracity of competing theories dealing with the evolution and history of the earth. The classic example of this is the evidence employed by Louis Agassiz in 1837 to suggest the operation of continental-scale glaciations in shaping the landscape of much of the Northern

Hemisphere. He had originally developed his 'Glacial theory' after observing the landforms left by receding glaciers in the Swiss Alps and after discussions with Jean de Charpentier in 1836, and subsequently identifying similar features outside the limits of contemporary glaciation. His ideas were rapidly applied elsewhere and these observations were eventually to help overturn the view that landscape change resulted from great floods (the 'diluvial' theory).

However, it wasn't until the mid-nineteenth century that physical geography and geology were used systematically to interpret landscapes and develop models to understand landscape change. In this context, W.M. Davis (1850–1934) is often seen as the founder of pre-WWII Anglo-American geomorphology. His appeal lies in stressing a large-scale historical and evolutionary approach to landscape evolution and his influential work on cycles of erosion was published at the end of the nineteenth century (Davis, 1899; see also Chapter 8 in this volume by Rhoads). His approach was geological in outlook although other workers such as G.K. Gilbert used the language and methods of physics, mechanics and engineering to develop alternative schemes. Davis stressed three important themes. First, his approach was regional and employed the drainage basin as the fundamental geomorphic unit. Second, he stressed the nature of change over long-term, geological, timescales. Third, he was particularly influenced by Hutton's theory of gradualism in understanding landscape change and by Darwin's evolutionary theories. This allowed Davis to create a model which embedded both of these concepts. He argued that landscape change was dominated by gradual denudation towards an end-state (the peneplain) and this change was evolutionary in the sense that change was irreversible and progressive. This meant that landscapes could be characterized as moving through a succession of characteristic states: youth, maturity and old age.

Davis's work was widely criticized, however, and this led to alternative methods of geomorphological understanding being constructed. The main criticisms were focused on Davis's epistemology. His schemes were seen as being excessively evolutionary and theoretical. However, Darwin's evolutionary theories were taken up by other geographers and used by environmental determinists such as Ellen Churchill Semple, who stressed the role of the physical landscape in influencing human behaviour. But set against the criteria of more systematic studies, that called for quantification and understanding of process, Davis's theories lacked a solid grounding in field observation and experiment. They were thus seen as lacking the empirical base, regarded as the necessary mark of scientific enterprise. Since his analyses of landscape change did not produce testable hypotheses (as it was non-experimental), Davis also fell foul of the Popperian criterion for falsifiability as a mark of a science. His work was further criticized by later geomorphologists as being too qualitative and descriptive, and of ignoring processes. The quantitative revolution of the 1950s and 1960s in physical geography can be seen as sounding the death knell of Davisian understandings of landscape change.

From the mid-twentieth century onwards, the advent of computers and powerful statistical models, allied to logical positivist philosophies of science, have allowed physical geographers and allied earth scientists to construct a new physical geography based on systems theory and on the language of mathematics and physics (Strahler 1950, 1952, 1980; Chorley 1962). This was an attempt to recognize and simplify the complexity of natural systems by modelling them as the result of transfers and storage of mass and energy. These approaches have created the dominant physical geography paradigm in British and American universities, often referred to simply as the process/form paradigm (see Chapter 8 in this volume by Rhoads). This physical geography has typically involved detailed studies of processes, often on a small scale, allied to sophisticated laboratory and field experiments, statistical treatment of the results and the application of computer modelling. The aim has been to understand the complexities of landscape-forming processes, boundary conditions and change at small spatial and temporal scales and to extrapolate this knowledge in order to explain change at the landscape scale. This approach has produced a powerful research methodology underpinned by detailed geomorphic theory and consideration of geotechnical properties. It can be seen to be the antithesis of the qualitative approach developed by Davis.

Allied to this systems and process methodology and associated with the advent of new technologies of data analysis and handling and remote sensing, are a number of other related themes in physical geography. These themes were not confined to physical geography, nor did they necessarily originate there. They were shared with related fields such as hydrology, climatology and geology. A concern with the quantitative morphological expression of landscapes followed from the work of hydrologists such as R.E. Horton who studied drainage networks from the 1940s onwards. In the 1950s, A.N. Strahler researched on drainage basins and slopes. These and allied researchers suggested that morphometric analyses (investigations into the shape and form of the land surface) and classifications of landforms and landscapes allowed insight to be gained into their evolution. Much of the impetus for this research was gained by the introduction of remote sensing, Digital Terrain Models and GIS techniques. Climatic geomorphology can also be seen to be a separate branch of the subject and this was especially taken up by German and French geomorphologists. Its rationale was that there is an identifiable relationship between landforms, geomorphological and biogeographical processes, and climate (e.g. Peltier, 1950). Its emphasis on morphological classifications and theory at the expense of detailed investigations of process meant that this approach has found little favour with British and North American physical geographers.

Key Debates: Reductionism, Emergence and Complexity

The process/form paradigm seems to have swept all before it, above all in geomorphology (see Chapter 8). Its adherents fill many of the most influential positions in British and North American universities and its methodologies have been adopted by many of the thematic programmes of the major grant-giving bodies. However, there appear to be a number of critical ways in which the paradigm fails, and this part of the chapter attempts to highlight some of these. In geomorphology the tension between small-scale, short-term understandings of processes and the large-scale, long-term development of landscapes can be seen to be the central scientific problem, particularly because one major role of physical geographers is to provide explanations of landscape change at the large scale (Spedding, 1997; Sugden et al., 1997). We have a sophisticated understanding of small-scale processes via knowledge gained from Newtonian classical mechanics. Such understandings may be viewed as *ahistorical* in that the equations describing the processes do not have a time dimension within them; that is, the equations can be run forwards or backwards in time without affecting the result. From this body of knowledge and these tools, we wish, however, to obtain an understanding of large-scale landscapes and landform development. In this case the processes are *historical*, where the landscape is seen as being created by the accumulation of processes over time operating on varying materials possessing varying properties. As a result, landscape change is dominated by processes governed by thermodynamics which means that change can only occur in one temporal direction and is irreversible. At the landscape scale, we can therefore see that change occurs as a function of time, and Davis elevated time to the status of a landscape-forming process.

The predominant process/form paradigm therefore aims to create explanations via what we might call a reductionist methodology, whereby understandings at the small scale are extrapolated upwards to provide explanations at the large scale. This view has been central to methods of explanation in science (e.g. Primas 1983). For instance, the physicist Anderson (1972: 393) argued that 'The reductionist hypothesis may still be a topic for controversy among philosophers, but among the great majority of active scientists I think it is accepted without question.' Such a view is still held by a number of physicists and, to a lesser or greater extent, by most process geomorphologists and those seeking to understand land*form* via process.

Alternative schemes in geomorphology (especially those of Davis) employed approaches based on explanations which were located within specific spatial and temporal scales (see Kennedy, 1977). In other words, these approaches stressed the emergent properties of landscapes. Here, the terms *reductionist* and *emergent* require elaboration. There are two ways in which researchers have attempted to overcome the problem of understanding landscape development. First, they have suggested that an understanding of complex systems can be gained by examining the component parts of the system; second, others have suggested that ex- planation is scale-dependent in that our best understandings follow from the examination of parts of complex systems at the scale at which we are interested. The first is reductionism; the second, an emergent strategy. The reductionist approach has two strands. Ontological reductionism argues that all that exists are the fundamental constituents of matter, or entities that are determined by them. Epistemological reductionism, on the other hand, argues that theories and conceptions about macroscopic entities can be reduced to theories about fundamental constituents. Reductionism therefore suggests that a fundamental theory is 'deeper', and has more explanatory power and provides a deeper understanding of the world than one using alternative methods (Silberstein, 2002). Emergence rejects such notions of fundamental ontologies and argues that explanation depends on scale; a plurality of theories may provide the deepest understanding.

While the reductionist programme might intuitively seem to be the most appropriate method for analysing complex systems such as landscapes, I believe that there are a number of practical and logical problems with it, which we must now examine. We might, for example, believe that the principles of processes governing physical geography are reducible to those of physics. However, it is clear that such 'intertheoretic' reductionism (where one subject is reduced to the fundaments of another) is often problematic. For instance, we would expect to be able to reduce the principles of chemistry to those of quantum mechanics, especially since the structure of the hydrogen atom was only successfully understood once a partial understanding of quantum theory had been developed. However, chemistry cannot be derived from the Schrödinger wave equations (Hendy 1998) and quantum wave functions cannot be used to support chemical inferences (Silberstein 2002). In fact, quantum mechanics shows us that the reductionist programme is *logically* (as well as perhaps practically) flawed. Reductionism cannot provide a coherent philosophy of science since the most fundamental theory which science possesses (and to which all other phenomena might be expected to reduce) is quantum theory, in which the system states display entanglement. This means that the state of the system is not constructed by the states of its parts. Further discussions on these issues in geomorphology are provided by Harrison and Dunham (1998; 1999).

Reductionism argues that determinist approaches to science and positivist views of causation are the appropriate methodologies for exploring complex, multi-faceted systems. It suggests that causal and effect relations are bound by linearity and that such 'one-to-one' relationships (Bohm, 1957) thus allow perfect prediction and retrodiction. This paradigm suggests that everything can be reduced to a set of quantitative laws governing the behaviour of basic forces and a few basic elementary particles and entities and, further, that all qualitative meso- and macroscopic properties of objects such as hardness, colour, texture etc. are subjective, epiphenomenal characteristics since they are absent in the basic laws governing atomic and sub-atomic behaviour. Reductionism therefore provides us with analysis, rather than synthesis, of complex systems. Deutsch (1998: 24) sums up the shortcomings of reductionism by suggesting that

> [It] misrepresents the structure of scientific knowledge. Not only does it assume that explanation always consists of analysing a system into smaller, simpler systems, it also assumes that all explanation is of later events in terms of earlier events; in other words, that the only way of explaining something is to state its *causes*. (emphasis in original)

Non-Linearity and Complexity

The landscape which many physical geographers study is, then, a very much more complex set of systems than the early positivist, quantitative practitioners expected (Harrison et al., 2004). It is driven by processes which are, in the main, non-linear and this obscures cause and effect relationships. Non-linear systems are those whose causal powers are not derivable from the aggregations of lower-level behaviour, since these cannot be known. In this sense, it may be that all cases of non-linearity are emergent (Küppers 1992; Kim 1992). One of the problems for reductionist explanations of landscapes is that many of these non-linear processes may also be non-computable and display algorithmic complexity (as do certain complex systems in subjects like biology) (see Fraenkel 1993; Casti and Karlqvist 1996). The solution of such (even simple) problems may be computationally intractable; some may be non-polynomial problems where the algorithm required for their solution grows quicker than any mathematical power of N (the number of individual components of the problem) (Barrow, 1998). In addition, owing to the non-linear and dynamic nature of many complex systems, any mistakes which are made in the specification of the state variables of the components of that system multiply rapidly to create huge uncertainties in the future state variables (Nicolis, 1996). We can therefore see that specification of the initial conditions of a system is not possible, which introduces an irreducible uncertainty into all systems (see Phillips, 1992; 1999, for discussions of deterministic uncertainty in landscapes).

Arising out of this complexity is the problem of equifinality whereby a landform or landscape may be created by a number of different processes operating at different times, together and individually (Culling, 1987; Beven, 1996). Thus the possibility of deriving useful information about past environments and processes from the nature and disposition of landforms and landscapes is made very problematic. An oft-quoted example of equifinality concerns the nature of the granite tors of Dartmoor (Linton, 1955; Palmer and Radley, 1961; Palmer and Neilson, 1962). Here, plausible theories accounting for their development involve either a two-stage model involving deep chemical weathering and subsequent exhumation; or a one-stage model involving periglacial weathering and mass-movement. Both of these competing theories produce similar landforms and this makes the deduction of the nature of landscape forming events on Dartmoor from the nature of the tors very difficult. Such equifinality can be seen in a very large number of geomorphological contexts including the development of alluvial fans, river terraces, rock glaciers, and solifluction sheets. While such equifinality may be seen to be a trivial problem of 'coarse-grained' classification, there appears to be no easy philosophical way to circumvent the problem.

As a result of these problems posed by complexity, there is the increasing recognition among some physical geographers (and many more scientists from other disciplines) that the way to treat such systems is to understand emergence (Harrison, 1999; 2001). While this approach was employed by Davis, who saw the drainage basin as the fundamental geomorphic unit, it is perhaps easier to see what an 'emergent' geomorphology would look like by using glaciated landscapes as an example. One of the recent ways in which glacial geomorphologists have tried to assess the impact of glaciation on landscapes has been to employ large-scale models called 'landsystems'. This idea originally came from Australian workers who tried to classify land based upon such parameters as topography, geology and climate (Ollier, 1977). These landsystems can be seen as areas with common attributes and a hierarchical scheme is employed. At the base is the 'land element', which represents individual landform types. Above this lies 'land facets' where similar land elements are grouped, and at the top of the structure are landsystems which comprise composites of land facets. Such landsystems can be made more dynamic by the insertion of process-form models, and, applied to the large scale, such models provide us with persuasive and coherent accounts of the temporal and spatial shifts in process domains during landform development. A number of landsystem models have been developed which attempt to integrate understandings of glacier morphology and dynamics in the construction of landform/ sediment associations (Eyles, 1983; Benn and Evans, 1998). Once such associations have been identified, it then becomes possible to assess the extent to which landscapes are the result of overprinting of glacial styles, and this is then further used for palaeoclimatic reconstructions. Such holistic models were constructed by Eyles (1983) for the subglacial landsystem, the supraglacial landsystem and the glaciated valley landsystem but have since been expanded to include landsystems describing the landforms and processes associated with retreating valley glaciers, lowland surging ice lobes and for understanding the landscapes associated with high latitude polythermal valley glaciers (e.g. Glasser and Hambrey, 2001). These large-scale explanations are very different in scope and form to small-scale process studies of glacial systems. Much of this latter work attempts to relate the physical nature of ice at different temperatures, sediment concentrations and pressure to the dynamics of glaciers and the nature of glacial processes. Useful reviews of such research includes Le Hooke (1998) and Paterson (1994).

A physical geography based upon the principles of emergence would therefore recognize that the relations between objects play a special role in the landscape and that landscape form is contingent upon a number of influences which may not be amenable to reductionist explanations. Such an 'interpretive' physical geography, as it has been called (Harrison, 1999;

Baker, 2000), would not be a return to a simple Davisian scheme since we now have a much more sophisticated understanding of the extrinsic and intrinsic factors that play a role in landscape evolution and development. These factors include those associated with tectonics, climate change, and internal system variability (see Summerfield, 2000; Thomas, 2001).

Conclusion

From the arguments put forward here, we can see that physical geography is a complex science comprising a collection of related subjects whose methodologies and foci of attention straddle the ranges of science. In geomorphology alone, there is a range from small-scale studies employing classical mechanics and stochastic interpretations of process, to large-scale narratives dominated by ideas of contingency, equifinality and non-linearity. I believe that we should see this range of approaches as a strength, and some researchers have contested that the greatest challenge facing physical geographers can be found here. They believe that developing methodologies that can bridge the scales is both achievable and desirable.

Such views may be misplaced if we adopt the view that geomorphological explanation is predicated on a 'question and answer logic' (Collingwood, 1994) where the answer obtained from the system under observation depends upon the type of question asked of it. For example, by 'asking' a small-scale process question of a landscape, we may obtain answers about the nature of soil creep on the hill slopes, the rate of sediment transfer in river channels, and so on. Landscape-scale questions will elicit answers about the nature and influence of tectonic processes, the effects of glaciation or the nature of uplift and denudation. The reductionist and emergent approaches therefore provide us with *complementary* rather than *competing* descriptions of landscape change. The future challenge for physical geographers may be to prescribe these approaches in greater detail and to recognize that the subject (and science in general) is like a commonwealth of knowledges, not an empire.

ACKNOWLEDGEMENTS

I would like to thank Steve Pile, Phil Dunham, Ali Rogers and Noel Castree for their incisive comments on an earlier draft of this chapter, and Nick Spedding for discussions on these issues.

ESSAY QUESTIONS AND FURTHER READING

1   'Problems of explanation in physical geography relate to methodological approaches to scale issues.' How far do you agree with this statement? This question is aimed at understanding the debate between reductionism and emergence. You should read Harrison (2001) who argues for a re-engagement of landscape scale study, but also Kennedy (1977). Sugden et al. (1997) widen the debate to call for a strategy to link short-term processes and landscape evolution. Spedding (2003) provides a readable and up-to-date review of some of the issues.

2   In what sense, if any, was the Davisian approach to landscape change scientific? This question attempts to bring out the distinction between historical, evolutionary narratives of landscape understanding and the more quantitative, process-based subject which emerged in the 1950s. Baker (2000) provides an interesting slant on this topic, and further insights can be found in Kennedy (1983) and Bishop (1980). To get a flavour of the origins of the debate, you should read the original works: Davis (1899) and Strahler (1950).

NOTE

1   Work by philosophers such as Reichenbach and Duhem shows that there are insuperable problems with falsifiability as a discriminator. Reichenbach (1970) reasons that the problem of induction (where the past success of a theory is used to highlight its future success) cannot be solved in a purely falsificationist way. It would also mean that science is only concerned with explanation and never with prediction. Duhem (1954) shows that auxiliary assumptions are always used to test the validity of deductive statements from observations (Worrell, 2002), therefore, no scientific theory can have empirical consequences in isolation from other assumptions and, as a result, falsification can never be conclusive. A more pragmatic objection is that it is unreasonable to require that a new theory be immediately rejected as soon as falsifying evidence is produced, since it does not accord with usual scientific practice which is to modify the theory and thus preserve it. Over-reliance on falsification makes serendipitous discoveries and flashes of intuition (both embedded in notions of 'revolutionary' science) much less likely. Yet these are often the means by which breakthroughs in scientific understanding are accomplished.

REFERENCES

Anderson, P.W. (1972) More is different: broken symmetry and the nature of the hierarchical structure of science. *Science* **177**, 393–396.

Baker, V.R. (2000) Conversing with the Earth: the geological approach to understanding. In Frodeman, R. (ed.) *Earth Matters: The Earth Sciences, Philosophy and the Claims of Community*. Prentice Hall, Englewood Cliffs, NJ, pp. 2–10.

Barrow, J.D. (1998) Impossibility: the limits of science and the science of limits. Oxford University Press, Oxford.

Benn, D.I. and Evans, D.J.A. (1998) *Glaciers and Glaciation*. Arnold, London.

Beven, K. (1996) Equifinality and uncertainty in geomorphological modelling. In Rhoads, B.L. and Thorn, C.E. (eds) *The Scientific Nature of Geomorphology*. Wiley, Chichester, pp. 289–313.

Bishop, P. (1980) Popper's principle of falsifiability and the irrefutability of the Davisian cycle. *The Professional Geographer* **32**, 310–315.

Bohm, D. (1957) *Causality and Chance in Modern Physics*. Routledge, London.

Casti, J.L. and Karlqvist A. (eds) (1996) *Boundaries and Barriers on the Limits to Scientific Knowledge*, Addison-Wesley, New York.

Chorley, R.J. (1962) *Geomorphology and General Systems Theory*. United States Geological Survey Professional Paper, 500B.

Collingwood, R.G. (1994) *The Idea of History*, revised edn. Oxford University Press, Oxford.

Culling, W.E.H. (1987) Equifinality: modern approaches to dynamical systems and their potential for geographical thought. *Transactions of the Institute of British Geographers* NS **12**, 57–72.

Davis, W.M. (1899) The geographical cycle. *Geographical Journal* **14**, 481–504.

Deutsch, D. (1998) *The Fabric of Reality*. Penguin, London.

Duhem, P. (1954) *Aim and Structure of Physical Theory*. Atheneum, New York.

Eyles, N.J. (ed.) (1983) *Glacial Geology: An Introduction for Engineers and Earth Scientists*. Pergamon, Oxford.

Fraenkel, A. (1993) Complexity of protein folding. *Bulletin of Mathematical Biology* **55**, 1199–1210.

Glasser, N.F. and Hambrey, M.J. (2001) Styles of sedimentation beneath Svalbard valley glaciers under changing dynamic and thermal regimes. *Journal of the Geological Society of London* **158**, 697–707.

Harrison, S. (1999) The problem with landscape: some philosophical and practical questions. *Geography* **84**, 355–363.

Harrison, S. (2001) On reductionism emergence in geomorphology. *Transactions of the Institute of British Geographers* NS **26**, 327–339.

Harrison, S. and Dunham, P. (1998) Decoherence, quantum theory and their implications for the philosophy of geomorphology. *Transactions of the Institute of British Geographers* NS **23**, 501–514.

Harrison, S. and Dunham, P. (1999) Practical inadequacy or inadequate practice? Quantum theory, 'reality' and the logical limits to realism. *Transactions of the Institute of British Geographers* NS **24**, 236–242.

Harrison, S., Pile, S. and Thrift, N.J. (2004) Grounding patterns: deciphering (dis)order in the entanglements of nature and culture. In Harrison, S., Pile, S.

and Thrift, N.J. (eds) *Patterned Ground: Entanglements of Nature and Culture.* Reaktion, London, pp. 15–42.

Hendy, R. (1998) Models and approximations in quantum chemistry. In Shanks, N. (ed.) *Idealization in Contemporary Physics.* Rodopi, Amsterdam, pp. 123–142.

Kennedy, B.A. (1977) A question of scale. *Progress in Physical Geography* 1, 154–157.

Kennedy, B.A. (1983) Outrageous hypotheses in geography. *Geography* 68, 326–330.

Kim, J. (1992) 'Downward causation' in emergent and non-reductive physicalism. In Beckermann, A., Flohr, H. and Kim, J. (eds) *Emergence or Reduction? Essays on the Prospects of Nonreductive Physicalism.* Walter de Gruyter, Berlin, pp. 119–138.

Küppers, B.-O. (1992) Understanding complexity. In Beckermann, A., Flohr, H. and Kim, J. (eds) *Emergence or Reduction?* Walter de Gruyter, Berlin, pp. 241–256.

Le Hooke, R.B. (1998) *Principles of Glacier Mechanics.* Prentice Hall, Englewood Cliffs, NJ.

Linton, D.L. (1955) The problem of tors. *Geographical Journal* 121, 470–487.

Nagel, E. (1961) *The Structure of Science: Problems in the Logic of Scientific Explanation.* Routledge and Kegan Paul, London.

Nicolis, G. (1996) Physics of far-from-equilibrium systems and self-organization. In Davies, P. (ed.) *The New Physics.* Cambridge University Press, Cambridge, pp. 316–347.

Ollier, C.D. (1977) Terrain classification, principles and applications. In Hails, J.R. (ed.) *Applied Geomorphology.* Elsevier, Amsterdam, pp. 277–316.

Palmer, J.A. and Neilson, R.A. (1962) The origin of granite tors on Dartmoor, Devonshire. *Proceedings of the Yorkshire Geological Society* 33, 315–339.

Palmer, J.A. and Radley, J. (1961) Gritstone tors of the English Pennines. *Zeitschrift für Geomorphologie* 5, 37–52.

Paterson, W.S.B. (1994) *The Physics of Glaciers.* Pergamon, Oxford.

Peltier, L.C. (1950) The geomorphic cycle in periglacial regions as it is related to climatic geomorphology. *Annals of the Association of American Geographers* 40, 214–236.

Phillips, J.D. (1992) Nonlinear dynamical systems in geomorphology: revolution or evolution? *Geomorphology* 5, 219–229.

Phillips, J.D. (1999) Spatial analysis in physical geography and the challenge of deterministic uncertainty. *Geographical Analysis* 31, 359–372.

Primas, H. (1983) *Chemistry, Quantum Mechanics and Reductionism.* Springer-Verlag, Berlin.

Reichenbach, H. (1970) *Experience and Prediction: An Analysis of the Foundations and the Structure of Knowledge.* University of Chicago Press, Chicago.

Silberstein, M. (2002) Reduction, emergence and explanation. In Machamer, P. and Silberstein, M. (eds) *Philosophy of Science.* Blackwell, Oxford, pp. 80–107.

Spedding, N. (1997) On growth and form in geomorphology. *Earth Surface Processes and Landforms* 22, 261–265.

Spedding, N. (2003) Landscape and environment: biophysical processes and biophysical forms. In Holloway, S.L., Rice, S.P. and Valentine, G. (eds) *Key Concepts in Geography*. Sage, London, pp. 268–281.

Strahler, A.N. (1950) Davis' concept of slope development viewed in the light of recent quantitative investigations. *Annals of the Association of American Geographers* **40**, 209–213.

Strahler, A.N. (1952) The dynamic basis of geomorphology. *Geological Society of America Bulletin* **63**, 923–938.

Strahler, A.N. (1980) Systems theory in physical geography. *Physical Geography* **1**, 1–27.

Sugden, D.E., Summerfield, M.A. and Burt, T.P. (1997) Linking short-term processes and landscape evolution. *Earth Surface Processes and Landforms* **22**, 193–194.

Summerfield, M.A. (ed.) (2000) *Geomorphology and Global Tectonics*. Wiley, Chichester.

Thomas, M.F. (2001) Landscape sensitivity in time and space: an introduction. *Catena* **42**, 83–98.

Worrall, J. (2002) Philosophy of science: classic debates, standard problems, future prospects. In Machamer, P. and Silberstein, M. (eds) *Philosophy of Science*. Blackwell, Oxford, pp. 18–36.

Beyond Science?
Human Geography, Interpretation and Critique

Maureen Hickey and Vicky Lawson

[F]rom its modern foundations, geography has designated itself a science, and it prospers less when this role diminishes.

(Turner, 2002: 53)

A real science is able to accept even the shameful, dirty stories of its beginning.

(Foucault, 1988, quoted in Kirby, 1994: 300)

As the title of this chapter indicates, there is an ongoing struggle over legitimate knowledge within human geography, centred around what many in the discipline identify as a science/beyond-science binary. While we do not deny that there are important debates on 'scientific' geography within the discipline, we argue that what we term 'critical human geography' is also scientific, and therefore not 'beyond science' at all. We argue that the very act of constructing a science/beyond science divide and then choosing to position oneself as a 'scientist' within it is, at the core, a deeply political move. As scientists in a variety of fields have pointed out, science is always part of larger social processes and invariably embedded in political circumstances and power relations (for an accessible overview, see Sardar et al., 2002). The same is true for geographic research that draws on scientific principles (Mattingly and Falconer-Al-Hindi, 1995). Therefore we argue that critical, interpretive human geography is not 'beyond science' but rather these approaches raise crucial questions about accountable scientific practice in geography. We demonstrate the analytical power of critical human geography and discursive approaches to knowledge. In doing so, we encourage the parties situated on the boundaries of the science/beyond science debate within geography to engage more productively with one another.

We argue that the science/beyond science debate obscures more than it reveals. If geography truly aspires to scientific status, it must grapple with debates within the sciences. Scientific knowledge, and what constitutes legitimate scientific practice, are deeply contested within a range of scientific communities. Within the 'hard' or natural sciences there are ongoing and often contentious debates about how scientific knowledge is to be generated and verified. These 'science debates' have been influenced by relativity theory, quantum mechanics and the incompleteness theory in mathematics (reviewed in Barnes, 1994). The epistemological and methodological issues that these debates have raised have 'undermined belief in the absolute foundations of knowledge' (Best and Kellner, 1997: 7) and have reverberated throughout scientific communities. As a result, social scientists who claim that their research derives legitimacy from scientific assumptions and practices are immediately drawn back into another of the central questions preoccupying critical human geographers, namely, how is knowledge about our world produced and legitimated? For us, scientific geography entails careful attention to both the ways in which humans construct *meanings* (or what we later term and define as 'discourses') to make sense of our world, as well accounts of the *material* world.

At this point, some might wonder at our insistence that critical human geography be placed within and not beyond 'science'. We claim 'scientific status' for critical human geography for two reasons. First, scientific research has tremendous legitimacy in academia as well as a great deal of political currency in wider society, which is simply too powerful to ignore for those engaged in critical approaches (see Lawson, 1995; McLafferty, 1995). Second, the work of critical scholars is often dismissed as 'unscientific' by its detractors. For example, in his address as president of the Association of American Geographers Reg Golledge wrote: 'a significant part of the quest for geographic knowledge has been detoured by attempts to understand the latest 'ism' rather than advancing geographic knowledge' (2002: 2). But his implication that one can either pursue philosophical debates or advance knowledge is without foundation. Science can never be separated or 'sealed off' from society and, in fact, it may actually be irresponsible and distorting to maintain a position that scientific practice is neutral, apolitical and purely objective (Mattingly and Falconer-Al-Hindi, 1995: 430). The recognition that scientific practice, interpretation and dissemination are socially constructed and deeply political actually *strengthens* knowledge claims. Rather than simply dismissing science, critical human geographers (among others) argue that acknowledging the ways in which science is embedded in society challenges us to pay closer attention to scientific knowledge while simultaneously holding scientists and scientific institutions accountable. We must constantly ask who is doing science, for whom, and to what ends.

The Question of Science

Few would deny that scientific knowledge has historically been used to promote certain political agendas, social programs and economic policies. Because of this tendency, the social discourses (the structures of meaning) that operate around and through science must be constantly and carefully interrogated. Examples abound of the ways in which science has been invoked in aid of questionable ends, and separating the practice of science from the ethical dimensions of human life in order to achieve 'objectivity' raises troubling political questions. Science plays a key role in society and in shaping social (and spatial) relations, and therefore the study of how science operates within society is no detour at all, but instead a legitimate and important object of inquiry within the social sciences.

We have emphasized two aspects of the 'non-innocence' of science. The first critically examines the relationship between science and politics and the second points to contestations of scientific knowledge among scientists themselves. In the next section of our chapter, we argue that the science/beyond-science binary in human geography obscures important continuities in research conducted by 'spatial scientists' and 'critical human geographers' over the past four decades. We will use the term 'spatial science', albeit cautiously, acknowledging that it is not a unified category. By 'spatial science' we refer to a range of approaches within geography emerging in the 1950s and 1960s, including systems analysis, spatial statistical analysis and behavioural geography (Livingston, 1992; Johnston, 1997; see also Chapter 4 in this volume by Castree). In broad terms, these approaches are characterized by the search for universal laws, generalization, and the formalization of abstract models through empirical testing of human and spatial phenomena. These approaches are also characterized by a particular version of objectivity that requires a sustained separation between the researcher and research object as essential to producing rigorous results. We acknowledge that while a commitment to these principles continues to define these approaches, there have been substantial debates within spatial science over rigid adherence to a positivist philosophy (see Livingstone, 1992, for an extended discussion).

Just as spatial science encompasses a variety of theories, critical human geography is not a unified category but rather encompasses theoretical arguments from feminist, Marxist, anti-racist, postcolonial and queer theory (McDowell and Sharp, 1999). Here, we adopt a broadly poststructural framework.[1] Drawing on poststructural theory, we demonstrate the analytical power of this version of critical human geography through a detailed example from development work. We do this because poststructural approaches have resonance with the goals in human geographic research. Specifically, poststructural theory in geography is characterized by concern with oppressive and unequal power relations; the historical and geographical contexts of privilege and marginalization; and a conceptual pluralism in which identities and subjectivities are theorized as complex and fluid. We must also clarify that the term 'critical' does not mean endless fault-finding, but rather that a critical approach signals an engaged, constructive, and socially accountable analysis.

As we noted earlier, a hardening of distinctions between approaches to explanation has emerged – expressed through struggles over the legitimacy of knowledge. In response we suggest that this binary is counterproductive and that there are important continuities within geographic research. Specifically, a central value across all geographic research involves revisiting and re-examining initial assumptions and questions in the face of evidence. In other words, geographers take seriously questions of reflexivity, open inquiry and rigor in their research. This point is particularly pertinent for debates over spatial science in geography, because few are adherents to a hard science position. Current geographic research across the science/beyond-science 'divide' is characterized by a common commitment to theory and explanation as the basis for knowledge-building within the discipline (Livingstone, 1992; Johnston, 1997).

Despite continuities, however, we argue that there are nevertheless important differences between critical human geography and spatial science approaches, particularly *in the ways in which* issues of reflexivity, open inquiry, and rigour are defined, debated and practised (Dixon and Jones, 1996; 1998; Johnston, 1997). There are also vigorous debates within critical human geography as to what constitutes reflexive and rigorous knowledge production (see Rose, 1997, for a summary). As a consequence, it is impossible for us to provide a comprehensive survey of either critical human geography or spatial science. Instead, we use an example from Critical Development Studies in our final section to illustrate our broader arguments.

Science, Reflexivity and Critique

A series of core values connect spatial science and critical human geography, including commitment to open inquiry, continual questioning, and reflexivity. These values serve as points of continuity across the discipline of human geographic research, uniting all geographers who seek to create rigorous understandings of the social world. Of these common values, we argue that reflexivity is key, because the principle of open inquiry ultimately rests on constant interrogation of our questions and evidence. Reflexivity is defined as the interdependence of what is observed and the observer(s). Reflexivity in the sciences and the social sciences is the conscious and continuous interrogation of research practice and results in light of this inseparability between the description and the describer. In other words, reflexive research practice requires us to probe the question of what is the connection between the scientist and the science and what impact does that connection have?

Although there is a common interest in reflexivity across human geography, we argue that there are *important differences* regarding the ways in which this and other core values are understood and deployed within the discipline. The following discussion highlights three key differences between spatial science and critical human geography. First, we note that critical human geographers question how categories, and our assumptions about them, come into being in our work (see Chapter 14 in this volume by Dorling). Second, critical human geography does not claim that specific research findings or data analyses are generalizable to all (or even most) situations. In other words, when presenting the results of research, critical human geographers are careful to place those results in context – to situate the research in time and in place. This process of 'locating' research, we argue, has the potential to produce accountable analyses of the social world – to produce research that captures the *differences* between places and people, which are every bit as important as the *similarities* that are captured through the approaches taken by spatial scientists. Third, critical human geographers question the objective basis of knowledge itself, arguing that meanings – the ways in which we understand the world – are not natural or universal, but instead constructed through specific power relations and through situated interactions and participation in the social world.

According to spatial scientists in geography, questioning and reflexivity are at the core of scientific practice. For example, geographer Fred Schaefer is remembered in geography for his 1953 landmark paper that called for an explicitly *scientific* geography, and his famous debate with regional geographer Richard Hartshorne. Schaefer's approach exemplifies one version of a reflexive approach to geographic science, arguing that geographic methodology is 'an active field [in which] concepts are continuously refined or entirely discarded' (quoted in Dixon and Jones, 1998: 256). Schaefer's statement suggests the need for a constant revision and reworking of categories and concepts, or, in other words, a particular kind of scientific reflexivity. Spatial scientists are committed to producing rigorous, generally applicable knowledge that answers important questions and improves our understanding of social and spatial processes.

However, the assumptions undergirding spatial science – namely those of a stable, stratified material reality that can be objectively observed – signal important differences from critical human geography. Spatial analysis is predicated on the assumption that the social world is comprised 'of discrete objects and events, spaces and times, and the cause–effect relationships that govern variability in the characteristics' of the social world (Dixon and Jones, 1998: 250). In other words, spatial scientists emphasize the high degree of similarity across time and space of certain kinds of people, places and situations. This makes it possible to assume broad 'sameness' within categories of social phenomena for counting and to utilize quantitative techniques. One advantage of this approach is the ability to organize and analyze large quantities of information, discern broad patterns and reveal new areas for further research. The goals of this work are to infer and generalize and, in some cases, attempt to predict (Barnes, 1994; Johnston, 1997: 144). Spatial science practises a kind of reflexivity that involves questioning and redefining categories in order to isolate and measure particular variables and to examine how those variables operate within models. However, spatial science approaches are not designed to engage in a more fundamental questioning of the very stability of evidence captured in those categorizations. Critical human geographers, by contrast, argue that such an engagement is important for the advancement of geographic research, and should therefore be central to the discipline.

We have argued that critical human geography is not 'beyond science' but instead that these approaches share with spatial science a commitment to reflexivity and open inquiry. Despite this common concern, there are important differences in epistemology (how we know what the world is like, i.e. through categorization, measurement, objectivity) and in ontology (what we can know, what is knowable, i.e. measures of observable phenomena, the unseen, such as power, discrimination, etc.). Critical approaches question the underlying assumptions that have led to the creation of commonly accepted categories, such as 'development' (see below). This questioning of the historical foundation of our categories signals a fundamental difference between spatial science and critical human geography.

Critical human geographers suggest that reflexivity must go even further than a constant reevaluation or fine-tuning of categories, arguing that social categories are not natural or essential but are constructed through power relations, cultural practices and representational processes (Gregory, 1994). Indeed, critical human geography engages in a rigorous application of key principles of scientific research through its constant inquiry into the histories, contexts and meanings that are produced in our work. Despite the perceived divide between spatial science and critical approaches in human geography, as well as important differences in epistemology and ontology, these two approaches often inform one another in practice. Many human geographers utilize both approaches to some extent, using statistical information and spatial models to identify new questions and areas for more intensive research, or using qualitative data and critical analyses to check assumptions, reformulate categories and pinpoint new avenues of exploration. Our example from Critical Development Studies below illustrates one way in which different approaches to research, and different kinds of data, can inform one another in a critical analysis.

Within Anglo-American human geography, interpretive and critical approaches have emerged from several literatures, but feminist geographers have been the group most actively engaged with advancing understandings of reflexivity (McDowell, 1992; England, 1994; Kobayashi, 1994). Feminist researchers are concerned with the positions of both the researcher and researched within social structures (positions within relations of gender, class, race, ethnicity, nationality, and so on). Considering these relations is crucial to reflexivity because social positions influence the choice of questions, what is revealed in the research encounter, and, ultimately, the analysis and the ways in which 'data' are interpreted. While some dismiss this concern with deep reflexivity as 'navel-gazing', we disagree, as these interrogations of the research relationship force us to understand that we ourselves, and our research, are produced through fields of power (Katz, 1994).[2] This realization has crucial political and practical implications because it requires us to constantly investigate and reevaluate every aspect of the research process.

Acknowledging the power-laden character of all aspects of our research does not, however, mean that we already know the answers to our research questions beforehand. Rather, critical approaches to producing knowledge share with science a commitment to open questioning and discovery. Donna Haraway, an important philosopher of science whose work connects feminist discussions of reflexivity to broader debates about scientific practices, asserts that open-ended questioning is a fundamental activity within all contemporary science. She argues for a new definition of objectivity that actively acknowledges that all perspectives are partial and contextual and that 'privileges contestation, deconstruction, passionate construction, webbed connections, and hope for transformation of systems of knowledge and ways of seeing' (1991: 191–192). Yet such openness to partial perspectives does not mean that 'anything goes' or that 'it is all relative'. Nor does it mean that we cannot seek a better world for the future, only that the possibilities for such a world are, in fact, expanded by the active recognition that·all knowledge is partial and incomplete. That is why Haraway argues that researchers in all fields

> [are] bound to seek perspective from those points of view, *which can never be known in advance*, which promises something quite extraordinary, that is, knowledge potent for constructing worlds less organized by axes of domination . . . Science has been utopian and visionary from the start; that is one reason 'we' need it. (ibid.: 192, emphasis ours)

Haraway's work reiterates our point that all perspectives are necessarily partial because all researchers are always, inescapably, positioned within (and constituted through) the social world. Our 'positionality', therefore, shapes what we know – and how we can know it – returning us once again to the issue of epistemology. Appreciating the complexities inherent in any research situation means that we need to 'place' all research within a broader historical and geographical context and not assume that what holds true in one study will necessarily hold true in other situations. This is a crucial distinction from spatial science approaches which take as a basic assumption that the 'facts speak for themselves' and researchers assume that 'the empirically observed world adequately represents the operations and mechanisms of the real world' (Staeheli and Lawson, 1995: 322).

Feminist arguments about reflexivity and awareness of our own partial perspectives have prompted critical human geographers to call into question the 'natural' or 'objective' basis of knowledge. Critical human geographers take seriously the ways in which meaning is constructed through histories, power relations, places and the very act of research itself. But if the 'facts' don't speak for themselves, then how are we to understand the ways in which knowledge is constructed? Critical human geographers use the term 'discourse' to describe and analyze the structures of knowledge and power that construct and shape the social realms of both everyday life and specialized knowledge. Discourses are 'ways of knowing' or 'regimes of truth' about the world, and as such are made up of ideas, ideals, social conventions, narratives, texts, institutions, individual and collective practices. Discourses help to create the institutions and individuals that they describe. For example, the power of the state exists not only in the threat or use of force, but also, and perhaps more importantly, in the way the institutions of the state shape everyday life through laws, bureaucratic procedures and socially accepted practices of behaviour. These dominant discourses are all the more powerful because they are understood not as historical constructions but instead as obvious knowledge about the 'natural' state of the world (Foucault, 1980a, 1980b; Gregory, 2000).[3]

The need to attend to discourse is especially an issue in geography and other social 'sciences' that seek to apply scientific principles, methods and metaphors to the social lives of human beings. In the past, scientific theories were often put forth to legitimate projects that now seem nonsensical or even offensive. Within geography, take, for example, the work of Ellen Churchill Semple, who made her name in geography as an advocate for the theory of environmental determinism. Semple's work on Appalachia (1901) was dedicated to demonstrating how mountain isolation and rugged conditions 'retarded' the development of the Anglo-Saxon race that, in her opinion, had achieved so much in other places. While these kinds of environmental determinist arguments have long been discredited in geography, they nonetheless continue to surface in contemporary academic and policy debates over economic and social development. A recent *Washington Post* newspaper article (1998) summarized the recent work of two Harvard economists, Jeffrey Sachs and John Luke Gallup, noting that these researchers found 'that two factors – a cool climate that holds down disease and good access to ocean-going trade – go a long way toward explaining why some regions are rich and others are poor'. These arguments, and others like them, disregard the specific histories of colonization that reoriented economies to extract and export resources and displaced local peoples. Furthermore, they also ignore contemporary political-economic relations of indebtedness and unequal markets in the current global system. Despite these shortcomings, such theories continue to have broad appeal and political legitimacy, by their appearance in major newspapers and other media outlets. Discourse analysis can draw out their connections and show how the direction of scientific inquiry was influenced by political (imperial) ideologies and practices (Driver, 1992).

An Example: Situating Scientific Development

Our aim is to problematize the science/beyond-science debate within geography and to argue that critical analyses of the conditions of knowledge production must be a fundamental element of advancing scientific understanding. We draw here on an example from development studies, to illustrate the importance of understanding knowledge as *situated* – situated in history, geography and social relations of difference and power. This choice reflects both our research interests and the process by which we came to this discussion. Lawson was schooled in quantitative and inferential geographic research in the early 1980s. Over the course of her career, she has become very interested in feminist discussions of the socialization of researchers and the social construction of knowledge and these debates have transformed her approach to development studies. Hickey, Lawson's doctoral student, came to graduate study in geography after spending seven years working in the fields of international development and environmental/population education. In the course of her professional experience she became interested in critically evaluating the ways in which institutions develop and justify development policies. As a result of our very different trajectories, both of us share a deep interest in the ways in which 'scientific' language and practices have shaped the field of international development.

'Science' is a powerful and contested terrain within development studies and institutions and so we start with the pervasive and influential 'science' discourses of economic development (modernization). Development institutions, such as the World Bank, draw much of their authority by claiming scientific status, universally applicable analyses and a narrow economic view of progress, all of which avoid any discussion of power or politics in discussions of development. We then go on to illustrate how resituating mainstream development discourses in their geographically specific political-economic contexts serves to critically reexamine popular representations of the 'Global South'. As we flesh out our example, we realize that 'development' also has a broader meaning, encompassing a range of material processes that includes policies, institutional practices, and the workings of economies and societies. It also encompasses systems of language, meaning and knowledge production that produce a particular discourse. For us, a reflexive and rigorous scientific human geography, exemplified here through our discussion of development, engages with complex issues around the material and discursive forms and processes of power.

One of the most enduring themes in development policy is that the countries of the Global South are poor, hungry and environmentally fragile because they are 'overpopulated'. In other words, they are bursting at the borders and filled with people of unbridled fertility. This enduring Western representation is fuelled on a number of fronts by anxieties over immigration to the USA and Europe from the Global South, and by environmental rhetorics that associate 'overpopulation' with environmental degradation (Connelly and Kennedy, 1994; Kaplan, 1994). Furthermore, in US classrooms, there is a particular geography to this representation. In teaching a large undergraduate development class, Lawson questions the students about which are the five most populous countries in the world. Students typically do name China and India as ranked one and two, but almost invariably Mexico is named as the third most populous country. Population data actually demonstrate that the United States is the third most populous country, followed by Indonesia and Brazil. In fact, Mexico doesn't even make the top-ten list! We can then re-pose the question to students: why do Americans continue to believe that Mexico is the world's third most populous country when the data incontrovertibly refute it?

The tenacity of the 'overpopulation' story is found not only in Western popular cultures, but also in the mainstream development 'industry' of funders and agencies engaged in a wide range development projects. We question why this belief that problems of hunger and poverty are a result of 'overpopulation' in the face of abundant evidence to the contrary continues to be so widespread and persistent. For us and our students, Timothy Mitchell's work 'America's Egypt' continues to be one of the most lucid and powerful examples of a political-economy and discursive critique of the commonly accepted 'overpopulation' argument circulating in international development institutions (Mitchell, 1991a; 1991b). Drawing on the empirical example of Egypt, he challenges the dominant representation of that country as a place with too many people and too little agricultural land. For development practitioners, these 'facts' are self-evident and continue to explain increasing hunger in the Egyptian countryside. What makes Mitchell's argument so powerful for students is that he refutes mainstream development arguments *first* by using the statistical measures and data employed by development institutions themselves, and *then* by situating the image of a crowded, hungry Egypt in its larger historical and political context.

Mitchell contests the scientific representation of the World Bank that hunger in Egypt is primarily a mathematical problem of too many people, on too little land, with too little technology to produce adequate food supplies. He employs data measuring numbers of people, food, growth rates, land densities and land ownership to demonstrate that the dominant understandings of the problem can be, and indeed have been, refuted using the very statistical measures commonly employed by development institutions. He argues, for example:

> Between 1965 and 1980, according to World Bank tables, the population of Egypt grew at an annual rate of 2.2 percent. Yet during the same period, the World Bank also shows, agricultural production grew at the even faster rate of 2.7 percent a year, agricultural growth continued to keep ahead. In 1987, food production per capita was 11 percent higher than at the beginning of the decade. So it is not true that the population has been growing faster than the country's ability to feed itself. (1991a: 20)

Nonetheless, even though data have been used to challenge this understanding of 'overpopulation' in Egypt and a myriad of other places (see, for example, Jarosz, 1996, and also Greenhalgh, 1996), mainstream explanations continue to influence both the policy field and popular understandings of Egypt in the West. Here again, as in our discussion of Mexico above, the claim of overpopulation has tenacity far beyond the existence of evidence to support it. This raises the central question of why this particular interpretation is so trenchant and suggests that something else – something deeper – is at work.

By now, students should be asking the question: 'What else is going on?' If the facts don't fit the picture, why does the 'overpopulation' interpretation persist? The answer revolves around issues of power, which mainstream science, based on assumptions of objectivity and universalism, is not designed to measure. By contrast, part of the 'science' of critical human geography is to use the facts to re-question initial assumptions and long-standing explanations. This is a reflexive approach in that it locates and situates explanation within a broader social context. But critical scholars go further, arguing that development categories themselves are socially constructed discourses, and that the salience and tenacity of discourses that explain poverty as the result of 'overpopulation' are actively produced through specific histories and power relations. Following from this reflexive analysis, critical development scholars argue that development categories themselves must be interrogated and perhaps rethought.

Part of our response to the students' question is that a complex problem like hunger (or poverty, or inequality, or fertility) results from the intersection of geo-political and economic power shaping material circumstances. After Mitchell demonstrates that despite strong evidence that agricultural growth rates have kept up with, and even exceeded, population growth rates, he then asks, 'Why has the country had to import ever increasing amounts of food?' (1991a: 20). He demonstrates that a closer look at the geo-political and economic history of Egypt in the world system offers potential explanations that are considerably more persuasive than the equation of 'too many people/too little land'. This richer analysis considers international commercial food interests, food aid tied to political agendas such as changing diets and opening markets for the West, and class and gender politics within Egypt itself:

> Let's look at the kinds of food being eaten and who gets to eat it...The 1974–75 consumer budget survey showed that among the urban population, the richest 27 percent consumed almost four times as much meat, poultry and eggs per year as the poorest 27 percent. In the subsequent oil-boom, income growth, together with massive U.S. and Egyptian government subsidies, encouraged a broader switch from legumes and maize (corn) to less healthy diets of wheat and meat products. (ibid,: 20–21)

To go still further, another response to our students' question is that the framing of 'overpopulation' as *the* problem is shaped through powerful discourses that set the terms of the debate in favour of Western interests. The focus on 'overpopulation' obscures scientists' ability to 'see' other framings of the problem, such as 'overconsumption'. By focusing on the 'numbers problem', framed as a scientific argument, hunger and poverty are constructed as technical problems that can be solved with the rational application of technocratic solutions. In contrast, from a critical perspective, hunger must be understood in terms of uneven access to resources in specific places and the ability of different groups to have an effective voice in defining both key issues and alternative ways of addressing them (Escobar, 1995).

Thus, our third response to the question: 'What else is going on?' is that students must examine the effects of mainstream development discourses *here* in the West. It is not only that these discourses have been limited, but that the persistence of certain discourses keeps the focus on 'them' and obscures the ways in which 'we' are implicated and benefit from dominant framings of development. Part of the explanation for the persistence of mainstream discourses is their *effects*, in other words, the role these discourses play in re-inscribing our place in the order of things. A fuller understanding of why discourses persist involves a reflexive analysis of our investments in them, whether we are aware of those investments or not. Keeping the focus on the Global South through attention to 'overpopulation', 'hunger', and 'poverty', allows those in the West to elide responsibility for changing *our* practices (such as 'over-consumption'), and more broadly, prevents us from having to critique the very market capitalist system we are both embedded in and continue to benefit from.

Lawson uses an exercise in her undergraduate development class to illustrate that one effect of critiquing mainstream discourse is that people become defensive when that interpretation of the world is challenged. Often to their own surprise, it turns out that students have substantial investments in the order of things; in terms of their material lifestyles; in terms of how they understand who they are; and in terms of the legitimacy of our entire social and economic system. Using a reading by Arturo Escobar (1995) which challenges the way poverty is constructed as the problem in mainstream development narratives and institutions, Lawson asks students to discuss how analyses of development and resultant policies would be different if 'overconsumption' were defined as the major problem in the development industry instead of 'poverty'.

This exercise produces three insights, and some surprisingly strong reactions from students. First, they became familiar with the idea that framing poverty as the problem and economic growth as the solution is *only one way* to understand global differences. Second, using Escobar (1995) together with a powerful personal narrative called 'On Becoming a Development Subject' by Nanda Shresthsa (1995) students investigate how development would look completely different if the problem were defined as 'overconsumption' and the solutions involved more equitable distribution and consumption of resources across the globe. When students see a completely different framing of (and possible alternative solutions for) the challenges of development they begin to see that the focus on 'too many people' in the Global South absolves them of the need to change or even to question their own lives. At the same time, Lawson points out that students themselves are unwittingly invested in a set of persistent discourses that point to the need for change *over there*, rather than *over here*. The very fact that some students become defensive, and even angry, when they are framed as the source of the problem, illustrates the depth of our collective investments, and how these investments are masked and hidden in our lives, in public discourse and even in the academy (including, of course, geography).

Conclusion

In our example we demonstrate that scientific discourses of development – pervasive in the media, popular culture, scholarship and indeed classrooms – have roots in dominant explanations of how economic development 'should' proceed, and how it is currently lacking (supposedly threatening the environment, food supply, etc.) in the Global South. We have also demonstrated that these discourses are remarkably tenacious and continue to persist because they are bolstered by a series of material and discursive power relations that re-inscribe our advantaged position in the world order. Our example challenges how we can, and should, think about the 'science' of development. On one hand, we value a range of kinds of evidence, including quantitative and technical information emanating from institutions such as the World Bank. As we show in our example, Mitchell uses World Bank data to demonstrate that the food supply is keeping up with population growth in Egypt. These forms of evidence are valuable because they often point directly to internal inconsistencies and contradictions within dominant explanations of phenomena such as 'overpopulation'. Indeed, similar analyses would reveal the discursive construction of 'sustainability', 'free trade' and 'globalization'. On the other hand, we demonstrate the importance of interrogating 'scientific' explanations to reveal the crucial historical, political-economic and discursive foundations for *all* interpretations of development. This type of critical analysis strengthens knowledge production and can make scientific development research more accountable to itself and its subjects.

Our larger point in building this example and in writing this chapter is to move beyond polarized debates over what is 'science' or 'beyond science' in geography. Our purpose is to reclaim 'science' as a critical, reflexive, politically accountable process of knowledge construction. Although we see important continuities within human geographic research involving reflexivity, open inquiry and rigour, we argue that critical human geography takes these practices further and that all kinds of geographic research can, and should, involve a constant re-examination of assumptions in the face of evidence. We illustrate that within human geography (and the social sciences more broadly), ideas of science are powerful and important to all of our work. As a result, our discussion stresses that it is not enough to simply refine our categories and questions. Rather we argue that scientific work is invested in, and has a strong tendency to reproduce, politically powerful discourses and material inequalities. For us, 'doing' critical science must involve a deeper analysis of the ways in which scientific knowledge is socially embedded and is always, inevitably and irrevocably, political. By building scientific knowledge that is accountable to its own embeddedness, we can construct 'worlds less organized by axes of domination' (Haraway, 1991: 192). The idea is not that there are no 'truths' or 'facts' in critical human geography, but rather that critical approaches within geography take seriously the notion that 'skepticism knows no bounds if it is really science' (Brown, pers. comm.., 2003).

ESSAY QUESTIONS AND FURTHER READING

1 How would mainstream development be practised differently if 'overconsumption' were the central problem defined by the development establishment rather than 'overpopulation'? Take a look at Escobar (1995: chapter 2) for background on how poverty has been defined as a central problem in development. Then take a look at Durning (1992) for an incisive critique of consumption practices. What would be some of the major obstacles to replacing the current emphasis on 'overpopulation' with your emphasis on 'overconsumption' and what does this reveal about the politics of discourse? Mitchell's (1991a) article and Shresthsa's (1995) essay both provide insights on the workings and consequences of development discourses.

2 Why is reflexivity important if human geography is to be fully scientific? Compare and contrast reflexivity as defined and practised in 'spatial science' and 'critical human geography'. Dixon and Jones (1998) and McDowell (1992) present overviews of these different positions on reflexivity. Feminist geographers in particular have articulated rich analyses of reflexivity for critical human geography, see England (1994), Kobayashi (1994) and Rose (1997). For a recent 'spatial science' reading of reflexivity, see Wai-chung Yeung (2003).

NOTES

1 Post-structuralism is distinct from 'postmodernism', a term that is loosely applied to historical epochs, artistic and architectural styles and strands of social theory. More broadly it is a wide-ranging movement of cultural critique which is sceptical of the ideals and scientific practices that have dominated Western science and society since the Enlightenment (Sim, 1998). Post-structural theory, as its name suggests, moves beyond structural analyses of society and rigorously questions the limits, inclusions and exclusions in all social theories (Sarup, 1993; Sim, 1998; McDowell and Sharp, 1999). Post-structural research is socially and politically accountable and committed to

building constructive practice. This distinction is important because postmodern research is often labeled as sceptical, nihilist and apolitical and yet most critical human geography is consciously, socially and politically engaged.

2   Nevertheless, as Rose (1997) cautions, the very concept of reflexivity requires reflexive scrutiny, and an acknowledgement of the difficulty of actually achieving it.

3   The examination of discourses and the rise of discourse theory in the humanities and the social sciences can be traced to the intense questioning by many scholars of Enlightenment theories of universal truth and meaning, in particular by Michel Foucault. For an introduction to Foucault's work, see the review essays Gordon (1980) and Rabinow (1984) and on his influence on geography, see Gregory (1998) and Philo (1992).

REFERENCES

Barnes, T. (1994) Probable writing: Derrida, deconstruction, and the quantitative revolution in geography. *Environment and Planning A* **26**, 1021–1040.

Barnes, T. and Duncan, J. (1992) Introduction: writing worlds. In Barnes, T. and Duncan, J. (eds) *Writing Worlds*. Routledge, London, pp. 1–17.

Best, S. and Kellner, D. (1997) *The Postmodern Turn*. Guildford Press, London.

Connelly, M. and Kennedy P. (1994) Must it be the West against the rest? *The Atlantic Monthly* **December**, 61–84.

Dixon, D. and Jones, J.P. (1996) For a supercalifragilisticexpialidocious scientific geography. *Annals of the Association of American Geographers* **86**, 767–779.

Dixon, D. and Jones, J.P. (1998) My dinner with Derrida, or spatial analysis and poststructuralism do lunch. *Environment and Planning A* **30**, 247–260.

Driver, F. (1992) Geography's empire: histories of geographical knowledge. *Environment and Planning D: Society and Space* **10**, 23–40.

Durning, A. (1992) *How Much is Enough?* W.W. Norton and Co., New York.

England, K. (1994) Getting personal: reflexivity, positionality and feminist research. *Professional Geographer* **46**, 80–89.

Escobar, A. (1995) *Encountering Development: The Making and Unmaking of the Third World*. Princeton University Press, Princeton, NJ.

Foucault, M. (1980a) Two lectures. In Gordon, C. (ed.) *Power/Knowledge: Selected Interviews and Other Writings 1972–1977*, trans. Gordon, C., Marshall, L., Mepham, J. and Soper, K. Pantheon Books, New York, pp. 78–108.

Foucault, M. (1980b) Truth and power. In Gordon, C. (ed.) *Power/Knowledge: Selected Interviews and Other Writings 1972–1977*, trans. Gordon, C., Marshall, L., Mepham, J. and Soper, K. Pantheon Books, New York, pp. 109–133.

Gordon, C. (1980) Afterword. In Gordon, C. (ed.) *Power/Knowledge: Selected Interviews and Other Writings 1972–1977*, trans. Gordon, C., Marshall, L., Mepham, J. and Soper, K. Pantheon Books, New York, pp. 229–260.

Greenhalgh, S. (1996) The social construction of population science. *Comparative Studies in Society and History* **38**, 26–66.

Gregory, D. (2000) Discourse. In Johnston, R.J., Gregory, D., Pratt, G. and Watts, M. (eds) *The Dictionary of Human Geography*, 4th edn. Blackwell, London, pp. 180–181.

Gregory, D. (1998) Power, knowledge and geography. *Geographische Zeitschrift* **86**, 70–93.

Gregory, D. (1994) *Geographical Imaginations*. Blackwell, Malden, MA.

Golledge, R. (2002) The nature of geographic knowledge. *Annals of the Association of American Geographers* **92**, 1–14.

Haraway, D.J. (1991) Situated knowledges: the science question in feminism and the privilege of partial perspective. In Haraway, D. *Simians, Cyborgs, and Women*. Routledge, London, pp. 183–202.

Jarosz, L. (1996) Defining deforestation in Madagascar. In Peet, R. and Watts, M. (eds) *Liberation Ecologies: Environment, Development, Social Movements*. Routledge, New York, pp. 148–164.

Johnston, R. (1997) *Geography and Geographers*, 5th edn. Arnold, London.

Jones, J. (1981) *Bad Blood: The Tuskegee Syphilis Experiment*. Free Press, New York.

Kaplan, R. (1994) The coming anarchy. *The Atlantic Monthly* **February**: 44–76.

Katz, C. (1994) Playing the field: questions of fieldwork in geography. *Professional Geographer* **46**, 67–72.

Kirby, A. (1994) What did you do in the war, Daddy? In Godlewska, A. and Smith, N. (eds) *Geography and Empire*. Blackwell, Oxford, pp. 300–315.

Kitchin, R. and Tate, N. (2000) *Conducting Research in Human Geography: Theory, Methodology and Practice*. Prentice Hall, Englewood Cliffs, NJ.

Kobayashi, A. (1994) Coloring the field: gender, 'race', and the politics of fieldwork. *Professional Geographer* **46**, 73–80.

Lawson, V. (1995) The politics of difference: examining the qualitative/quantitative dualism in post-structuralist feminist research. *Professional Geographer* **47**, 449–457.

Livingstone, D. (1992) *The Geographical Tradition*. Blackwell, Oxford.

Mattingly, D. and Falconer-Al-Hindi, K. (1995) Should women count? A context for debate. *Professional Geographer* **47**, 427–435.

McDowell, L. (1992) Doing gender: feminism, feminists and research methods in human geography. *Transactions of the Institute of British Geographers* NS **17**, 399–416.

McDowell, L. and Sharp, J. (1999) *A Feminist Glossary of Human Geography*. Arnold, London.

McLafferty, S. (1995) Counting for women. *Professional Geographer* **47**, 436–441.

Mitchell, T. (1991a) America's Egypt: discourse of the development industry. *Middle East Report* **March–April**, 18–34.

Mitchell, T. (1991b) *Colonising Egypt*. University of California Press, Berkeley, CA.

Philo, C. (1992) Foucault's geography. *Environment and Planning D: Society and Space* **10**, 137–161.

Rabinow, P. (1984) Introduction. In Rabinow, P. (ed.) *The Foucault Reader*. Pantheon Books, New York, pp. 3–30.

Rose, G. (1997) Situating knowledges. *Progress in Human Geography* **21**, 305–320.

Rosenau, P. (1992) *Postmodernism and the Social Sciences*. Princeton University Press, Princeton, NJ.

Sardar, Z., Van Loon, B. and Appignanesi, R. (2002) *Introducing Science Studies*. Totem Books, Kallista, Australia.

Sarup, M. (1993) *An Introductory Guide to Post-Structuralism and Postmodernism*, 2nd edn. Harvester Wheatsheaf, New York.

Schaefer, F. (1953) Exceptionalism in geography: a methodological examination. *Annals of the Association of American Geographers* **43**, 226–249.

Semple, E.C. (1901) The Anglo-Saxons of the Kentucky Mountains. *Geographical Journal* **17**, 588–623.

Shresthsa, N. (1995) On becoming a development subject. In Crush, J. (ed.) *Power of Development*. Routledge, London, pp. 266–277.

Sim, S. (1998) *The Icon Critical Dictionary of Postmodern Thought*. Icon Books, Cambridge.

Staeheli, L.A. and Lawson, V.A. (1995) Feminism, praxis, and human geography. *Geographical Analysis* **27**, 321–338.

Turner, B.L. (2002) Contested identities: human-environment geography and disciplinary implications in a restructuring academy. *Annals of the Association of American Geographers* **92**, 52–74.

Wai-chung Yeung, H. (2003) Practicing new economic geographies: a methodological examination. *Annals of the Association of American Geographers* **93**, 445–466.

Washington Post (1998) Tropical and landlocked make a poor combination. Byline Steven Pearlstein, 23 April.

Key Debates in Geography

7

General/Particular

Tim Burt

Particular . . . of a single person or thing; applying only to some of a class.

General . . . not limited to one part or section of a whole; concerning all, or almost all, members of a class.

(The Penguin English Dictionary, 2nd edn, 1969)

The aim of this chapter is to consider two related and venerable intellectual issues in geography: first, whether the discipline of geography should study the particular or the general and, second, the extent to which wider generalizations can be made on the basis of specific investigations. To the fraught undergraduate, the subject matter might, on first sight, appear unimportant or even just plain boring. However, I want to argue that the debate remains just as crucial today as it was a century or two ago, and that, like it or not, it is an argument that we just cannot dodge or ignore. Put another way, this chapter is about whether geography is a science or not; Noel Castree and Stephan Harrison address this issue in their own ways (Chapters 4 and 5) and provide a complementary approach to this same question elsewhere in this volume.

Explanation lies at the heart of all we do, whether student or professor, and we immediately face a simple choice. Do we restrict ourselves to the study of unique objects, one by one, or do we try to do more? Within science there is a fundamental distinction between observation and theory: theories make claims that go beyond the available data and will yield predictions about cases that have not yet been examined (Brown, 1996). In other words, theory allows us to reduce an unexpected outcome to an expected one. It follows that description and classification are not enough: we need to explain what we have observed.

Explain . . . To make plain or intelligible. To interpret. To account for.
(*The Shorter Oxford English Dictionary*, 3rd edn, 1983)

In simple terms, a scientific explanation is no more than a satisfactory account of the facts before us. What exactly we choose to study is up to us – presumably, as geographers, we have a particular interest in some things (e.g. cities, beaches) and not so much in others (e.g. DNA, Uranus). But, having made our topical choice, we immediately face a dilemma: to restrict ourselves to individual cases (on the grounds that everything is unique) or to sacrifice uniqueness in an attempt to produce general statements that cover more than one item of interest. Here I follow Marshall (1985) in taking a very broad view of science: geography simply *is* a science by virtue of the fact that it is a rational discipline whose subject matter consists of empirical observations. On this basis, 'scientific method' denotes the logical structure of the process by which the search for trustworthy knowledge advances (Marshall, 1985). As scientists (in the broadest sense), geographers seek to make 'trustworthy' (i.e. honest and reliable) explanations; the important point is that any such explanation allows us to move on to deal with other examples of the same thing, things or events as yet unknown. Now, not all geographers would even go this far – and the argument about the particular *versus* the general is by no means a new one!

Kant's Stones

Some time in the autumn of 1971, I wrote an undergraduate essay with the following title: 'Is Geography an idiographic or nomothetic discipline?' My tutor's main criticism was that I had not defined my terms, so to avoid making the same mistake twice:

Idiograph, one's private mark or signature; hence **Idiographic** *a*.

Nomothete. A lawgiver or legislator; hence **Nomothetic, -al** *a*. law-giving; legislative. (*The Shorter Oxford English Dictionary*, 3rd edn, 1983)

The two words, idiographic and nomothetic, have been used over many decades to distinguish between contrasting approaches to scholarly work. The nomothetic way of thinking indicates a desire to produce law-like statements that encompass a number of individual cases, whereas an idiographic stance implies a concern with the uniqueness of individual phenomena or events (Marshall, 1985). There has, however, been much dispute between those who believe that generalization of facts in theory is possible in geography and those who believe that geographical fact is unique so that nothing beyond description and interpretation of individual places is possible. The idea of unique objects stems from the writings of the German philosopher, Immanuel Kant (1724–1804), who argued the idiographic stance that geography studied objects unique in place while history studied events unique in time. Kant's ideas eventually developed into regional geography, an approach that dominated the first half of the twentieth century and was championed in particular by Richard Hartshorne (1939). No comparison is possible as each region is a unique assemblage of objects at a particular place. In short, no two regions are alike, so it is no good looking for general laws. Moreover, the failure of environmental determinism (which attempted to explain human activity simply in terms of the physical environment) convinced regionalists that geography was concerned only with the idiographic, literally the unique signature of each region; no more was possible because of the uniqueness of objects at any given place. Having exhausted their description of one district, the regionalists moved inexorably on to the next one. In my own experience at high school, this meant progressing from Anglo-America to the Mediterranean Lands! (see Gould, 1985: Chapter 2, for an amusing account of the 'inventory' style of regional geography research).

Fred K. Schaefer (1953) emphasized the 'exceptionalism' of regional geography as he sought to counter Hartshorne's argument that geography could only be concerned with particular places.

> **Exception**. Something that is excepted; a person, thing or case to which the general rule is not applicable. (*The Shorter Oxford English Dictionary*, 3rd edn, 1983)

Kant's argument was based on the fact that no two stones could ever be exactly alike. More recently, Kant's fellow German, Max Weber (1864–1920), reflected that uniqueness proves too much; in other words, we must not confuse the unique with the individual. Everything is a matter of degree and, in order to generalize, one must sacrifice the precision of uniqueness for the efficiencies of generalization. In Kant's exceptionalist approach, where everything is unique, explanation becomes tautological, description equals explanation, and no extrapolation beyond the particular case being studied is possible. As we might well imagine, such an approach eventually becomes stultifying. This brings us back to science and the advantages of a theoretical (nomothetical) approach.

Theory lies at the heart of science since it unites logic and fact, and is thus the key to solving the puzzles of reality – producing order out of a chaotic set of facts. A theory must be predictive as well as explanatory; science therefore deals with unique – or rather, individual – events as well as with generalized statements. As Bambrough (1964) wrote: 'All reasoning, including all mathematical, scientific and moral reasoning, is ultimately concerned with particular cases, and laws, rules and principles are devices for bringing particular cases to bear on other particular cases.' The point is that, with generalization, it is the variable aspects of objects, not the objects themselves, which are of interest. Thus, we study the size, shape and degree of sorting of stones on the bed of a river channel, rather than each stone in turn for its own sake. As Marshall (1985) points out, the terms 'idiographic' and 'nomothetic' are not antonyms (opposites): rather, they identify attitudes that are distinct from one another but by no means mutually incompatible, complementary rather than competitive. Nevertheless, some subjects lean heavily one way or the other, for example, history, classics and theology are strongly idiographic, while chemistry and physics are strongly nomothetic. We might wonder where geography falls along this scale.

Black Swans

Let us reflect on idiograph as signature. Each signature is unique, of course – it remains the basis on which shops verify our possession of a valid credit card, for example. But if we begin to think about signatures, we can begin to distinguish styles – 'Timothy P. Burt', 'T.P. Burt' and 'Tim Burt' in my case. We can also think of those that are legible and those that are not! We have begun to classify, but it does not take us very far. We cannot predict how the next person, say, Noel Castree, will sign on the basis of all we have seen before. However, it is not far from this position to one type of science – *induction* – in which we use evidence as the basis for generalization.

Many scientific investigations proceed by slowly and carefully building up a set of measurements about the phenomenon of interest. Usually, through repeated exploration of the data, a regular pattern becomes apparent. Where possible, scientists try to express this regularity in the form of an equation; in many cases this is a regression equation, summarizing (regression) and quantifying (correlation) the degree of association between a dependent variable and one or more controlling factors. Take the case where we have paired observations between an independent variable (X) that is considered to control the dependent variable (Y). A scattergram describes the relationship between X and Y. The regression line (of the form $Y = a + b\,X$) defines the best-fit relationship between X and Y, while the dimensionless correlation coefficient (r) quantifies the goodness-of-fit (degree of scatter around the line) of the regression equation. An example might be the relationship between rain gauge altitude and average annual rainfall in the Northern Pennine hills, UK (Figure 7.1). Knowing something about the general nature of orographic rainfall, I expect there to be a simple and straightforward relationship between these two variables for any similar environment. Observations of rainfall gradients lead to explanations that lead to expectations.

In the grand scheme of things, this kind of relationship is hardly a 'law of nature'. Nevertheless it is a 'rule' of some sort and as such has some value. It provides a (limited) basis for further work: we can try to explain why the relationship exists, and we can attempt to make predictions. In terms of explanation, we know that altitude does not directly 'cause' rainfall – X is not the true cause of Y. In our case, X is the cause of Y only via several intermediate variables. Nevertheless, the linkage is easy enough to explain and might well form the foundation for deductive investigations (see below). Our regression equation also allows predictions to be made – about rainfall totals at places where no measurements have so far been made. This is where, using the inductive method, we must make a leap of faith (Mitchell, 1985) – the reliance of a general rule

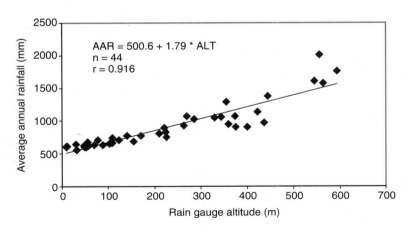

Figure. 7.1 The relationship between rain gauge altitude and average annual rainfall in the Northern Pennine hills, UK.

on a set of observations. Probably, our regression equation would yield reasonable estimations of average annual rainfall within the Tees or Wear basins in England, where the data were collected, but it would be less reliable as we moved to different localities (e.g. the Lake District) or outside the range of observations. For example, might the relationship change for the very highest global elevations and the greatest changes in elevation? And indeed it does. Continuing our rainfall example, we know well enough that a British rainfall gradient should not be expected to hold elsewhere – rainfall gradients reverse at high altitude in mountainous areas, for example. And at the micro-topographic scale, the distribution of rainfall is likely to be much more related to slope angle and aspect, rather than to altitude *per se*.

Our simple example of upland rainfall demonstrates the tension between the idiographic and nomothetic approaches – the difficulty of using specific cases as the basis for generalization. In geography, very often the problem is compounded from the need to apply the results of one scale of analysis at different scales. This may entail *upscaling* of results from smaller to larger areas, for example, extending results from small catchment studies to large river basins. Or, in some circumstances, it can involve *downscaling*, for example, applying the results of general circulation models (global scale) to particular regions. It has long been known that generalizations made at one level do not necessarily hold at another, and that conclusions derived at one scale may be invalid at another (Haggett, 1965). One common approach to the upscaling problem in catchment hydrology is to use 'nested' experiments, each one designed to fit neatly inside the next. Thus, we might move from bounded plots through instrumented hill slopes and small catchments to a large river basin study. In this way we can show how small-scale processes have a more general impact; on the other hand, as scale changes, so too do the main controlling variables. Thus, in small basins, hillslope topography is the major control of storm runoff response, whereas, in large basins, the nature of the channel network is more likely to control flood response (see Anderson and Burt, 1978, and Burt, 1989, for examples).

The standard textbook example of induction – extended empirical generalization – is: 'All swans are white'. Despite countless observations that all swans were white, David Hume (1711–1776), the Scottish philosopher, pointed out that the truth of the statement could not be guaranteed because all swans had not been observed Eventually, black swans were discovered in Australia. This shows how difficult it is to generalize on the basis of specific investigations; empirical generalizations can only be proved beyond doubt if each and every possibility can be examined.

The Proof of the Pudding

Proof. Evidence sufficient to establish a fact or produce belief. The action or an act of making trial of anything . . . test, experiment, examination.

(*The Shorter Oxford English Dictionary*, 3rd edn, 1983)

There are two routes to scientific explanation: the inductive route already described, and the alternative, deductive route (see Figure 4.1 in Chapter 4 by Castreee, if you want a reminder). The deductive route depends on a clear distinction between the origin and testing of theories. It requires first the formulation of an idealized view or model of reality. The models may then be tested, either to confirm that it remains an acceptable (if idealized) reflection of the real world, or, if this is not the case, so that it may be revised and improved so as to become one, or rejected. The testing of a theory involves the independent collection of data. Thus, explanation of individual objects or events becomes, under the deductive approach, a more efficient process since general statements are produced to cover all such events, rather than producing a unique account of just one object or event (Anderson and Burt, 1990).

Karl Popper (1902–94) argued that the purpose of scientific experiments is to attempt to falsify theories: the best established theories are those that have withstood a gruelling procedure of testing or a long period of time. By ruling out what is false, a theory approaches the truth: though supported, it can never be conclusively verified since it remains possible that it will be falsified in the future. Such an approach comes close to the deductive route to explanation outlined by Harvey (1969). As noted above, the word 'prove' has two meanings: to test (thus, 'the proof of the pudding is in the eating'); and, to confirm the truth. Popperian logic would seem to favour the former, although in practice, in the absence of unequivocal truth, we do tend to corroborate (i.e. confirm) our theories until such time they can be shown to be false. Thus, most articles in research journals appear confidently to 'prove' (rather than verify) their point, and the possibility of refutation is kept firmly in the background. Even one refutation need not condemn a theory outright, since the theory may not have been given a fair trial, perhaps because the quality of experimental data is open to doubt. Only when refutations accumulate do we abandon the theory. Even then, a theory widely acknowledged to be unsatisfactory will normally survive until a superior alternative theory is devised (Marshall, 1985). W.M. Davis' Cycle of

Erosion is one that springs immediately to mind: it was concerned with the long-term, progressive evolution of landforms and envisaged a gradual reduction of relief as the landscape moved towards the end-state of peneplain. The Cycle is referred to again, in a little more detail, later on (see also Chapters 5 and 8 in this volume by Harrison and Rhoads).

Hypotheses lie at the heart of the deductive route to explanation. Of course, they need to be devised in the first place, a point often forgotten. Where do hypotheses come from? Sometimes, they are literally invented or dreamt up, sometimes insanely. In other cases, they emerge from empirical, inductive work; in this sense, the inductive route can be thought of as preceding the deductive route. Thus, the particular case (e.g. rainfall in the North Pennine hills) can form the basis for a theory-led approach; further work involves more data collection to test the ideas generated earlier. We must also consider the way in which theoretical ideas are formulated. While the ideal is to use the formal logic of mathematics, very often we are unable to achieve this level of sophistication. Statements may be qualitative rather than quantitative, and commonly we use visual analogy (we might call them iconic models) to shape our ideas. While analogy can never be fully satisfactory, it can be especially useful in exploratory work (Church, 1984). A good example in geomorphology would be a sequence of profiles showing the evolution of slope form over time (this example is discussed in more detail below). Field measurements would be used to provide data against which to test the 'model' sequence and, in this case, appropriate causal mechanisms would be invoked to explain linkage between process and form.

In geomorphology, the traditional approach to explanation by W.M. Davis and his followers was to use verbal reasoning to argue a case (for evolution of landforms over time); very often, the only evidence provided was a series of drawings of the landforms in question showing the alleged change in form over time. However, from the 1950s onward, it became increasingly accepted that independent data collection was required for theory testing. Initially, the approach was statistical and explanations were regarded as 'functional' (statistical) rather than 'realist' (mechanical) – for example, the hydraulic geometry studies of Luna B. Leopold and his co-workers in the USA. However, quite quickly an interest in process mechanics developed. Channel studies borrowed ideas from civil engineering, for example. In recent times, many areas of geography have taken advantage of the ready availability of powerful computers to produce numerical simulation models. Such models, by definition, can only resemble the real world at an abstract, mathematical level, unlike the visual models mentioned earlier. However, just as physical resemblance does not guarantee that a model is effective, nor does mathematical structure. It is easy, and plainly wrong, to assume that, because the computer model relies on abstract mathematical expressions, it must be right in its forecasts (Kirkby et al., 1993). Nevertheless, computer models have allowed much progress to be made, at least in some areas like hydrology. Very often, such models are incredibly complex so that even the people who wrote the model in the first place cannot always anticipate their outcomes. The basis of the model may well be a series of essentially simple statements (like Darcy's Law on flow through porous media) but in a computer model, these theoretical building blocks build up into very complex structures. This can make theory testing difficult (do we know the model is right for the right reasons?) and is undoubtedly one of the challenges for the future.

We can use the study of hillslope geomorphology to illustrate the evolution of theory building in geography from iconic models and verbal reasoning, through mathematical theory to computer simulation models. More importantly here, we can see how a particular location can be used, not as a unique instance, but as a particular case against which a theory can be tested. The sequence of research is as follows:

1   W.M. Davis formulates a theory to describe and explain the evolution of hillslope form through time (see, for example, Sparks [1960] for a summary).

2   R.A.G. Savigear (1952) describes a series of slope profiles in South Wales and in so doing produces one of the most widely quoted papers in the history of geomorphology. It is one of the most frequently cited examples of a space–time substitution: that is, the set of slope profiles in space may be regarded as demonstrating the pattern of slope evolution over time. Briefly, following Holocene sea level rise, a spit grows from west to east, progressively cutting off the inland slope from marine erosion. Today, we see a series of slope forms, with concave foot-slopes to the west, an active cliff to the east, and intermediate forms in between. Savigear interprets the spatial pattern as an evolutionary sequence, in his view, a demonstration of the Davisian model. Unusually within the Davisian paradigm, field evidence is used to provide independent testing of a theory.

3   M.J. Kirkby (1971) develops a mathematical model relating slope process to characteristic form. In his view, rather than time being the dominant factor, shape (form) is controlled by the action of the processes operating on the slope.

4   Kirkby (1984) translates his original mathematical theory into a computer simulation model and is thereby able to model the effect of various processes (creep/solifluction, wash and mass movement) over time. The simulations confirm that the eastern slopes could have evolved as proposed by Savigear, with cliffs being buried by scree once isolated from marine undercutting. The simulations also illustrate a point implicit in Savigear's original work, that the upper slope convexities are very much older than the cliff-scree forms. The Kirkby model shows how a cliff degrades over time: the angle of the straight-slope section gradually declines over time while an upper convexity develops as a result of creep/solifluction processes (see Burt, 2003).

Our example shows how theory and field data (in this case, slope profiles) go hand in hand. The idiographic and nomothetic are not opposites: indeed, the whole point, as Bambrough (1967) noted, is that all theoretical reasoning is ultimately concerned with individual cases.

In more complex situations, it may be necessary to bring several theories to bear on a particular case. The Kirkby slope model does this by including several erosion processes. In general, as we raise our sights and study larger areas, a combination of ideas will be needed to address a problem. In studying the carbon balance of upland catchments, for example, it is necessary to combine expertise in hydrology (runoff processes), soil science (nutrient cycling in soils), micrometeorology (gas exchange between soil and atmosphere), and aquatic ecology (in-stream nutrient dynamics). If we add in management issues, the list grows further, to include land use, planning, tourism and nature conservation. Even here, however, it remains important to take a general view and avoid working on a case-by-case basis. If we are given a premise of 'integrated catchment management', we immediately have a way to structure our thinking in terms of how to view the drainage basin system. Of course, as we move along the road from pure through applied science to 'management' issues, our theories can become somewhat detached from the work in hand. Nevertheless, they continue to provide the basis of trustworthy knowledge on which we base our decisions about the particular case before us.

Conclusion: Newton's Apple

This chapter has been almost entirely about physical geography. This will disappoint the editors, who were, no doubt, hoping for a more balanced assessment of the topic. But like the cobbler sticking to his last, it seemed safer for me to keep to the world I know, rather than venturing into someone else's. My world is one of water and soil. That is not to say that I'm not interested in people or in how my scientific knowledge can be used to better people's lives – far from it – but in research terms it's a question of emphasis.

Some geographers, especially on the human side of the subject, will not accept my argument that geography is a scientific enterprise. They believe that scientific method is inappropriate to the subject matter of geography (as discussed in Chapter 4). I can see the difficulties of the participant-observer: having to examine a world of which we are an integral part, not disinterested spectators. Nevertheless, the narratives of humanistic geography seem subjective and anti-theoretical to me, promising little more than a return to the exceptionalist tradition. Apparently there are no regularities we can bring to each new situation, except ourselves. Sometimes it is claimed that the human world is so much more complex than the physical world that no generalities are possible; I may have missed something but ecosystems and drainage basins are pretty complicated structures too. The complexity of human response does not in itself seem to me an excuse for abandoning all attempts to generalize. Ron Johnston (1985) posits a scale stretching from the 'voyeuristic' geography of place in the exceptionalist tradition, to the arid, placeless spatial science of the positivist tradition: the latter assumes that all is general, whereas the former assumes that nothing is. Johnston concludes that, as is so often the case, a middle ground is needed. You might conclude that I am far out in the scientific desert therefore – but there is the odd oasis of hope: my research is firmly grounded in places chosen as field sites, as well as space, and conclusions drawn from specific sites do help improve theories and illuminate future studies.

Physical geographers must address the unique as well as the general, taking interest in the exceptional event as well as in the regular and predictable. We do – the notion is inherent in our examination of outliers in regression analyses, for instance. But even when we approach something as rare as the 1952 flood in Lynmouth, England, we do so in a context of knowledge about the hydraulic of river channels and their associated bedforms. Physical geographers must also acknowledge contingency, the particular history of the site in question. Savigear's study illustrates this well: in some respects the rather specific cliff-scree sequence, the product of Holocene sea-level rise, stands apart from the more general conclusions about slope evolution as informed by the Kirkby model.

Notwithstanding its attempts to follow a scientific approach, physical geography remains, in some ways, an infant science. Twenty years ago, I reflected that much of our fieldwork remains empirical, just another case study, attempting simply to describe the response of yet another small catchment (Burt and Walling, 1984). There has been progress, I think, with more active collaboration between field scientists and theoreticians, and planned research projects aimed at producing useful generalizations. No doubt though, many studies remain largely site-specific and only loosely connected to the wider theoretical context. We tend these days to have very sophisticated measurement techniques; what may be sometimes lacking is a rigorous scientific framework within which the data are collected. While things have moved forward, helped in part by computerization, Dunne's (1981) lament remains partly true, as we seek to place ourselves properly between the two poles of idiographic and nomothetic. It is also a fitting conclusion:

> Science progresses through the making of generalizations in the face of the complexity of nature. But if Isaac Newton had reported his reaction to a falling apple in the manner that we commonly use, he would have described the gauging station by which he was sitting, the uniqueness of the weather patterns during the preceding three years, the particular apple, and his plans to spend the next three years sitting there to observe other apples, in the hope that at the end of his data collection program, he or someone else would be able to decide what it all meant! ... We need to plan our next research projects with the express intention of developing some useful generalizations that will expand the theoretical framework of the science. More emphasis needs to be placed on planning field measurement programs that will generate the critical data required for modelling rather than just the data that are easy to obtain. Such planning requires that from the outset the study should be designed either by someone skilled in both theory and fieldwork or by a partnership of such interests. (Dunne, 1981: 114)

ESSAY QUESTIONS AND FURTHER READING

1 Reflect on your own studies, perhaps a dissertation or project you are working on or have recently completed. Following Marshall (1985), ask yourself to what extent you have achieved a scientific approach:

   (i)   Have you clearly stated the *problem*?
   (ii) Have you (or has someone else) formulated an appropriate *theory*?
   (iii) Have you derived some *hypotheses* that can be tested?

(iv) Have you collected relevant data and carried out *empirical tests*?
(v)   Have you evaluated your results, and provided an *explanation* in terms of the causal mechanisms operating at your site?

2 Is geography an idiographic or nomothetic discipline? This chapter and the references below will help you answer this question, and a good account of the philosophical issues concerned can be found in Entrikin and Brunn (1989). Marshall (1985) and Harvey (1969) are good places to start. Think about how geography compares with other disciplines, physics, history or anthropology, for example?

REFERENCES

Anderson, M.G. and Burt, T.P. (1978) The role of topography in controlling throughflow generation. *Earth Surface Processes* **29**, 331–334.
Anderson, M.G. and Burt, T.P. (1990) Geomorphological techniques – part one: introduction. In Goudie, A.S. (ed.) *Geomorphological Techniques*, 2nd edn. Unwin Hyman, London, pp. 1–29.
Bambrough, (1967) *Plato, Popper and Politics*. Barnes & Noble, New York.
Brown, H.I. (1996) The methodological roles of theory in science. In Rhoads, B.L. and Thorn, C.E. (eds) *The Scientific Nature of Geomorphology*. Wiley, Chichester, pp. 3–20.
Burt, T.P. (1989) Storm runoff generation in small catchments in relation to the flood response of large basins. In Beven, K.J. and Carling, P.A. (eds) *Floods*. Wiley, Chichester, pp. 11–36.
Burt, T.P. (2003) Some observations on slope development in South Wales: Savigear and Kirkby revisited. *Progress in Physical Geography* **27**, 581–595.
Burt, T.P. and Walling, D.E. (1984) Catchment experiments in fluvial geomorphology: a review of objectives and methodology. In Burt, T.P. and Walling, D.E. (eds) *Catchment Experiments in Fluvial Geomorphology*. Geo Books, Norwich, pp. 3–20.
Church, M. (1984) On experimental methodology in geomorphology. In Burt, T.P. and Walling, D.F. (eds) *Catchment Experiments in Fluvial Geomorphology*. Geo Books, Norwich, pp. 563–580.
Dunne, T. (1981) Concluding comments to the Christchurch Symposium on 'Erosion and Sediment Transport in Pacific Rim Steeplands'. *Journal of Hydrology NZ* **20**, 111–114.
Entrikin, J.N. and Brunn, S.D. (eds) (1989) *Reflections on Richard Hartshorne's 'The Nature of Geography'* (Occasional Publications of the Association of American Geographers). Association of America Geographers, Washington, DC.
Gould, P. (1985) *The Geographer at Work*. Routledge and Kegan Paul, London.

Haggett, P. (1965) *Locational Analysis in Human Geography*. Edward Arnold, London.

Hartshorne, R. (1939) *The Nature of Geography*. Association of American Geographers, Washington, DC.

Harvey, D.W. (1969) *Explanation in Geography*. Edward Arnold, London.

Johnston, R.J. (1985) Introduction: exploring the future of geography. In Johnston, R.J. (ed.) *The Future of Geography*. Methuen, London, pp. 3–24.

Kirkby, M.J. (1971) Hillslope process-response models based on the continuity equation. *Transactions of the Institute of British Geographers* Special Publication No. 3, 15–30.

Kirkby, M.J. (1984) Modelling cliff development in South Wales: Savigear reviewed. *Zeitschrift für Geomorphologie* **28**, 405–426.

Kirkby, M.J., Naden, P.S., Burt, T.P. and Butcher, D.P. (1993) *Computer Simulation in Physical Geography*, 2nd edn. Wiley, Chichester.

Marshall, J.U. (1985) Geography as a scientific enterprise. In Johnston, R.J. (ed.) *The Future of Geography*. Methuen, London, pp. 113–128.

Savigear, R.A.G. (1952) Some observations on slope development in South Wales. *Transactions of the Institute of British Geographers* **18**, 31–52.

Schaefer, F. (1953) Exceptionalism in geography: a methodological examination. *Annals of the Association of American Geographers* **43**, 226–249.

Sparks, B.W. (1960) *Geomorphology*. Longmans, Green & Co., London.

Process/Form

Bruce L. Rhoads

The way we think about the world shapes human inquiry. The purpose of the categorical concepts we use is to organize thought so that distinctions among ideas about the world can be discerned. Once an initial set of categories has been developed, inquiry becomes possible by associating characteristics of the world with ideas embedded in relevant concepts. Enmeshed within categorical concepts are ontological and epistemological presuppositions, i.e. underlying philosophical notions about the constitution of the world and how specific concepts connect with this constitution. In some cases, underlying presuppositions may be apparent. More commonly, presuppositions become obscured through habitual use that ingrains intuitive meaning and legitimizes an unquestioned connection between the concept and characteristics of the world. The latter tendency typifies many of our most common concepts, including two of particular importance in geography: *process* and *form*. Crystallization of meaning yields concepts that are convenient, widely 'understood' conceptual tools for scholarly inquiry. Impediments to understanding can develop, however, when awareness of presuppositions fades, conceptual legitimacy shifts toward conceptual authority and the concept's usefulness cedes to supremacy.

The aim of this chapter is to examine the evolving nature of the concepts of process and form within the discipline of geography, focusing mainly on geomorphology and selected themes within human geography. In particular, it addresses the question: What conceptual roles do process and form play in modern geographical inquiry? Geography, it is often stated, studies the visible landscape (material forms). But since the landscape is shaped by physical and human actions (processes), then the process-form relationship is fundamental to geographical inquiry. Furthermore, current conceptions of process and form derive mainly from presuppositions that laid the foundations for the emergence of the modern scientific world-view during the sixteenth and seventeenth centuries – a world-view that has dominated Western thinking since that time, including geographical thought (see Leclerc, 1972, and Urban and Rhoads, 2003).

Process and Form in Modern Geography

In the United States, geography as an academic discipline emerged mainly through the initiative of geologists *cum* geographers. The most prominent and influential individual in this regard was William Morris Davis. As a champion of geography, Davis had a profound impact on virtually the entire intellectual domain of the fledgling discipline; however, his legacy derived mainly from advocacy for two theories: the cycle of erosion and environmental determinism. The former dominated not only geomorphology, but all of physical geography for over half of the twentieth century. The latter served as the conceptual framework for human geography for the first two decades of that century.

Davisian geomorphology

Davis described the main ideas of the cycle of erosion as *structure*, *process* and *stage*, but the emphasis was on stage, rather than process or structure. Although based on a rudimentary, but misguided consideration of erosional action by water (Strahler, 1950), the scheme did not promote detailed investigations of *landform-sculpting processes*. Erosional mechanisms underlying the cycle remained largely unspecified, but were assumed to lead in aggregate to progressive, sequential change in landscape form over time. To Davis, process meant simply whether the landscape was dominated by fluvial, glacial, arid-region, or karstic erosion and thus he developed different cyclic schemes for each of these 'processes' with fluvial being viewed as the 'normal' cycle (Davis, 1899).

The cycle of erosion, with its emphasis on sequential stages (youth, maturity and old age) of landscape change is clearly an evolutionary theory with organic connotations. Davis himself noted that the 'evolution of the earth and the evolution of organic forms are doctrines that have reinforced one another' (1904: 675). Although biological evolution emphasizes change over time as an undirected process influenced by natural selection operating in conjunction with random variation, Davis envisioned the cycle of erosion as analogous to *developmental* change in biological systems. This developmental perspective equates process with time:

> 'Time', thus became, at least for many of those concerned with adapting the evolutionary notion to wider fields, almost synonymous with 'development' and 'change', such that it was viewed not merely as a temporal framework within which events occur but as *a process itself*. It was in this sense that Davis employed the concept of evolution as the basis for the cycle of erosion. (Chorley et al., 1973: 193)

Because the sequential evolution inherent to the cycle of erosion was inevitable, this evolution, rather than details of erosional action, became the overarching process of landscape development.

Form entered Davisian geomorphology as the empirical basis for using the cycle of erosion to generate explanations for the genesis of specific landscapes. The focus on 'morphogenesis' was central to Davisian explanation, i.e. how has the form of a landscape changed through time to yield the extant form? The idealized cycle was inherently deductive in the sense that effect (extant form) could be inferred from cause (antecedent stages of landform evolution). However, application of the cycle to specific landscapes involved abductive reasoning, whereby cause (antecedent stages of evolution) was inferred from effect (extant form) (Rhoads and Thorn, 1993, 1996a). Observations of effect were largely visual and involved assigning the extant form to a morphogenetic category corresponding to a particular stage in the cycle of erosion. This genetically classified form was then used in conjunction with the ideal cyclic model to infer the sequence of landform development that produced the extant landscape.

From the perspective of natural science, Davis's method often involved objectionable circularity because both the genetic classification of extant forms and the abductive inference of landscape history were rooted in the theoretical content of the cycle. This strong dependence of the data to be explained on the inferred explanation undermined any pretence to objective analysis (Rhoads and Thorn, 1996a). Despite its development at a time when logical empiricism was becoming the dominant philosophical perspective on science, the Davisian method was a decidedly nonempiricist approach to landform analysis. In the words of Davis: 'But the prime fact remains that explanatory concepts, deduced from general principles, are much more intimately and reasonably knowable than empirical concepts or even than facts of observation usually are, and in this quality of being intimately and reasonably knowable lies their highest value' (1912: 106).

Environmental determinism

The type of explanation presumed in environmental determinism is captured succinctly in W.M. Davis's (1906) assertion that a statement of geographical quality is one that defines a relation between an inorganic control and organic response, including human response. This perspective was similar to the cycle of erosion in that the 'process' responsible for structuring the 'form' of human cultures and the cultural landscape was assumed to be known. The environment, like time in the cycle of erosion, became an overarching 'process' that guided human response, yielding characteristics of individuals and societies. Within this naturalistic framework, humans were an organism responding to 'geographic' conditions: 'Certain geographic conditions... apply certain stimuli to which man, like the lower animals, responds by an adaptation of his organism to his environment' (Semple, 1911: 22).

The exact mechanisms by which the environment influenced human action remained for the most part unspecified, resulting in the use of metaphorical language to describe its effects. Thus, the environment could 'stimulate', 'conspire' or 'lure' people into certain kinds of actions, 'enter mind and soul', 'direct thoughts' or 'sharpen wits' (Peet, 1985). The capacity for consciousness to transcend environmental influence or the mediation of human interaction with the environment through society was often ignored. Insidious explanations included unsubstantiated claims about the influence of environment on the temperaments of people of different races, on the sophistication of religious doctrine of different cultures and on the manifest destiny and national superiority of the United States (ibid.).

Historical and regional geography

Dissatisfaction with the strong influence of physical geography and natural science on the content of geography led to two major perspectives on American geography between 1930 and 1960: the cultural historical approach advocated by Carl Sauer, and regional geography as outlined by Richard Hartshorne. Both of these perspectives emphasized the influence of humans on the natural environment and the transformation of this environment into a *cultural* landscape. Thus, cultural processes were viewed as the prevailing influence shaping the form of landscapes – a complete reversal of environmental determinism.

Historical geography examined 'processes, or sequences of events' to provide an explanation for the observed form of landscapes (Martin and

James, 1993: 349). This approach adopted the view that 'whatever interests us in the contemporary scene is to be understood only in terms of the processes at work to produce it' (Clark, 1954: 71). In particular, interest centred on *human* occupancy of an area and the *cultural* processes of change that led to the configuration of natural and cultural features. Much of this work bordered on the anthropological, attempting to trace processes of landscape change from pre-human occupancy to the present. It also emphasized inductive empiricism, whereby conclusions about the processes that transformed a cultural landscape should be drawn from observed facts, rather than from *a priori* theory.

The concept of areal differentiation achieved prominence in regional studies advocated by Hartshorne (1939). Such studies stressed the interrelatedness of observable phenomena and the extent to which phenomena and their interrelations are uniform or homogenous over specific portions of the earth's surface – the basis for identifying regions. Inductive synthesis, rather than deductive explanation, became the point of emphasis. Hartshorne viewed geography as 'a field that dealt with *all* the characteristics of areas (physical, social, economic, political, etc.) in combination rather than as a subject that analyzed the processes which produce combinations of phenomena in areas' (Agnew, 1989: 126; see also Chapter 7 in this volume by Burt). Thus, regional geography focused mainly on the form, or pattern, of observable features and, to preserve the goal of scientific objectivity, did not seek to delve beyond the empirical level of analysis (Entrikin, 1989). This perspective has been described as 'antithetical to "process"' – a view that contributed to the isolation of geography from mainstream social science during the middle part of the twentieth century (Smith, 1989).

Geography since 1950: The Turn to Process

Near the middle of the twentieth century, a sea change took place throughout geography. The initial hallmark of this shift was an adoption of the 'scientific method', particularly the method associated with logical empiricism, which at this time was reaching its zenith of influence throughout science. Approaches to geographical analysis shifted from largely descriptive to largely quantitative in both human and physical geography, bringing the two sides of the discipline closer together. Since 1970 physical geography and human geography have diverged philosophically and methodologically, but a common theme over the past half century has been an emphasis on the investigation of *processes* underlying relations among empirically observable geographical phenomena (i.e. forms), and the need to ground explanations of these relations within a *theoretical* understanding of underlying processes.

Physical geography

In 1950 physical geography was in serious decline. The strong aversion to any hint of environmental determinism in regional or historical studies and the emphasis on patterns of cultural features conspired to marginalize physical geography to the role of providing the climatic, geomorphological and biotic contexts within which cultural regions develop. According to Hartshorne (1939: 123), geographical studies require 'a knowledge of the environment, but this knowledge is logically subordinate, not to be studied for its own sake'. In geomorphology, Davis's influence persisted well into the 1950s; Wooldridge (1958: 31) noted that 'geomorphology is primarily concerned with the interpretation of forms, not the study of processes'. However, by the time this statement was made, much had already changed in geomorphology.

One of the first signs of impending change was Robert Horton's (1945) theoretical treatment of the erosional development of stream channels and stream networks based on physical reasoning about the mechanical effects of flowing water on earth materials – a type of analysis alien to Davisian geomorphology. The clarion call for change, however, was Arthur Strahler's provocation for a new geomorphology

> grounded in basic principles of mechanics and fluid dynamics, that will enable geomorphic processes to be treated as manifestations of various types of shear stresses, both gravitational and molecular, acting upon any type of earth material to produce the varieties of strain, or failure, which we recognize as the manifold processes of weathering, erosion, transportation and deposition. (Strahler 1952: 923)

Soon after, the focus of geomorphological inquiry shifted from descriptive morphogenetic studies of landform evolution to quantitative empirical and theoretical investigations of geomorphological processes and the physical/chemical mechanisms underlying these processes. By providing an attractive alternative for an increasing number of geomorphologists dissatisfied with the Davisian approach (Rhoads and Thorn, 1996a), Strahler's paper inspired a new mode of inquiry that continues to the present and has extended beyond geomorphology into other domains of physical geography (Gregory, 2000).

Conceptually and methodologically, geomorphology since 1952 can be characterized as a 'return to Gilbert', i.e. to the type of geomorphological inquiry conducted by G.K. Gilbert, a contemporary of William Morris Davis (Rhoads and Thorn, 1996a). Gilbert, whose background included training in engineering mechanics and geology, 'looked upon physics as a given body of techniques and concepts by use of which he could solve geologic problems' (Pyne, 1980: 96). He employed Newtonian mechanics, quantitative methods and systems concepts, especially the notion of equilibrium, to explore how geomorphologic processes shape landscapes. In this sense he is viewed as the 'father of modern American geomorphology' (Ritter, 1978: 4) and the 'first process geomorphologist' of the modern era (Huggett, 2003: 9). Until the 1950s, however, Gilbert had at most a minor influence on physical geography due to the overwhelming authority accorded to W.M. Davis.

Systems concepts provide a convenient context within which to view relations between process and form in modern geomorphology and physical geography (Chorley and Kennedy, 1971; Strahler, 1980). Within the systems framework, the mechanistic conception of process is clear: process can be defined as the action produced when a force induces a change, either chemical or physical, in the materials or forms at the earth's surface (Ritter, 1986). In turn, form consists of geometrical attributes of material at the earth's surface, i.e. landscape morphology. Although geomorphological processes are the natural agents that shape the landscape, the latter affects the operation of geomorphological processes through its influence on the magnitude and directionality of physical forces. Thus, process and form are interactive: the operation of a process changes form and the changed form influences the operation of the process.

One important aspect of the systems perspective is the distinction between time-independent and time-dependent behaviour (Strahler, 1952). The interaction of processes and forms in open geomorphic systems does not necessitate landform evolution, but can be an integral component of the *maintenance* of the characteristic, or steady state, morphology of landforms. Thus, for example, the form of the channel bed in a meander bend may remain constant despite the ongoing process of sediment transport because the form is mutually adjusted with the process to yield a balanced flux of sediment throughout the bend (Dietrich, 1987). The period between 1950 and 1970 was the 'era of equilibrium' in which process-based investigations emphasized the attainment of characteristic forms in the face of ongoing processes. Since 1970 recognition of nonlinear and threshold-related dynamics has called attention to unsteady, time-dependent behaviour of many geomorphic systems (Phillips, 1999). Thus, nonlinear interaction of lateral migration among successive bends of a meandering river may lead to a continuous meander evolution in which the suite of meanders never achieves a stable, characteristic form (Stolum, 1996).

The quantitative expertise of geomorphologists has become increasingly sophisticated and mathematical modelling, once rare, 'is no longer merely common in geomorphology, but pervasive' (Wilcock and Iverson, 2003: vii). In part, this tendency reflects the presupposition that geomorphic processes have a deterministic basis in Newtonian mechanics. Deterministic models consisting of sets of partial differential equations that define adjustments among geomorphic processes and forms over time and space currently represent for some the path to 'geomorphic nirvana' (Bras et al., 2003). Such modelling is, however, scale dependent and currently most physically based mathematical models of process-form relations are constrained to relatively small time and space scales. As scale increases, mathematical modelling is still appropriate, but heuristic rather than physically based models may be used to explore or simulate the dynamics of geomorphological systems. Heuristic models do not violate physical principles, but are based on summary (rather than detailed) representations of these principles. Advanced mathematical modelling is complemented by field studies of geomorphic processes based on increasingly sophisticated observational methods. Such studies are capable of yielding detailed information on process dynamics at small time and space scales for comparison with model predictions. As time and space scales increase, however, information density per unit of time and space generally decreases, resulting in enhanced uncertainty in inferences about process-form relations (Rhoads and Thorn, 1993).

Mathematical modelling is still a long way from predicting the development of specific landscapes, leading to some incongruity between process-based studies and geohistorical investigations (Rhoads and Thorn, 1996c). In his landmark paper, Strahler (1952: 925) argued that 'better knowledge of how processes operate and normal forms evolve will increase the effectiveness of historical studies and reduce the likelihood of drawing erroneous inferences about past events. Whether or not this promise has been fulfilled is debatable' (Douglas, 1982), but improved understanding of geomorphic processes has greatly enhanced the capacity to interpret modes of landform evolution. In geohistorical studies, the emphasis is to determine the events that have produced landscape characteristics, where an event is a mixture of environmental/historical contingency and general processes governed by physical laws (Rhoads and Thorn, 1996a). This type of investigation often relies on abductive logic in which the cause, or landform-shaping process or event, is inferred from extant landform characteristics and knowledge of the types of processes or events that could produce these characteristics (ibid.). Exemplars of this type of geohistorical analysis are the studies by J. Harlan Bretz and others of the Channeled Scablands (Baker, 1987).

Contemporary inquiry in geomorphology is unified not by an all-encompassing theory such as the cycle of erosion, but by tacit acceptance of the validity of established chemical, physical and biological principles, that provide the theoretical basis for process-based models (Rhoads and Thorn, 1996a). The philosophical foundations of the process perspective have not been explored in detail, but could be characterized as an amalgam of empiricism and mechanistic materialism. From an epistemological standpoint, theoretical principles from the basic sciences (e.g. continuum Newtonian mechanics), because they are viewed as 'established' by geomorphologists, play an evidential role in rational decisions among competing hypotheses – a perspective consistent with scientific realism (Rhoads and Thorn, 1994). The evidential role of theory explains the preference for models that are explicitly expressed as mechanical formulations. If two competing models predict patterns of observational data equally well, but one is physically based (i.e. it specifies process mechanics in detail) and the other is heuristic (it only approximates process mechanics in an attempt to reproduce accurately a particular set of observations), the physically based model generally will be preferred because of the perceived evidential role of the detailed mechanical formulation (Iverson, 2003).

Interest in scientific realism has focused not only on epistemological issues (Richards, 1990; Rhoads, 1994; Rhoads and Thorn, 1994), but has led to preliminary exploration of the ontology of geomorphological processes and forms (Rhoads and Thorn, 1996b; Keylock, 2003). The adoption of theoretical principles from the basic sciences as foundational ones for geomorphology can be interpreted as a form of reductionism that fixes the ultimate source of geomorphic process-form causality in concepts of energy, force and matter. It also requires that one look to physics for answers to ontological questions. Unfortunately, this path, if followed, does not lead to clarity because the ontology of physics is highly controversial. Newtonian continuum mechanics has yet to be satisfactorily reconciled with quantum mechanics and represents only a heuristic approximation of the dynamics of low-speed, small-mass systems when viewed from the perspective of relativity theory. The ontology of 'forces', 'fields', 'spacetime' and other physical entities remains controversial despite the empirical success of physical mathematical theories that incorporate terms representing these concepts (Jones, 1991).

Human geography

Quantitative spatial science Like Strahler's (1952) paper in geomorphology, an article by Fred K. Schaefer (1953), an economist *cum* geographer, has been identified as seminal in the transformation of geography into quantitative spatial science (Johnston, 1997). This transformation has been characterized as a turn toward positivist geographic research. Quantification and the use of statistical analysis to identify laws of spatial relations became standards for geographic scholarship. Theory development, not application, was emphasized and theory itself was viewed as an inductive construction of interconnected empirical (quantitative) laws – a perspective consistent with logical empiricism (Abler et al., 1971). Schaefer advocated that quantitative geographic laws should define *morphological* relations of empirically defined spatial covariates and that geographers must turn to the more 'basic' social sciences to determine the *processes* responsible for these laws.

By 1970, human geography was characterized as the study of spatial organization expressed as patterns and processes (Taaffe, 1970). Patterns and processes referred primarily to empirical phenomena that could be defined by quantitative data and subjected to statistical analysis. The overwhelming 'empirical, inductive' nature of geographic investigations restricted analysis predominantly to aggregate measures, or variables defined from large data sets, that could be incorporated into statistical procedures. Such measures were most readily acquired from published economic and population censuses; thus, emphasis shifted toward economic, demographic and social investigations, whereas historical, cultural and regional studies became marginalized (Johnston, 1997).

Despite the retrospective characterization of this era as 'positivist', at the time little or no attention was paid to philosophical issues, including epistemological or ontological analysis of notions of process and form. Even Harvey's (1969) spatial-science manifesto *Explanation in Geography* dealt mainly with methodological issues and did not extensively discuss philosophical implications of logical empiricism (Johnston, 1986). Human geography had become more 'scientific', but also ensnared unreflectively in the implicit privileging accorded to knowledge generated by the positivist scientific methodology.

Humanistic geography By the early 1970s, human geography's foray into positivist research had led to growing discontent. Concern was raised that humans were being reduced to mechanistic 'preconditioned responders to stimuli' (Johnston, 1997: 191) and that space was reduced purely to an absolute geometrical 'container'. Some geographers, especially historical and cultural geographers, never subscribed to the approach in the first place and felt its methods were irrelevant to their work. In many cases, prediction was poor, explanation weak and understanding insufficient.

One response was to reject empiricism. Geographers followed much the same course in the early 1970s, developing humanistic approaches to geography as an antithesis to positivist spatial science. These approaches focused on the individual and were grounded in idealism, existentialism and phenomenology (Johnston, 1986). Common to humanistic perspectives is an emphasis on the subjectivity of knowledge, i.e. the notion that all knowledge of the world is obtained through individual human experience. Thus, knowledge necessarily embodies the individual's 'geographical behavior as well as their feelings and ideas in regard to space and place' (Tuan, 1976: 266). At the level of the individual, thought, meaning and intentionality become important mental processes underlying human action and the manifestations of this action. 'The human geographer simply attempts to reconstruct the thought behind the actions that were taken' (Guelke, 1974: 198) through a 'method by which one can rethink the thoughts of those whose actions he seeks to explain' (ibid.: 193). Humanistic geography acknowledges mind–matter dualism and centres itself firmly within the mental component of this dualism: 'mental activity has a life of its own which is not controlled by material things and processes' (Guelke, 1981: 133).

The focus of humanistic geography is on the individual and the cognitive processes through which different individuals appraise the world, but may involve a 'search for the common (imprinted not agreed) elements among those appraisals' (Johnston, 1997; 189). One seeks an 'understanding of actions as those involved understand them, rather than in terms of abstract, outsider-imposed models and theories' (ibid.: 192). Humanistic inquiry emphasizes process-based understanding, or 'a view of the world from the vantage of *process metageography*', where metageography seeks 'the principles lying behind perceptions of reality, and transcending them' (Berry, 1973: 9). Important issues of concern deal with how human geographic constructions, such as places and landscapes, are repositories of meaning, intentionality and even desire, and how such constructions may vary over time, according to process-based change in the underlying processes. Thus, at the individual level, space and time are intimately connected within a processual framework when examined from the perspective of human experience and behaviour.

Marxism   Neither humanistic geography nor spatial science dealt effectively with *general* social processes. Concerns about the role of human geography as a *social* science led to an upsurge of Marxist approaches to geographical inquiry beginning in the 1970s. Marxism is founded in materialist doctrine, except in this case the underlying philosophical base is not the mechanistic materialism of the natural sciences, but the historical materialism of Karl Marx and Frederich Engels. Historical materialism maintains that all social processes are founded on a materialist base – the production of material goods. Social relations represent realizations of underlying, fundamental economic processes (the infrastructure), especially modes of production, that generate forms of observable socio-economic phenomena (the superstructure) (e.g. inequities in wealth, class divisions, housing patterns). In contrast to mechanistic materialism, Marxism is not a variety of determinism. Humans are not mere invariant respondents to 'inhuman' economic processes, but instead interpret these processes through human agency. Because the interpretation of the processes can differ from one group to the next, different manifestations of human action (superstructure) can occur even if underlying processes are similar.

Economic processes within the infrastructure are specific to particular geographical and historical contexts. Because realizations of underlying processes in the superstructure are contingent upon these contexts, regularities among empirical phenomena, the basis of positivist analysis, do not provide a basis for inferences about underlying processes. Thus, Marxism is a critique of positivist science. Empirical analysis of observable forms (patterns of data) is not a path to process-based understanding; instead, causal processes and mechanisms must be identified from Marxist theory and evaluation involves the development of explanations of patterns in the superstructure that are consistent with outcomes that could be produced from postulated economic processes.

Geographers have found that Marxism provides a powerful tool for explaining spatial organization of social patterns. A good example is the work by Harvey (1974, 1982), who showed how interpretations of basic mechanisms of production, i.e. the desire to generate profits, by those who manage finance capital reproduce class differences through residential segregation. The underlying economic processes not only lead to spatial clustering of classes of people and house types through the generation of spatially separated housing markets, but also, in large part, overwhelm the capacity of individuals to choose freely *where* to live. Thus, the process of uneven geographical development is an essential part of capitalism (Harvey, 1982). Urbanization is perhaps the most visible manifestation of this process, which arises as 'the profit-seeking (cost-reducing) proclivities of producers lead to the dense spatial massing of units of capital and, as a corollary, of labor' (Scott, 1985: 481). However, the connection is not necessarily solely one of the social production of space through the dominant influence of the economic infrastructure; instead, an interactive relation may exist between the mode of production (infrastructure) and specific spatial manifestations (superstructure) – a dialectical process referred to as spatiality (Soja, 1980; Johnston, 1986).

Concern about an over-emphasis on general economic processes has led progressively to perspectives that highlight the scale-dependence of economic processes and the importance of locality in interpretations of social relations and organization (Johnston, 1997). The crux of this concern can be represented as a tension between structure and agency: to what extent is the substantial geographic variability in characteristics of the superstructure the result solely of general infrastructural economic processes and to what extent are local non-economic processes, including human agency, responsible for specific superstructural characteristics? The theory of structuration represents an attempt to reconcile this tension by acknowledging a role for both structure and agency in the spatial organization of social, economic and political life. This interactive view of processes operating at different scales has paved the way for the latest perspective on human geography: one grounded in postmodernism.

Postmodernism   Since the late 1980s increasing concern both within human geography and the social sciences at large about the complexity of social relations has led to a new perspective that celebrates difference and diversity, both of social processes and of explanations of these processes. This perspective embraces a geographical inquiry consistent with what has come to be known as postmodernism (Johnston, 1997). The emphasis on difference and diversity has called attention to the importance of factors such as race, gender, religion, sexuality, positionality and power relations in attempts to understand social processes. Cultural processes have thus taken centre stage with economic processes in geographical explanation. In particular, feminist approaches to geography, which at their core tend to be rooted in concerns about 'difference', have a close alliance with the postmodernist viewpoint.

Criticism has been aimed specifically at 'totalizing' theories such as Marxism, which adopts an essentialist perspective on truth by ultimately casting all explanations within a historical materialist framework which is assumed to embody 'truth'. Thus, postmodernism is anti-realist; it affirms a strong relativist perspective on knowledge and inquiry in which 'no single explanation can be identified in any study and no single "entry point" to . . . analysis can be privileged over any other' (ibid.: 269). Rather than a focus on the *orderly* workings of social processes and the manifestations of these processes, postmodernism explicitly stresses the *disordered*, fragmented character of the social realm and the tendency of those adhering to totalizing visions of society to impose order where it does not exist. Instead, change, flux, and the time–space specificity of geographical knowledge are points of emphasis. Within geography, difference and diversity have been examined within the context of renewed concern about heterogeneity, particularity and uniqueness (Gregory, 1989), especially with regard to spatial representations of social processes and forms. The focus of concern includes notions of how social constructions of meaning, identity and power relations are related to geographical understandings of 'place' and 'region'. In contrast to Hartshornian regionalism, however, this reassertion of the importance of areal differentiation is not explicitly atheoretical, but embraces theory and adopts the view that diversity in theoretical perspectives leads to enhanced richness of theoretical understandings.

Conclusion

The concepts of process and form are pivotal to inquiry within contemporary physical and human geography. In the past 50 years, the discipline has exhibited an increased concern for enhanced 'depth of understanding' of processes or process mechanisms underlying empirical manifestations, or forms, of geographic phenomena. Process-based understanding is viewed as the key to developing adequate comprehension of how physical and human systems change in form or are sustained in dynamic, yet enduring configurations. It also is perceived as enriching the theoretical content of the discipline. Because processes or process mechanisms are unobservable or difficult to observe, inferences about processes rely heavily on theoretical analysis. The extent to which a discipline relies on theory in the development of new understandings of the world plays an important role in communal assessments of its intellectual quality. This factor certainly has contributed to geography's development over the past 50 years. Virtually all appeals for, or assessments of, conceptual change within geography, from Davisian to process-based geomorphology, from spatial science to Marxism, and from Marxism to postmodernism have emphasized the value of such change in enhancing the discipline's 'image' within the realm of the earth or social sciences. Conceptual change may have as much to do with sociological concerns as it does intellectual interests.

Although both sides of the discipline have turned toward process-based understanding, as a whole, geography is still entrenched deeply in the Cartesian dualism of mind and matter that has dominated science since the advent of mechanistic materialism in the seventeenth century (Urban and Rhoads, 2003). Physical geography rests largely on a mechanistic materialist foundation of Newtonian physics with its conception of space as an inert 'container' with absolute dimensions. Human geography, on the other hand, while partly embracing mechanistic materialism within the context of 'positivist' spatial science, has largely embedded inquiry within conceptual contexts that emphasize human processes. Human geographers largely subscribe to theoretical notions based heavily on the 'mind' side of mind–matter dualism. Human processes – social, political, economic, cultural – are seen not only as primary to understanding the structure of society, but as consummate. Environmental influences on human behaviour, if they occur at all, always are mediated strongly by socio-cultural processes.

The continuing influence of dualism on contemporary geography indicates that the discipline still is embedded within Enlightenment thinking, postmodernism notwithstanding. Although postmodernists may argue that they have transcended such thinking, such claims cannot be applied to the discipline as a whole. Moreover, even within postmodernism, elements of Enlightenment thinking can be discerned. Many postmodernists are interested in relations between underlying causal processes and empirical manifestations of these processes, while allowing for multi-theoretical, highly contextualized understandings of these relations. Nevertheless, the contemporary notion of process-form connections largely emerged within the context of the mechanistic materialism of the seventeenth century, when process-form relations largely were reduced to 'locomotion' or simple rearrangement or material transformations of material bodies. Under this conception, the notion of 'force' or 'causal mechanism' emerged as primary in producing change, i.e. as the basis for 'process'. Strict empiricist interpretations of force or causal mechanisms are noncommittal regarding ontology, whereas realist interpretations view such forces or mechanisms as actual existents. Relativists, including humanists and postmodernists, may deny any claims of ontological status or allow for multiple ontologies, but in either case embrace the epistemic richness provided by unequivocal multitheoretical explanations of causality. Such a view derives at least in part from idealist philosophies, including that of Kant, which arose in response to mind–matter dualism instigated by mechanistic materialism.

Cause–effect thinking remains a deep-seated presupposition in a wide range of contemporary geographical inquiry and this thinking is often expressed in terms of process-form relations. Such a perspective contrasts greatly with, for example, the Aristotelian view of the world wherein form is primary and process emanates from form without the need for a causal relation between the two. Under this conception, process and form are inextricably interwoven, and being and becoming involve holistic, irreducible self-actualization at multiple scales of time and space. Although the Aristotelian view of the world may seem irrelevant in the light of the findings of contemporary natural science, such is not the case. Contemporary science, especially quantum and relativistic physics, has established a remarkable theoretical framework for empirical predictability at the expense of a difficult, varied and highly contentious ontological interpretation of this framework.

What are the implications for geography? The discipline always has looked elsewhere for philosophical and methodological inspiration and this trend seems likely to continue. Process-form conceptions are only one element of a largely derivative conceptual foundation. Breaking out of this derivative mould may be beyond the capacity of the discipline, but it probably also is not necessary. The future of geography will be guided by sociological factors as much as it will by intellectual ones. Philosophy, however, is not irrelevant to this future for it often can be a source of inspiration for innovation by those seeking to become the discipline's next 'fashion dude' (Sherman, 1996).

ESSAY QUESTIONS AND FURTHER READING

1   How far do you agree with the view that process-based studies rescued physical geography from its state of 'serious decline' in the 1950s? Good background material to this question can be found in Gregory (2000) and Huggett (2003), while you should also read Strahler (1952), Chorley and Kennedy (1971) and Rhoads and Thorn (1996a).

2   Contrast the way concepts of process and form appear in spatial science and Marxist geography. Start with Johnston (1986; 1997), and follow this up with Abler et al. (1971), Harvey (1974), Scott (1985) and Soja (1980). You might also read Schaefer's (1953) original paper.

REFERENCES

Abler, R.F., Adams, J.S. and Gould, P.R. (1971) *Spatial Organization: The Geographer's View of the World*. Prentice Hall, Englewood Cliffs, NJ.

Agnew, J.A. (1989) Sameness and difference: Hartshorne's *The Nature of Geography* and geography as areal variation. In Entrikin, J.N. and Brunn, S.D. (eds) *Reflections on Richard Hartshorne's 'The Nature of Geography'* (Occasional Publications of the Association of American Geographers). Association of American Geographers, Washington, DC, pp. 121–139.

Baker, V.R. (1987) The Spokane Flood and its legacy. In Graf, W.L. (ed.) *Geomorphic Systems of North America* (Centennial Volume 2). Geological Society of America, Boulder, CO, pp. 416–423.

Berry, B.J.L. (1973) A paradigm for modern geography. In Chorley, R.J. (ed.) *Directions in Geography*. Methuen, London, pp. 3–22.

Bigelow, J., Ellis, B. and Pargetter, R. (1988) Forces. *Philosophy of Science* **55**, 614–630.

Bishop, P. (1980) Popper's principle of falsifiability and the irrefutability of the Davisian cycle. *The Professional Geographer* **32**, 310–315.

Bras, R.L., Tucker, G.E. and Teles, V. (2003) Six myths about mathematical modeling in geomorphology. In Wilcock, P.R. and Iverson, R.M. (eds) *Prediction in Geomorphology*. American Geophysical Union, Washington, DC, pp. 63–79.

Buttimer, A. (1979) Erewhon or nowhere land. In Gale, S. and Olsson, G. (eds) *Philosophy in Geography*. D. Reidel, Dordrecht, pp. 9–38.

Chorley, R.J., Beckinsdale, R.P. and Dunn, A.J. (1973) *The History of the Study of Landforms*, Vol. 2: *The Life and Work of William Morris Davis*. Methuen, London.

Chorley, R.J. and Kennedy, B.A. (1971) *Physical Geography: A Systems Approach*. Prentice Hall, London.

Clark, A.H. (1954) Historical geography. In James, P.E. and Jones, C.F. (eds) *American Geography: Inventory and Prospect*. Syracuse University Press, Syracuse, NY, pp. 70–105.

Davis, W.M. (1899) The geographical cycle. *Geographical Journal* **14**, 481–504.

Davis, W.M. (1900) The physical geography of the lands. *Popular Science Monthly* **57**, 157–170.

Davis, W.M. (1902) Systematic geography. *Proceedings of the American Philosophical Society* **41**, 235–259.

Davis, W.M. (1904) The relations of the earth sciences in view of their progress in the nineteenth century. *Journal of Geology* **12**, 669–687.

Davis, W.M. (1906) An inductive study of the content of geography. *Bulletin of the American Geographical Society* **38**, 67–84.

Davis, W.M. (1912) Relation of geography to geology. *Geological Society of America Bulletin* **23**, 93–124.

Davis, W.M. (1915) The principles of geographical description. *Annals of the Association of American Geographers* **5**, 61–105.

Dietrich, W.E. (1987) Mechanics of flow and sediment transport in river bends. In Richards, K.S. (ed.) *River Channels Environment and Process.* Blackwell, Oxford, pp. 179–227.

Dietrich, W.E., Bellugi, D.G., Sklar, L.S. and Stock, J.D. (2003) Geomorphic transport laws for predicting landscape form and dynamics. In Wilcock, P.R. and Iverson, R.M. (eds) *Prediction in Geomorphology.* American Geophysical Union, Washington, DC, pp. 83–94.

Douglas, I. (1982) The unfulfilled promise: earth surface processes as a key to landform evolution. *Earth Surface Processes and Landforms* **7**, 101.

Entrikin, J. (1989) Introduction. In Entrikin, J. and Brunn, S.D. (eds) *Reflection on Richard Hartshorne's 'The Nature of Geography.'* American Association of Geographers, Washington DC.

Golledge, R.G. (1981) Misconceptions, misinterpretations, and misrepresentations of behavioral approaches in human geography. *Environmental and Planning A* **13**, 1325–1344.

Gregory, D. (1989) Areal differentiation and post-modern human geography. In Gregory, D. and Walford, R. (eds) *Horizons in Human Geography.* Macmillan, London, pp. 67–96.

Gregory, K.J. (2000) *The Changing Nature of Physical Geography.* Arnold, London.

Guelke, L. (1974) An idealist alternative in human geography. *Annals of the Association of American Geographers* **14**, 193–202.

Guelke, L. (1981) Idealism. In Harvey, M.E. and Holly, B.P. (eds) *Themes in Geographic Thought.* Croom Helm, London, pp. 133–147.

Hartshorne, R. (1939) *The Nature of Geography.* Association of American Geographers, Lancaster, PA.

Harvey, D. (1969) *Explanation in Geography.* Arnold, London.

Harvey, D. (1974) Class-monopoly rent, finance capital and the urban revolution. *Regional Studies* **8**, 239–255.

Harvey, D. (1982) *The Limits to Capital.* Blackwell, Oxford.

Horton, R.E. (1945) Erosional development of streams and their drainage basins: hydrophysical approach to quantitative morphology. *Geological Society of America Bulletin* **56**, 275–370.

Huggett, R.J. (2003) *Fundamentals of Geomorphology.* Routledge, London.

Iverson, R.M. (2003) How should mathematical models of geomorphic processes be judged? In Wilcock, P.R. and Iverson, R.M. (eds) *Prediction in Geomorphology.* American Geophysical Union, Washington, DC, pp. 83–94.

Johnston, R.J. (1986) *Philosophy and Human Geography.* Arnold, London.

Johnston, R.J. (1997) *Geography and Geographers.* Arnold, London.

Jones, R. (1991) Realism about what? *Philosophy of Science* **58**, 185–202.

Keylock, C. (2003) The natural science of geomorphology? In Trudgill, S. and Roy, A. (eds) *Contemporary Meanings in Physical Geography*. Arnold, London, pp. 87–101.

Leclerc, I. (1972) *The Nature of Physical Existence*. Allen and Unwin, London.

Martin, G.J. and James, P.E. (1993) *All Possible Worlds: A History of Geographical Ideas*. Wiley and Sons, New York.

Peet, R. (1985) The social origins of environmental determinism. *Annals of the Association of American Geographers* **75**, 309–333.

Phillips, J.D. (1999) *Earth Surface Systems: Complexity, Order and Scale*. Blackwell, Malden, MA.

Pyne, S.J. (1980) *Grove Karl Gilbert: A Great Engine of Research*. University of Texas Press, Austin, TX.

Rhoads, B.L. (1994) On being a 'real' geomorphologist. *Earth Surface Processes and Landforms* **19**, 269–272.

Rhoads, B.L. and Thorn, C.E. (1993) Geomorphology as science: the role of theory. *Geomorphology* **6**, 287–307.

Rhoads, B.L. and Thorn, C.E. (1994) Contemporary philosophical perspectives on physical geography with emphasis on geomorphology. *Geographical Review* **84**, 90–101.

Rhoads, B.L. and Thorn, C.E. (1996a) Observation in geomorphology. In Rhoads, B.L. and Thorn, C.E. (eds) *The Scientific Nature of Geomorphology*. Wiley, Chichester, pp. 21–56.

Rhoads, B.L. and Thorn, C.E. (1996b) Toward a philosophy of geomorphology. In Rhoads, B.L. and Thorn, C.E. (eds) *The Scientific Nature of Geomorphology*. Wiley, Chichester, 115–143.

Rhoads, B.L. and Thorn, C.E. (1996c) Preface. In Rhoads, B.L. and Thorn, C.E. (eds) *The Scientific Nature of Geomorphology*. Wiley, Chichester, pp. ix–xi.

Richards, K.S. (1990) 'Real' geomorphology. *Earth Surface Processes and Landforms* **15**, 195–197.

Ritter, D.F. (1978) *Process Geomorphology*. W.C. Brown, Dubuque, IA.

Ritter, D.F. (1986) *Process Geomorphology*. W.C. Brown, Dubuque, IA.

Schaefer, F.K. (1953) Exceptionalism in geography: a methodological examination. *Annals of the Association of American Geographers* **43**, 226–249.

Scott, A.J. (1985) Location processes, urbanization, and territorial development: an exploratory essay. *Environment and Planning A* **17**, 479–501.

Semple, E.C. (1911) *Influences of Geographic Environment*. Russell and Russell, New York.

Sherman, D.J. (1996) Fashion in geomorphology. In Rhoads, B.L. and Thorn, C.E. (eds) *The Scientific Nature of Geomorphology*. Wiley, Chichester, pp. 87–114.

Smith, N. (1989) Geography as museum: private history and conservative idealism in *The Nature of Geography*. In Entrikin, J.N. and Brunn, S.D. (eds) *Reflections on Richard Hartshorne's 'The Nature of Geography'* (Occasional Publications of the

Association of American Geographers). Association of American Geographers, Washington, DC, pp. 89–120.

Soja, E.W. (1980) The socio-spatial dialectic. *Annals of the Association of American Geographers* **70**, 207–225.

Stolum, H.H. (1996) River meandering as a self-organization process. *Science* **271**, 1710–1713.

Strahler, A.N. (1950) Davis' concepts of slope development viewed in the light of recent quantitative investigations. *Annals of the Association of American Geographers* **40**, 209–213.

Strahler, A.N. (1952) Dynamic basis of geomorphology. *Geological Society of America Bulletin* **63**, 923–938.

Strahler, A.N. (1980) Systems theory in physical geography. *Physical Geography* **1**, 1–27.

Taaffe, E.J. (1970) *Geography*. Prentice Hall, Englewood Cliffs, NJ.

Tuan, Y.-F. (1976) Humanistic geography. *Annals of the Association of American Geographers* **66**, 266–276.

Urban, M.A. and Rhoads, B.L. (2003) Conceptions of nature: implications for an integrated geography. In Trudgill, S. and Roy, A. (eds) *Contemporary Meanings in Physical Geography*. Arnold, London, pp. 211–231.

Wilcock, P.R. and Iverson, R.M. (2003) Preface. In Wilcock, P.R. and Iverson, R.M. (eds) *Prediction in Geomorphology*. American Geophysical Union, Washington, DC, p. vii.

Wooldridge, S.W. (1958) The trend of geomorphology. *Transactions of the Institute of British Geographers* **25**, 29–36.

Representation/Reality

Matthew Hannah

Most people are aware that representations of the world, whether personal impressions, maps, news reports, or what have you, do not always 'match' the reality they are supposed to represent. It is almost impossible at the beginning of the twenty-first century to go about one's daily life without running into controversies about whether some story or image (some representation) is misleading. It has been assumed that scholarly knowledge produces representations more firmly linked to reality than those that make up our casual, everyday consciousness of the world. However, in many fields of scholarly inquiry, including human geography, the past 20 years have seen a major shift in thinking about the relation between scholarly representation and the reality it is supposed to represent. It is no longer possible to take for granted that academics produce 'objective' knowledge, knowledge that represents reality 'more accurately' than lay knowledge. Indeed, the success of all kinds of knowledge has been fundamentally called into question. It is not just a matter of 'realism' (reality exists independently of us, and there is a best way to represent it) versus 'relativism' or 'perspectivism' (the world exists independently, but there is no 'best way' to represent it, it's a matter of perspective). Both realism and relativism take for granted a funda-mental difference between reality and representation. As we shall see below, recent developments in academic thinking about knowledge have called this difference into question. This challenge is, among other things, an attack on the old philosophical distinction between epistemology (the study of how knowledge 'works' and is produced, how representations are forged so as to reflect reality) and ontology (the study of reality 'itself,' of how beings exist, and of what existence means more generally).

Human geographers are social scientists. That means we try to understand 'society', with particular reference to 'spatial relationships', 'place', 'spatial distributions', 'movements', and so on. But what do all these terms in quotation marks, all these *representations*, actually represent? Are they neutral categories describing really-existing phenomena? Or do they, in fact, concoct the 'realities' they seem merely to describe? Geographers, of late, have entered into heated debates over these questions – questions about what 'grounds' our knowledge of the world. Some still believe that our scholarly representations can 'correctly' capture a material world 'out there'. Others argue that some representations are tainted (by bias or prejudice, however unconscious), while some are true. Still others (like poststructuralists) maintain that we can never exit the 'web' of language that we necessarily use to make sense of a world that cannot speak for itself. Whatever their personal view, geographers continue to produce representations we hope will be useful in improving the world. And these representations continue to be accepted, modified or rejected by students, other scholars and the lay public according to how *persuasive* they appear to be. Though it may seem paradoxical or inconsistent, what counts as 'persuasive' representation continues to be at least partly a matter of evidence, coherent reasoning, and so on, *even for scholars who no longer believe in objectivity*. All knowledge may be political (in the sense of 'contestable'), but that doesn't mean scholars should or even can abandon the search for 'better' knowledge. It is just that the meaning of 'better' has become more complicated. In short, the field of knowledge has become, for many geographers, a bed of hot coals, across which we must learn to walk or dance. Every representation we rely upon is unstable, contestable, 'hot'. Yet we have no choice but to rely upon representations. All paths lead across this 'bed'; none lead around it.

Students of human geography need to be aware of this predicament, because many of the representations of the world presented in the classroom these days, such as the journal articles and other readings through which students are initiated into geography, are produced with all of this in mind. It is impossible to understand human geography as a body of knowledge unless one understands recent shifts in scholarly conceptions of the relation between representations and reality, on the one hand, and the concrete, material conditions in which scholars produce geographical knowledge, on the other. As Noel Castree writes in Chapter 17, 'Whose geography?', all knowledge is political. By focusing on the representation/reality dualism, we can deepen our understanding of why this is so.

Four Ways of Dancing on Hot Coals

In this section, I briefly indicate four types of response critical human geographers have offered to the predicament described above. I focus on these geographers in particular because they have tackled the predicament head on. My purpose is not to give a full summary of the various arguments, but to engage them *only* as responses to the challenge of dancing over hot coals. Thus, only one or a small number of illustrative texts are selected to stand for each category. Many human geographers work in and draw from more than one of these 'ideal-types', and the distinctions between them are fluid. But as starting points they can be helpful in distinguishing different priorities and emphases in working out strategies for the production of knowledge.

Actor-network theory and geographies of knowledge

The most sophisticated and comprehensive attempt thus far to 'accept' poststructuralist theory while continuing to defend the possibility of verifiable links between representations and reality is the critical realism of Roy Bhaskar (a philosopher of science), of which Castree writes in Chapter 4 (see Sayer, [1984] 1992; Bhaskar, 1986; Collier, 1994). Bhaskar sees the ultimate disproof of poststructuralism in the undeniable success of natural science. He is willing to grant that the conclusions of poststructuralism hold in the cultural realm and even for every specific theory produced by the sciences. But he argues that the overall progress science has made in uncovering ever-deeper workings of the natural and social worlds is irrefutable proof of the independent existence of a real world.

Critical science studies or science and technology studies (STS) directly confronts this faith in science as the 'last bastion' of objective knowledge by entering into the innermost sancta of science (the world of the laboratory experiment, the mathematical proof) as uncommitted observers. They show that the purportedly isolated workings of 'nature' are impossible to distinguish from social, political or cultural dynamics (see Law, 1991; Callon, 1995; Barnes et al., 1996). The most accessible and provocative research programme within critical science studies has been that of Bruno Latour. In his books *Laboratory Life* (Latour and Woolgar, 1979 [1986]) and *Science in Action* (1987), Latour adopts the perspective of an anthropologist whose business is 'following scientists around' (see Murdoch, 1997, for an excellent overview, and Hetherington and Law,

2000). Suspending the common-sense belief that the activities of scientists merely 'transmit' truth about 'nature' in a transparent way, Latour focuses on the complex ways in which scientists and laboratories have *constructed* the seemingly pre-given split between nature and society. A key move in this approach to science is to stop thinking of the 'objects' of inquiry (microbes, subatomic particles, genes or what have you) as inert, passive, lifeless and obedient to 'laws,' and to start thinking of them instead as *actants*, that is, as players who may or may not cooperate with scientists, who behave or misbehave to the benefit or detriment of different investigators. The concept of the actant constitutes a direct challenge to the subject/object dualism. Actants become important for the activities of scientists through the extension of *networks* composed of laboratories, schools, communication media, journals, etc. Networks extend the conditions of science into the world, and enable the translation of the world into scientific places and terms. As such, they directly contradict the nature/society dualism at the root of traditional philosophies of science.

Actor-Network Theory (ANT) has proven interesting to geographers because its extremely literal and concrete understanding of networks of knowledge production (Latour, 1999) dovetails nicely with the long-standing geographical sensitivity to spatial relations (Murdoch, 1997). It also offers a persuasive argument that scientific knowledge is always geographically specific, marked by its production in particular places and deeply reliant on the physical movement of people, things and information. The most robust and promising effects of an encounter with ANT appear in recent critical work on the social construction of nature carried out by geographers with at least one foot in poststructuralist theory (Braun and Castree, 1998). Barnes has also drawn on actor-network theory to begin to retell the story of the 'quantitative revolution' in more critical terms (Barnes, 1998; 2002).

Actor-Network Theory has two features worth noting. The first of these (particularly in the case of Latour) is a certain fearlessness in relying on some 'common-sense' distinctions (for example, 'description' as opposed to 'interpretation' or 'judgment' as the proper activity of ANT practitioners; see Murdoch, 1997) while insistently rejecting and avoiding others, most prominently the nature/society and subject/object dualisms. Murdoch (1997) notes that Latour's 'ethics' seem to amount to an avoidance of those concepts that have accumulated the most power to control aspects of the world. But surely the description/judgement distinction, closely linked as it is with the fact/value dualism, has been as intimately involved in extending the power of science as have those dualisms so carefully avoided by ANT theorists. The particular choices Latour makes in retaining some dualisms as pillars of his analysis are of course debatable; the need to make such choices in some way is not.

Epistemological activism

A second pattern of response to the basic problem of social-constructionist knowledge has two variants, one originating in the Marxist tradition and the other in postcolonial theory. Both are more expressly political in orientation than is ANT. The work of Gibson-Graham (1996) in the area of 'anti-essentialist Marxist' geography is a particularly interesting attempt to work toward social and economic justice in full awareness of the poststructuralist critique of stable representation. To be anti-essentialist is to refuse to attribute a stable essence or root meaning to a category such as 'capitalism', but to think of it instead as a provisional construction whose meaning is *produced* by the very discourses that claim only to try to *understand* it. Gibson-Graham acknowledges that every conceptual 'entry point' from which something like 'capitalism' can be studied is at one level 'indefensible', but they nevertheless insist that choosing an entry point remains unavoidable (Graham, 1990). They attempt then to re-think that entry point ('class processes') in a way that brings together different sorts of 'exploitation'. These include the traditional Marxist focus of surplus value production in the workplace but also gender-based and other forms of exploitation. One lesson of poststructuralist theory was that apparently monolithic categories always turn out to be less solid and 'natural' than previously supposed. In line with this insight, Gibson-Graham rethink 'capitalism' as a ragged, heterogeneous and only loosely connected system, in which there are in fact many openings for the development and extension of non-exploitative, indeed, non-capitalist practices. Similarly, Castree's treatment of the concept of nature in Marxist theory combines a commitment to progressive politics with a sophisticated understanding of the pitfalls of representation (Castree, 1995). Castree argues that in addressing ecological issues, Marxists should become more savvy about the politics of 'cerning' (treating categories temporarily or tactically as unproblematic) and 'dis-cerning' (focusing attention on concepts from a critical perspective in order to highlight their instabilities).

Strategic essentialists differ significantly from the anti-essentialist approach of Gibson-Graham, holding on to the assumption that something which at least *appears* more defensible than a mere 'entry point' is needed if an argument is to be convincing, especially to wider political audiences or 'the lay public'. For strategic essentialists, it may be the case that any starting concepts they choose are *ultimately* unstable and deconstructable. But these concepts will not be of much political use unless they involve some sort of claim that they are in fact more adequate or truer than other possible entry points. However hard we may try to remain continuously aware of the contestability of the terms we use, we *cannot help* but consider the bulk of our representations of the world to be accurate. Moreover, it is arguably not enough for human beings merely *not to question* our assumptions; it may be necessary *actively to believe* things in order to make our assumptions useful in practical life, where we may have no alternative to being essentialists, however anti-essentialist we try to be as scholars. This 'seat-of-the-pants' essentialism need not rest upon a realist view of the world; it may simply be a result of our inability to pay critical attention to everything (or even a significant proportion of our worlds) at once (Hannah, 1999). This is how I understand the present chapter: as a strategic essentialist narrative.

An influential example of strategic essentialism comes out of the work of the postcolonial theorist Gayatri Spivak. She developed the notion of strategic essentialism while thinking about the writings of a group of Indian scholars known as the Subaltern Studies group (Spivak, [1985] 1996; Best, 1999). These scholars have grappled with the problem of how formerly colonized peoples can understand their history and desire for self-determination in ways not undermined from the beginning by reliance upon Western notions of nationhood, independence, etc. These notions, however nice they may sound to Western ears, have also helped to justify racism and colonial conquest, and thus cannot be seen simply as positive. In her accessible introduction to Spivak, Beverley Best puts the problem in terms of essentialism: 'once we have registered that the constitutive paradox of essentialism and anti-essentialism is irreducible, that our most painstaking anti-essentialist readings are marked by an irreducible essentialist moment, then what?' (1999: 479). Once we realize that we cannot avoid talking about some things as if they are accurate representations that capture the essence of real things, how can we avoid all the bad politics that seem to come along with this assumption? Spivak's notion of *catachresis* (summarized by Best) is intended to capture this tension:

> [I]f one chooses to take the risk of representation, one has to start somewhere, and where one starts is with a name. The name which has no literal or adequate referent . . . , *but is used as if it did*, temporarily and strategically, so that a narrative can be constructed around it, temporarily and strategically, for scrupulously visible political interests, is a *catachresis*. (ibid.: 481)

A catachresis, in other words, is a representation used by someone who knows better than to trust representations, but who also knows it is impossible not to use representations at all. Spivak is very careful to insist that this is unavoidable.

All these efforts can be seen as examples of 'epistemological activism' in the sense that what counts as knowledge (that is, which representations are treated as provisionally 'true') becomes the focus of deliberate political decisions based on the expected effects of producing *this* knowledge rather than *that* knowledge. That *some* representations will have to play the role of true knowledge is at least implicitly accepted by epistemological activists. The term 'epistemological activism' is also intended to allude to the relatively accessible style of these geographers, who consider it worthwhile to build their stories out of widely accessible language.

Theories and categories that aren't

The third strategic response to the problem of knowledge after poststructuralism takes a variety of forms, but all involve trying to find theoretical approaches and categories that (a) avoid the problems identified by poststructuralist analysis; but (b) allow geographers to continue writing about social world(s). The epistemological activists have resigned themselves to the fact that only imperfect and faulty tools will ever be available for them to use. Geographers in this third category have not. They continue to hope that language can be found which does *at least some* of what language is supposed to do without contributing to injustice. One such approach, developed in the work of Soja (1996) and Pile (1994) involves the category of 'thirdspace'. In addition to the complicated ontological arguments associated with this term (left aside here), 'thirdspace' represents a 'political-instrumental' response to the problem of dualism outlined above. That is, if dualisms have been tainted by their involvement in various forms of domination, perhaps the best response is to attempt to get beyond the use of dualisms altogether by inventing more 'hybrid' concepts less fraught with undesirable politics. In an early discussion of 'thirdspaces', Pile argued that 'if we accept these dualisms then we collude in the reproduction of the power-ridden values they help to sustain. Moreover, ... because dualistic architectures are not as fixed, stable or natural as they are meant to be ... it is possible to refuse them' (1994: 255). 'Thirdspace' is supposed to 'refuse' dualisms by indicating a character of 'betweenness'. The '/' which seems to separate dualistically opposed terms (such as subject and object) is suggested as its own place, as a place from which more liberating and socially useful ways of representing the world could come. Like some other approaches summarized here, this one acknowledges a heavy debt to postcolonial theory (ibid.). 'Thirdspace' stands for a much more widespread pattern. The signatures of this pattern are phrases to the effect that 'we need an understanding of knowledge that . . . ' or 'in order properly to work toward emancipation, our epistemology must be able to . . . '. Epistemologies are, in other words, 'custom-tailored' to avoid intellectual problems and to fit perceived political needs.

A second instance of this general approach is to be found in the 'non-representational theory' espoused by Nigel Thrift and others. He, too, takes as one of his points of departure the claim that 'we need a form of writing [which] . . . ' (Thrift, 2000: 213). For my purposes, what comes after the 'which' is less important than the more fundamental idea that if we need something, we'll be able to provide it. This idea is so deeply embedded in Western ways of thinking about knowledge that hardly anybody stops to think about it. But why should we assume that we'll be able to develop representations of the world that do something we want them to do, just because we think we need to? Does the fact that we seem to need some kind of theory mean it will become available? And if we invent a theory to meet a perceived need, how can we know it will be adequate in ways not related to the reason we invented it? These are big questions, conundrums that underlie much of what this chapter is about. But we'll leave them aside for now. Returning to the idea of non-representational theory, Thrift wants 'to provide a body of work which values *creative* praxis. This will not be easy as – with a few exceptions – most academics nowadays still tend towards impoverished views of praxis which leave remarkably little room for creative exorbitance' (ibid.: 213). Another difficulty is that this creative praxis is largely extra-discursive, a dimension of human life not easily (if at all) captured in language. He insists, quoting the philosopher Polanyi, that 'we know more than we can tell' (Thrift, 1999: 316). This 'more' has to do with creativity, with the fact that human beings always act and think about our actions out of an embodied position, and that we *perform* our way through life on the basis of bodily skills and creative engagement with spontaneous situations. To put it briefly, we *embody* knowledge in ways we cannot easily 'know' in the more conventional sense.

The term 'performance' is central for Thrift, and indeed for a large swath of critical geographic work, so it deserves a bit more explanation here (see also Dewsbury, 2000). Originating in the work of Goffman on symbolic interactionism, in sociological studies of modernity, in cultural theory (especially the work of Judith Butler and Gilles Deleuze) and in research on theatre and dance (Thrift, 2000), the concept of performance has acquired major significance for human geography. Although theories of performance and performativity have grown increasingly complex and varied, the insights they offer can be boiled down for the sake of brevity by returning to the idea of social constructionism introduced above. If social constructionism is the recognition that social life and its institutions and routines are not natural, rigid and static but constructed and always contestable, performance can be thought of as the complement or flipside of social constructionism. If our ways of life are not as rigid and unchangeable as they appear, it follows that they only persist because most people continue to *perform* them in ways that don't pose a challenge. The apparent stability of institutions and broader habits of life depends centrally on repeated performances of their rules and patterns. To say that society is constructed is also to say that social life is performative: if we begin to perform differently, we begin to re-construct society in new ways. The performative character of even the most everyday tasks means that, whether we're aware of it or not, there is always an element of unpredictability, potential innovation and creativity, even the possibility of theatricality in what we do. Much emphasis in recent years has centred on the performativity of gender roles and sexuality, but the principle can easily be extended to all spheres of social life.

Thrift is interested in deepening the notion of performativity by showing how tied up the performance of everyday life is with a kind of difficult-to-capture bodily knowledge best illustrated in dance and writings about dance. He hopes to work out an 'alternative "nonrepresentational" style of work' (Thrift, 2000: 216) better able to point toward this whole dimension of life. His theory is 'nonrepresentational' both because he understands and accepts all the critiques of representation summarized above and because the feature of social life he wants to indicate is itself particularly difficult to represent. All of this makes his work, like that of Soja and Pile, unusually well suited to illustrate the problem of 'dancing over hot coals'. In a passage near the beginning of his extended 'Afterwords' piece, he writes: 'this is *not* a new theoretical edifice that is being constructed, but a means of *valuing* and *working with* everyday practical *activities* as they occur' (ibid.: 216). He is clearly struggling with the conflicting desires, on the one hand, to point to something beyond the possibility of representation, and on the other, to keep writing and thinking about 'it'. At the end of this piece, he asks, 'So how to understand a paper which keeps on saying more when there is nothing more to be said?' His first answer: 'As a plea.' To try to keep it from disappearing into the geographic goulash of new theories, Thrift identifies his work not as a theory but as a new 'style' of writing. The term 'style' is supposed, here, to function similarly to the term 'thirdspace': as a category whose definition is dictated above all by what it is trying to avoid. Similarly, Thrift couches his survey of related theories in terms of ideas he 'likes' and 'dislikes', instead of ideas that are 'right' or 'wrong'.

The ultimate hope in Thrift's work, like that of Soja and Pile, is to make helpful representations, Gregory's (1978) 'committed explanation in geography'. But these authors are not satisfied with strategic essentialism: they are searching for styles and categories that can still function as indicators or pointers without really buying into the whole, problematic world of conventional representation.

Poststructuralism 'proper'

The most difficult and demanding response to the poststructuralist turn takes the basic impulse of Thrift, Pile and Soja to an Olympian (or Dantean, depending on how one sees the matter) level of theoretical sophistication, especially in the work of Marcus Doel (1993; 1999). Here the difference between a 'critical' or 'deconstructive' and a 'positive' or 'useful' mode of knowledge-production disappears entirely. Doel's work refuses any internal division of labour between apparently successful communication on the one hand, and the disruptions, shifts and surprises that interfere with such effects by exposing their duplicity on the other. He takes turbocharged flight from all conventional involvement in the use of categories, and tries to liberate creative energies of thought by demonstrating alternative ways of living in language. Drawing on the work of Deleuze, Derrida and others, Doel takes poststructuralist literary 'play' to an extreme pitch, but insists throughout that concrete geographies, indeed geographical *science*, remain his point of orientation.

The chief dualism that falls prey to Doel's representational play is a spatial one: the inside/outside dualism. In a sense, this dualism undergirds many of the others discussed above. The science/society dualism is usually called upon to defend the notion that, however insupportable the goings-on *outside*, at least *inside* the realm of scientific praxis, the polluting influences of society are absent. Similarly, the individual human subject, whether set off against society or against the object of knowledge, has traditionally been understood to represent a stable, private 'inside'. Doel insists that everything is surface, and that what appears to have the character of separateness or depth, for example the human subject, can be understood instead as folds, ripples, twists and pleats. The notion of a fold as a figure which constructs an 'inside' from entirely exterior material nicely illustrates a major strand of the poststructuralist critique of subjectivity.

To return to the image of 'dancing on hot coals', such poststructuralist writing performs the nimblest dance among the four strategies covered here. Doel and other poststructuralists keep their conceptual 'feet' moving as fast as possible, flashing over the coals and resting on any one representation only long enough to find vanishingly brief footing for the next movement of thought. The advantage of this kind of dance is that one avoids burning one's feet, unlike, say, strategic essentialists, who balance far longer on certain concepts in order to problematize others, and thereby run a greater risk of getting bogged down in 'bad' politics. The dance of the poststructuralists is a dance of continuous 'plausible deniability'. Confronted by the accusation that they do, after all, rely on representational assumptions about language, Doel and company could always answer, 'We didn't inhale'.

Putting Our Feet Down

Although all four of the strategies reviewed above *implicitly* acknowledge the predicament of dancing on hot coals, only one side of this predicament has been thoroughly dealt with by scholars. Human geographers now have a fairly sophisticated sense of the instability of the representations that make up our stock of knowledge. But we still struggle to come to terms with the other side, the inevitability of taking a great deal for granted, of putting our feet down somewhere. I have argued elsewhere that the inescapable need to rely on unjustifiable assumptions is best understood as a matter of *finitude of scope* (Hannah, 1999). Finitude of scope is a basic feature of human beings, but is rarely remarked upon in studies of human knowledge. The term recognizes that individual human beings are the indispensable hosts, the only 'homes' for 'knowledge'. However impressive the accumulation of knowledge at a societal scale, however powerful the 'stock' of scientific knowledge, it can only ever be produced and treated as knowledge, accessed, understood, interpreted and reproduced by individual human knowers. But we knowers are fundamentally limited; we cannot 'pay attention critically to everything at once', indeed, we cannot call into question more than a tiny fraction of our fields of engagement. The fact that we can only be at one place at any one time, and can only do a finite number of things, is fundamental to our nature as materially embodied beings. This limitation was recognized decades ago in geographical discussions of social action in a general sense, but it applies also to specifically intellectual activities. In this section of the chapter I take some time to flesh out the notion of finitude. The point here is to set the stage for thinking about how geographers produce and debate representations. This, too, is of immediate relevance to students of the subject. The more students know about the details of where scholarly representations come from, the easier it will be to recognize the common ground they share with their teachers as 'incomplete knowers'. This in turn should make it easier to see learning as properly a matter of dialogue rather than authoritative dispensing of 'truth' by the experts to the uninitiated.

Again, many professors are very aware of the changes in human geography that have been described in this chapter. We understand the representations we offer in lectures, seminars and readings are very often contestable, both because of the impossibility of 'non-political' knowledge and because of the selectivity imposed by our finitude as individuals. Not only do we not know anything *beyond all shadow of a doubt*, we are also necessarily very selective in the issues with which we are *at all* familiar. This may come as a surprise, given that many professors appear to 'know everything'. Social scientists do indeed have a sort of 'head start' in discussing the issues with students because of the sheer amount of time and energy we're obligated to put into thinking about such things. It is, after all, our job. Most people, even if they wanted to, could only think carefully and systematically about the way societies work for at most a couple hours out of every day: their energies are absorbed by other occupations. But this 'head start' of academics have should not seem as intimidating as it may once have appeared. In the larger scheme of things, even the 'head start' doesn't get scholars very far. The most widely read scholar on earth (were it possible to determine who that is) would still never have a hope of developing an informed opinion about more than a microscopically tiny fraction of all there is to think about. And, based on the arguments given above, even that tiny fraction of hard-won knowledge would be inherently debatable.

Let me make some schematic suggestions about how best to take advantage of the new openness to debate which students can and should expect from their professors. First, if representations *construct* realities, and if human geographers are aware of this, it is fair to ask why professors construct their representations of the world the way they do. Why do we represent 'globalization' the way we do? Why does this professor use the term 'Third World' and that one not? Sometimes, the answer will be simply 'For convenience', or 'Because the textbook does it this way'. But sometimes there are more interesting thought processes behind such decisions, and by asking professors to be explicit about them, students can get a more complete sense of what they're learning (and perhaps also help the professors organize their own thoughts more systematically). Second, it is worth keeping a special eye out for dualisms. Since they are practically unavoidable, they will pop up from time to time. But *which ones* do professors rely upon and which ones not? Does a particular instructor seem to buy into the gender dualism, and treat domestic work as though it's unimportant and inferior to work in the public sphere? Ask about it. You might get a wide range of reactions, from genuine engagement to nervous, defensive dismissal. But even in the latter case, asking the question in the first place will help you and your fellow students get a better sense of the limits of what's being presented to you.

In principle, of course, there are no limits to the representations students can (and should feel free to) challenge in the classroom. But even the most omniscient professors must choose to rely upon countless concepts as though they are unproblematic, so it's rather cheap and easy to make the accusation of 'incompleteness' or 'neglect to mention something'. It will always be possible to bring up some consideration a professor has neglected, or point out a way in which an explanation is incomplete. A more difficult but also more useful skill to cultivate is to be able to recognize when the holes and gaps are important and when they are not. And anyway, as finite beings themselves, students cannot truly question everything at once. Trying to be totally critical of everything is generally a pointless exercise. The key, again, is to learn to think carefully about how to *select* those representations one would like to challenge. Here a couple of rules of thumb may prove useful: you could either (a) single out those concepts *the professor* seems to rely upon most frequently and uncritically; or (b) try to identify those representations *you yourself* take most deeply for granted. The latter path is the more difficult one, as it requires a higher degree of critical reflection on one's *own* assumptions. But it is also a very fruitful exercise.

Another strategy for directing critical energy in the classroom, suggested by a number of the schools of thought mentioned above, is also tremendously useful beyond the halls of education. According to this strategy, critical attention should be paid first and foremost to those representations put forward by *powerful individuals and institutions*. What are the representations most strenuously and deliberately put forward by the scientific establishment, national governments or other large organizations (such as major newspapers or other multinational corporations)? Does the way these representations construct the world have anything to do with the fact that these institutions enjoy a great deal of prestige, influence, and economic power? In many cases, the answer is yes. A good experiment is to look for different ways in which the term 'globalization' is used. Almost invariably, organizations which benefit from globalization in its current form will represent it as *natural* or *inevitable*. This is because they benefit from it. By encouraging people the world over to accept the inevitability of globalization, they help fulfil their own prophecy and ensure their own prosperity...the particular form of globalization we now see will indeed become inevitable if nobody takes the trouble to think through and work toward (that is, *perform*) alternative forms. In many areas of human geographic scholarship, the government documents and media reporting that supply us with such representations are important sources of information, and need to be examined carefully.

In a sense, all these suggestions merely amount to an updated version of the famous ancient dictum: *the unexamined life is not worth living*. This has always been especially true for life in the classroom, though that fact has been obscured by the authority granted professors as the keepers of privileged representation. As a result of recent developments in the way representation and reality are understood, professors of human geography are now free to step down from the pedestal. And students should feel free to give the pedestal a helpful nudge. In this spirit, it is appropriate to close with an adaptation of another hallowed piece of wisdom: 'Truth will not make us free, but taking control of the production of truth will' (Hardt and Negri, 2000: 156).

ESSAY QUESTIONS AND FURTHER READING

1   'Representations do not simply "express" reality.' Discuss this proposition on the basis of the following reading about science, a practice normally thought to produce accurate representations of the world: Latour (1987, Chapters 1, 2) and Demerritt (1998).
2   'Maps, as representations of the world, are inherently political.' Discuss this statement on the basis of the following readings: J.B. Harley (1989) and the chapters on maps in Barnes and Duncan (1992).

REFERENCES

Barnes, T. (1998) A history of regression: actors, networks, machines and numbers. *Environment and Planning A* **30**, 203–223.

Barnes, T. (2002) Performing economic geography: two men, two books, and a cast of thousands. *Environment and Planning A* **34**, 487–512.

Barnes, B., Bloor, D. and Henry, J. (1996) *Scientific Knowledge: A Sociological Analysis*. University of Chicago Press, Chicago.

Barnes, T. and Duncan, J. (eds) (1992) *Writing Worlds*. Routledge, London.

Best, B. (1999) Postcolonialism and the deconstructive scenario: representing Gayatri Spivak. *Environment and Planning D: Society and Space* **17**, 475–494.

Bhaskar, R. (1986) *Scientific Realism and Human Emancipation*. Verso, New York.

Braun, B. and Castree, N. (eds) (1998) *Remaking Reality: Nature at the Millennium*. Routledge, New York.

Butler, J. (1993) *Bodies That Matter*. Routledge, New York.

Callon, M. (1995) Four models for the dynamics of science. In Janasoff, S., Markle, G., Petersen, J. and Pinch, T. (eds) *Handbook of Science and Technology Studies*. Sage, New York, pp. 29–63.

Castree, N. (1995) The nature of produced nature and knowledge construction in Marxism. *Antipode* **27**, 12–48.

Collier, A. (1994) *Critical Realism: An Introduction to Roy Bhaskar's Philosophy*. Verso, New York.

Cosgrove, D. (1992) Orders and a new world: cultural geography 1990–1991. *Progress in Human Geography* **16**, 272–280.

Demerritt, D. (1998) Science, social constructivism and nature. In Braun, B. and Castree, N. (eds) *Remaking Reality*. Routledge, New York, pp. 173–193.

Demeritt, D. (2001) Being constructive about nature. In Castree, N. and Braun, B. (eds) *Social Nature: Theory, Practice, Politics*. Blackwell, Oxford, pp. 22–40.

Dewsbury, J.-D. (2000) Performativity and the event: enacting a philosophy of difference. *Environment and Planning D: Society and Space* **18**, 473–496.

Doel, M. (1993) Proverbs for paranoids: writing geography on hollowed ground. *Transactions of the Institute of British Geographers* **18**, 377–394.

Doel, M. (1999) *Poststructuralist Geographies*. Rowman and Littlefield, New York.

Gibson-Graham, J.-K. (1996) *The End of Capitalism (As We Knew It)*. Blackwell, Oxford.

Graham, J. (1990) Theory and essentialism in Marxist geography. *Antipode* **22**, 53–66.

Gregory, D. (1978) *Ideology, Science and Human Geography*. St Martin's Press, New York.

Gregory, D. (1994) *Geographical Imaginations*. Blackwell, Oxford.

Hannah, M. (1999) Skeptical realism: from either/or to both-and. *Environment and Planning D: Society and Space* **17**, 17–34.

Hardt, M. and Negri, A. (2000) *Empire*. Harvard University Press, Cambridge, MA.

Harley, J.B. (1989) Deconstructing the map. *Cartographica* **26**, 1–20.

Hetherington, K. and Law, J. (2000) After networks. *Environment and Planning D: Society and Space* **18**, 127–132.

Latour, B. (1987) *Science in Action*. Harvard University Press, Cambridge, MA.

Latour, B. (1999) Circulating reference. In Latour, B. *Pandora's Hope: Essays on the Reality of Science Studies*. Harvard University Press, Cambridge, MA, pp. 24–79.

Latour, B. and Woolgar, S. ([1979] 1986) *Laboratory Life: The Construction of Scientific Facts*. Princeton University Press, Princeton, NJ.

Law, J. (ed.) (1991) *A Sociology of Monsters*. Routledge, New York.

Murdoch, J. (1997) Inhuman/nonhuman/human. *Environment and Planning D: Society and Space* **15**, 731–756.

Peet, R. (1998) *Modern Geographical Thought*. Blackwell, Oxford.

Pile, S. (1994) Masculinism, the use of dualistic epistemologies and third spaces. *Antipode* **26**, 255–277.

Sayer, A. ([1984] 1992) *Method in Social Science: A Realist Approach*. Routledge, New York.

Sidaway, J. (2000) Recontextualising positionality. *Antipode* **32**, 260–270.

Soja, E. (1996) *Thirdspace*. Blackwell, Oxford.

Spivak, G. ([1985] 1996) Subaltern studies: deconstructing historiography. In Landry, D. and Maclean, G. (eds) *The Spivak Reader*. Routledge, New York, pp. 203–236.

Thrift, N. (1999) Steps to an ecology of place. In Massey, D., Allen, J. and Sarre, P. (eds) *Human Geography Today*. Blackwell, Malden, MA, pp. 295–322.

Thrift, N. (2000) Afterwords. *Environment and Planning D: Society and Space* **18**, 213–255.

Meta-Theory/Many Theories

Michael R. Curry

Geographers speak of themselves as being involved with 'theory' perhaps more than ever before. On the face of it, this seems both a simple
matter and one that is obviously true. For most of us, hardly a day goes
by in which we do not either hear, read, utter, or write the term. But here,
as elsewhere, the very commonness of the term should raise a cautionary
flag. And, indeed, if we reflect on our own use of the term, we see that it
is routinely employed in a wide range of ways, ones that in many cases
seem unrelated, or even contradictory.

My task here is not to delineate the proper use of the term 'theory', nor
to describe how the term is in fact used, how theories are constructed,
tested, and applied within the discipline of geography (see Chapter 15 in
this volume by Graham). Rather, I shall concern myself here with the
ways in which geographers have over the past 30 or so years developed
an awareness of and interest in theory, and as a consequence of metatheory, of the very general features that are shared by, that underlie, or that
ought to underlie different theories. But we shall see that if for a time it
seemed as though metatheoretical analysis might lead geography on the
path to a more conceptually integrated discipline, by the 1980s it had
come to be challenged by the claim that the whole idea of a metatheory
was merely an ideological construct, one that developed within and now
supported a particular set of social formations. On this, sometimes
termed a 'postmodern' view, the very idea of a coherent discipline was
rejected, replaced instead by the view that we have, and can only have,
many theories.

What follows will be in two parts. First, I will point to what is surely a
central feature of geography, the ways in which we typically conceptualize the relationships between the world, how we know about it, and
who we are. These ways of thinking about geography and geographical

knowledge are so common that they are seldom commented upon; they are taken to be natural. Yet one can hardly make sense of the discipline without paying attention to the ways in which it is organized. Second, I shall show that the first way of thinking has been fundamental to a view in which geographical knowledge is a kind of edifice. On this view different approaches to geography may be sorted into types, and those types are differentiated in terms of their *meta*-theoretical features. Here we shall see that the attack on metatheory and the rise of an alternative understanding of the nature of geography emerge out of an increasing understanding of the extent to which all human knowledge (from the most mundane to the most abstruse) is a product of people situated in particular places at particular times. From this newer point of view, the very idea that anyone could take up a standpoint that would allow him or her to judge the differences between theories without at the same time appealing to and buying into a theory was sheer arrogance. From that point of view, we need to understand that we are all in the thick of things, making judgments about the world from a particular vantage point, from a place. This, in fact, has a further implication: this alternative way of thinking about geography and its parts suggests that the idea that geography will one day become a discipline unified by a web of well-articulated concepts and facts is simply a pipe-dream.

World, Knowledge and Discipline

Geographers are fond of saying that what 'ties the discipline together' is an attention to phenomena insofar as they are distributed in space. At the same time, and like other scholars, geographers tend to see their discipline as divided into subdisciplines. There is economic geography, biogeography, and so on. Here a similar strategy is invoked: it is held that economic geography concerns spatial aspects of economic phenomena, that biogeography concerns spatial aspects of living things, and so on. It is common to imagine that below disciplines and sub-subdisciplines are research areas, and finally the work of single individuals.

We see just this view in Brian Berry's famous 'cube' (Figure 10.1), where the discipline is divided into human and physical parts, which are in turn subdivided into the economic, the social, and so on, and where the discipline can be further divided orthogonally, in terms of the geographical area or scale that is being studied, or of the time period that is being studied. Although Berry created his cube during the quantitative revolution of the 1960s, this way of thinking was by no means

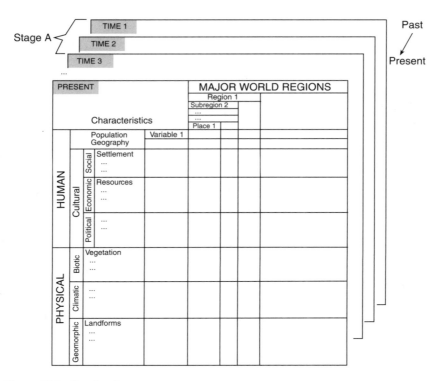

Figure 10.1 Berry's cube.

new to – nor is it a relic of – that era. We see an earlier version in Freeman and Raup's 1949 *Essentials of Geography* (1949: 8) (Figure 10.2).

And it appears more recently in de Blij and Murphy's *Human Geography* (2003: 5) (which though entitled 'human geography' also includes physical geography and environmental studies) (Figure 10.3).

Indeed, in the case of geography we can find a similar project even as far back as the ancient Greek geographer Ptolemy (AD 90–168), where geography is described in what looks like a familiar way, as the study of places, regions, and the 'figure' or shape of the earth itself, a figure that is to be captured in mathematical terms. So there seems to be good reason, on historical grounds, for thinking of geography as a discipline that is ultimately defined in ontological terms, in terms of the objects that it studies. And this should be no surprise – geographers are not alone in looking at disciplines in this way. A look at an introductory textbook in almost any discipline will reveal something similar, a diagram or

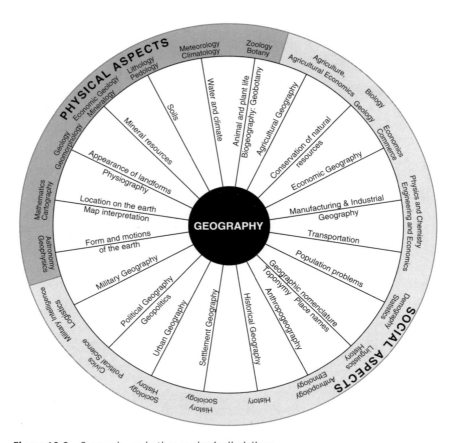

Figure 10.2 Geography and other academic disciplines.

chart – often a pie chart – laying out the structure of the discipline, and pointing to the place of that discipline among all disciplines.

But it is important to note that in geography, as elsewhere, these illustrations are fundamentally ambiguous. They may refer to a discipline in terms of the objects that it studies, as in Berry's cube where geomorphologists study landforms, or in Freeman and Raup, where there are geographers who study population problems, or in de Blij and Murphy where some geographers study environmental problems. But the illustrations often seem to suggest something different, that disciplines and subdisciplines need to be seen not as reflections of the structure of the world, but as the way we structure of our *knowledge* of the world. So Berry sees economic geographers not simply as looking at 'economies', but also

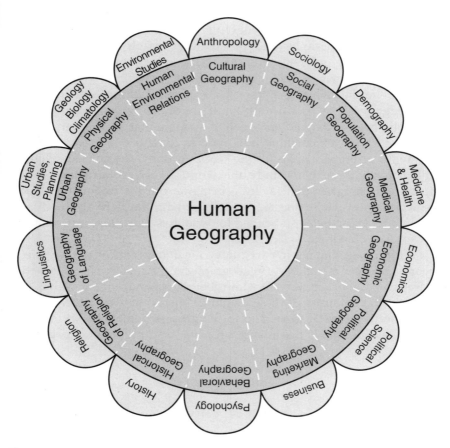

Figure 10.3   Human geography.

as asking economic questions about the world, and for de Blij and Murphy, cultural geographers ask cultural questions. In a sense, each can be said to be looking at the world through a particular lens, economic, cultural, and so on. From that perspective the illustrations are very much like the systems used in libraries for the classification of published materials and of written knowledge, systems such as the American Library of Congress and Dewey Decimal classification systems.

But this is not all. The illustrations may in fact be read a third way; they may be seen as laying out the structure of the discipline itself. So there is a subdiscipline called economic geography that creates economic-geographical knowledge of economic-geographical aspects of the world, and so on. There are people called 'biogeographers' and 'economic geographers'. They publish in biogeography and economic geography journals, go to biogeography and economic geography conferences, and belong to biogeography and economic geography organizations.

These three ways of looking at academic disciplines – in terms of the nature of the objects that they study, in terms of the structure of the knowledge that they produce, and in terms of their social organization – have long been widely accepted. Note, though, that as different as they may be, they have something important in common; each envisions the possibility of unity, a unity of the world, a unity of knowledge, and a unity among those who study the world. The very structure of the illustrations suggests that far from being an unruly, fragmented place, the world is an interconnected whole that with the right approach and the right tools can be apprehended for what it is. It is a structure that can be captured on a page.

It is this image that has in part guided the understanding of the place of theory, and later metatheory, in geography and elsewhere in science. But as we shall see, in recent years some geographers have made claims that undercut the authority of these diagrams, just as they call into question the authority of metatheory, and in the process demote theory. On this newer view, academic disciplines can never be captured on a page.

On Metatheory

Like members of other disciplines, geographers have routinely felt it necessary to define their discipline, and to differentiate it from others; but in the 1960s this process of definition became increasingly one of *re*definition, as the question 'What is geography?' seemed to take on a new urgency. For some time a standard answer had been that geography was the study of the way in which the earth is divided into different regions (Hartshorne, 1939). But a new generation of geographers claimed that this was an old-fashioned view, one that went with an old-fashioned world. From their point of view, geographers needed to recognize that geography needed to become a science, rather than the descriptive enterprise laid out in Freeman and Raup's illustration in Figure 10.2; and they needed to recognize that this required that it become theoretical. It was not enough to *describe* the economic or biological phenomena on the earth's surface; one needed to develop means for *explaining* them theoretically.

Although there has over the years been a tremendous amount of discussion and discord among philosophers and historians of science

→ Part of the "tension"
→ Maybe Systematic turns it to a Science
Whereas "Regional" turns it to a Description Enterprise
As indicated by Freeman & Raups (ABOVE)

about just what a theory is, geographers in the 1960s by and large sidestepped that work and adopted a simple and pragmatic definition. Elaborated in classic works like David Harvey's *Explanation in Geography* (1969) and William Bunge's *Theoretical Geography* (1962), it was often drawn from work in related fields, such as economics. On this view, a theoretical geography needed to be one that started from observations gathered from the world ('I see an object with these characteristics', where the objects might be a person, a plant, or a body of water). These observations were then categorized ('All of these bodies of water are perennial streams', or 'All of these individuals are recent immigrants'). And the relations among those types of objects were captured in an abstract structure, so 'The streambeds of perennial streams are all alike in these ways, because of these factors,' or 'All immigrants go through these phases as they become permanent residents of a new place'). Finally, the theory itself, a structure of abstractions describing the relationships among various sorts of objects, can be tested against new observations. Although theories need not be mathematical, when geographers spoke of the need for theory, they very often meant that geography needed to be quantitative, that it ought to use statistical methods (such as the calculation of means or of regression coefficients), or that the theories themselves needed to be in the form of mathematical structures (as in the gravity model, where $I = d^n p_1 p_2$).

From the point of view of its advocates, only by adopting the use of theory could one begin to make connections among the work of people in other subdisciplines and other disciplines. Moreover, the turn to theory was necessary because of the state of the world – the old world of regions was fading and being replaced by a new spatial world in which goods and people and ideas were increasingly mobile; because of the state of knowledge – which was increasingly interconnected; and because of the state of academic and scientific disciplines – where to remain a traditional descriptive discipline was to risk obscurity and death. Geography needed to be spatial, theoretical, and integrated with other sciences.

Although in the 1960s and 1970s geographers did not use the term 'metatheory', in retrospect, these arguments were just that, metatheoretical arguments. Here, as elsewhere, the term 'meta' refers to that which is beyond or above. For example, metaphysics in a sense steps back from physics, and looks broadly at what physics is, at its structure and presuppositions (or, in contemporary usage, looks at the limits or possibilities of existence). Similarly, a 'metatheory' is a theory about theory; it sorts, characterizes, and explains theories according to their structures or goals.

[handwritten margin notes: "this is More like Regana", "Empirical"]

Metatheoris'al
& Spatial.

There are others, but in geography special attention was at that point given to three metatheoretical divides. First, from a metatheoretical point of view, one might distinguish between theories that attempt to describe the world as it is, and ones that create abstract images of the constituents of the world, and model the behaviour of those constituents. So in the first case one would have theories that take the flows of industrial commodities and using statistical methods describe their interrelations; in the second case, one might ask about the decisions that a purely rational and all-knowing individual would make about what to ship where and in what way. In a way, the first models the real, the second the ideal. And indeed, in the 1960s and 1970s, one major criticism levelled by younger geographers was the metatheoretical argument that geography was 'stuck' in the real, while science operated by peeling back everyday appearances in order to discern the ideal structure that lies behind.

We see just this argument in the famous Hartshorne–Schaefer dispute, as discussed by Castree and Burt in Chapters 4 and 7. There, newcomer Fred Schaefer (1953) took on Richard Hartshorne, whose book *The Nature of Geography* (1939) was seen by many as a kind of grand summation of the discipline. Schaefer argued that far from doing the right thing badly, Hartshorne was doing the wrong thing entirely. He claimed that no one ought to be doing regional geography in the way that Hartshorne had been doing it, and that geographers ought instead to be engaging in work that sees the fundamental geographical unit as the individual person or object, and that sees interrelationships among those elements as definable in abstract and mathematical and spatial terms.

Many of the advocates of the view that geography ought to be a spatial science held that one of the failings of traditional geography lay in its inability to be objective, in its overt introduction into geography of evaluative or normative notions. But others in this era championed the introduction of such values. Works as otherwise different as Anne Buttimer's *Values in Geography* (1974) and David Harvey's *Social Justice and the City* (1973) took issue with quantitative and spatial geography's claim that values ought to be excised from geography, and argued that all science ought to make explicit the ways in which it incorporates and promotes particular sets of values. So a second metatheoretical divide was between accounts whose goal is to describe the way in which the world works, and those that are normative, describing the ways in which the world should and could work.

In the 1970s there emerged what one might term a counter-revolution against the new, spatial and theoretical, geography. There, humanistic geographers began to argue that geography was not about – or at least, not simply about – region and space, but rather about place (Tuan, 1974; Relph, 1976). This counter-revolution was typically non-theoretical; it shared that with earlier regional geographers. But in another way it claimed that both older regional geographers and newer spatial geographers were off the mark; it argued that central to understanding the workings of the world is not the way the world is – in either the descriptive way advocated by regional geographers or the theoretical way championed by the new spatial scientists. Drawing on works by scholars like Max Weber, Ludwig Wittgenstein, and Peter Winch, it argued that one needs to begin, at least in the human side of the discipline, with an understanding that people act not on the basis of how the world is, but rather on the basis of how they *believe* the world to be. This was the third divide, between those who believed that one could in principle discover – or create – knowledge that was from a God's-eye point of view, and those who believed that everything that we know and might know is inexorably the product of human thought, perception, and action.

Metatheory and the dream of a guiding light

Although in the 1960s and 1970s one commonly heard the sorts of metatheoretical debates that I have described above, at the same time there emerged a second way of thinking about the differences among geographers and geography, one that was metatheoretical in rather a different sense. On this view, the discipline was sorting itself into groups of people, each of which claimed allegiance to a single set of theories and theoretical ideas. Most visibly, economic geographers looked to classic works on central places (by Walter Christaller and August Lösch), industrial location (by Alfred Weber), and agricultural location (by von Thünen), all of which were seen as providing a sense of the way in which this integrated science might develop. For Berry, and many others, it seemed possible that one might develop a comprehensive, systematic geography, as a science of spatial behaviour.

But this was only one of several such projects; and paralleling it were others. There was, for example, a behavioural geography based upon psychology (Downs and Stea, 1973; Gould and White, 1974) that drew in part on the idea that people approached the world in terms of 'mental maps'. And, perhaps most visibly, there were attempts to develop a Marxist geography (Harvey, 1973).

Alongside these projects, all of which envisioned the development of a theory that in some ways looked like the sort glorified in parts of the natural sciences, one that was reductive and mathematical, there remained alternatives that rejected that model of knowledge and instead suggested that the roots of a new geography needed to be found outside science, perhaps in philosophers such as Heidegger, Merleau-Ponty, Collingwood or Croce (Tuan, 1974; Relph, 1976; Guelke, 1982).

But on this view, whether in the mainstream or the alternative camps, a central motivating idea was that it would be possible to encompass the interests of geographers under one very large and general theory, such as Marxism or behaviourism or Darwinian evolution. If we turn back to Figures 10.1, 10.2 and 10.3, one could have a Marxist version of Figure 10.3, presumably competing with an alternative version, based on Christaller and von Thünen and Weber, and so on. And in the end, it was imagined (or hoped), these theories having fought it out, one would become victorious. The Marxist version of Figure 10.3 would perhaps vanquish the neoclassical version, just as modernist, Newtonian physics had vanquished Aristotelian physics.

Here metatheory does not operate from what it sees as a timeless set of purified concepts, like 'ought' and 'is', or 'description' and 'theory', with the idea that it is sorting real from pseudo knowledge. Rather, one begins to see the idea that the choice was one of what might be best termed a 'theoretical approach'. One could choose to be a 'mainstream' geographer, or a Marxist geographer, or a humanist. And in fact, this approach to theory cut across the earlier one. One could be a Marxist geographer and still share with mainstream geographers a view of the need for abstraction; or one could be a Marxist and share with humanists a view of the importance of values. Metatheory became less a set of rules than a guiding light.

Here, and not surprisingly, the widest metatheoretical rift was clearly on the human side of geography. In contrast, in physical geography, beginning with climatology and then spreading across the spectrum, there was a more unified attempt to abandon the descriptive and historical features of older work and to take on the mantle of a theoretical science much like that promoted by many human geographers. In physical geography, this move was further supported by a powerful and widely accepted view, wherein one might in principle move from the micro level, from the level of the atom and its constituent parts, up to successively higher levels of aggregation, and thereby come to an integrated understanding of the operation of phenomena as diverse as systems of oceanic and atmospheric circulation, the development of ecosystems and the extinction of organisms, and the role of human activities in atmospheric chemistry. Here the fact that the discipline was the home both of remote sensing and imaging systems and of geographic information systems provided technological support for that view of science and offered as a guiding image the powerful view of the earth from above (Cosgrove, 2001). Using that image, many advocates of geography as a theoretical, mathematical science went further; they suggested that in the perhaps-near future it was possible that the remaining barriers between human and physical geography would fall away, and that geography would fulfil its role as a synoptic science, one that emerged from the marriage of chemistry and physics, psychology and evolutionary theory.

As I suggested at the outset, this image is still alive, and is often propounded in introductory textbooks, where human geography texts promote the view that, starting with people, we quickly move to issues of resources and environmental impacts, and physical texts, beginning with 'strictly' physical processes, move to humans as agents or factors of change. But when we move beyond the hopefulness of introductory texts, we find that the discipline has developed in ways that are very different from those that were expected.

Postmodernism and the Decline of Metatheory

The potential for a unified discipline has been fundamentally called into question by the emergence of a view that sees metatheory less as a universal standard against which any theory ought to be measured than as a rhetorical or ideological device used in the service of some already-chosen theory.

From metatheory to metanarrative

In the 1980s discussions of the nature of theory and metatheory were dramatically recast. One can point, symbolically, at least, to three texts that were key to this change. First, Hayden White's *Metahistory* (1973) showed in a compelling way that historical accounts embody the standard plots found in fictional works. The clear inference, though one about which White himself seemed ambivalent, was that historians inexorably bring to their work attitudes, either individual or cultural, about the direction and meaning of history. Second, in anthropology, Clifford and Marcus's (1986) *Writing Culture* showed that anthropologists, and by implication others in the social sciences, were in their written works constantly, rather than simply at the margins, using language in ways that defined and maintained power relations between the author and the object of inquiry. For Geertz, anthropologists established their authority to speak for others by writing in a monological mode, as if they were but conduits of truth about the world. And finally, Jean-François Lyotard's *The Postmodern Condition* (1984) helped once again to open the door to continental European thought. Lyotard argued that since the Enlightenment, Western academics had supposed that reality (social and environmental) could be understood through one or other intellectual framework. For him, these master frameworks threatened to squeeze out more modest, more local *petits récits* (or small stories about the world).

Each of these works gave support to the idea that a metatheory is very often – perhaps always – a disguised metanarrative. It is, that is to say, a 'big story'; it emplots a historical epoch, or even more, by giving it a direction, a beginning, a middle, and an end, as in the stories told by archaeologists, anthropologists, and geographers of 'man's role in changing the face of the earth' (Thomas, 1956). In a way, of course, this had long been admitted. For example, central to a common view (recall the earlier discussion of theory) is that science is a whole, but one that consists of a large set of parts. Here the idea has been that science is not yet, but will someday be, complete, a tidy package of theories and facts, all connected together; it will be a package that leaves no gaps, leaves nothing unexplained. In the interim there are, of course, plenty of gaps, but on the popular view this fact does not vitiate the power of the whole, because the structure of science, one of observation, hypothesis formation, testing, and so on, is fundamentally sound; it is a timeless model of knowledge and of the means of its acquisition and synthesis. And that structure, if followed scrupulously, will in the end lead to a fully articulated body of knowledge about the operation of the world. Here, and again as suggested earlier, the idea has been that scientific knowledge of the world has a structure, and that the world itself has a structure. Science, to use a famous phrase, reads the 'book of nature', and scientists then write it for all to read.

This metaphor, of the book of nature, has a long history. In science, of course, it has come to be associated with the notion that one is reading the structure of natural systems. But in geography it also suggests something rather more literal, namely the idea that the world is there to be mapped, and that mapping is a process of reading the natural and human patterning of the globe and translating it into cartographic form, so that the structure, too, is there, waiting to be discovered (rather than, say, invented). Indeed, in the light of the image elaborated by Ptolemy of an earth laced with numerical gridlines, where every object and action could potentially be defined in terms of what we now think of as latitude and longitude, of X- and Y-axes, geography's task could be seen as simply a matter of filling things in, of determining and recording those locations.

Here, though, a meta-*theory* seemed clearly to imply a meta-*narrative*, of a natural move from less to more knowledge. But as elsewhere in science, many viewed this metanarrative as non-historical. It was imagined that it described a matter not of historical change, but of the natural working out of a process intrinsic to the system of latitude and longitude itself. From the point of view of those who saw it as non-historical, to say that it was historical would be rather like claiming that counting from one to one hundred is a historical process, simply because it occurs in time; for them, the entire process is 'already there' and the process of articulating it is simply one of discovery.

But, according to White and Clifford, and especially Lyotard, the turn to metanarrative undercuts the foundations of the set of metatheories that were so popular through the first three-quarters of the twentieth century. It does so in two ways. First, if we think of creating a theory simply as a matter of discovering 'the way things are', then it is easy to imagine that a theory has no creator, no author. But essential to the idea of metanarra- tive was that it always had an author (though the author might very well be a culture or group or even God!). And for that reason, a metanarrative always expressed a point of view. Second, a metanarrative is always in some sense provisional, and never final. Historians need routinely to revisit their subjects, just because as the present becomes the past it recasts the context within which events must be understood; this is the other side of the fact that we cannot predict the future. Indeed, as White and Lyotard would insist, metanarratives very often operate outside the categories of 'true' and 'false', and ought instead to be seen as expressive of deep-seated beliefs about human nature and the nature of society, beliefs that from the point of view of those who hold them are not subject to falsification.

So from a metanarrative point of view, even those works of science that claim to be neutral and timeless are in fact suffused with narrative elements, with expressions of a belief in progress or decline, of growing order or disorder, of the rightness of certain developments, or perhaps of the utter meaningless of the world and everything in it. They express the belief, one perhaps held by a group of neighbours, colleagues, or coun- trymen, that the world works in a particular way and is moving in a particular direction. This belief often takes that direction to be normal and natural, and sees it not as an expression of a set of values, but rather as the taken-for-granted background of everyday life.

With this appeal to metanarrative, geographers and others proclaimed that they could see through the claim of mainstream geography to be neutral and objective in its description of the development of democracy, capitalism, and social, cultural, racial, and economic conditions; they suggested that the stories told by such geographers were simply stories, and stories that very often served their own purposes.

Postmodernism and the local turn

One might usefully see the development of the view that scientific accounts of the world are expressive of metanarratives as one part of the postmodern turn in social theory.[1] And, in fact, if metanarrative operated at and attempted to take over the level previously occupied by metatheory, at the lower level of theory and knowledge acquisition there was a parallel development.

Here, as the appeal to the idea of metanarrative developed, one very important metaphor came to the fore. Led by anthropologist Clifford Geertz (1983), many geographers began to claim that all knowledge is *local*, i.e. it reflects the people and the specific context out of which it emerges. This idea of local knowledge was in fact articulated in various versions. From what might be termed a weak perspective, knowledge consists strictly of ideas. On that view, it is possible to argue that all knowledge is local, but that one can translate from one locality's knowledge to that of another. This way of looking at science leaves intact the earlier relationship between the world, knowledge, and disciplines.

But a strong version of local knowledge has more radical consequences. Drawing upon earlier work in the history and sociology of science, including parts of Kuhn's (1970, original 1962) work that were little noticed, it sees science as consisting not simply of ideas, but also of local practices, in part what Michael Polanyi (1958) had termed 'tacit knowledge', and institutions. As some would put it, these practices 'go all the way down'; there is nothing underneath, no more universal 'stuff' supporting or underpinning them. Knowledge, there, is irredeemably local. Metatheories are in the end just slicker versions of stories told around a campfire.

In both its strong and weak forms, the idea of local knowledge has suggested that all knowledge is in some sense relative, relative perhaps to where one is, to who one is, to one's gender, ethnicity, or social class (see Chapter 9 in this volume by Hannah). But on the weak form, where knowledge consists merely of ideas, different local knowledges are commensurable, and hence one may be translated into another. In contrast, on the strong view there are a great many ways to core a tree, for example, and the similarities between the ways used by members of two groups are at best simply the result of both groups having been trained within the same times and places, in the same institutions, using the same tools. On this view one need not – and cannot – suppose that those individuals 'share' or have 'the same' ideas of what they are doing; it is neither possible nor necessary that there be agreement about the particular objects used, say, in a laboratory. As Star and others have noted in appealing to the concept of a 'boundary object', objects within a laboratory can be used within a team by a variety of individuals who in fact have very different understandings of the nature of the object; they need only to be able to articulate their uses of the objects in question (Star and Griesemer, 1989; Fujimura, 1992).

The idea that knowledge is local has had a long history in geography, but against the background of these theoretical developments it developed a new life. In the history of cartography, for example, Harley (1988; 1989) showed that far from being neutral representations of the world, maps embody multiple sets of power relations, and that, in fact, they embody diverse narratives, of the process of human habitation, of the naturalness of certain physical or biological processes, or of the undesirability of other processes. These claims have since been adumbrated in a wide range of works on cartography (Black, 1997) and on scientific representation more generally (Hankins and Silverman, 1995).

So, under the sway of the same forces that have supported the move from metatheory to metanarrative, some have begun to insist that just as what were thought to be timeless metatheories have turned out to be metanarratives, always told at particular times and places by particular individuals and groups, what we had thought were timeless theories themselves, on inspection, turn out to be merely local. We are all, in the end, engaged in work that will pass away, created by people who will pass away, in places that will pass away. What remains will be taken up by those who follow us, but almost certainly in ways that we would find strange and even implausible. If we had a dream of 'theory', we will when all is said and done, have only 'theories'.

In Conclusion

Attempting to make sense of the theoretical choices within geography is never easy. This is all the more so because it was only very recently, the 1970s, that geographers began to engage in a discourse that appealed to some of the common distinctions that had been at the centre of debate in the philosophy of science, and then the philosophies of the social sciences and of history. In part, for that reason, attempts to connect the literature in geography with that elsewhere are always more difficult than they would otherwise be. One can, nonetheless, look at the theoretical positions adduced in the 1970s and 1980s and see individuals and groups as having taken stands in favour, say, of individualism over holism, or in favour of seeing science as neutral, rather than as expressive of particular values. To do so is to engage in a metatheoretical inquiry.

But in the 1980s, under the banner of postmodernism, some geographers in effect denied the relevance or importance of metatheoretical inquiry. They did so by claiming that the metatheoretical enterprise was in fact not an inquiry into a set of permanent and timeless categories – as had been argued within the philosophies of science and the social sciences – but was instead an artifact of a particular era, the modern era, from which we were in the process of emerging. One needed, they countered, to look at the world, and people's accounts of the world, as always expressing a particular point of view, as always situated. If for many who pressed the metatheoretical approach it was possible to imagine a science without an author, a science that emerged from an interplay between the world and a modest witness, for the postmodernists there was always, in a sense, an author – though that did not mean that the author had control of the text.

In this piece I have described the move from modernist to postmodernist geographies as one in which metanarrative attempted to vanquish metatheory. If scholars differ in their judgements of the success of that undertaking, it is surely true that it has as a consequence become increasingly difficult to maintain the modernist view that some day science will fulfil its destiny and become unified.

Although it does seem clear to me that the fulfilment of this dream of a unified science – or even a unified geography – has become increasingly difficult to count on, it is only fair to note that for many geographers, and others, the idea of a modernist science and the belief in the utility of metatheoretical analyses remain very real indeed.

In a sense, we see here a battle between those who believe in the primacy of conceptual analyses and those who believe in the primacy of historical analyses. How might we adjudicate that dispute? In a set of provocative pieces in the 1960s and 1970s philosopher Louis Mink (e.g. Mink, 1978) argued that there can be no adjudication. Rather, he argued, we live in a world in which there really are three main types of intellectual discourse, philosophy (or conceptual analysis), history (or narrative analysis), and science (or causal analysis). As Mink saw the matter, each attempts to comprehend the others; there is a philosophy of science and a philosophy of history, a history of science and of philosophy, and even a science of philosophy (cognitive science or psychology) and of history (perhaps sociology, or even economics). If each claims primacy over the others, none can in fact establish that primacy without making assumptions that the others would not make.[2]

This to some is an intellectually appealing position, but it remains one that for many is emotionally unsatisfying. Just as to many people metatheoretical analyses retain their power, so to others does the postmodern idea that today's science, too, will pass, and the idea that one must be more true than the other. What does seem likely is that the ideals of a science unified through a universal theory will continue to come up against those forces – including the desire for a unified discipline[3] – that foster the demotion of theory into theories.

ESSAY QUESTION AND FURTHER READING

If we believe that there cannot be a unified, theoretical geography, but rather can only be a series of stories and voices, does it make sense to talk about progress within geography? Here consider the essays in Sack (2002), especially those by Vale, a biogeographer, and Lowenthal, a historical geographer. See also Bassett (1999). How do these authors deal with the issues raised by Michael Dear (1988) and Trevor Barnes (1996)?

NOTES

1 This view, that there is something 'beyond' modernism, was not entirely new. By the 1970s architects had begun to develop a family of styles that they termed 'postmodern', and social theorists like Jürgen Habermas had begun to explore the concept at around the same time (Habermas, 1981). But drawing on influential works by Fredric Jameson (1984) and Lyotard (1984), geographers in the late 1980s began systematically to explore the concept (see Dear, 1988; Harvey, 1989; Soja, 1989).

2 Mink here echoes a similar claim made in 1917 by anthropologist Alfred Kroeber, who in an article on 'The Superorganic', claimed that anthropology and history share a method, of looking directly at phenomena, while science always involves looking past the phenomena, with an eye to underlying processes.

3   Note that the idea of a unified discipline resonates with the romantic idea that one might bring together into some larger social and moral whole the isolated, modern, individual scientist (Tinder, 1986).

REFERENCES

Barnes, T.J. (1996) *Logics of Dislocation: Models, Metaphors, and Meanings of Economic Space*. Guildford Press, New York.
Bassett, K. (1999) Is there progress in human geography? *Progress in Human Geography* **23**, 27–47.
Berry, B.J.L. (1964) Approaches to regional analysis: a synthesis. *Annals of the Association of American Geographers* **54**, 2–11.
Black, J. (1997) *Maps and History: Constructing Images of the Past*. New Haven, CT, Yale University Press.
Bunge, W. (1962) *Theoretical Geography*. C.W.K. Gleerup, Lund.
Buttimer, A. (1974) *Values in Geography*. Association of American Geographers, Washington, DC.
Clifford, J. and Marcus, G. (eds) (1986) *Writing Culture: The Poetics and Politics of Ethnography*. University of California Press, Berkeley, CA.
Cosgrove, D.E. (2001) *Apollo's Eye: A Cartographic Genealogy of the Earth in the Western Imagination*. Johns Hopkins University Press, Baltimore, MD.
Dear, M.J. (1988) The postmodern challenge: reconstructing human geography. *Transactions of the Institute of British Geographers* NS **13**, 262–274.
de Blij, H.J. and Murphy, A.B. (2003) *Human Geography*. John Wiley, New York.
Downs, R. and Stea, D. (1973) *Image and Environment*. Edward Arnold, London.
Freeman, O.W. and Raup, H.F. (1949) *Essentials of Geography*. McGraw-Hill, New York.
Fujimura, J.H. (1992) Crafting science: standardized packages, boundary objects, and 'translation'. In Pickering, A. (ed.) *Science as Practice and Culture*. University of Chicago Press, Chicago, pp. 169–211.
Geertz, C. (1983) *Local Knowledge*. Basic Books, New York.
Gould, P. and White, R. (1974) *Mental Maps*. Penguin, Harmondsworth.
Guelke, L. (1982) *Historical Understanding in Geography: An Idealist Approach*. Cambridge University Press, Cambridge.
Habermas, J. (1981) Modernity versus postmodernity. *New German Critique* **22**, 3–14.
Hankins, T.L. and Silverman, R.J. (1995) *Instruments and the Imagination*. Princeton University Press, Princeton, NJ.
Harley, J.B. (1988) Maps, knowledge, and power. In Cosgrove, D. and Daniels, S. (eds) *The Iconography of Landscape: Essays on the Symbolic Representation, Design, and Use of Past Environments*. Cambridge University Press, Cambridge, pp. 277–312.
Harley, J.B. (1989) Deconstructing the map. *Cartographica* **26**, 1–20.

Hartshorne, R. (1939) *The Nature of Geography*. Association of American Geographers, Lancaster, PA.

Harvey, D. (1969) *Explanation in Geography*. Edward Arnold, London.

Harvey, D. (1973) *Social Justice and the City*. Johns Hopkins University Press, Baltimore, MD.

Harvey, D. (1989) *The Condition of Postmodernity*. Basil Blackwell, Oxford.

Jameson, F. (1984) Postmodernism, or the cultural logic of late capitalism. *New Left Review* **146**, 53–92.

Kroeber, A.L. (1917) The superorganic. *American Anthropologist* **19**, 163–213.

Kuhn, T.S. ([1962] 1970) *The Structure of Scientific Revolutions*. University of Chicago Press, Chicago.

Lyotard, J-F. (1984) *The Postmodern Condition*. University of Minnesota Press, Minneapolis.

Mink, L.O. (1978) Narrative form as a cognitive instrument. In Canary, R.H. and Kozicki, H. (eds) *The Writing of History*. University of Wisconsin Press, Madison, WI, pp. 129–149.

Polanyi, M. (1958) *Personal Knowledge*. Routledge and Kegan Paul, London.

Ptolemy (1948) The elements of geography. In Cohen, M.R. (ed.) *A Source Book in Greek Science*. Harvard University Press, Cambridge, MA, pp. 162–181.

Relph, E. (1976) *Place and Placelessness*. Pion, London.

Sack, R.D. (2002) *Progress: Geographical Essays*. Johns Hopkins University Press, Baltimore, MD.

Schaefer, F.K. (1953) Exceptionalism in geography. *Annals of the Association of American Geographers* **43**, 226–249.

Soja, E.W. (1989) *Postmodern Geographies*. Verso, London.

Star, S.L. and Griesemer, J.R. (1989) Institutional ecology, translations, and boundary objects. *Social Studies of Science* **19**, 387–420.

Thomas, W.L., Jr. (ed.) (1956) *Man's Role in Changing the Face of the Earth*. University of Chicago Press, Chicago.

Tinder, G. (1986) *Community: The Tragic Ideal*. Louisiana State University Press, Baton Rouge.

Tuan, Y.-F. (1974) Space and place: a humanistic perspective. In Board, C., Chorley, R.J., Haggett, P. et al. (eds) *Progress in Geography: International Reviews of Current Research*. Edward Arnold, London, pp. 211–252.

White, H. (1973) *Metahistory: The Historical Imagination in Nineteenth-Century Europe*. Johns Hopkins University Press, Baltimore, MD.

The Practice of Geography

Cartography and Visualization

Scott Orford

The International Cartographic Association (ICA) describes a map as 'a symbolized image of geographical reality, representing selected features or characteristics' (ICA, 1995: 1). Maps have been representing 'selected features or characteristics of geographical reality' for millennia and considerably longer than the discipline called 'geography' has been recognized and taught. But being useful, effective and well-established tools in representing the world around us, maps were readily adopted by geography as an infant discipline. Although the phrase 'geography is about maps, history is about chaps' may no longer hold true, maps still have a central role in geographical thinking. Indeed, maps and mapping are features that are still common to both the human and physical sides of the discipline. Visualization, or more precisely, scientific visualization is a much more recent concept than maps, one that uses the power of computers and computer graphics as means of constructing knowledge about the world (McCormick et al., 1987). The rationale behind scientific visualization is to 'see the unseen' in increasingly large and complex digital datasets by drawing pictures of the data using computer technology. Geographers and cartographers have adopted this rationale and are applying it to the very large and complex digital spatial datasets that are now available to geographers such as the UK's decennial Census of Population and the Landmap Project database. The result is that the traditional concept of maps and cartography – that of drawing a graphical representation of the world by hand on to a piece of paper – is slowly being replaced by computational cartography with more and more maps being created and stored electronically.

This chapter is therefore concerned not only with maps in their traditional sense but also with the new computational mapping that has developed in recent years. By examining two key issues relevant to map use – exploring geographical information and communicating geo-graphical information – the chapter will explain that the recent emphasis upon scientific visualization is not only changing what we can do with maps, but it is also changing who can map and the concept of what a map actually is. Rather than reinforcing the traditional view of maps as tech-nical products, the chapter will discuss how visualization is actually drawing attention to the social aspects of map making. First, however, the role and power of maps will be introduced by a discussion of one of the best-known (and misunderstood) maps to have been drawn: Dr John Snow's map of cholera deaths in Soho, London in 1854.

Map Making and Myth-Making: A Classic Example of Map Use

One of my first recollections of being interested in maps and mapping was at school when I watched a TV series about Victorian London. The series was concerned with the social conditions of London and one programme was about the frequent cholera epidemics of the mid-nineteenth century. It was this programme that grabbed my attention since it told a very interesting story of how the link was made between cholera and dirty drinking water by the use of a map. At the time, it was generally accepted that cholera was caused by miasmas – noxious gases and smells emanating from London's sewers and spoil heaps. However, during a major cholera epidemic in 1854, the programme described how Dr John Snow, an emi-nent London physician, had isolated the real source of the epidemic. He did this by drawing a map of deaths from cholera that had occurred in a small number of streets in the vicinity of Golden Square in Soho and saw that they centred upon a particular water pump in Broad Street (Figure 11.1). When the handle was removed from the pump, deaths from cholera abated. This was regarded by Dr Snow as proof that cholera was being spread, not by air-borne gases as was generally accepted, but through contaminated drinking water although it would not be until 1884 before the actual pathogen was discovered (the cholera bacteria *Vibrio Cholarae*).

Looking back, this story of how Dr Snow used a map to discover the cause of cholera is interesting for two reasons. First, because it provides a powerful illustration of how maps can be used as tools for undertaking research and for knowledge discovery. By plotting deaths from cholera on to a map and revealing the geographical relationship between deaths and the location of the Broad Street pump, Dr Snow had showed how maps could provide a unique insight into the patterns, processes and relationships of spatial phenomena. The relationship between polluted

Figure 11.1   Part of Dr Snow's map of deaths from cholera, Soho, 1854.

drinking water and cholera was not self-evident and had to be graphic-ally displayed before the connection could be made. The second reason why this famous story is interesting is because it is not true!

Contrary to popular belief, Dr Snow did not discover that cholera was spread by contaminated drinking water by drawing a map of cholera deaths clustered around the Broad Street pump (Brody et al., 2000). He had hypothesized that cholera was transmitted through dirty drinking water six years earlier, following the south London cholera epidemic of 1848. With the arrival of the 1854 epidemic, Dr Snow had decided to test his controversial hypothesis and was in the process of undertaking a large-scale study of the relationship between cholera deaths and the water supply in south London when Broad Street witnessed its first death. Due to the severity of the outbreak (more than 500 people died

L.T - mentioned this in her presentation.

in a 10-day period) and also its localized nature, Dr Snow realized that the Soho epidemic would also be a good place to test his polluted water supply hypothesis. By enquiring where the people who had died had obtained their drinking water, he quickly isolated the Broad Street pump as the likely source of the outbreak. With this information and with other anecdotal evidence, he got the handle of the pump removed. So where did his now famous map fit into the story?

Dr Snow actually drew his map of cholera some time after the epidemic had abated and definitely after the handle of the pump had been removed. The map formed part of a report written by Dr Snow on the Soho epidemic that had been commissioned by the officials of St James's parish where Broad Street was located. The map was drawn purely as an illustrative device to show the spatial correlation between the cholera deaths and the water pump. The majority of the report focused upon other evidence that linked the Broad Street pump to the cholera deaths. The map was used simply to add weight to this evidence rather than being the crux of the argument. In actual fact, it has been suggested (Brody et al., 2000) that Dr Snow may have been inspired to use a map to illustrate his report by a map in Shapter's (1849) earlier study on cholera in Exeter, which Dr Snow had cited in his own work. Even after the publication of the map and the report, not everybody was convinced by Dr Snow's claims and his hypothesis remained controversial for some time.

So what does the story of Dr Snow's map tell us, apart from not believing everything we are told? First, it demonstrates the different uses that maps can have. From Dr Snow's point of view, the map was used purely as an illustrative device to present what he already knew about the spread of cholera through drinking water to a wider, lay audience – in this case, the officials on the parish committee. The map was used to communicate information in a visually striking – and at the time innovative – way. However, from the point of view of the programme makers over one hundred years later, the map had taken on a different role. The re-telling of the story has it that Dr Snow had generated his contaminated water hypothesis from examining the cluster of cholera deaths on his map and their relationship to the Broad Street pump. Rather than a communicator of knowledge, Dr Snow's map had become a tool for constructing knowledge in an exploratory and highly inductive way. The main role of the map had been switched from a communicatory to an exploratory device.

The second thing the story tells us is something about the power of maps. Dr Snow must have realized the utility of drawing a map of cholera deaths in Soho to have included it in his report. In fact, evidence suggests that the map was re-drawn several times to include additional information such as a boundary indicating the homes that were closest to the pump in terms of walking distance. The time and effort devoted to re-drafting the map by hand implies that Dr Snow must have appreciated how the map could help legitimate his controversial claims on the spread of cholera to a then sceptical audience. Although he had not needed to draw a map to convince himself of the validity of his hypothesis, the evidence that had persuaded him of the link between cholera and dirty water was obviously not enough to convince other people. A visual aid was needed to coerce others into accepting his argument. And this visual aid was so powerful that over one hundred years later it is the map that people remember and not the real chain of events.

Exploration and Communication: A Typology of Map Use

The different stories associated with Dr Snow's map clearly demonstrate how maps have multiple uses. In order to formalize these uses, DiBiase (1990) conceptualized map use as a continuum from maps that are used to explore geographic information to maps that are used to present or communicate geographic information. Maps along this continuum fall into a typology of four main uses: (1) exploration (2) confirmation; (3) synthesis; and (4) presentation. Naturally, these four categories do not have well-defined boundaries along the continuum and it can be argued that any particular map can fall into more than one category. Maps that are used to explore geographic information are used in a research capacity. They help investigators to search for properties in the data such as geographic patterns and relationships that may not be obvious or intuitive. They represent an inductive approach to knowledge discovery and are important tools in the formation of geographic theories and the generation of hypotheses. Dr Snow's map in the later re-telling of the story falls into this category of map use. Maps associated with presenting geographic information are used to communicate facts to a general audience. This may be to illustrate a point, to present ideas or to demonstrate relationships. Dr Snow's actual use of the cholera map falls into this category since it was used to aid his arguments to the parish committee.

An important distinction between these different map uses is whether they are used in a public or private domain. Generally, maps used in an exploratory capacity or used to confirm and synthesize ideas tend to only be seen in the private domain of the researcher. They are not intended for

Rapid development
of comp. tech .

publication and are normally not seen by a wide audience. In contrast, the maps seen by the public are those used in a presentation capacity since these are the ones that are published. Therefore, there are many 'hidden' processes of map use that are rarely seen in the public domain but which are highly critical. In some cases the published map only represents the last of four stages of map use. It is known that Dr Snow drafted and re-drafted his map several times but only one appeared in the report to the parish committee. This distinction between the public and private uses of maps – what is originally mapped and what the public eventually sees – is an issue that will be returned to later in the chapter.

Maps and cartography have changed a great deal since Dr Snow first published his map in 1854. These changes have been especially fast during the past 30 years, being associated with the rapid development of computer technology, the increased availability of digital spatial data and a growing need to understand an ever more complex world. Computers have qualitatively changed what people can do with maps. Unlike the cholera map, maps are now very rarely drawn by hand – anyone with access to a computer, mapping software and spatial data can now create a map digitally and with relative ease. More importantly, computerized or computational mapping allows the user a high degree of interactivity with the map. As a result, MacEachren (1994a) has adapted DiBiase's conceptual model of map use by incorporating the interactive and dynamic elements afforded by computer technology. This model of map use is known as [CARTOGRAPHY][3] and a graphical representation is given in Figure 11.2.

The cube contains three dimensions with the axes of each dimension relating to a particular aspect of map use. One of the dimensions (Data) corresponds to DiBiase's continuum of map use ranging from maps used to explore and reveal unknown facts in geographic data to maps used to present known facts. The second dimension (Map User) refers to whether the map is used in a public or private domain. The third dimension (Interactivity) refers to the degree of interaction in the mapping environment from the high interactivity of a computer environment to the low interactivity of a paper map. The space inside the cube summarizes map use along these three dimensions and makes the distinction between two qualitatively different approaches to map use. In one of the approaches, cartographic communication, maps are used to communicate known facts in a non-interactive environment to a general (public) audience. In the other approach, cartographic visualization, mapping is a private activity in which unknown geographic facts are revealed to the researcher in a

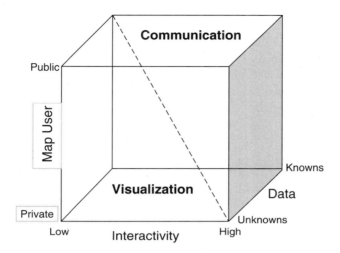

Figure 11.2   [CARTOGRAPHY]³ – a graphical representation of how maps are used.

highly interactive environment. Both of these approaches to map use are equally applicable to human, physical and applied geography, with the different parts of the discipline often sharing ideas, methods and techniques. Hence in the past it has not been unusual for human geographers to borrow mapping techniques from physical geographers when mapping social science data and vice versa. Indeed, the recent development of cartographic visualization has seen both human and physical geographers (and computer scientists in some cases) working together to create new mapping and visualization methods. Some of these new methods will be discussed later in the chapter. Cartographic visualization and cartographic communication have evolved out of different concerns for mapping and therefore have different agendas. These different agendas have been the focus of a recent critical re-appraisal of cartography, one that has stressed the importance of understanding the social relations in maps and map making.

Cartographic communication: presenting geography

All maps that have been published have been done so to communicate geographic information of one type or another to a general audience. Maps are different from other types of media representing the world by the fact that they are crammed full of readable information.

However, it is only since the second half of the twentieth century that issues concerned with map design and how people use and interpret maps have become important. Prior to then, cartography and map making were less rigorous and less attention was paid to the importance of clarity and the user's expertise and familiarity with interpreting maps. Arthur Robinson, author of one of the standard textbooks in cartography, helped initiate this concern by introducing a scientific approach to cartography, in which maps are models for communicating information. The approach was scientific in the sense that map design was to be based upon psychological and cognitive experiments of how different map users interpreted and extracted information from maps. If the aim of a map was to communicate information, then it was important that it did so in a clear and unambiguous way. The traditional cartographic concern for map aesthetics was replaced by an emphasis on a series of scientifically informed rules and procedures that standardized map design.

The goal of cartographic communication is to produce a single, best map that presents information clearly based upon cognitive and psychological understandings of map use. The key words in producing this best map are clarity, accuracy and certainty and these pervade all the stages of the map design process. The first stage is to identify the purpose of the map together with the intended audience. It is important to be clear about what you are going to say and to whom you are going to say it. The second stage is to obtain the appropriate spatial data and address issues such as planimetric position, projection and scale. In the third stage these data are simplified by identifying the spatial dimensions of the features being mapped and classified according to the scale of the data. Map design tends to simplify geographic features into three basic spatial objects: points, lines and polygons (areas), and data into four scales: nominal, ordinal, interval and ratio. These simplified features are then mapped in stage four using standardized graphics in a process called symbolization.

Symbolization is where clarity issues become paramount and has been the focus of a great deal of cartographic research. Although maps contain a lot of different types of graphics, these can all be classified into eight basic visual variables: size, colour value, texture, colour hue, orientation, shape and the two dimensions of the plane of a piece of paper (Bertin, 1983: 42). Table 11.1, adapted from MacEachren (1994b), shows how these eight visual variables relate to the spatial dimension and data scale of the particular feature to be mapped. Since visual variables vary in their ability to display different types of information on a map, psychological and cognitive experiments have been undertaken in order to identify

Table 11.1 The relationships between visual variables and the characteristics of the features to be mapped.

	Nominal	Ordinal	Interval/Ratio	Point	Line	Polygon
Location	G	G	G	G	G	G
Size	P	G	G	G	G	M
Colour Value	P	G	M	G	G	G
Colour Hue	G	M	M	G	G	G
Texture	G	M	M	M	P	G
Orientation	G	M	M	G	P	G
Shape	G	P	P	G	M	G

G = Good; M = Marginally effective; P = Poor
Source: Adapted from MacEachren (1994b), Fig. 2.28.

which ones are best in which circumstances. Bertin's framework has since been adapted and expanded to include new visual variables such as pattern, clarity (MacEachren, 1995) and projection (Dorling, 1994). These allow a greater degree of detail to be added to a map. Once the data have been symbolized, other graphical elements, such as a legend, are added so that the map communicates the information clearly and with as little ambiguity as possible. In the final stage of the map design process, the map is assessed to determine whether users would find it useful and informative. When the map is finished it should appear visually balanced with no large empty spaces and the minimum of clutter (Tufte, 1983).

The communication model of cartography therefore stresses the technical aspects of map making. Other aspects, such as the social and the cultural, are of little importance or have been removed altogether.

Cartographic visualization: exploring geography

In contrast to the communication model of cartography, the visualization model of cartography is relatively new and still evolving. Currently there are very few rules, procedures and consensus governing the process of cartographic visualization. Instead the emphasis is upon the user's own personal preferences, ideas and agendas with the aim of discovering something new (and hopefully interesting) about the world. The purpose of cartographic visualization is to facilitate data exploration, allowing the data to be investigated for unknown relationships, to reveal patterns, to flag unusual events and outliers and to generally support inductive reasoning and hypothesis generation. Cartographic visualization is seen by many geographers as the only means by which increasingly large and complex digital spatial datasets can be analysed effectively.

The key to cartographic visualization is the high degree of interaction and dynamism afforded by computer technology. Cartographic visualizations allow panning, zooming, rotation, dynamic re-expression, dynamic comparisons and brushing as part of their functionality (Dykes, 1997). Panning, zooming and rotation allow the user to navigate around the map, change the orientation of the map in three dimensions and increase or decrease the scale at which the map is viewed. Dynamic re-expression allows the map to be updated automatically when a change has been made to the dataset. Dynamic comparisons allow the map to be linked to different views of the data, such as a table, a graph or another map. Choosing a point in one view will highlight the same point in the different views. Brushing allows users to select areas by dragging the mouse across the map. These functions are useful in the exploratory analysis of spatial data, particularly when not much is known about the nature of the data. The Cartographic Data Visualizer (cdv), shown in Figure 11.3, is an example of recent software that allows exploratory spatial data analysis using an interactive map as the platform (Dykes, 1998).

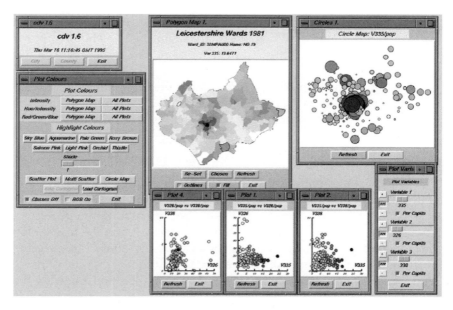

Figure 11.3   A view of the Cartographic Data Visualizer (cdv).

Cartographic visualization has also benefited from new dynamic visual variables complementing the existing set of visual variables used in traditional cartographic design. These new dynamic visual variables include animation, multi-media and virtual reality. Animation allows movement on the map, which can be useful when exploring changes through time and across space. For instance, it can be used when investigating flow data such as migration patterns or the movement of water through river channels. Animation can also depict the growth and change of city structures or vegetation cover in upland areas. Multimedia are the use of more than one medium such as photographic images, video footage, text-based data and even sound to represent and convey information (Cartwright, 1999). This qualitative information can provide context and meaning to a traditional cartographic representation. It allows the map user to see, hear and perhaps experience what a place is like rather than relying upon traditional abstract and (typically) statistical representations.

Virtual reality is an exciting prospect, although its impact on cartographic visualization is still unclear. An example of its use in geography and cartography has been the creation of Virtual Worlds (Fisher and Unwin, 2002). Virtual Worlds is a cheap and simple version of virtual reality that has been used to visualize landscapes within multi-user environments and usually on a PC. It does not involve the creation of a three-dimensional model of reality within which a viewer is immersed, but instead uses linked images to produce a 'through the window' navigable scene. The use of perspectives and user navigation allows an adequate impression of the virtual environment to be maintained. In geography Virtual Worlds are best known within the context of Virtual Field Courses that are used in teaching and learning contexts (Dykes et al., 1999). Virtual Worlds have also been used in the visualization of the built and natural environments in which users can fly through actual or planned three-dimensional landscapes. This is becoming an important feature in urban planning and resource management, allowing the user to explore the outcome of different scenarios upon existing landscapes.

The growth of the Internet has also had major impacts upon cartographic visualization, fostering the development of web-cartography (Kraak and Brown, 2001). The Internet's interactivity and flexibility have enabled mapping on demand (Cartwright, 1997) and there are a number of websites that allow people to log on, design and download their own maps. The Internet's highly graphical nature, its ability to support multimedia, animation and virtual reality also means that it is an ideal medium for producing cartographic visualizations.

Web-cartography is seen as a way of democratizing map making with visualization providing a common language enabling the collaboration of different groups of people in interactive, learning multi-user environments (MacEachren and Kraak, 1997).

Communication versus Visualization: Maps, Power and Knowledge

The recent move towards a more complex visualization in cartography has coincided with a growing critical awareness in geography of maps and mapping. The cultural and postmodern turns in geography have drawn attention to the power relations inherent in map making and in the communication model of cartography. The rationale behind cartographic communication is to take maps apart to see when they work and when they don't work, in order to produce a set of rules for map production. By following these rules, the map produced is the best or optimal map that represents the real world clearly and unambiguously. However, by taking the process of map making apart – to try and understand maps and how they represent the world – it soon became apparent that 'the scientific and objective character of maps is simply an illusion' (Edney, 1993: 177). It was the cartographer Brian Harley who was the first person to really draw attention to the concept that maps are socially constructed texts and therefore can be interpreted in multiple ways. There is now a growing school of thought that cartography is actually about social control, with maps being constructed to serve the designs of their creators rather than to inform the general public (Wood, 1992; Pickles, 2004). In this view, cartographic design is not purely a technical process of translating reality on to paper as is often thought. Rather, it is about governments and other powerful organizations that control map production choosing what information is collected and mapped. The concerns central to cartographic communication – accuracy, clarity and certainty – are seen as a smoke screen for the actual purpose and origins of most maps; for showing certain things but not including others. Since there are an infinite number of maps that can be drawn of any place, the role of cartographic communication is to privilege certain forms of maps (and hence the geographical knowledge they represent) because they are more scientific (i.e. more accurate). Common reasons for why some maps deliberately exclude certain features usually cite issues of national security, such as the removal of secret military installations on maps during the Cold War. However, other less acknowledged and more subtle examples of cartographic censorship exist, such as the exclusion of the poor and other disadvantaged groups from maps (Dorling and Fairbairn, 1997).

The concept that maps are social products as well as technical products challenges the concept of authority in mapping. In the conventional cartographic communication model, a map is 'better' and therefore more authoritative the more accurately it resembles the world in miniature. And since in the cartographic communication model there can only be one 'best' or optimal map, this 'best' map represses other competing world-views (Crampton, 2001). Hence critics have argued that a map does not derive its authority from its accuracy, but rather from the authority of the person who draws it (Wood, 1993). There are clear power relations in map production connecting the patrons of the map, the makers of the map and the users of the map. The confusion between the benevolence and self-interest of those who fund and undertake the production of maps is not a new one. It has long been recognized that political maps, or maps drawn in times of war, contain elements of propaganda (Monmonier, 1996). What is new, however, is the increasing acceptance that the criticisms made of propaganda maps can be applied to *all* maps and not just those that are overtly political/territorial (Pickles, 2004).

Interestingly, the new emphasis upon cartographic visualization, with its concern with the exploration and construction of geographical knowledge rather than its communication, could challenge these power relations. With exploration favoured over presentation, maps become transient rather than near permanent, constantly changing with a push of a button. Since multiple presentations of data mean multiple maps are produced, there is no such thing as the 'best' map; rather, different maps showing different things in different contexts. Cartographic visualization blurs the distinction between map maker and map user – the map maker is the map user and vice versa – with the development of web-cartography bringing cartographic visualizations to a wide audience. Maps can now be drawn outside traditional organizations, such as universities, governments and large companies, which look 'technically correct' (i.e. the follow the 'rules' of cartographic communication), even if, in a traditional sense, they are not (e.g. they represent disadvantaged groups).

The significance of cartographic visualization and web-cartography in challenging conventional claims to geographical knowledge and authority in map making should not be overstated, however. Web-cartography relies on access to the Internet and this remains highly unequal between different groups of people and between different countries of the world.

Just as traditional cartography can be viewed as Eurocentric and having a Western bias, so currently is the majority of web-cartography. And since cartographic visualizations constructed on the Internet are constrained by the software and data hosted on particular websites, power relations are still an important consideration, particularly when a government or other major organization hosts the website. It is important to appreciate that new technology does not necessarily alter the underlying social and political structures affecting cartography.

Future of Cartography: Back to Basics?

Maps have been used for communicating geographical information for thousands of years and it is not difficult to understand why. It is the most efficient method we have of representing the world around us in detail on a single sheet of paper or computer screen. New advances in computer technology have had a huge impact upon cartography. Not only has it changed what can be done with maps but importantly it has also changed who can map. Cartographic visualization has opened up the door to exploration and discovery on a qualitatively different scale than previously possible. Given the increasingly large digital spatial datasets of the world that are now available, cartographic visualization maybe the only way we have of analysing them. The Internet can allow cartography to be accessible to a wider range of people, who can create their own maps and thus be less reliant upon maps produced by governments and other powerful organizations. This, and the changing emphasis on what it is important to map, mean that there could be a real democratization in map making although there are still problems with the web-cartography model.

Even so, it is important not to throw the baby out with the bathwater. Democratizing map making and putting a greater emphasis upon exploration and knowledge discovery are important, but then so is a well-designed map. The emphasis of cartographic communication upon clarity and accuracy remains essential if a map is to communicate geographic information, and a person's ideas, effectively. Remember that in many cases the hypothesis or decisions which the individual or group of people are investigating needs to be confirmed or displayed to a wider audience to be accepted. The development of computerized and web-cartography may have enabled a partial democratization of map making but it unfortunately has also resulted in a proliferation of rather inadequate maps (Kraak and Brown, 2001). As Dr John Snow must have appreciated, maps and other graphical devices are a powerful means of legitimating knowledge claims and coercing others into accepting your arguments. It would now seem that the Broad Street map has, over time, transcended the text that it was drawn to illustrate and has become somewhat iconic: an exemplar of the perfect map (Tufte, 1997). This reveals something interesting and important about the power and status of maps in communicating information. A well-designed map that supports queries and communicates facts effectively to different users is still as important today as it has always been, as different people and organizations demand speedier access to geographical knowledge and information.

ESSAY QUESTIONS AND FURTHER READING

1   In what ways do the stories of Dr John Snow and the Broad Street pump help us understand the nature and power of maps and map use? Brody et al. (2000) critically re-evaluate the context of the Soho cholera epidemic and show that the oft-cited version of how Dr John Snow first drew his famous map, and how he used it, is historically incorrect. Tufte (1997) provides a good example of this historical oversight when discussing best practice in map making. Monmonier (1996) provides a broader view of how maps have been used to 'lie' throughout history and Wood (1992) and Dorling and Fairbairn (1997) provide a critical introduction to the concepts of maps and map use, showing how maps are not just technical devices but are also social products that can be used to legitimate different world-views.

2   To what extent does cartographic visualization challenge the power relations associated with the traditional communication model of cartography? MacEarchren and Kraak (1997) and Cartwright (1997; 1999) provide an overview of the new developments in cartographic visualization. Crampton (2001) and Crampton and Monmonier (2002) examine the power relations behind map making and map use in relation to cartographic visualization technologies.

REFERENCES

Bertin, J. (1983) *The Semiology of Graphics.* University of Wisconsin Press, Madison.

Brody, H., Rip, M.R., Vinten-Johansen, P., Paneth, N. and Rachman, S. (2000) Map-making and myth-making in Broad Street: the London cholera epidemic, 1854. *The Lancet* **356**, 64–68.

Cartwright, W. (1997) New media and their application to the production of map products. *Computer and GeoSciences* **23**, 447–456.

Cartwright, W. (1999) Extending the map metaphor using web delivered multimedia. *International Journal of Geographic Information Systems* **13**, 335–353.

Crampton, J.W. (2001) Maps as social constructions: power, communication and visualization. *Progress in Human Geography* **25**, 235–252.

Crampton, J.W and Monmonier, M. (2002) Maps, politics and history. *Environment and Planning D: Society and Space* **20**, 637–646.

DiBiase, D. (1990) Visualization in the earth sciences. *Earth and Mineral Sciences, Bulletin of the College of Earth and Mineral Sciences, PSU* **59**, 13–18.

Dorling, D. (1992) Visualizing people in space and time. *Environment and Planning B* **19**, 613–637.

Dorling, D. (1994) Cartograms for visualizing human geography. In Unwin, D. and Hearnshaw, H. (eds) *Visualization and GIS*. Belhaven, London, pp. 85–102.

Dorling, D. and Fairbairn, D. (1997) *Mapping: Ways of Representing the World*. Longman, London.

Dykes, J. (1997) Exploring spatial data representation with dynamic graphics. *Computers and GeoScience* **23**, 345–370.

Dykes, J. (1998) Cartographic visualization: exploratory spatial data analysis with local indicators of spatial association using Tcl/Tk and cdv. *Journal of the Royal Statistical Society Series D: The Statistician* **47**, 485–497.

Dykes, J., Moore, K., and Wood, J. (1999) Virtual environments for student fieldwork using networked components. *International Journal of Geographic Information Science* **13**, 397–416.

Edney, M. (1993) J.B. Harley (1932–1991): questioning maps, questioning cartography, questioning cartographers. *Cartography and Geographic Information Systems* **19**, 175–178.

Fisher, P. and Unwin, D. (2002) *Virtual Reality in Geography*. Taylor and Francis, London.

International Cartographic Association (1995) *Achievements of the ICA, 1991–95*. Institut Géographique National, Paris.

Kraak, M.J. and Brown, A. (eds) (2001) *Web Cartography*. Taylor and Francis, London.

MacEachren, A.M. (1994a) Visualization in modern cartography: setting the agenda. In MacEachren, A.M. and Taylor, D.R.F. (eds) *Visualization in Modern Cartography*. Pergamon, Oxford, pp. 1–12.

MacEachren, A.M. (1994b) *Some Truth with Maps: A Primer on Symbolization and Design*. Association of American Geographers, Washington, DC.

MacEachren, A.M. (1995) *How Maps Work: Representation and Visualisation*. Guildford, New York.

MacEachren, A.M. and Kraak, M.J. (1997) Exploratory cartographic visualization: advancing the agenda. *Computers and GeoSciences* **23**, 64–81.

McCormick, B.H., DeFanti, T.A. and Brown, M.D. (eds) (1987) Visualization in scientific computing: a synopsis. *IEEE Computer Graphics and Applications* **7**, 61–70.

Monmonier, M. (1996) *How to Lie with Maps*, 2nd edn. University of Chicago Press, Chicago.

Pickles, J. (2004) *A History of Spaces: Cartographic Reason, Mapping and the Geo-coded World*. Routledge, London.

Shapter, T. (1849) *The History of Cholera in Exeter in 1832*. J. Churchill, London.

Tufte, E.R. (1983) *The Visual Display of Quantitative Information*. Graphics Press, Cheshire, CT.

Tufte, E.R. (1997) *Visual Explanations: Images and Quantities, Evidence and Narrative*. Graphics Press, Cheshire, CT.

Wood, D. (1992) *The Power of Maps*. Guildford Press, New York.

Wood, D. (1993) What makes a map a map? *Cartographica* **30**, 81–86.

Models, Modelling, and Geography

David Demeritt and John Wainwright

From forecasting the weather to the economy, models have become ubiquitous, if little-noticed, features of modern life. Models of various sorts are used to predict and thereby manage everything from whether it's likely to rain on your picnic to the responses of consumers to changes in interest rates. In turn, those practical applications depend upon and help to inform the development and use of models in the context of pure research. Modelling has arguably become the most widespread and influential research practice in the discipline of geography, as indeed within the sciences more generally.

Models have assumed such prominence because they provide a method for understanding and predicting the operation of systems that either for practical and political reasons or because of their complexity, spatio-temporal scale, or both do not lend themselves to experimental methods of parameter or control group manipulation. Consider the case of global climate change. Although anthropogenic increases in the concentration of greenhouse gases in the atmosphere can be likened to an 'experiment' on the planet, we don't have a second untreated 'control group' planet to compare the results of our 'experiment' against. Even if we did, we will not be able to observe the full results of our experiment for another 50 years or more. By then it will be impossible to re-do the 'experiment' if we discover that our planet is no longer inhabitable. Thus other methods are required if we wish to understand the dynamics of the climate system and predict its response to emissions of greenhouse gases from fossil fuels in time to do anything about them (USGCRP, 2000).

In this chapter we want to provide a brief overview of the variety of models and modelling practices commonly used by geographers. Though now largely synonymous with computer-based techniques of numerical computation, models and modelling encompass a much wider variety of forms and practices as we demonstrate in the first part of this chapter. Nevertheless many of the early programmatic statements of the so-called quantitative revolution in geography claimed that the techniques of mathematical modelling would provide the method to unite the discipline and ensure its scientific status (e.g. Chorley and Haggett, 1967). Those early claims both about the methodological unity of geography and about the potential for models to produce valid, explanatory laws of causation and prediction have sparked considerable debate (Macmillan, 1989), which we consider in the second part of this chapter. Proper understanding of these somewhat abstract, philosophical debates about the possibility of prediction and model validation has taken on added importance now that complicated computer models are increasingly used to inform contentious public policy decisions about climate change, economic policy, and other matters.

Typology of Models

What is a model? A model might be defined as a simplified representation or 'abstraction of reality'. By this broadest of definitions, models would encompass everything from physical analogues and scale models to conceptual, box-and-arrow schematic diagrams and various forms of (typically computer-based) mathematical modelling. Insofar as a model is a *model* of something else rather than the thing itself, modelling demands that geographers make analytical choices about what to concentrate on modelling and what can be simplified or even ignored altogether. Furthermore, insofar as the practice of modelling typically involves the use of highly formalized and widely understood procedures of abstraction, such as formal logic and mathematics, it can also help facilitate the integration of multi-disciplinary research, such as on global climate change (USGCRP, 2000).

Working with different kinds of models involves different craft skills and traditions of practice. In turn, those modelling practices depend on a variety of philosophical understandings of science and of the relationships between theory, models, and the systems they purport to represent. However, we would suggest that part of the confusion in the use of models within geography stems from a failure to distinguish clearly enough between types of models and the philosophical stances their uses imply. To address this concern, we provide a brief typology of models and modelling practices, before turning in the second part of the chapter to debates about their philosophical underpinnings and practical applications.

Physical analogues and scale models

These models are physical systems whose form or observable behaviour or both are in some way analogous to those of the actual system of interest. For instance, one way to explore the movement of sediment in a river channel is to build a reduced scale model of it in a laboratory using a sediment-filled flume. By manipulating the size and slope of the sediment or the volume and velocity of water in the laboratory flume, it is possible to predict how sediment would be transported in the actual river, whose conditions are less convenient (or not even possible) to control experimentally. Another kind of physical model is the natural analogue model described by Chorley (1964). Analogue models are real objects or events that are somehow analogous to some other process or object of scientific interest. Thus, one way to predict the possible responses to future increased greenhouse gas concentrations would be to use the natural analogue provided by past periods of earth history when greenhouse-gas concentrations were higher than they are now.

Scale, both spatial and temporal, is an important issue in building such physical models, as indeed, in any kind of model. Some watershed processes, like the action of water on sediment particles, are easier to scale down (both in terms of their physical size and the resulting kinematic forces) to the laboratory scale than others, such as the effects of tree roots in holding on to that sediment. Having made allowances for these distortions between the spatial scale of the watershed and that of the physical model, the investigator is still faced with the question of temporal scale and how to extrapolate the short-term sediment-transport processes measured in the lab over the long temporal scales involved in the evolution of actual landforms.

While scaling models most clearly involves the construction of physical analogues, some philosophers have argued that in fact *all* forms of modelling are based on building of analogues of one sort or another. The philosopher of science Mary Hesse (1966) insists that all models work by analogy: they bring theory to bear on the world by seeing one domain in terms of another. For example, some of the earliest economic models were based on the analogy of monetary circulation to the flow of water. From Hesse's perspective, the relationship between the model and the system to which it is being compared is suggestive and metaphorical rather than mimetic. That is to say, the model is not intended to mirror what it models in any kind of one-to-one or photographic sense and should not be evaluated in terms of how exactly it corresponds to the system it is modelling. Rather, from Hesse's perspective, the truth value of the model, like that of a metaphor, is more subjective and lies in the quality of insight it provides, in the way the comparison of model to modelled renders aspects of the previously strange and unfamiliar familiar and understandable.

Conceptual models

A conceptual model is an abstract representation designed to articulate the processes operating in a system of interest. A conceptual model may take narrative form and use words to describe the system at hand, but with their long spatial science tradition, geographers have frequently drawn on geometry and graphical forms of visual representation to render their conceptual models. For instance, Figure 12.1 provides a schematic diagram of the physical processes involved in maintaining the earth's radiation balance, popularly known as 'the greenhouse effect'. While the phrase 'greenhouse effect' relies on the physical analogy between the earth's atmosphere and a glass greenhouse, this schematic diagram doesn't work by positing an analogy to something else, as Hesse's definition of modelling as analogy building suggests. Rather, it

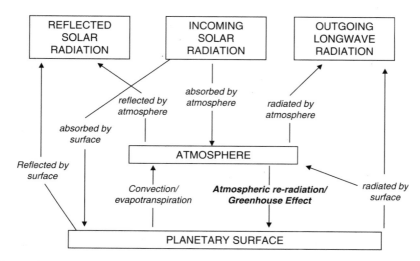

Figure 12.1   A conceptual model of the processes involved in the greenhouse effect.

seeks to conceptualize how the fundamental laws of physics apply in the particular case of the earth's atmosphere. From this perspective, the work of modelling is at once theoretical, helping to flesh out theory and make it more explicit and applicable, and experimental: manipulating model phenomena so as to test their correspondence to theory and to independent observations of the phenomena they are models *of*.

Despite the important role of conceptual modelling in linking theory to data, conceptual models can be difficult to apply empirically because they do not specify parameter values and boundary conditions. It is only by specifying the magnitude of the flows depicted in Figure 12.1 that our model of the greenhouse effect can be applied specifically to planet Earth rather than to Venus, for example. Without such empirical specification, this conceptual model can neither be tested against independent observations nor used in an applied context to generate precise predictions that might inform subsequent policy decisions. To those two ends, many geographers seek to convert their conceptual models into mathematical ones. But that move is by no means universal. As we discuss in the second part of this chapter, fierce debates about the philosophy of theory testing and the politics of applied science have led other geographers to resist mathematical modelling.

Mathematical models

Mathematical models use formal equations to represent the relationships among system components, their various state conditions, and rates of change to them. Such models can range from simple equations to complex software codes applying many interlinked equations to calculate spatially explicit results dynamically over discrete time steps. It is possible to distinguish two broad approaches to mathematical modelling – empirical-statistical and deductive-deterministic – but in practice most large models, at least in physical geography, combine both approaches.

Empirical-statistical models   Empirical-statistical modelling uses statistical techniques to derive mathematical equations representing the operation of a system based on past observations. Such 'fit-to-data' models are often used in applied contexts, such as flood control engineering, to generate quantitative predictions about the future behaviour of the system. But empirical-statistical modelling is also important in pure research. As a stage of exploratory data analysis, the construction of formal, empirical statistical models provides one way to search for patterns in large data sets and generate hypotheses for explaining their origin and implications.

Advocates of geocomputation believe that computer automation will make this kind of inductive approach to data-mining and hypothesis generation increasingly important in geographical research (Openshaw, 1998).

Typically, the formal equations in an empirical statistical model are derived from existing data sets using statistical measures of association, such as regression analysis. Regression is a parametric statistical technique that takes previously observed statistical associations among variables and fits an equation to them that allows you to predict the value of any variables you deem to be 'dependent', such as, for example, streamflow Q [m^{3}s^{-1}], for any given value of those variables you deem 'independent', such as rainfall R [mm day^{-1}], as in equation 1:

$$Q = a + b\ R^c + \varepsilon \tag{12.1}$$

In this equation, Q and R are called variables because their values change dynamically from one application or time-step iteration of the model to the next. By contrast, the other terms in this equation are called parameters because their values, once assigned through a process called parameterization (see below), remain constant and set the boundary conditions for any run of the model. The parameter ε is an error term that expresses uncertainty in the relationship between Q and R, due either to measurement error or perhaps also because Q may, in addition to R, also be influenced by other variables not accounted for directly in our model.

The process of assigning values to parameters is called parameterization. The work of generating and improving parameterizations often makes up the largest part of constructing a mathematical model. While parameter values may be initially set based on empirical estimates, it is also common, in the process of model construction, to use mathematical optimization techniques to tailor values so as to increase the goodness of fit (a statistical measure of correspondence) between model predictions and observed data. As a result of having had their precise parameter values 'tuned' in this way, empirical-statistical models often provide very accurate predictions about the association among variables in the particular place and period of time for which their performance has been optimized. For example, the Universal Soil Loss Equation (USLE), an empirical-statistical model based on tens of thousands of data points, can still produce estimates of soil-erosion rates that are at least as good as much more sophisticated process-based models (Tiwari et al., 2000). Where there are good theoretical reasons to support such empirical-statistical approximation, physical geographers sometimes refer to the resulting model or parameterization as 'physically based', although 'process based' is probably a better term in this case because it is not based on the physics of the system but instead on a simplification to the assumed process at work.

Two implications follow from the practice of model parameterization and optimization. First, the calibration of parameter values creates logical problems of circularity in model validation and may result in the model getting the 'right' answer (in the sense of matching observations) but for the wrong reason (i.e. physically unrealistic parameter values). Second, precisely because they have been tuned to one particular time and place, empirical-statistical models often perform very poorly if generalized and used to make predictions about *other* places or times in which the associations among variables and parameters may be very different.

Empirical-statistical models sometimes include variables and parameters whose values are calculated stochastically. Stochastic values are ones that are calculated randomly within an ascribed probability distribution range. For example, Markov Chain models calculate the value of a variable at time interval t as a probabilistic function of its value at the previous time interval t-1. We might use this technique to derive stochastic values for rainfall (R) in equation (12.1) above and thereby generate a probability distribution of high and low flows over a given time period (i.e. the 100-year flood or drought), such as might be useful for flood-defence planning. If we make the simplifying assumption that a day is either completely wet or dry, the following matrix would define the complete set of possible sequences of wet and dry days:

Day 1

	Dry	Wet
Dry	p_{dd}	p_{wd}
Wet	p_{dw}	p_{ww}

Day 2

(12.2)

where: p_{dd} represents the probability of a dry day being followed by a second dry day, p_{dw} the probability of a dry day being followed by a wet day, p_{ww} the probability of a wet day being followed by a wet day and p_{wd} the probability of a wet day being followed by a dry day.

Since $p_{dw} = 1 - p_{dd}$ and $p_{wd} = 1 - p_{ww}$ by definition, this Markov model is defined by only two parameters, which can be estimated empirically by looking at relative frequencies of actual dry and wet days in a climate record. Such stochastic techniques provide a way to take account of the fact that some model parameters or variables may either be determined by chance or known so imprecisely that their values are better treated as if they were random.

Exponential growth in the computational power of modern computers has enabled geographers to build progressively more complex and computationally demanding mathematical models that link together and solve many equations simultaneously. In particular, geographers have pioneered the development of spatially explicit mathematical models. Whereas the model in equation (12.1) describes streamflow over time for an undifferentiated area, we might produce a spatially distributed model that would calculate values for streamflow Q in each sub-unit of space by linking together and simultaneously solving equations describing processes operating within each spatial unit with other equations describing how flows operate between the spatial units (often cells or pixels, for example, in a GIS image). In the simplest case, we could employ equation (12.1) for each spatial unit individually, and then, using topographic information to determine which units are interlinked, calculate the total streamflow in that unit as the sum of the streamflows in the upstream contributing area. This approach would give a spatially explicit but temporally simplified approximation. To incorporate temporal variability, we can use a form of the continuity or mass balance equation:

$$Q_{x,t} = Q_{in} - Q_{out} \qquad (12.3)$$

This states that the flow Q in the current spatial unit x at time t is equal to the inflow from upslope (Q_{in}) less the outflow from the current location (Q_{out}). This equation would be employed iteratively, so that the value of Q_{out} would be the previous value of flow in the spatial unit (i.e. $Q_{x,\,t-1}$) and Q_{in} the previous value of flow in the upslope unit (i.e. $Q_{x-1,\,t-1}$).

Empirical-statistical models are sometimes called input–output models because they assume that the value of the dependent variable output by the model – in equation (12.1) streamflow Q – is determined solely by those of the independent variables input into the model (e.g. rainfall R in equation (12.1) above). Not that economic geographers and regional scientists reserve the term 'input–output model' for an application of empirical-statistical techniques to economic modelling of inter-industry linkages of inputs and outputs (of labour, capital, etc.) within an economy. Insofar as empirical-statistical models calculate dependent variable values as a mathematical function of independent variable values, they are sometimes called black box models because they do not specify anything about how or why inputs are transformed into outputs.

Thus empirical-statistical models run the risk of making spurious associations between variables whose statistical correlation may either be purely coincidental or contingent upon some intervening process ignored by the model.

For this reason, critical realists reject empirical-statistical modelling. They claim that it commits the inductivist fallacy of affirming the consequent and failing to explain why the value of a dependent variable necessarily depends on that of an independent variable (Sayer, 1992). As we discuss in more detail below, the objective in many applied contexts is simply to forecast some output. So long as that result can be accurately predicted, a simple black box model may be more appropriate than a more complicated one that specifies so many processes in such great detail that it becomes difficult to test and interpret or requires a super-computer to run. For the purposes of pure research, by contrast, understanding the relationships among variables is the objective in building the model. But practical considerations often induce modellers to set some parameter or variable values based on past empirical observations rather than using deductive-deterministic methods to model the process dynamically based on first order physics.

Deductive-deterministic approaches Deductive-deterministic approaches to modelling start from first order theoretical principles and specify mathematical equations from which to deduce the interactions within a system and thereby explain and predict the dynamic behaviour of the system as a whole. This approach to modelling raises a number of important philosophical questions. Are processes at higher scales entirely reducible to those operating at lower ones (and thus could a grand unifying theory explain everything from the sub-atomic to the inter-planetary)? To what extent are human geographies of behaviour and meaning determined by universal (and thus predictable) laws of social physics in the same way as physical geographies of soil particle motion are deducible from first-order physical principles?

Although physical geographers have not ignored these philosophical questions (e.g. Richards, 1990), they have tended to be more concerned with the practical and computational difficulties of a strictly deductive-deterministic approach to process modelling. Two technical problems, in particular, have dogged efforts to apply deductive-deterministic approaches.

First, as we have already seen, the laws of physics are often so abstract that we have to specify certain boundary and initial conditions in order to provide a bridge between our theory and the particular context at hand.

In many cases these values are incompletely known. The process of parameterization links model to field and other data, but can be time-consuming and expensive. As it is generally not possible to measure all such parameters directly, it is usually necessary to combine empirical-statistical and deductive-deterministic approaches. An important implication is that many models – especially the widely used ones such as USLE or WEPP for erosion estimates – contain *implicit parameterizations* that are only applicable to the original domain of application. It is thus important to ensure that a model test in a new domain accounts for this issue. It may be the implicit parameters that are at fault rather than the model itself.

Second, even when the processes at hand are well enough understood to represent them dynamically based on the first-order laws of physics, it is often very difficult to identify equations that are both appropriate and analytically tractable. Returning to the example of streamflow modelling, we can describe the rate of change to the flows between cells in equation (12.3) above, with the following equation:

$$\frac{\partial A}{\partial t} + \frac{\partial Q}{\partial x} = e_x \tag{12.4}$$

This is called the kinematic wave equation, where A is the cross-sectional area of the flow (m^2), t is time (s), Q is the flow discharge ($m^3\ s^{-1}$), x is the distance (m) and e_x any unit lateral inflow into the system ($m^2\ s^{-1}$ – usually the difference between rainfall and infiltration rates). This kind of equation is derived from calculus, the branch of mathematics used to describe rates of change over time. Insofar as environmental modelling is concerned with rates of change in time and space, such equations figure centrally. Furthermore, most models consist of non-linear differential equations, which are unfortunately very difficult to solve. As a result, modellers have had to find various ways to approximate them using methods such as numerical iteration or finite difference calculation that provide analytically tractable solutions (for a basic introduction, see Mulligan and Wainwright, 2003).

The Contested Heritage: Models and Modelling in Geography

Modelling was widely celebrated during the heyday of the so-called quantitative revolution as providing a methodological foundation for the unity of geography as a discipline. Those claims were never uncontested, and many now, particularly in human geography, reject modelling. In order to appreciate both the promise and the problems of modelling, it is worth revisiting three long-running debates about the aims and methodology of science, the practice of model validation, and the political applications of modelling. These debates raise important questions about its place in the discipline as a whole and its potential role as a bridge between human and physical geographers.

Modelling = Systematic

Modelling and the methodology of geography as science

Modelling has figured centrally in long-standing methodological debates over the definition of geography, its status as science, and the relative merits of qualitative versus quantitative approaches to its practice. Especially among physical geographers mathematical modelling is sometimes opposed to field-based methods of empirical research. That opposition is a false one, insofar as modelling almost always depends on field and other data for both model construction and calibration as well as for subsequent model validation. The practices of mathematical modelling provide one of the most important means of integrating different kinds of data from the field and other methods, like remote sensing, with each other and with relevant theory.

Methodological discussion of the advantages of modelling relative to other research techniques often involves theoretical questions about the definition and philosophy of science. Consider, for example, the early debates about mathematical modelling among geomorphologists. Arthur Strahler (1952) extolled the importance of mathematical modelling to the discovery of fundamental laws. By contrast, S.W. Wooldridge (1958) rejected this 'narrowly physico-mathematical approach' to geomorphology as he called it, favouring the qualitative observation of landforms in the field (Thornes, 1978). He was defending an older, more idiographic conception of geomorphology as a branch of regional geography, concerned not with the nomothetic search for universally predictive laws of general physical process but with understanding the unique history of particular landforms and regions. Recent developments in physical geography have also begun to recognize that the nomothetic approach may be limited, as each location to be modelled has its own unique characteristics (e.g. Beven, 2000; Wainwright et al., 2000).

Among human geographers much of the debate about modelling has turned on this same issue about the goals of geography and its status as science. In the 1950s and 1960s, early proponents of the quantitative revolution attributed the lowly status of the discipline to its inductive tradition of regional studies and landscape description. They hoped that the application of quantitative methods and mathematical modelling would 'increase the scope and reliability of geographic knowledge' and reorient the discipline around the nomothetic 'search for and development of laws concerning spatial relations' (Golledge and Amedeo, 1968). Whereas Wooldridge had feared that mathematical modelling would splinter physical from human geography, many of its early proponents hoped that it would transform the discipline of geography into a unified 'science of locations, seeking to predict locations where before there was contentment simply with describing' (Bunge, 1966: xvi).

Humanistic geographers rejected this idea, complaining that the universalizing project of a predictive spatial science was dehumanizing, because its quantitative methods ignore questions of human value, emotion, and meaning (e.g. Ley and Samuels, 1978). Furthermore, insofar as they do, mathematical models tend to rely on simplistic and falsely universalizing conceptual models of the human subject, such as the rational economic actor (*Homo economicus*), and thus, critics charge (e.g. Barnes, 1996), are unlikely to meet spatial scientists' ambition of universal prediction. For example, empirical-statistical gravity models of migration are based on the analogy between the gravitational pull of planetary objects and of cities. Treating migrants as automata, this kind of social physics ignores human agency and the capacity of people to respond to their environments in creative, emotional, and unpredictable ways. Humanistic geographers also reject the underlying predictive ambition of modelling and with it the long-standing idea (common both to spatial science and to the old-style regional geography of Wooldridge that it succeeded) of human and physical geography as being united by a single scientific methodology. Instead, they insist that human geography should not model itself on the law-seeking experimental sciences but on the interpretative arts and humanities.

Validation, induction and emergence

A second bone of contention concerns the practice, indeed even the very possibility, of validating a model. Among modellers there is extensive technical discussion about how to test and evaluate a mathematical model. They distinguish two discrete testing practices. First, what is often called *verification* involves debugging computer code to remove typographical or programming errors that may have arisen during model construction as well as testing to ensure that the resulting mathematical model is producing analytically correct solutions to its equations.

Second, *validation* involves comparing model outputs against some independent measurements of those same variables so as to test the empirical adequacy of their simulation. This practice is far from straight-forward. First, there is a question of which variables to evaluate, since a complex model may simulate many different variables. For some pur-poses the ability to simulate just a few critical variables very accurately may be preferable to getting them all more or less right. Even with just one variable to validate, as in our simple runoff model in equation (12.1) above, we would still need to decide whether the best test of our model, for the particular purpose at hand, is our model's ability to reproduce the magnitude of maximum runoff, its timing, or perhaps its spatial pattern. Having decided on which empirical aspect of our model's performance we wish to evaluate, there are often problems about the availability of data at the appropriate spatial or temporal (or both) scale to compare against our model outputs. Then, there is a question of which evaluation methods to use in validation. In addition to 'eyeballing' scatterplots of model outputs against independent data, there are also a number of more formal statistical techniques for measuring model goodness-of-fit (e.g., coefficient of determination, r^2; root mean square error). Each of these measures is sensitive to a different aspect of model behaviour.

While these technical difficulties with model validation occupy much of the modelling literature, some more fundamental philosophical issues have caught the attention of modelling critics. Philosophers of science have long noted that the logical problem of induction makes it impossible to validate a model in the everyday sense of establishing the truth and accuracy of its hypotheses. Unlike the formal analytical language of equations, such as '$2 + 2 = 4$', whose truth is defined by a closed system of internal logic that can be tested through verification (in the sense of above), a model's empirical claims pertain to open systems, and so must face the logical problem of induction: just because every previous time you've seen someone with an umbrella it has been raining, does not give you a purely logical basis for making the inductive inference that if you see her again with an umbrella, it must therefore be raining. To do so is to commit the fallacy of affirming the consequent, because as Sayer (1984: 110) puts it, 'what causes an event has nothing to do with the number of times that it has been observed to occur'. It may well be that she is carrying an umbrella for other reasons, perhaps to shield herself from the sun. Likewise, just because the data available to test our model in equation (12.1) happen to match its predictions of the streamflow Q resulting from a given quantity of rainfall R, we have no logical basis for validating the model and assuming the model's empirical predictions will continue to hold in future. Natural systems are dynamic and open. Future conditions may well change in ways that our model has not accounted for. 'If a model fails to reproduce observed data, then...the model is faulty in some way, but the reverse is never the case' (Oreskes et al., 1994: 643).

Accordingly, some modellers have advocated the critical rationalist approach of seeking to falsify, rather than verify, their models (e.g. Haines-Young and Petch, 1986). In practice, however, this falsification principle turns out to be no less problematic. It is often difficult to decide whether an inconsistency between a model and some empirical test of it is due to a problem with the testing procedure (i.e. our auxiliary assumption that the test data are representative may be false) or the falsity of the model itself.

Critical realists offer a somewhat different response to these logical problems with induction and validation. They complain that the problem with mathematical models, especially empirical-statistical models, is that they merely describe and do not explain the processes by which dependent variables are related to and dependent upon independent variable values:

> The use of mathematical models as an aid to causal explanation is inevitably problematic because, as a language, mathematics is acausal and astructural. It lacks the categories of 'producing', 'generating', or 'forcing' which we take to indicate causality. Mathematical functions such as $y = f(x)$ say nothing about what makes y or x, only that quantitative variation in y is formally (not substantially) related in some way to quantitative variation in x. The $=$ sign in an equation does not, of course, mean that the so-called independent variable is the cause of the changes in the 'dependent variable', but merely that the quantities on either side are equal! Any imputations of causality associated with the decision to define one variable as independent and the other as dependent must be based on non-mathematical, causal criteria. (Sayer, 1984: 179)

As a result of this failure, they are unable to explain qualitative change or how new properties might emerge. Critical realists emphasize the importance of conceptualization – what we have called conceptual modelling – to distinguish the necessary mechanisms responsible for causation from purely contingent statistical associations. The response to this critique of mathematical modelling has been quite different in human and physical geography. Physical geographers sympathetic to critical realism have responded by trying, as much as possible, to replace empirical-statistical methods in favour of more physically-based mathematical modelling approaches, such as physically-based parameterization or deductive-deterministic modelling methods. By contrast, human geographers have tended to abandon mathematical modelling altogether in favour of theoretical conceptualization.

Applications, politics and relevance

A third line of criticism turns on the applications of modelling and the politics they involve. Much of the initial enthusiasm for mathematical modelling in geography was driven by the hope that the development of such quantitative techniques would advance the status of geography as a science. While geographers were soon making important contributions to such areas of pure research as spatial autocorrelation, almost from the very dawn of the quantitative revolution, there were also concerns about the wider relevance of modelling and the implications of this kind of research both for society at large and for the future of geography as an academic discipline.

Such concerns fuelled two distinct, and to some extent opposed, responses that echo to this day. On the one hand, there are those for whom the problem was – and still is – that ivory-tower geographers are 'locked in private debate, preoccupied with trivia, mending and qualifying accepted ideas' (Prince, 1971: 153). Initially, this complaint about the irrelevance of academic geography was directed against all forms of geographical research. More recently, however, this cry has been taken up by those advocating a more central role for mathematical modelling, alongside remote sensing, GIS, and other quantitative techniques, in the discipline. Thus, the recent U.S. National Research Council's (1997: vii) *Rediscovering Geography: New Relevance for Science and Society* begins by emphasizing how these 'tools are being used by educators, business people, researchers, and policy makers to address a wide range of scientific and societal needs'. The report urges that the discipline's 'supply capacity' be brought into balance with the 'demand' this kind of applied expertise (ibid.: 171).

On the other hand, the radical geographers complained that such applied research tended to address narrowly technical questions at the expense of wider political critique. Reflecting on the first 20 years of modelling in geography, David Harvey (1989: 212–213) wrote:

> I accept that we can now model spatial behaviours like journey-to-work, retail activity, the spread of measles epidemics, the atmospheric dispersion and the like, with much greater security and precision than once was the

case. And I accept that this represents no mean achievement. But what can we say about the sudden explosion of third world debt in the 1970s, the remarkable push into new and seemingly quite different modes of flexible accumulation, the rise of geopolitical tensions, even the definition of key ecological problems? What more do we know about major historical-geographical transitions (the rise of capitalism, world wars, socialist revolutions, and the like)?

Whereas radical critics argued that geographers should abandon mathematical modelling in favour of conceptual modelling to inform political critique, more recent work by human geographers has sought to explore the social contexts and consequences of using models in political decision-making (Demeritt, 2001). There are important questions both about how such technical knowledge is actually used to inform the policy process and about how the demand for policy relevant science is shaping evolution of geographical knowledge (Demeritt, 2000).

Conclusion

Even if you do not plan to engage directly with models and modelling as part of your dissertation or other research work, we believe that all geographers should have a solid understanding of models. Aside from its increasingly important role in public policy-making, modelling occupies a central place in the history and practice of geography as a scientific discipline. While its role in providing human and physical geography with a unifying methodological framework remains hotly contested, there can be little doubt that the practice of modelling provides an important point of unity among the otherwise divergent sub-disciplines of physical geography (Gregory et al., 2002).

Much of the critical debate about modelling has focused on mathematical modelling without always acknowledging that it is not, as we have tried to demonstrate in this chapter, the only kind of modelling. It is important to recognize the different practices and associated philosophical assumptions involved in different kinds of modelling. Ironically, some of the most strident critics of mathematical modelling are themselves engaged in forms of conceptual modelling based on graphic and narrative, rather than mathematical, forms of abstraction (Sayer 1984). In turn, defenders of modelling have responded in turn with blanket denunciations of 'soft' geography and social theory (e.g. Openshaw 1998; Dorling and Shaw 2002). But if thinking and representation were reconceived as forms of conceptual modelling, then it might be possible to move forward collectively to explore the common ground shared by all geographers around the important questions, at once practical and theoretical, of appropriate scale, empirical adequacy, and methods of abstraction involved in modelling, whether it be conceptual, mathematical, or both.

It is time for a truce in the long-running battle between qualitative and quantitative approaches. There is, as Cosgrove (1989: 242) notes, a 'formal affinity between geographical models expressed in mathematical and statistical form and a landscape painting'. Constructed 'according to formal rules and conventions', both 'represent an idealized world ... [by] arrang[ing] objects within the space they create in order to clarify the relations between those objects.' Rather than rejecting modelling and quantitative approaches to geography altogether, it would be more helpful to recognize 'numerical modelling as a mode of geographical description ... alongside a range of alternatives' (Cosgrove, 1989: 244).

ESSAY QUESTIONS AND FURTHER READING

1   What is the proper role of models in geographical research? While Openshaw (1998) advances an inductive, geocomputational response to this question, the critical rationalist tradition of Popper is well articulated by Haines-Young and Petch (1986). That orthodoxy has been challenged both by advocates of critical realism, such as Sayer (1984) and Richards (1990; 1994), and by philosophers of science, such as Hesse (1966) and Cartwright (1983). The practical concerns relating to model definition are covered in Beven and Binley (1992) and Mulligan and Wainwright (2003).

2   How appropriate is it to apply the modelling techniques used by physical geographers to the practice of human geography? Humanistic geographers, such as Ley and Samuels (1978), rejected the affirmative claims advanced by early proponents of models in geography, such as Bunge (1996) and Chorley and Haggett (1967) for a single methodology in geography. These debates are helpfully reviewed in Macmillan (1989), which also provides an introduction to the concerns of critical theorists about the applications of models. Some further considerations of how model building may progress in geography are given by Wainwright and Mulligan (2003).

To both questions, Kirkby (1987) and Lane (2002) provide brief and accessible introductions to modelling in physical geography, while Willmott and Gaile (1992) provide an overview that covers both human and physical geography. A more technical discussion of actual model construction is available in

Mulligan and Wainwright (2003) and the other chapters in that edited collection, while the chapters in Macmillan (1989) provide a good starting point for philosophical debates about the nature, purpose, and politics of models in geography.

REFERENCES

Barnes, T.J. (1996) *Logics of Dislocation: Models, Meanings, and Metaphors of Economic Space*. Guildford, New York.

Beven, K.J. (2000) Uniqueness of place and process representations in hydrological modelling. *Hydrology and Earth System Sciences* **4**, 203–213.

Beven, K.J. and Binley, A.M. (1992) The future of distributed models: model calibration and predictive uncertainty. *Hydrological Processes* **6**, 279–298.

Bunge, W. (1966) *Theoretical Geography*, 2nd edn (Studies in Geography, Ser.C, no. 1). Royal University of Lund, Lund.

Cartwright, (1983) *How the Laws of Physics Lie*. Clarendon Press, Oxford.

Chorley, R. (1964) Geography and analogue theory. *Annals of the Association of American Geographers* **54**, 127–147.

Chorley, R. and Haggett, P. (eds) (1967) *Models in Geography*. Methuen, London.

Church, M. (1996) Space time and the mountain: how do we order what we see? In Rhoads, B.L. and Thorne, C.E. (eds) *The Scientific Nature of Geomorphology*. Wiley, New York, pp. 147–170.

Cosgrove, D. (1989) Models, description, and imagination in geography. In Macmillan, B. (ed.) *Remodelling Geography*. Basil Blackwell, Oxford, pp. 230–244.

Demeritt, D. (2000) The new social contract for science: accountability, relevance, and value in US and UK science and research policy. *Antipode* **32**, 308–329.

Demeritt, D. (2001) The construction of global warming and the politics of science. *Annals of the Association of American Geographers* **91**, 307–337.

Dorling, D. and Shaw, M. (2002) Geographies of the agenda: public policy, the discipline and its (re)'turns'. *Progress in Human Geography* **26**, 629–641.

Golledge, R. and Amedeo, D. (1968) On laws in geography. *Annals of the Association of American Geographers* **58**, 760–774.

Gregory, K.J., Gurnell, A.M. and Petts, G.E. (2002) Restructuring physical geography. *Transactions of the Institute of British Geographers* **27**, 136–154.

Haines-Young, R. and Petch, J. (1986) *Physical Geography: Its Nature and Methods*. Paul Chapman, London.

Harvey, D. (1989) From models to Marx: notes on the project to 'remodel' contemporary geography. In Macmillan, B. (ed.) *Remodelling Geography*. Blackwell, Oxford, pp. 211–216.

Harvey, L.D.D. (2000) *Global Warming: The Hard Science*. Pearson, Harlow.

Hesse, M. (1966) *Models and Analogues in Science*. Notre Dame University Press, New York.

Kirkby, M.J. (1987) Models in physical geography. In Clark, M.J., Gregory, K.J. and Gurnell, A.M. (eds) *Horizons in Physical Geography*. Macmillan, Basingstoke, pp. 47–61.

Lane, S. (2002) Environmental modelling. In Rogers, A. and Viles, H. (eds) *Student's Companion to Geography*, 2nd edn. Blackwell, Oxford, pp. 64–76.

Ley, D. and Samuels, M. (eds) (1978) *Humanistic Geography: Prospects and Problems*. Croom Helm, London.

Macmillan, B. (ed.) (1989) *Remodelling Geography*. Basil Blackwell, Oxford.

Mulligan, M. and Wainwright, J. (2003) Modelling and model building. In Wainwright, J. and Mulligan, M. (eds) *Environmental Modelling: Finding Simplicity in Complexity*. John Wiley, Chichester, pp. 7–73.

Openshaw, S. (1998) Towards a more computationally minded scientific human geography. *Environment and Planning A* **30**, 317–332.

Oreskes, N., Shrader-Frechette, K. and Belitz, K. (1994) Verification, validation, and confirmation of numerical models in the earth sciences. *Science* **263**, 641–646.

Prince, H.C. (1971) Questions of social relevance. *Area* **3**, 150–153.

Ragin, C. (1987) *The Comparative Method*. University of California Press, Berkeley, CA.

Rhoads, B. (1994) On being a 'real' geomorphologist. *Earth Surface Processes and Landforms* **19**, 269–272.

Rhoads, B. and Thorn, C. (1994) Contemporary philosophical perspectives on physical geography with emphasis on geomorphology. *Geographical Review* **84**, 90–101.

Richards, K.S. (1990) 'Real' geomorphology. *Earth Surface Processes and Landforms* **15**, 195–197.

Richards, K.S. (1994) Real geomorphology revisited. *Earth Surface Processes and Landforms* **19**, 277–281.

Sayer, A. (1984) *Method in Social Science*. Routledge, London.

Sayer, A. (1992) *Method in Social Science*. 2nd edn. Routledge, London.

Strahler, A.N. (1952) Dynamic basis of geomorphology. *Bulletin of the Geological Society of America* **63**, 923–938.

Thornes, J. (1978) Introduction. In Embleton, C., Brunsden, D. and Jones, D.K.C. (eds) *Geomorphology: Present Problems and Future Prospects*. Oxford University Press, Oxford, pp. ix–xiv.

Tiwari, A.K., Risse, L.M. and Nearing, M.A. (2000) Evaluation of WEPP and its comparison with USLE and RUSLE. *Transactions of the ASAE* **43**, 1129–1135.

USGCRP (2000) *Our Changing Planet: The FY 2000 US Global Change Research Program*. US Global Change Research Program, Washington, DC.

U.S. National Research Council (1997) *Rediscovering Geography*. National Academies Press, Washington, DC.

Wainwright, J. and Mulligan, M. (2003) Pointers for the future. In Wainwright, J. and Mulligan, M. (eds) *Environmental Modelling: Finding Simplicity in Complexity*. John Wiley, Chichester, pp. 389–396.

Wainwright, J., Parsons, A.J. and Abrahams, A.D. (2000) Plot-scale studies of vegetation, overland flow and erosion interactions: case studies from Arizona and New Mexico. *Hydrological Processes* **14**, 2921–2943.

Willmott, C.J. and Gaile, G.L. (1992) Modeling. In Abler, R.F., Marcus, M.G. and Olson, J.M. (eds) *Geography's Inner Worlds: Pervasive Themes in Contemporary American Geography.* Rutgers University Press, New Brunswick, NJ, pp. 163–186.

Wooldridge, S.W. (1958) The trend of geomorphology. *Transactions of the Institute of British Geographers* **25**, 29–35.

Ethnography and Fieldwork

Steve Herbert, Jacqueline Gallagher and Garth Myers

The history of the discipline of geography is grounded in fieldwork expertise. Long before quantitative analysis and critical theory, geography's emphasis on earth description necessitated a direct engagement with the physical landscape and the people inhabiting it (Zelinksy, 2001: 3–4). Of course, much of the early cataloguing of the earth, its resources and its peoples was done in the name of colonialism, and thus is a history that some geographers understandably disparage (Godlewska and Smith, 1994; Driver, 2001). For others, the legacy of fieldwork carries with it overly romanticized and masculinist overtones that deservedly call the enterprise into question (Rose, 1993). But many geographers possess an abiding interest in exploration, as a means to understand how the landscape is shaped, and how humans interact with it. The history of both physical and human geography contains pivotal figures who expected students to engage directly with the landscape and those who populated it. Well into the twentieth century, the association between fieldwork and geography remained strong.

By the 1960s, however, this association began to weaken (Rundstrom and Kenzer, 1989), in large part due to the so-called 'quantitative revolution'. Because quantitative work sought to discover abstract laws that ostensibly govern physical and human processes, the contextual analysis involved in fieldwork became delegitimated. Analyses of individual cases, from this perspective, involved too many idiosyncratic particulars whose study frustrated the drive to discover propositions that would hold true everywhere; geographic context became less important than allegedly placeless laws.[1]

However, there are increasing suggestions in the discipline of a re-invigorated enthusiasm for fieldwork (*Geographical Review*, 2001; Herbert, 2000; Simandan, 2002). There is a simple logic to this, in the recognition that being a geographer means working to deepen one's awareness of the landscapes around us, the forces – human and non-human – that create them, and the values we enact by moulding and interpreting them as we do. One of the joys of being a geographer means being able to 'do' geography anywhere and anytime, in locales both strange and familiar. It's one of the reasons students choose to study geography at university. Landscapes can always teach us, if we take the time to observe and to ask the right questions.

Questions, Theories, and the Challenges of Fieldwork

In short, simple curiosity about the world compels many geographers to head to the field. But landscapes do not always deliver their mysteries in any transparent fashion. And, as interpreters of landscapes, we always employ some set of cognitive schemes to make sense of what we are witnessing. The processes of probing and interpreting places are thus complicated and time-consuming. How does one channel one's innate curiosity into the pursuit and analysis of data that enable one to say something meaningful and significant? How does a researcher do field-work in a fashion that is comprehensive and comprehensible? How does one know what to take as significant from the wealth of data that a landscape presents? How does one interpret that data? And how does one use those interpretations in the service of an explanatory narrative that others, with no familiarity with the place, can understand?

As these difficult questions suggest, even if fieldwork is a compelling endeavour, it is also a rigorous, demanding and often frustrating experi-ence. In this chapter, we hope to make plain why we've found fieldwork both enjoyable and challenging. Collectively, we have spent several years in the field, pursuing a range of questions in a range of settings. We draw upon those experiences to explain what motivated our explorations and what confronted us as challenges to resolve. In the first-person accounts that follow, we address some of the more central challenges that field-workers face. In particular, we are interested in addressing three ques-tions: (1) How does a fieldworker balance a desire to make broad, general claims about a place with the need to respect the complexities and idio-syncrasies of that place?; (2) How does a fieldworker employ the right methods to answer any such questions comprehensively?; and (3) How does one manage the relationships that one inevitably makes in the field?

The first of these is addressed in Steve Herbert's discussion of his ethnographic fieldwork with the Los Angeles Police Department. For

Herbert, as for other academic fieldworkers, research questions emerge from an engagement with matters of theory. That is because academic geographers wish to converse with others about the forces that shape the creation and appreciation of landscapes. To make these conversations possible across a range of times and places, one must invoke theories that detail the wider forces that structure landscapes. For example, two different cities can be analysed by common reference to theorized patterns of settlement, or two different fluvial systems can be analysed by invoking the theoretical notion of equilibrium. But this key attribute of theory – its abstracted nature that enables cross-case comparison – is simultaneously its danger. To drift into too abstracted a universe is to elide the complexities of landscape. The fieldworker's quest to embrace the multiplex nature of experience thus places him or her in a tense relationship with theory; the fieldworker is simultaneously attracted and repulsed by the desire to generalize. So, while geographers rely upon theory to help them determine what questions to ask, they also try to ensure a capacity to discover what the theory might occlude. And what often gets hidden by theory is the complexity of the field. Herbert explains how his observations of the LAPD led him to understand the limitations of existing theories, and thus motivated him to develop his own theoretical schema that enabled sufficient flexibility to comprehend the complex reality of policing.

As Jacqueline Gallagher makes plain, matters of theory are somewhat less perplexing for physical geographers who engage in fieldwork. The central questions of theory are considered largely settled, and are drawn upon to develop hypotheses to help explain particular phenomena. But that hardly means that fieldwork is any easier in physical geography than in human geography. As Gallagher vividly illustrates in her discussion of her current work on the history of Lake Okeechobee in Florida, explaining a particular landform requires efforts on many fronts. She thus ably demonstrates the centrality of our second key challenge: the task of employing many means to decode the significance of a landscape. Likening herself to a detective trying to solve a mystery, Gallagher explains how the multiple effects on landscapes require multiple methodologies. Each line of evidence must be pursued in the hope that a coherent narrative of causation can be developed. Thus, the complexities of landscape formation pose a significant challenge for geomorphologists like Gallagher: to try and tie all the loose strands of fieldwork data together into a plausible and defensible historical account. This is especially tricky in geomorphological work, because the causal factors are all hidden from view, and must be inferred from the wide range of relevant data.

Garth Myers addresses the different, but no less compelling, challenge of negotiating relationships in the field. Myers's fieldwork takes him to Africa, specifically Zanzibar, Lilongwe and Lusaka, where he seeks to answer questions about the politics of urban development. But how can he, as a Western outsider, come to understand how some Africans inter-pret landscapes? And is there a way of involving local informants in the research that is not exploitative? Myers explains how he increasingly relies upon research collaborations as a means of addressing these important questions. By working with local research partners, Myers seeks to both enrich his own understanding of the places he studies and to provide an active role for those partners. He shows how he and his partners learn together, through reliance on their respective expertise. He also shows how the data he subsequently gathers enrich his understanding of urban development, by making clear how cities are understood by those who use them, not just those who plan them.

The first-person accounts that follow document these critical dilemmas that emerge from the fieldworker's task to understand and explain the sites that he/she visits. We each describe strategies to capture the many-sided nature of the social and physical realities we investigate. As our accounts make plain, fieldwork is enriching and challenging. Landscapes and the processes, both human and physical, that shape them, are never simple. It only follows that neither are our attempts to make sense of these processes.

Capturing the Complexities of Territorial Control: Making and Marking Space with the Los Angeles Police Department (Steve Herbert)

Like all fieldworkers in the human sciences, I chose to enter the field because I possessed a strong curiosity about the people I wished to understand. When I was in graduate school in Los Angeles in the early 1990s, there were few social institutions attracting more attention than the Los Angeles Police Department. For years, the LAPD had been accused of being overly aggressive and racially biased. As a consequence, when the brutal beating its officers administered to an African-American citizen named Rodney King was videotaped and shown on television in 1991, the Department became the focus of intense public debate. A year later, the officers involved in the beating were acquitted of all charges in the case, and the city erupted in civil unrest that caused millions of dollars of damage and left more than 50 people dead. I watched the unrest on television for hours, horrified by its violence and compelled to wonder how an incident with the police could spark such an explosion.

This more visceral interest in the police dovetailed for me with a more academic interest in a set of theoretical questions. At the time, there was a discussion emerging, both inside and outside the discipline of geography, focused on how the exercise of power was importantly connected with the control of space. Some of this work was inspired by the French historian, Michel Foucault, who, among other things, sought to describe how modern forms of power relied upon the categorization and control of territory. Foucault was interested in documenting how power infused even the smallest of spaces (see, for example, Foucault, 1977). This more micro-oriented approach contrasted with other work on the power–space connection, which drew on the German sociologist Max Weber's interest in the territorial structure of the modern nation–state. State-making, from this perspective, relies heavily on securing borders and then pacifying the population within those borders, through such activities as census-taking, conscription, and policing (see Giddens, 1985; Mann, 1986). This was a more centralized approach to the spatialization of power, focused as it was on the formal institution of the nation–state.

While these discussions were thought-provoking, their abstracted nature frustrated me; they lacked rich empirical data to substantiate their theoretical claims. Given the public prominence of the LAPD, I decided to investigate the power–space connection via an ethnographic study of the police. What better way, I thought, to see whether and how the control of space, sometimes referred to as territoriality (see Sack, 1986), was central to the exercise of power. No other method could provide the same insight. Surveys of officers might have been instructive in helping understand what factors shaped their understanding of their work and the places they patrolled. Less structured interviews would also have provided important data. But only ethnography could provide direct insights into police *action*. It is one thing to understand the world-view of the police – how its officers understand the city and the various peoples that inhabit its neighbourhoods. It is quite another to understand how that world-view helps explain specific acts that the police engage in during their daily routines in urban space. For this, only ethnography would suffice.

As a consequence, I spent several months riding with officers in a particularly diverse and busy patrol division in the LAPD. In a typical week, I visited the patrol station two or three times, and spent four to six hours accompanying an officer on his or her tour of duty. The officers were invariably consumed with the immense number of calls for which they were responsible, and thus I observed much police activity. These police actions also provided fodder for my conversations with the officers. They would naturally wish to describe what they had done and why, and I would follow up with questions to deepen my understandings. My 'interviews' simply evolved from the day's course of events.

My theoretical focus prompted an interest in the police's exercise of territoriality. It became obvious to me that, without the power to control space, officers would largely be impotent to enforce law or maintain order. As I then wrote (Herbert, 1997: 11):

> Officers typically bring domestic and business disputes under control by segregating the combatants and often by convincing at least one party to leave the scene. They end loud parties by sending people home. They regularly sweep gang members from street corners, underage youths from saloons, prostitutes from the fronts of cheap motels, homeless people from commercial thoroughfares. Further, one of their most potent means of exercising control is to jail, an especially severe territorial act – a suspect is transported from one place and confined to another. Simply put, many police strategies to create public order involve enacting boundaries and restricting access; police power rests upon a political geography. As one officer said about his strategies for a house where drugs were sold, 'Basically I do whatever I can to get them to move along.'

To demonstrate the centrality of territoriality to policing was a fairly easy project of description – I merely outlined the range of the officers' territorial practices. The harder task was to explain that territoriality. How did the police understand the spaces they patrolled, and how did they justify their territorial actions? How did their social organization structure their understandings of space, and their actions in space? Here, I sought to make general statements about the social structure of policing and how it translated into geographical practice.

To accomplish this, I both drew upon and expanded existing theory. In essence, my approach was to steer a middle theoretical course between the Weberian focus on formal institutions and the Foucauldian focus on the diffuse nature of power. There were obvious ways in which police behaviour was dictated by formal legal rules and organizational regulations. For example, I often witnessed officers trying to decide whether an activity of a citizen could be categorized as a legal infraction. However, too much of what the police did was impelled by norms and values reinforced in the subcultural world officers built for themselves. And these subcultural norms often trumped legal considerations, most obviously when officers conducted searches of citizens that were legally questionable, given the US Constitutional guarantees against searches without 'probable cause'. Officers justified these searches in the name of a value – safety – that was regularly reinforced within their subculture. The work of Foucault made me sensitive to these less formal structurings of power. Unfortunately, it did not provide any analytic frames for explaining them.

For these reasons, and with assistance from some theoretical work in organizational and cultural sociology, I devised a theoretical scheme that provided significant analytic purchase to explain police territoriality. I mobilized the term, normative order, and defined it in a particular way, as a set of rules and practices organized around a central value. I argued that six such orders – law, bureaucratic control, adventure/machismo, safety, competence and morality – deeply shaped how officers understood and sought to control territory. The first two of these orders, law and bureaucratic control, reinforced the Weberian emphasis on formalized and centralized dictates; these largely defined space and proper spatial behaviour for the police. The other four, however, were more internally-constructed, and reflected the power of the subculture.

I arrived at this theoretical conclusion through a protracted process of moving back and forth between the field notes I constructed during the ethnography and the theoretical work I engaged. This was necessary because my field data did not map neatly on to any pre-existing theoretical framework; the complexities of the realities on the ground were considerably more vast than the abstracted theories that I consulted allowed. My fieldwork experience was thus an opportunity to flesh out existing theories in a way that provided some greater capacity to understand the complex world of policing.

Geomorphologist as Detective: Solving the Mystery of Lake Okeechobee (Jacqueline Gallagher)

For me, as a geomorphologist primarily interested in landscape evolution and paleoenvironmental reconstruction, fieldwork means long days and vigorous physical activity with one or more 'assistants'. It also usually means getting wet and muddy. There is a great deal of planning beforehand, and much laboratory work afterwards. Not a whole lot of this *seems* all that theoretical to those who do physical geographic fieldwork. Indeed, many physical geographers deny the presence of theory in their discipline, for such an admission puts them in an office with a book, not out in 'the field' with water, mud, soil, rocks, etc. Thorn stated that, 'pursuit of theoretical knowledge is not generally a favoured activity in geomorphology. The old saw that "geography is learnt through the soles of your feet" is clearly also a widely accepted view of the way to approach geomorphology' (1988: 1). Or, as Chorley quipped, 'whenever anyone mentions theory to a geomorphologist, he instinctively reaches for his soil auger' (1978: 1).

In practice, physical geographers work according to a few dominant theories, and then test for the exact conditions of their primary interest. Most researchers view themselves as scientists – they follow the tenets of physics and chemistry, and formulate testable hypotheses within the framework(s) of accepted theories or models. But all of this sounds very serious and academic in a way that is seldom considered when *doing* fieldwork. Fieldwork in geomorphology requires knowledge of some or all of the following: erosion, transportation and deposition in fluvial, coastal, aeolian and glacial environments; hillslope processes and mass movements; climatic change (including sea level change); and plate motion. For the most part, these processes are considered factual since geomorphologists, like geologists, work in the uniformitarian paradigm under the adage 'the present is the key to the past'.

Thus, doing fieldwork in physical geography requires some familiarity with the broad theories that explain landscape formation. These theories help one to develop various hypotheses about how a particular landscape was created. But once in the field, the actual research involves grappling with the complexities of a given place. The best analogy, for work in Quaternary geomorphology, is to a detective story: you are given the 'answer' and have to find out the story behind it. It's like finding a corpse and determining who was the murderer! You never really know for sure if you are correct because you can never go back in time and no one was there to tell you – so the more pieces of corroborating data, the better your interpretation. Thus it is a good idea to have multiple lines of evidence. Or, as Rhoads and Thorn (1996: 50) put it: 'It is essential to construct a web of evidence, each piece of which provides an independent element of support for a particular explanation while at least some of the same data serve as disconfirmatory evidence for competing explanations.'

For example, the detective story that occupies me at present is the existence of Lake Okeechobee in southern Florida. The second largest freshwater lake in the coterminous United States, Lake Okeechobee is basically an inland sea, occupying a depression that was an embayment during an earlier interglacial high sea level stand. We already know that the lake is young, about 5,000 years. There is little literature on its formation, and hence my big questions: Why was Lake Okeechobee formed, and when? Unfortunately, I cannot address that big question without addressing some smaller, more manageable questions first: What was the original nature of the lake? Did it act like an inland sea, with shorelines, wave-cut benches, and littoral drift? What was the original nature of the lakeshore? How old are apparent previous shorelines north and east of the lake?

At present, I am focusing on these old shorelines, visible as sand ridges to the east and north of a modern dike. These ridges are invisible on topographic maps but seen on satellite images. They could have been created by humans, in recent or pre-historical times, or by the lake prior to its enclosure and control, or potentially by the sea at some high level. They could be ancient, or might represent a not-too-distant flood event of potential concern to today's inhabitants. One problem is that there are few good records of modifications to the lake, and so much has been changed by the sugar industry, the US Army Corps of Engineers, and the water management districts. In some areas, it is difficult to find anything natural!

To get to the bottom of the story, then, I have worked to develop my own data bases, and have done so through multiple methods. After reading and reconnaissance, and with teams of students, I took several cores of varying depth from a number of locations. These were analysed for textural content and for age. I surveyed the ridge to get accurate height and slope dimensions. I visited the modern shore to collect samples and see if ongoing processes might be comparable. I spoke to long-time residents of the area who knew Lake Okeechobee before it was enclosed by a dike, and asked about currents, beaches and shorelines. I visited the rivers feeding into the lake and sampled them for sand content. I graphed records of lake stage over time and tied them to wind strength and direction data obtained from the South Florida Water Management District. I examined old aerial photos and maps to look for methods by which the ridges could have been deposited. And then I will repeat each of these steps as necessary.

Like a good detective, then, I approach the scene of the crime in a comprehensive fashion, using multiple methods to understand the principal causes of Lake Okeechobee's development. I rely upon my pre-existing theoretical understandings of the basic processes of modern and ancient lakes in uniformitarian/dynamic equilibrium paradigms. This theoretical knowledge is essential for my fieldwork, but any given lake, like Okeechobee, cannot be simply explained via abstract theory. Its existence is a consequence of a complex range of processes, and my task as a fieldworker is to embrace and explain that complexity. One question leads to another, for which there is no clear answer without many avenues of research.

Not all of these avenues of research, of course, actually require my presence in the field. I am like all fieldworkers, in both physical and human geography, in that I rely upon data I gather from a variety of sources. However, the importance of being in the field cannot be over-stressed. Part of that, of course, is that the cores and other physical material I need to analyse can only be extracted from my field site. But part of it is the inescapable need to actually see 'the scene of the crime'. I must examine landscape in its entirety, assess how the various components of that landscape relate to one another, and visualize what it might have looked like in the past. Only by seeing the landscape whole, and seeing how the parts interrelate, can I fully grasp the confluence of forces that structure a place like Lake Okeechobee.

As for my current mystery, at the moment, I think the ridges in question are, in fact, original shorelines, produced by high wave energy. I need to prove it beyond doubt and then figure out their significance. To do so will require continued used of varied methods, and continued exploration of various hypotheses. I will likely encounter numerous dead ends. I will also get very wet and muddy.

Relations as Vehicles for Understanding: Planning from the Ground Up in Africa (Garth Myers)

Fieldwork must be a big deal to me. When I count the days, it becomes apparent that I have spent more than two of the last dozen years of my life 'in the field'. What it means, to me, to be in the field is that the whole of daily life becomes a vehicle for learning. The experience of sharing life with people in Zanzibar, Lilongwe, or Lusaka helps inform my understanding of urban processes and the various urban planning projects I have been studying over these years of fieldwork.

Edward Said (1983: 216) wrote that '[there] is no vantage outside the actuality of relationships between cultures... that might allow one the epistemological privilege of somehow judging, evaluating and interpreting free of the encumbering interests, emotions, and engagements of the ongoing relationships themselves'. I often return to this quotation to remind me that my conceptions of the world and my identity within it inevitably carry over into my research. But what Said sees as 'encumbering' can be *enriching* interests, emotions, and engagements. Sharing our lives with friends and walking around with our eyes open can teach us a world of things about places, in an incidental and yet profound way. Nothing, simply nothing, can replace the learning that happens because of those 'ongoing relationships themselves' in fieldwork contexts.

Let me provide one visceral example of why fieldwork can offer something from these ongoing relationships that is irreplaceable. Zanzibar city's historic working-class heart is the neighbourhood area known as Ng'ambo, literally 'the Other Side'. It is closely built and disorderly to Western eyes, a system of twisted alleys that seems like a hedge maze for visitors. Planners from the 1920s onward have sought to rebuild Ng'ambo to make it orderly, with wide roads, streetlights and drains. By living in such a neighbourhood and observing everyday spatial behaviour I came to understand that the majority of women residents of Ng'ambo walk through alleys rather than on those wide streets that have been created. They do so because the alleys are cooler, more comforting, and less likely to bring them under the scrutiny of groups of young men who gather on stoops of main streets, often under street lights. Lighting, women often said, was a major priority for them, but lighting for the alleys, not the streets. I am confident that, as a Western male, I could never have gained this understanding without the female friendships my fieldwork experience generated.

Fieldwork, of course, often involves more structured activities besides simply 'hanging out' with groups of people, activities such as in-depth interviews, door-to-door questionnaires, and field maps. In this sense, I'm like Jacqueline Gallagher, travelling down several avenues in search of relevant data. But nothing can quite replace 'hanging out' as a means of measuring the full depth of social life in the places I visit, of getting closer to the complex whole of what places mean to people. In addition, ethnography's close association with storytelling enables me to bring my understanding – however partial – to a wider audience more creatively and, I feel, more engagingly than a more scientific presentation of 'data' or 'results' could.

That said, an important question remains about how to negotiate relationships in the process of this type of research. I do some of these activities alone, but usually I work in collaboration with local researchers. I increasingly believe that such collaboration must be increased for fieldwork to re-emerge at the centre of geographic inquiry. In a way, the more the expertise is decentralized and distanced from the central (outsider) researcher, the stronger the project.

As an example of this, let me again return to Zanzibar. In 1999 I conducted research on natural resource management in the Chwaka Bay area on Zanzibar island's east coast, in collaboration with my long-time research partners, M.A. Muhajir and Ali Hasan Ali. I know little about fishing, and even less about fish; my interests reside in the politics of development planning. Muhajir was raised in a fishing village, and Ali spent 15 years as a fisherman. Chwaka village is more than 99 per cent Muslim, and both Muhajir and Ali are Muslim while I am not. Chwaka fisherfolk were far more likely to have a useful conversation with Ali about fishing methods, or the habitats and behaviours of particular species, than with me, given my ineptitude with a fishing basket. On the other hand, the combination of Ali's expertise and my own eagerness to at least get out in the boat and try to pull up the baskets gained us both a measure of respect. Likewise, Ali's regular attendance five times per day in the mosque in which these fishermen prayed gave him a far stronger understanding of community life than I could ever claim. In combination, Ali and I learned things that I never would have learned alone (Myers, 2002).

I survived a doctoral programme heavily laced with social theory; I was required to read the latest influential thinking in human geography, particularly works from Marxist, feminist, and poststructuralist perspectives. A particularly important, and continuing, source of inspiration for me is the concept of cultural hegemony, as developed by the Italian Marxist, Antonio Gramsci. This concept has been usefully transcribed into cultural studies and cultural geography via Raymond Williams, Denis Cosgrove, and others. Briefly, the construct goes like this: a dominant group in society maintains that dominance by manufacturing the consent of the governed through consensual and discursive persuasion backed by the threat of force. However, this attempted cultural hegemony is contested via alternatives from non-dominant groups, and all of that is played out in the urban landscape. So, my challenge is to understand how hegemony is both expressed *and* resisted. To hold too dearly to the concept of hegemony might leave me stranded in 'theoretically-created puzzles that hinder empirical investigations' (Mouzelis, 1991: 5). In other words, to overemphasize hegemony might lead me to miss resistance.

Hence the experience of conducting fieldwork constantly tests my Gramscian thinking. I still hold to the gist of hegemony theory as a general explanation for what I find baffling. What I find when I do field research is that the most interesting questions were not really those surrounding the ways in which the dominant group sought to project its hegemony on to the landscape. Instead, I became preoccupied with questions of how the urban majority of Zanzibar, in Ng'ambo, reframed the city in accordance with their own faith and customary practices, and within their own circumscribed power. After more than a hundred

interviews in which ordinary people, even while claiming their neighbourhoods were 'unplanned', talked about how the built environment
depended upon the *uwezo* (power), *desturi* (customs), and *imani* (faith) of
inhabitants, I began to think of that triumvirate of terms as, in fact, the
system by which planning happened. The three became, to paraphrase
Mouzelis (1991), my meso-level working concepts derived from the
ground up. In articulating them further and elaborating upon them,
I sought to suggest an alternative to Eurocentric social theoretical approaches to African cities (Myers, 1994), something I still work towards in
my current fieldwork.

Clifford Geertz (1983: 57) once wrote that fieldwork demands that we
'see ourselves among others', and that we seek balance between ourselves and others, as well as between our theories and our empiricism. In
that balance, Geertz believed, we would find 'an interpretation of the way
a people live which is neither imprisoned within their mental horizons,
an ethnography of witchcraft as written by a witch, nor systematically
deaf to the tonalities of existence, an ethnography of witchcraft as written
by a geometer'. I see that balance not only as a worthy goal for human
geography fieldwork, but as a convincing reason for reasserting the value
of field study to the discipline.

Conclusion

Academic geographers are by no means unique in possessing a love of
landscapes and a desire to understand those landscapes more completely. This curiosity about place impels many to travel, to explore,
and to peruse atlases. Such curiosity explains our love of fieldwork; it
motivates us to understand how places are formed, controlled, planned
and experienced. Our principal challenge as academic fieldworkers is to
channel our curiosity so that we are able to tell comprehensible and
instructive narratives about the places we study. This, it turns out, is no
simple matter, because landscapes, and the peoples who inhabit them,
are always opaque; the stories of the places that interest us rarely an-
nounce themselves. Our goal here is to make clear some strategies we use
to uncover the secrets of place, the methods we employ to ask good
questions and get educative answers.

We have immensely enjoyed the various challenges we have confronted in the field, from trying to understand how police officers read
the landscape, to uncovering the mysteries of landscape formation, to
discerning how various members of Zanzibar society understand the

logic of their city. These experiences have enabled us to do geography in the richest possible way. We work to see the world through the eyes of others, or as it once existed in the past; we see landscapes as the product of the many forces that shape them. To plunge into fieldwork is to plunge into the world in all its complexity, and with deep respect for that complexity. The analytic challenge of making some modest sense of that complexity is what compels us to do geography. Our hope is that we can inspire others to follow our example. If nothing else, we hope to breathe continued life into what we consider geography's central tradition: its animating commitment to the field, its compulsion to experience, probe and explain the spaces that surround us.

ESSAY QUESTIONS AND FURTHER READING

1   In their jointly-authored contribution to the *Annals of the Association of American Geographers* (1999) forum on methodology in physical geography, Bernard Bauer, Thomas Veblen and Julie Winkler liken the different methodologies employed by physical geographers to shoes of different styles. Given that the papers in the Forum represent individual views held by purveyors of distinct sub-disciplines of physical geography, how important do field studies appear to be in this shoe closet? The forum, entitled 'On Methodology in Physical Geography', appears in vol. 89, pp. 677–778. Further help can be found in a special issue of *Geographical Review* (2001) 'Doing fieldwork', vol. 91, pp. 1–508. See also Rhoads and Thorn (1996).

2   Can ethnography help poor and marginalized communities in their struggles, and, if so, how? Or is ethnography hopelessly exploitative of the subjects of research? In addition to the two special issues listed above, see also Nast (1994). Additional insights can be found in Herbert (2000) and Shurmer-Smith (2002).

NOTE

1   It is important not to overstate the effects of the embrace of quantification on the tradition of doing fieldwork in geography. For one thing, the distinction between quantification and fieldwork was significant only in human geography, not physical geography, where quantification was used to enhance the analysis of field data. Also, even during the height of the 'quantitative revolution', many human geographers continued to embrace the practice of fieldwork and other qualitative methods of gathering and interpreting data.

REFERENCES

Bauer, O. (ed.) (1999) Forum: on methodology in physical geography. *Annals of the Association of American Geographers* **89**, 677–778.

Chorley, R.J. (1978) Bases for theory in geomorphology. In Embleton, C., Brunsden, D. and Jones, D. (eds) *Geomorphology: Present Problems and Future Prospects*. Oxford University Press, Oxford, pp. 1–13.

Driver, F. (2001) *Geography Militant: Cultures of Exploration and Empire*. Blackwell, Oxford.

Foucault, M. (1977) *Discipline and Punish: The Birth of the Prison*. Vintage, New York.

Geertz, C. (1983) *Local Knowledge*. Basic Books, New York.

Geographical Review (2001) Special issues on 'Doing fieldwork', Delyser, D. and Starrs, P.F. (eds) *Geographical Review* **91**, 1–2.

Giddens, A. (1985) *The Nation-State and Violence*. University of California Press, Berkeley, CA.

Godlweska, A. and Smith, N. (eds) (1994) *Geography and Empire*. Basil Blackwell, Oxford.

Herbert, S. (1997) *Policing Space: Territoriality and the Los Angeles Police Department*. University of Minnesota Press, Minneapolis.

Herbert, S. (2000) For ethnography. *Progress in Human Geography* **24**, 550–568.

Mann, M. (1986) *States, Wars and Capitalism*. Basil Blackwell, Oxford.

Mouzelis, N. (1991) *Back to Sociological Theory*. St Martin's Press, New York.

Myers, G. (1994) Eurocentrism and African urbanization: the case of Zanzibar's other side. *Antipode* **26**, 195–215.

Myers, G. (2002) Local communities and the new environmental planning: a case study from Zanzibar. *Area* **34**, 149–159.

Nast, H.J. (1994) Methods and techniques: women in the field. *Professional Geographer* **46**, 54–102

Rhoads, B. and Thorn, C. (1996) Observation in geomorphology. In Rhoads, B. and Thorn, C. (eds) *The Scientific Nature of Geomorphology*. Wiley, Chichester, pp. 21–56.

Rose, G. (1993) *Feminism and Geography: The Limits of Geographical Knowledge*. University of Minnesota Press, Minneapolis.

Rundstrom, R. and Kenzer, M. (1989) The decline of fieldwork in human geography. *Professional Geographer* **41**, 294–303.

Sack, R. (1986) *Human Territoriality: Its Theory and History*. Cambridge University Press, Cambridge.

Said, E. (1983) Opponents, audiences, constituencies, and community. In Foster, H. (ed.) *The Anti-Aesthetic*. Bay Press, Port Townsend, Australia, pp. 135–156.

Shurmer-Smith, P. (2002) *Doing Cultural Geography*. Sage, London.

Simandan, D. (2002) On what it takes to be a good geographer. *Area* **34**, 284–293.

Thorn, C. (1988) *Introduction to Theoretical Geomorphology*. Allen and Unwin, Winchester, MA.

Zelinsky, W. (2001) The geographer as voyeur. *Geographical Review* **91**, 1–8.

Counting and Measuring
Happy Valentine's Day

Danny Dorling

On Valentine's Day 2003 the geographers of the United Kingdom received a truckload of cards. The 'cards' came in the form of innumerable press releases and tables of statistics concerning the geography of the UK signed, mysteriously and variously, ONS, GRO(S), and NISRA. The first of the 2001 Census data concerning the characteristics of the population of Britain had been both released and instantly interpreted on our behalf at 11 a.m. the previous day. If you are not reading this in Britain, please keep reading; this story has wider implications. The cards made the headlines on 14 February. These cards were not just delivered to geographers of course. But it was geographers who were most excited about what they might reveal, because the Census, far more than any other survey, contains geographical data. What could the data be telling us? What secrets lay within it? We (and particularly quantitative geographers) felt loved and needed. Our meal ticket for several years of research had come in. Newspaper and television pundits were talking about what we did. The people of the UK had studiously filled in their forms for our delectation and delight; and so many forms, producing so many numbers, and so many headlines. We could hardly contain our excitement. But then we began to read what was being written about these numbers, to see something of the purposes for which numbers had been made up, we began to see an agenda forming whereby the data, supposedly collected for one purpose, was being used for many others, and we began to look at the numbers themselves.

In writing this chapter, I want to try and answer a few simple questions in relation to human geography: what can and should be counted and how does one measure and quantify and to what end? To try to answer these questions, I have used my experience of Valentine's Day 2003 with excerpts from the press cuttings and news releases, tables and summary statistics of that day. These were just the first substantive results from the 2001 Census, many more will follow, and their substance and interpretation will shape both the work of geographers and the picture of the human geography of the UK that is painted for a decade to come. The key question is, how should you decide what to work on when presented with such sources of information? Whose picture really is being painted by these numbers?

The Big Story

One story dominated census reporting on Valentine's Day 2003. The headlines below are emboldened only when they were so in the original stories. Most of the text below is taken from the Internet and hence the text appears there a day before it appears in print in the following morning's newspapers. The evening television news on almost all channels also led with this story when discussing the 2001 Census. An operation costing a quarter of a billion pounds and collecting millions upon millions of statistics was boiled down by the press (with the assistance of the census authorities) to just two numbers: 39 and 45.

Blacks and Asians overtake whites in two areas of Britain (headline, David Barrett and Lyndsay Moss, PA News, *The Independent*, 13 February 2003)

More diverse, caring and single – the new face of Britain. Whites in minority in two boroughs, census reveals (headline and sub-heading, main census story, John Carvel, Social Affairs Editor, *The Guardian*, 14 February 2003)

Top 10 facts from the 2001 census ... [Fact number one] Two boroughs of Britain had more blacks and Asians than white people for the first time ever. (David Batty, SocietyGuardian.co.uk, 13 February 2003)

Ethnic groups growing – census Two areas of Britain have more black people and Asians than white people for the first time ever ... (BBC, lead census story, 13 February 2003)

Census results unveiled ... the census findings, published by the Office for National Statistics, reveal that two areas of Britain have more blacks and Asians than white people for the first time ever. (ITV news website, 13 February 2003)

Population snapshot ... Two areas of Britain have more blacks and Asians than white people for the first time ever: In Newham, East London, 39.4 [*sic*] of people are white, and in Brent, north-west London, 45.3 per cent are white. (Channel 4 News, lead census story, 13 February 2003)

I could go on and on – but hopefully the list above gives you an idea of how this one story dominated the first reports of the substantive census results (simple population counts by age and sex had been released earlier). Thankfully, perhaps, at least from the point of view of census reporting, the stormclouds of war were gathering on 14 February and the front pages of most newspapers and the first item on most news channels led with the news on the forthcoming war in Iraq and the preparations for what turned out to be the largest UK peace demonstrations of all time over the weekend that followed. I say thankfully, because the census was not designed to produce scare stories over 'white' people becoming a minority in a couple of places. How, then, did this turn out to be the story that was so extensively reported?

The similarity of the quotations suggests a single source and that source, interestingly, was not the government agency that released the figures; at least not directly. The main press release of the National Statistics stressed in its fourth paragraph that the big picture the census paints is 'a complex rather than a simple picture. Ideas of divisions between north and south or town and country hide the contrasting ways that people experience life in each area of the country' (ONS press release, 13 February 2003). Neither their main press release nor the more detailed press release (on ethnicity and religion in England and Wales) contained the two numbers that became the big census story. However, the tables that they released along with their summaries made it possible to calculate those numbers. By working back in time, it would appear that the most likely initial source of the numbers was the Press Association (see first quotation above). Someone there, armed only with a calculator, or perhaps just pen and paper, calculated the statistics that became the story.

The government agency clearly did not want this to be the lead story, their press releases painted a much more nuanced picture of the results, avoiding crudely lumping together groups and highlighting the sensational. However, they provided the numbers that made such a story possible and had the experience to know what happens when they do so. They also failed to provide the press with an alternative big story – suggesting in their earliest of releases that the big story was a decline in Gaelic speaking in Scotland! If the powers that be had not realized what the story would have turned into, then they have a very low level of competency in spinning the news. I think they did know and there are several reasons to think this. First, concerned, some organizations had clearly been pre-warned and had their press releases ready to distribute on the morning of 13 February. Chief among these was the Commission for Racial Equality which led with a story, the bones of which imply, don't be concerned, there are fewer black people than you think!

> **2001 census: replacing myths with facts**... The figures released today reveal that many commentators have over-estimated the size of the ethnic minority population. A recent MORI poll found that people estimated that ethnic minorities comprised 22.5% of the total population, nearly three times the actual size. (Beverley Bernard, Acting Chair of the Commission for Racial Equality, press release, 13 February 2003)

Operation Black Vote and the Muslim Council of Britain also released press stories at the same time although *without* the same bizarre message of 'don't worry, there aren't many of us!'.

Second, the main national statistical agency, the Office for National Statistics (ONS), chose not to release other statistics (which may be released later) which could easily have become the big story. Most obviously among these, the 2001 Census contained the first-ever count in Britain of same-sex couples who cohabited. Hidden within the ONS press releases was the statement that cohabiting couple families had risen from 5.5 per cent of households in 1991 to 8.3 per cent in 2001, with London having the highest proportion of adults who are cohabiting (10.3 per cent) and then: 'At local level though it is Brighton and Hove that shows the highest proportions of all. Cohabiting households make up 11.5 per cent and 14.8 per cent of all adults are cohabiting' (Census 2001 – families of England and Wales, ONS press release, 13 February 2003). At no point in that press release did ONS point out that the definition of cohabiting couples had changed to include same-sex couples, nor have they provided the figures that would allow members of the press to calculate that proportion. If they had, I suspect the big story on census day would have been something along the lines of '1 million gay "marriages" ', or 'Brighton, gay capital of Britain, married couples in minority'.

Third, and most importantly, the census authorities chose which questions to ask in the census and it is this which had by far the largest effect on what the 'big story' is, both on the day of release and for the ten years of research which will follow. Despite an overwhelming case being made by the academic community and many others for the 2001 Census to include a question on income, this was rejected at the last minute and, instead, a new question on religion was asked (Dorling, 1999). Had the income question been asked, as it is asked in the United States (and if higher incomes had been included), the big story would have almost certainly been: 'Census reveals huge income gap' followed by 'in two areas of Britain a majority of the population are living on the breadline', 'census results show extreme divide between two-earner households and pensioners', 'Black Britons paid less for the same work', 'People with disabilities are the poorest', 'Salaries now five times the average in posh place', 'I'm alright John society', and so on. The academic papers that would have flowed out as the detailed results were released would have concentrated on income inequalities. Government and public policy would be influenced first directly and then incrementally, with each drip of facts and analysis. People in Britain find income inequalities extremely uncomfortable, which is mainly why the question was not asked. Living with the unfolding statistical story of income inequalities would have been even more uncomfortable. Research papers from study-ing people's chances for having good health to doing well in education would quickly begin to make the refrain 'we find income explains the majority of variation', a research cliché. Academics would no longer be using pitiful proxies, such as the number of cars people have access to or whether they have a mortgage. We know this because income is asked in almost all other official surveys, but they are surveys, not censuses. Above all else, the census helps to make statistics 'real', because it puts them in place. When you talk about half the homes in a city rather than 'the poor', when you can say where the people you are talking about are, when you can identify the few places where the minority of the very affluent who live there have access to resources, through money, equiva-lent to that which has to be shared out between thousands of others, the numbers, analysis and implications come alive. But none of this hap-pened, because the tick boxes were removed from the forms before they were printed.

Why am I telling you this story, a story of one source of data and one set of press releases about one country? I am telling it because I think it summarizes what should not be counted. More subtly, it is an example of what should not be counted and presented in this way. I have no great objection to asking about ethnic origin on census forms. I do have great objection to crude and potentially harmful newspaper stories emerging from either malicious or unthinking actions by those paid to collect and disseminate statistics. One day you could have a job that involves counting, measuring and disseminating. Who would you have helped, had you sent the story around the world that: 'Ethnic minority groups on the rise in England . . . Blacks and Asians outnumber whites in two boroughs; the overall ethnic population rises to 9%, census shows' (*The* [Singapore] *Straits Times*, 15 February 2003)? Would it have been people interested in how parts of Britain are becoming more heterogeneous in their population's origins, or people wishing to start scare stories over immigration?

Returning to the Question

In the introduction to this chapter I set out a few apparently simple questions. It's now time to answer them.

'What can and should be counted and how does one measure and quantify and to what end?' The Valentine's Day reporting of the UK Census was unfortunate, to say the least. You may be wondering why I think this and here we come to the crux of the problem of counting and measuring in geography in particular and social science more generally. As I see it, the census paints a very different picture of ethnicity in the UK. The UK is full of ghettos but they are all, *without exception*, ghettos of people who ticked the 'White British' option. The vast majority of the Britain is made up of communities, neighbourhoods, villages and towns where over 95 per cent of the population, when asked, labels themselves as White Britons. There are only some 250 wards, out of over 10,000, where less than half the population label themselves as White Britons. Even in those diverse wards, the largest single ethnic group, constituting about a third of the population, are White Britons! What is remarkable about the geography of ethnicity in Britain is that most of the country is made up of ghettos and *all* the ghettos are White British ghettos. There are a few mixed areas and even fewer diverse areas (the 250 areas described above), but the reality (as I call my stories) of the geography of ethnicity is almost the opposite of the stories (what you are most likely to read as being the reality, as highlighted above).

You can apply the above example to many, if not most, other subjects quantified in geography. You can find a set of popular stories, a common knowledge and understanding, a spin put on a subject that is flawed. Compare those stories to your perception of reality: if they do not equate, ask further questions. Next, you ask where those stories came from, what were the source and the impetus for the line that was taken? Observe how usually there is a single origin for the line taken, in the case above, the Press Association. Then return to the source that was used and see whether, if looked at in another light, it really does merit what you are reading about. If it does not, then you have two further tasks: first, to try to understand why that spin was placed on the story and, second, to re-interpret the source as you think it would have been better interpreted in the first place. How do you decide what is better? You begin with the last question I set myself in writing this chapter: 'To what end?' Almost anything can be counted, measured and quantified; in innumerable ways. There are 'scientific rules' that govern such things, but they are so open to interpretation that they can be followed without determining the result and almost an infinite number of 'scientifically correct' results can be attained. What matters is to what end you are working. That, above all else, will influence what you find and will narrow down the options. What you find will be influenced by the data and what you find may alter what you think, but how and where and why you look matter most.

To return to our example, the stories depend very little on the source, the census. Whatever the census had reported, the newspapers were almost certainly going to run with the stories they did. It did not matter that the government agencies did not feed them those stories directly. The agencies would have had to have gone a long way out of their way to have produced press releases that would have led to another line being taken. They didn't, I believe, partly because they saw their job as providing the statistics that others would interpret (although they did release press releases which interpreted that data). Perhaps they too thought that what the census showed was the emergence of Black and/or Asian ghettos in parts of London. Almost all the people involved in writing these stories were White. In Britain at the start of the twenty-first century most White people were brought up in areas where almost no-one was not White. Areas where a tenth or a fifth of the population are not White are now routinely labelled as ethnic minority areas in popular conversation, in the media, and in academic studies (for instance, 'inner cities with a high proportion of Black Minority Ethnic Populations'). The fact that usually 90 or 80 per cent of the population is White in these areas is largely ignored. The world is always seen and described through particular lenses. Even in a situation as absurd as I claim the initial reporting of ethnicity from the census was, it is not seen as absurd; as it has been done before, and as it is usual to do it in this way, it is seen as normal to carry on in this way. To see if it is right to carry on in this way, think how you would feel if you were counted like this. Given these criteria, here are some possible answers to the questions of this chapter:

- 'What can be counted?' Almost anything can be counted as long as it should be counted. Almost anything that is simple can be counted. Counting love, happiness, despair, aspirations, opinions, feelings, beauty, evil and good are much more difficult. However, there are researchers who do attempt to count things which add up to issues, such as morality. Interestingly there is a current surge in interest in economics in counting 'happiness' (Dorling and Ward, 2003).

- 'What should be counted?' What matters to people and does not harm them in the counting. As an example, consider the current proposal that the ethnicity of babies should be counted upon birth registration in Britain. In other words each child's parents should be asked what they consider the most appropriate label for their newborn baby to be. Could being labelled by their parents be harmful to a child in the future? Possibly it could. Many people are shocked to find out later in life they have been adopted, or that their father is not named on their birth certificate, why then should it not be expected that some people will be harmed in the future when they find out how their parents chose to label them in the past?

- 'How does one measure?' To measure is to compare. Again, the answer to 'how' is carefully and considering that you too might be measured in the way you are proposing to measure. Take the statistic above that in about 250 wards out of over 10,000 in the Britain, less than half the population are White Britons. The category used to make that measurement are 'wards' and this is not really a sensible division of space. Wards are areas designed to have roughly equal numbers of electors in local government, but they were not designed to analyse how society is changing spatially.

- Ethnicity as measured by the 2001 Census is presented as a sensible division of people. Is it? White Briton is presented as a sensible reference category. Why? And 50 per cent has some kind of meaning. Again, why? Note also that I've ignored ethnicity in Northern Ireland or questions of religion in Scotland for that matter. Every assumption can and should be questioned. However, for many people currently working in geography, asking questions is seen to be enough. Providing answers is a little more difficult but equally, if not more, important. If you really want to say that you think someone's interpretation is wrong, then try saying not only what is wrong with it, but how you would have interpreted the information yourself.

- 'How does one quantify?' To quantify is to turn experience into numbers, not necessarily to demean or reduce it. Turning millions of experiences into thousands of numbers and portraying the complexity of human life can enrich it as much as other forms of analysis reduce the meaning of experience. In short, what I try to do (and often fail) is quantify in ways which do not reduce my understanding, despite my need to reduce the variety of life to categories. Most importantly, do not quantify in a way you would not like to be labelled. For instance, if you would describe yourself as White, but not White British on a census form, or you think others might not, then don't mindlessly amalgamate these labels. It's a simple way to proceed, just try to imagine how you would feel, were you described as you might describe others.

- 'To what end?' This is by far the most important question. If you do not know why you are looking at data, if you are looking just to find a story with little idea of what may matter, you are very likely to make a mistake in how you then quantify, measure and count. You should know why you are interested in what you are looking at before you try and determine what is happening. Having looked, you may change your mind, but if you begin looking without thinking, you are likely to get into trouble: by producing results which make or imply assumptions that you would not want made about you, were you in that situation.

Where can one turn for more information on counting and measuring? I could point you towards books and papers, but unless you are a very odd individual with both plenty of time on your hands and access to such things, you are unlikely to follow those up. Instead there are three groups in Britain which are currently quite active in trying to answer questions in these areas and have active websites. I have also added a source from the United States on sources of information on poverty, inequality and globalization to try to mitigate my parochial obsession with one country. The four boxes below provide examples and links to much other work. The first is the Radical Statistics Group, over a quarter of a century old, and this group has produced many examples of the mis-use of statistics over the years of relevance to geography. The second is the Statistics Commission, established by the government in 2000 and largely but not completely transparent in operation. It is the official watchdog on statistics in the UK. The third is the Royal Statistic Society, established by charter in 1834, and this is the body that has monitored and used statistics about the population for the longest time in the United Kingdom. The fourth is a more *ad hoc* collection of sources, concerning issues of relevance world-wide.

Box 14.1   The Radical Statistics Group

http://www.radstats.org.uk/

> We believe that statistics can be used to support radical campaigns for progressive social change. Statistics should inform, not drive policies. Social problems should not be disguised by technical language.

Many of its publications are now available on its website, for instance, on poverty and inequality.

Box 14.2   The Statistics Commission

http://www.statscom.org.uk

This commission is currently chaired by Professor David Rhind, who began his career in geography. The commission has the following remit:

> The Statistics Commission has been set up to advise on the quality, quality assurance and priority-setting for National Statistics, and on the procedures designed to deliver statistical integrity, to help ensure National Statistics are trustworthy and responsive to public needs. It is independent both of Ministers and of the producers of National Statistics. It operates in a transparent way with the minutes of its meetings, correspondence and evidence it receives, and advice it gives, all normally publicly available for scrutiny.

Examples of its recent reports include:

INTERIM REPORT ON THE 2001 CENSUS IN WESTMINSTER

> The Statistics Commission will publish its interim report on the 2001 Census in Westminster on Thursday 23 October at 2 pm. Copies of the report will be available from the ground floor reception desk at our offices, 10 Great George Street, and in pdf format on the Commission's website: www.statscom.org.uk.

STATISTICS USERS' COUNCIL ANNUAL CONFERENCE

> The Statistics Commission is sponsoring the Statistics Users' Council Annual Conference: Is it possible to impartially monitor the Government's performance with the available statistics?

Box 14.3 The Royal Statistical Society

Part of the society's mission is to 'disseminate and promote the use of statistical data, where it would be of benefit to the broader community and advance the welfare of society in general'.

Its website can be found at: http://www.rss.org.uk/

Box 14.4 Poverty, Inequality and Globalization Resources for Researchers

- A website provided by academics associated with the University of Berkeley in California, at: *http://are.berkeley.edu/~harrison/globalpoverty/*. Examples of its content include links to 'anti-globalization' websites/books.
- Trade Observatory Website (formerly known as WTO watch). Centred on trade agreements and institutions, but a high quality website.
- Oxfam International. Oxfam has a very broad range of interests, but it produces some of the best quality and most balanced critiques of the current global trading system. Searchable website of their statements and publications. See in particular 'Rigged Rules and Double Standards: Trade, Globalisation and the Fight against Poverty'.
- ATTAC. ATTAC is an international network of academics and intellectuals. The website includes searchable archive of their newsletters.
- Project for the First People's Century. Rojas is an academic and consultant. His website contains an impressive set of links to papers, publications, data sources, and other relevant websites.

Discussion

Statistics are powerful. When an argument is backed up by numbers it tends to carry more weight. Often that weight is warranted. The work has been carefully carried out, assumptions thought through, implications considered. Arguments about society not backed up by numbers, unless eloquently presented, and often unless they play to the prejudices a reader already holds, are less likely to hold sway. Given this fact, it is sensible to count, measure and quantify if you know to what end. But remember, people will also attempt to do these things without thinking too clearly about what they are doing.

When next you read, 'another study shows . . . ', and it concerns something of interest to you, ask yourself, 'Is that true?', ask yourself, 'How do I know it is true?', ask yourself, 'Where did it come from?' (where did it *really* come from?), ask yourself, 'Who wanted me to know that?' (paid for it to appear and why); ask yourself, 'What are the alternative explanations, stories, spin and interpretation?' And then ask yourself, 'Could I have done better?' To bring this chapter to a close I will return again to the British census, but the one held in 1971 rather than 2001, and to what has happened to counting and measuring in human geography over that period.

The following excerpt is taken from a flyer that was given to all households in Britain over 30 years ago along with their 1971 Census form. It would be an interesting question to ask to what extent the 1971 Census was ever used to meet the aims it specified. Processing of the 1971 Census was delayed due to the complexity of handling so much data at the time. The final printed volume of 1971 Census data was not published until 1979. Only a few centres in the country could handle the unpublished data (much the same is true in 2001). In 1979, of course, a new government (led by Mrs Thatcher) was elected in Britain that saw the market rather than state planning as the main mechanism to determine who benefits. Were the people of Britain duped?

Why this census is so vital

The Census is about Britain. How many of us live here? How many children? Are we well or badly housed? And how many of us have cars? What kinds of jobs do we do? And how many of us are on the move, or have been, from one part of the country to another?

The Census is to get facts [*sic*]. Facts, good and bad, about Britain – now – in 1971 at the beginning of a new decade. For how can we make plans to improve Britain, to build houses, schools, hospitals where we need them if we are ignorant of ourselves as a people? We can't guess our way into the future by assuming that we're this and that when, for all we know, we may be nothing of the sort. The Census is to help us plan ahead from facts. (OPCS and GRO(S) flyer, 1971).

Conclusion: Ask Who Benefits

The 1971 Census was never really used to plan how Britain should develop in the 1970s. By the time it finally appeared, the government were no longer interested and a new census was on its way. When the 1981 Census was released, it revealed a country that had just been gripped by mass unemployment following deindustrialization and by riots which were often labelled as 'race riots'. When the 1991 Census was released, it showed that there were almost no coal miners left in the country but many more households with lots of cars. What it showed that was new and could not be predicted was the size of Britain's self-declared ethnic minorities. People were asked their ethnicity in 1991, partly because it was thought a mistake that they had not been asked in 1981, given the riots of that summer. At the time of the 1991 Census, it was said that these statistics had been collected to help identify and reduce inequalities between ethnic groups in Britain.

The censuses have become increasingly used in resource allocation (although, even for that, more up-to-date statistics are now seen as vital). Who then benefits from the release of the 2001 Census? Initially, the very first number released was a huge surprise. It told us that there were roughly a million fewer people living in the country than we had thought (which shows just how bad our surveys and data fusion techniques are for those who worry about surveillance!). The immediate beneficiary of this, however, will be the Treasury, as the areas where fewer people now live will, in a few years time, receive less money. These tend, although not exclusively, to be poorer inner city areas. In the short term, these places will be penalized for having lost their populations, and more will likely leave these areas as a result. Some local authorities have questioned the results and those which questioned most vigorously have been awarded a few more people by the counting authorities.

The big story that this chapter has used as an example is that whites are a minority in two boroughs. This story clearly benefits right-wing groups in the way it was told and those who wish to claim that Britain is being 'swamped'. It is very hard to show that the asking of a skin-colour-based ethnic minority question in 1991 benefited people assigned to ethnic minorities other than the answers being used to calculate police force recruitment targets. It was not at all expected (when the question was asked) that the police, largely exempt from the 1976 Race Relations Act, would use the census data, but nor was it expected that it would be used for little else of tangible benefit to those minority groups listed who then dutifully recorded their ethnicity. In the event, the 2001 Census is beginning to show that, in terms of their position in society, Black and Asian ethnic minority groups' lot improved markedly between 1991 and 2001. The censuses tend to record what has happened rather than be used as tools to help shape the future.

Who benefits from the implications of what else was released for consumption on Valentine's Day? It depends very much on how the figures behind the headlines are measured and analysed in the coming days, months and years. I am not pessimistic over this but it is not hard to show that very little good came of the first asking of this particular question in Britain. An established geographer, David Harvey, once said that 'mapping even more evidence of man's patent inhumanity to man is counter-revolutionary in the sense that it allows the bleeding-heart liberal in us to pretend we are contributing to a solution when in fact we are not' (1973: 144). I disagree. I believe far too few maps have been drawn, often far too badly with far too little forethought. As a result, people in Britain, including most teachers of geography in universities, have very little idea of simple facts such as what average incomes are in their district and region, that there are only White ghettos in this country, or how many students are studying at university (2 million) and what really determines their chances of entry (geographical location). Around the time the established geographer questioned the drawing of maps of inhumanity, many human geographers began to stop counting or measuring. Very few human geographers in Britain now count and it is worth briefly addressing the issue, asking whether this is because there is something implicitly wrong with counting.

I would claim that Harvey's sentence had more impact on research in human geography over the course of the past 30 years than any other. For those of you too young to remember the 1970s, 'counter-revolutionary' was a term of insult some people mainly working in what were then extremely exclusive universities used to annoy each other. For those too young to remember the 1980s and 1990s also, human geographers abandoning mapping did not hasten the revolution. Bleeding-heart liberals found other outlets for their worries using words rather than statistics.

Qualitative methods boomed in popularity partly as a means of over-coming the problems seen as inherent in quantitative approaches. All kinds of new ways of conceptualizing the world were tried out resulting in a plethora of 'isms' that undergraduate geographers are often now taught by rote. And almost no maps were drawn. The last comprehensive maps of the prevalence of death from various diseases in Britain, for instance, were drawn by Melvyn Howe in 1970.

There is nothing inherently problematic with social statistics compared to any other form of information collected about people, no matter how sensitively and participatory alternative forms of information gathering may be. I find there is something a little bit painful about well-meaning, almost always middle-class, academics discussing other people's lives with them in a sensitive and caring manner. Empathy only gets you so far, experience gets you further and you can't be taught it. The much blunter tools of the census form, birth, marriage and death certificates, unemployment and benefit records, tax records, death duties and school exam results, routine blood sample analysis (for prevalence of drug consumption) have the advantages of not noticeably influencing people's lives as you try to measure them. You do not leave the pensioner you just spent two hours talking to in their home with the abiding question of whether the reason her state pension is so low is because the state is funding research such as yours, nice as you may be. An ethical and moral case can be made as to why counting and measuring are extremely valid and responsible was of undertaking social research.

So who does benefit from counting and measuring, and to what end? The state is the principal beneficiary. Its ability to shape people's lives, encourage them to conform, guide them through education, bump them up with Sure Start schemes, encourage and cajole them to go to university, to get a job, get a mortgage, have kids, get married, pay their taxes, consume large amounts of goods, vote to maintain the status quo, retire quietly and die even more quietly (if possible) requires the collection and analysis of a huge quantity of statistics. That is why the state pays a quarter of a billion pounds for the census and billions more for the collection and analysis of many more numbers. Individuals benefit too, however. Without social statistics and the work that has been done to analyse them and popularize them, it is unlikely that the living conditions of poorer people in the UK would have been raised so that they almost always appear to be similar to those enjoyed by the majority a generation before (see Davey Smith et al., 2001 for more than two centuries of evidence that such research matters).

In countries that collect and analyse fewer numbers (and at times within the UK when this has been so) it is not surprising to find the social gaps between groups of people growing. The most socially surveyed populations in the world live in Scandinavia. The least socially surveyed live in the world's poorest nations. However, not all countries that survey their population in detail and not all researchers that study such information do so with the interests of people at heart. Ministries of Truth and police states abound. It is not the information that is good or evil, it is what you do with it and who then benefits. Mapping, counting, measuring and analysing may not help make the world a better place. However, given that human geographers have largely abstained from such practices in the past 30 years, I think it fair to conclude that not doing so has not helped much either (Dorling and Shaw, 2002). It is time to come in from the innumerate wilderness and start counting again.

ESSAY QUESTION AND FURTHER READING

As an illustration of the effective use of simple quantification in maps see Howe (1970). For mapping of the world, including Britain, the best example is still the project inspired by Michael Kidron's Pluto Press Project (Kidron and Segal 1984; Fothergill and Vincent, 1985). For mapping of the 1991 UK Census, the work of two researchers based in a Social Policy Department was most influential (Forrest and Gordon, 1993). In the USA, the *Atlas of Community Economic Health and Distress in America (1960–2003)* is worth studying.

REFERENCES

Atlas of Community Economic Health and Distress in America (1960–2003). Available on http://www.onenation.psu.edu/projects/atlas

Davey Smith, G., Dorling, D. and Shaw, M. (eds) (2001) *Poverty, Inequality and Health: 1800–2000: A Reader*. Policy Press: Bristol.

Dorling, D. (1999) Who's afraid of income inequality? *Environment and Planning A* **31**, 571–574.

Dorling, D. and Shaw, M. (2002) Geographies of the agenda: public policy, the discipline and its (re)'turns'. *Progress in Human Geography* **26**, 629–646.

Dorling, D. and Simpson, S. (eds) (2000) *Statistics in Society: The Arithmetic of Politics*. Arnold, London.

Dorling, D. and Ward, N. (2003) Commentary: Social Science, public policy, and the search for happiness. *Environment and Planning A* **35**, 954–957.

Forrest, R. and Gordon, D. (1993) *People and Places: A 1991 Census Atlas of England*. SAUS Publications, Bristol.

Fothergill, S. and Vincent, J. (1985) *The State of the Nation*. Heinemann, London.

Harvey, D. (1973) *Social Justice and the City*. Arnold, London.

Howe, G.M. (1970) *National Atlas of Disease Mortality in the United Kingdom*, revised and enlarged edn. Nelson, London.

Kidron, M. and Segal, R. (1984) *The New State of the World Atlas*. Heinemann, London.

Theory and Theorizing

Elspeth Graham

This chapter is about theory. It is not about any particular theory or theorist but about the role of theory more generally in geography and about the associated activity of theorizing. Most geographers, during the course of their undergraduate studies, are introduced to a number of different theories. In many cases the content of these theories relates to the subject matter of sub-specialisms within geography. Thus, geomorphologists will be familiar with boundary–layer theory and the theory of plate tectonics, population geographers with demographic transition theory, and development geographers with dependency theory. Other theories, with apparently wider remits, also permeate the consciousness of geographers. General systems theory, chaos theory, social theory and game theory, to name but a few, are all mentioned in the geographical literature and have become common currency for some.

It must be admitted from the outset that human geographers have shown a far greater enthusiasm for thinking about theory than have physical geographers. 'New' human geographies have evolved from theoretical reflection on the meanings of 'culture' or 'regions', and calls for (re)theorization in health geography (Litva and Eyles, 1995) and population geography (Graham, 2000) seek similar transformations for these sub-specialisms. Yet other geographers remain profoundly suspicious of theory, regarding theorists as the worst kind of armchair academics whose obfuscating language and abstract concerns so remove them from the empirical world that they can legitimately be ignored. It is thus timely to take stock and ask some difficult questions about the nature and role of theory in contemporary geography.

Not only does the notion of 'theory' have many layers and different interpretations but its role in the various traditions within geography is hotly contested. Contemporary geography is characterized by a kaleidoscope of theories that overlap and nest in complex ways. Reflecting on what Jay (1998: 29) calls 'the dynamic force field of theories' inevitably takes us into the difficult terrain of philosophy and thus to questions of epistemology (theories about how knowledge of the world can be acquired) and ontology (theories about what can be said to exist). Such questions are myriad and it would not be possible to rehearse them all in one short chapter. The following discussion is, therefore, both partial and selective. I have chosen to focus on only a few 'big' theories – including those of Darwin and Marx – as exemplars. Most of these have their origins in the work of non-geographers but all have influenced both theoretical developments within geography and the ways in which geographers think about theory. In questioning 'theory', I hope to convey that:

- Theory itself is a contested concept. There are different ways of thinking about theory and its role in intellectual inquiry.
- Thinking about theory is challenging and exciting. Theorizing is a creative activity requiring critical engagement, which, at its best, results in new ways of understanding the world.
- Thinking about theory is not an optional extra but a necessary part of doing geographical research because theory helps us to make sense of the world.

What Is a Theory?

There is considerable debate about how we should conceptualize 'theory' and the meaning of the term 'theory' is 'extraordinarily disunified and elastic' (Jay, 1998: 18). Its etymology can be traced back to the classical Greek word *theoria* suggesting a visually-based contemplation of the world from afar. Theories are thus what Einstein called 'free creations of the human mind'. In this sense, we all indulge in theorizing when we specu- late about why something occurred. Imagine the following exchange:

> *Robin*: But why did Tony Blair support the Americans in the war against Iraq?
> *Kathy*: Well, I have a theory about that. All this talk about weapons of mass destruction – it's just a diversionary tactic. What you need to under- stand is that the war is really about oil. George Bush is, after all, a Texan and ...

Whether or not we would be convinced by Kathy's theory, it is apparent that theory and explanation are closely associated in ordinary language.

Moreover, theories are open to judgements about whether they do indeed provide or allow sound explanations. Are Kathy's claims more than speculative fantasy? How do we judge? One answer is that we must see whether the theory fits the 'facts' of the case but this is not as straightforward as it might seem. For a start, we are faced with the problem of deciding which 'facts' count. George Bush is a Texan, but to what extent does this 'fact' provide evidence for the claim that the war against Iraq is really about oil? More generally, separating 'theory' from 'fact', as we shall see, gets us into all sorts of philosophical hot water.

Kathy's theory relates to a particular historical event and many scientists, and some social scientists, would not count it as a theory at all. For them, theoretical understandings must be built upon well-founded scientific laws. And scientific laws are universal propositions about phenomena in the (natural) world based on the careful observation and measurement of these phenomena. Boyle's law states that 'for a fixed mass of gas at a constant temperature, the product of pressure and volume is constant', and it is accepted as a scientific law because it is supported by empirical evidence and expresses a constant order. History, on this account, is atheoretical – some would say anti-theoretical – because historians generally shun a search for constant order and lack sound standards for 'testing' their speculative theories. In science, theories provide frameworks that help us to make sense of the world in terms of scientific laws. And the most famous of these theories, such as Einstein's theories of special and general relativity, subsume other theories and their laws, creating a hierarchy of theories of increasing generality or abstraction. When we think about 'theory', however, we must recognize that what *counts as* a theory varies among different academic traditions.

While Kathy's 'theory' is directed at the explanation of a particular event, we also commonly talk about theories in a more generic sense. In everyday speech, the term 'theory' is frequently contrasted with 'practice'. For example, something may be said to be 'true in theory but not in practice'. Theory, in this sense, tells us what we might expect to happen, whereas practice (or experience) encourages a sceptical attitude to such expectations. As a popular understanding of theory, this view owes much to science and is clearly reflected in the way that physical geographers in particular tend to think of theory. Three features of what I will call the traditional scientific view of theory are evident even from this brief example. First, theory is distinct from, but can be related to, practice; second, theories yield predictions (and explanations); and third, theories can be judged true (or false). These interrelated features require elaboration in order to introduce some of the questions facing scientists who hold this view of theory. Since scientists have attempted to assert hegemonic power over what is to count as a theory, and since physical geographers often claim to be earth scientists, I want to open up the discussion by turning first to understandings of theory in physical geography. These understandings were once common across geography as a whole, but today have been challenged by newer ones.

Theory and Context

Theory without history (or geography)

In a recent forum on methodology in physical geography, Hirschboeck (1999) notes a tension between 'theory development' (often equated with mathematical modelling) and 'practice' (often equated with field observation) in hydrology. She argues that a dissociation between these two pursuits can lead to dilettantism, with modellers developing theory for theory's sake and remaining apart from their colleagues in field measurement. She sees future promise in combining both, but more worries that 'there is rarely any hypothesis testing of model performance to evaluate the validity of the underlying theory' (ibid.: 701).

Theory, on this view, is macroscale and expressed in mathematical terms but the crisis arises because its predictions do not accord with the empirical evidence of flow processes collected in the field. Hirschboek's is a so-called positivist view of theory, one common in hydrology and physical geography more widely. What counts as a theory is a set of universal propositions about the behaviour of drainage channels that have been 'tested' against detailed observation of particular cases. The crisis identified in hydrology, or so it seems to me, can be broadened to the whole of geography for its roots lie in a fundamental tension between the universal and the particular (see Chapter 7 in this volume by Burt). The positivist account of theory emphasizes universality, thus treating historical time and geographical space as immaterial in science. Think of Boyle's law and its constant order. The expectation encapsulated in this law is that gases will behave in the same basic way whenever and wherever they are encountered; and, we may add, whoever might be 'testing' their behaviour. Theory in science thus becomes theory without history (or geography). If we are to accept such a positivist view of theory, we must face the serious question of whether geography could ever be either theoretical or a science.

Bringing context back in

Physical geographers who reflect on these matters recognize a tension between a scientific interest in the general and a geographical interest in the particular (Spedding, 1997). The problem for theorizing in geography is that the traditional scientific view of what counts as a theory appears to exclude both time and space, at least in the sense of historical time and geographical space. There are two main responses to this (beyond deny-ing the possibility of 'geographical' theory[1]). The first is to challenge the received view of scientific theory by arguing that not all theory worthy of the adjective 'scientific' ignores historical time. Theory in evolutionary biology might provide some ammunition here. Moreover, the argument might be extended to encompass the thornier issue of geographical space by appealing more generally to the time–space context. The second broad response would be an outright rejection of the traditional scientific view of theory as inappropriate to geography and the substitution of a different account of the nature of theory and its role in geographical understanding. Most human geographers have adopted this last strategy and long since abandoned any aspiration to be theoretical scientists in the positivist mode, although it is worth noting that the legacies of positivism are more pervasive than is often recognized. I will examine both these possible responses to the apparent incompatibility of scientific theory and geographical inquiry but, before I do, a word of warning: it is easy to slip into dualistic thinking that equates physical geography with 'hard' sci-ence and human geography with non-scientific approaches to theorizing. Indeed, the present discussion may even encourage such thinking. This would be unfortunate because, on the matter of theory, the division between physical and human geography is much more fluid.

Evolutionary theory   Charles Darwin is one of the heroes of modern Western science. He presented his evolutionary theory in *The Origin of Species* in 1859 and it would be difficult to exaggerate the influence of what became known as Darwinism on the understanding of the biological world over the next century. Nor were geographers immune; W. M. Davis's cycle of erosion, Friedrich Ratzel's views on the state as an organism and Harlan Barrows' call for geography as human ecology are a few among many examples of evolutionary ideas percolating into geographers' thinking (Stoddart, 1966). In these circumstances it might seem foolhardy to challenge the scientific credentials of Darwin's theory, although it is pertinent to note that the borrowing of Darwinian ideas by geographers has not had the enduring impact that the original theory still retains in biology.

Darwin's evolutionary theory provided an account of the origins of life that famously challenged creationism. Rather than a world, in all its variety, created by God several thousand years ago, Darwin argued that all life on Earth has evolved by a process of random mutation and natural selection in favour of variants that fit within their niche. To many of us now, this evolutionary explanation seems much more convincing and scientific than the creationist view. But why is this so? On what grounds do we prefer one theory over another? We might try to argue that our preferred theory fits better with the empirical evidence. Darwin's hypotheses entail that human beings evolved from other species. If we assume that primates like the ape are closest to humans, then evolutionary theory leads us to expect (predicts) that there must have been species intermediate in the evolutionary chain between humans and apes. And since Darwin's time evidence of such hominids has literally been unearthed. Evolutionary theory, it would seem, has observational evidence on its side.

The problem that taxes philosophers of science, however, is that such evidence does not seem to justify choosing evolution over creation because the creationists can use exactly the same evidence to support their theory. What if God created the world with all the supposed evidence of evolution already there? The discovery of skulls and bones of the so-called hominids could be seen as part of God's plan and taken as empirical evidence for creationism. Although your inclination may be to think that there is something wrong with this argument, it does highlight one of the difficulties of judging between competing theories that has challenged philosophers. This is the problem of under-determination, namely, that the empirical data are often insufficient to determine which of several theories should be (provisionally) accepted as true. Further, the relationship between theory and observational evidence may be especially problematic for those theories that take context seriously.

Classical evolutionary theory embraces a conception of time as process (a process of adaptation) and space as a general container, without specific geographical location (the ecological niche). Neither time nor space is constitutive of the mechanism of change; cause is separated from context. This provides only the thinnest view of context because the mechanisms of change remain universal. Process geomorphology and geographical climatology take context more seriously insofar as they explore differential ways in which universal processes play out on the surface of the Earth. Scale and scale-switching thus become methodological issues but the universalizing imperative of normative science retains its hold: 'our goal may be to produce methodologies that allow an interpretable, comprehensive representation across all spatial and temporal scales that is somehow simpler and more compelling than a representation that includes all the separate components' (Bauer et al., 1999). Whether or not this is possible, the temptation is to conclude that it is a fit goal for 'proper' science.

The philosopher Karl Popper's project in the philosophy of science began with a search for a demarcation between science and pseudo-science. At one time, he was critical of the theory of evolution because he thought the hypothesis that the fittest species survive was tautological, or true by definition (Ladyman, 2002). In Popper's terms, this meant that the theory was not falsifiable and thus not science. However, Popper reserved his main attack for the social sciences, especially the theories of psychoanalysis and Marxism, which he deemed pseudo-science. His critique of Marxism (Popper, 1945; 1960) challenged the claim, made by Frederick Engels at Marx's funeral, that Marx had discovered the *scientific* principles underlying the development of societies and raises questions about the nature of social theory.

Social theory

Marx's ideas about the structure of society (usually referred to as historical materialism) have greatly influenced theoretical thinking throughout the social sciences and continue to be developed by theorists in human geography. In particular, geographers such as David Harvey, Neil Smith, Richard Peet and Dick Walker have used the theoretical framework of Marxism to expand understandings of the structuring of space under capitalism (see Peet, 1991). Marx's historical materialism is only one example of social theory and has many variants but its importance within geography, its claims to scientific status and the parallels (and contrasts) that can be drawn with evolutionary theory in biology make this set of theoretical ideas specially apposite to the current discussion.

Any social theory is directed towards the understanding/explanation of the nature of society. The task assumed by social theorists is to identify, or articulate, the basic components of the social world and the mechanisms that drive social change. In this context, we can see how one set of theoretical ideas can spawn another, leading to new ways of seeing the world. For Marx, society has its roots in the material conditions of life; human beings satisfy their material needs through productive social labour and, therefore, of necessity enter into relations of production. The real foundation of society is thus its economic structure, on which is built a legal and political superstructure. Many philosophers of social science have criticized Marxist social theory as being deterministic, denying the significance of intentional human action in shaping society, and a similar criticism has been voiced by geographers (Duncan and Ley, 1982).

This directs us towards a further question of philosophical interest. Is there a fundamental difference between the social world and the natural world such that the former cannot be explained or understood in the same way as the latter? One argument is that human behaviour cannot be conceived in terms of constant order (i.e. there are no laws of human behaviour) because, unlike volcanoes or rivers, human actions involve intentionality and free will. In short, humans choose to act, volcanoes and rivers do not. If this is so, then it suggests that theories in social science might be rather different from theories in the natural sciences. In the absence of laws, predictions are harder to define and the whole edifice of scientific method begins to seem inappropriate. Somers (1998: 756) comments, 'It is obvious in the social sciences ... that the test of falsification – in which a single counter-observation can falsify a theory – is virtually never practiced.' She ascribes this absence to the fact that more than one theoretical construction can almost always be placed on a body of evidence. Further, social theories often make claims about unobservable entities, such as social structures, classes or market forces, for which there could only be indirect empirical evidence. Although theories in natural science also make reference to unobservables (think of gravity or electrons), their predictions are, arguably, more amenable to testing. The reason for this, according to Chouinard et al. (1984), is that while research in natural science deals with closed systems, human societies are essentially open systems.[2]

In the absence of a rigorous methodology for testing theoretical claims, or so the argument goes, theories become self-referential; theory guides observation which is, in turn, (mistakenly) taken to validate the theory. Another way of putting this is that observation is theory-laden. The possibility that no interesting observational descriptions are theory-neutral is, of course, as much a problem for the physical sciences as the social sciences but I raise it here to demonstrate the need for careful consideration of this issue in relation to social theory. If empirical evidence cannot decide on the validity of a given social theory in an unambiguous way, then what other grounds might there be for preferring one over the other?

The answer provided by Sayer (1984) proved an attractive option to some human geographers. Sayer argues for a 'critical realist' philosophy of science which contrasts sharply with positivism, most notably in its view of causation. Realism also provides us with an alternative way of warranting social theory. Rather than look to observational evidence for validation (the singular strategy of the positivists), realism emphasizes conceptual coherence and, above all, practical adequacy. Thus a theory can be accepted if it proves an adequate theory to live by. Whether practical adequacy provides a more secure grounding for theory choice than correspondence between theoretical predictions and observational evidence is debatable, but Sayer's realism introduces the possibility that there may be ways of justifying theories beyond the empirical 'testing' at the heart of positivism. Moreover, realism encourages us to theorize about underlying realities beyond the confines of the observable.

There are many theories across the social sciences that offer conceptualizations of society. Marxists theories view social relations as the product of material conditions and thus emphasize class. Feminist theorists focus on the fundamentally patriarchal nature of societies and have criticized Marxists for not giving equal weight to gender (Massey, 1991). Despite substantive differences in content, theorists in this social theory tradition share a common goal in the development of a general theory of society. The impetus for generalization harks back to the claimed scientific status of classical Marxism, and the search for such 'grand theory' has been identified with the modernist project of the Enlightenment (Barnes and Gregory, 1997). It is also a goal that has been challenged by those who doubt the capacity of any single theoretical framework to represent the (social) world.

'Post-'Theories

Philosophical questions concerning theory and explanation in the sciences and in the social sciences tend to be addressed separately in the philosophical literature. Nevertheless, when Thomas Kuhn published *The Structure of Scientific Revolutions* in 1962 the shockwaves were eventually felt across all disciplines. Kuhn stresses that the history of Western science is not one of a smooth and progressive development of theory; and practising scientists do not adjudicate theories primarily on the basis of a positivist logic of justification. Indeed, Kuhn argues that, in periods of 'normal' science, anomalies are often blamed on poor instrumentation, treated as an invitation to amend the theory in order to accommodate the observation, or swept under the carpet. Further, in moments of scientific 'crisis', the same piece of evidence can assume an entirely different

significance. Rather than an orderly sequence of conjectures and refutations, science experiences a revolution in which one scientific 'paradigm'
is replaced by another.[3] That scientists were not behaving in the way that
textbooks on the scientific method said they did apparently came as a
revelation, but it is Kuhn's central thesis that has caused the greatest
consternation for he maintained that scientific change – from one 'paradigm' to another – cannot be properly understood without taking account of its social and historical context. As Hollis (1994: 85) observes,
Kuhn's thesis 'threatened to put paid to the whole Positivist programme
by showing that science depended on elements which had no possible
place in the Logical Positivists' scheme'.

The historicity of science identified by Kuhn has inspired a reinterpret-
ation of the nature of scientific theorizing. Donna Haraway (1991) uses
the term 'situated knowledge' to encapsulate this new understanding
which stresses social construction and embodiment. The traditional conception of scientific practice, she argues, relies on the illusion of a 'god
trick', or view from nowhere. Disembodied science, though, is impossible
and thus knowledge is always a view from somewhere – partial, incomplete, embodied, situated. This is a powerful critique from feminist
cultural studies of the received view of theory and science and one that
has encouraged the 'cultural turn' in contemporary geography. Along
with the postmodern challenge to the meta-narratives of grand theory
(see Chapter 10 in this volume by Curry), it opens up other possibilities
for the ways in which the nature and role of theory might be understood
and allows the refashioning of the practice of theorizing.

New theoretical understandings of 'texts' serve well as an exemplar.
Texts are about communication and may take several forms, including
the printed word, film and music. Academic books, for example, communicate the 'findings' of researchers through the conventions of language. Landscapes too are susceptible to textual interpretation. 'Reading'
a text, or so many literary theorists claim, involves decoding its meanings
and thus communication is not as unproblematic as is sometimes assumed. Hubbard et al. (2002: 125) state: 'When subject to critical interpretation, texts of all kinds begin to reveal partial, simplified and
distorted representations of people and place, often shot through with
notions that serve to reproduce social inequality.'

Texts are social productions and may also be seen as constitutive of
larger discourses, characterized by Barnes and Duncan (1992: 8) as
'frameworks that embrace particular combinations of narratives, concepts, ideologies and signifying practices, each relevant to a particular
realm of social action'. Communication between discourses breaks down

because words have no natural connection with referents outside the discourse. Put simply, language (and discourse) does not reflect the world, as in a mirror, rather, it gives us our world. Thus, the plurality of discourses produces many worlds. Discourse is a key concept in post-modernism since it removes one of the central tenets associated with modernist science, namely, the presumption that there could be a neutral language of observation.[4] This is a rich vein of theorizing, but two rather general implications of 'post-'theories are worth considering.

The first concerns how we are to understand the relationship between language and theory in the light of the postmodern crisis of representation. If writing theory is like writing worlds, then theoretical texts are as much prisoners of discourse as are other texts. They too are unable to appeal to a world beyond the discourse of which they are part. So how then do we decide whether to believe a particular theory or product of theorizing? One answer might be that judgements are made according to the prevailing conventions of the discourse. And, if, like discourses themselves, these conventions are not fixed but 'subject to challenge, negotiation and transformation' (Barnes and Duncan, 1992: 8), then the possibility arises that the grounds for accepting a theory will vary over time, as well as between (geographically situated?) language communities. Questions of who sets the conventions, how processes of transformation work and how individual language speakers relate to the structures of discourse then become relevant. Without an ability to stand outside our own discourse/s, however, it is difficult to know how such questions might be answered in relation to 'other' discourses. On this account, knowledges become relative (or relational) and culturally produced in a way that problematizes knowledge of 'others'.

Second, if language gives us our worlds and there is no world beyond language – or at least no world we can know – then the temptation is to 'play' with language thinking it will change the world. Without underestimating the power of words, there are surely dangers in ignoring the materiality of existence. I have no doubt that changing the way we represent the world can change our experience of it. The feminist questioning of female domesticity as part of a 'natural order' is a case in point. However, to put it (perhaps excessively) crudely, if we have no food we die, whatever language of representation we employ.

The thought that the world has a physicality beyond our representations of it has a common-sense appeal that is probably shared by (all) physical geographers and more than a few human geographers. Yet the 'reality' of the world, as distinct from our representations of it, seems impossible to establish, at least through empirical investigation. We cannot claim our theories tell us what the world is actually like because there is no neutral ground – no God's eye view – from which we could compare the two. If we retreat to the multiple worlds of relationality, however, how then do we make judgements about which theory to believe? And such judgements matter, for without them we are left with a diversity that 'unsettle(s) theories of social justice' (McDowell, 2002: 307) and renders political action problematic. Further, as Castree (2003) recognizes, the ability to judge 'better' or 'worse' theories has a heightened importance in the light of perceived environmental problems such as greenhouse warming and species extinction. Perhaps the pre-eminent theoretical challenge in geography today is to reconcile our conceptions of a material 'nature' with those of a relational 'culture'. This is a project that some geographers have begun in their rethinking of nature–culture (Castree and Braun, 2001) and it is an exciting, if daunting, one since it holds the potential to reach across, as well as beyond, the discipline.

Conclusion: Rethinking Theory

Theory provides a framework for our thinking but, even in the most positivist account of science, it is not something fixed and immovable. Indeed, the postmodern view of theorizing as a continuous process emphasizes the transitory, as well as situated, nature of theory. Even our best-regarded theories are only provisionally warranted and there is always the possibility that once-abandoned theories may influence future theorizing. Theories are imaginaries, creations of the human imagination, and constitutive of the way we understand the world. Rethinking theory thus changes our world/s and profoundly influences research practice. Without Darwin, the bones of past inhabitants of the Earth are not evidence for evolution. Without Marx, social (and spatial) inequalities lose their significance as outcomes of the internal logic of capitalism.

Debates about what counts as a theory, as we have seen, are debates about conventions that govern how theories are warranted – what is considered adequate evidence and argument, and how that evidence relates to the principal propositions of the theory itself. These conventions reflect how we understand 'observation', which is always more complex than a naïve gathering of the 'facts'. Further, conventions are contested since they rest on epistemological and ontological assumptions that are matters of philosophical uncertainty. In geography, the apparent clash between those convinced of the materiality of the world beyond

representation and those who emphasize the situatedness of all knowledges turns on a debate about what can be said to exist and how we can
acquire knowledge of it, in which even this dualism is subject to critical
scrutiny.

Theorizing requires contemplation, seeing connections in the otherwise
messy world of human experience. In this sense, theorizing entails 'a view
from afar', not from some Archimedian point but a reflexive self-distan-
cing that encounters a tension between reaching beyond particularities
and recognizing the diversity and difference of people and places (Gregory, 1994). Understanding nature/culture in all its variety is the life-blood
of geographical research, for explaining difference and diversity is geography's *raison d'être* (McDowell, 2002). Thus, the tension recognized by
Gregory has particular resonance across our discipline. Theorizing requires a critical engagement with all these debates, and without theory
geographers would have little of significance to say about the world.

ESSAY QUESTIONS AND FURTHER READING

1 Do assumptions about the nature of theory in physical geography conflict
   with a recognition that geographical context matters? Spedding's (1997) argument for reinventing geomorphology provides some support for an affirmative answer. Ken Gregory (2000: Chapters 1, 3) summarizes recent (post-
   positivist?) developments in physical geography, as well as outlining the
   positivist approach in science. However, note the tension between the general
   and the particular reflected in the discussions of Hirschboeck (1999),
   Meadows (2001) and Hall et al. (2002). What assumptions do physical geographers make about the nature of theory? And how do they deal with geographical context? Massey (1999) takes the argument further by suggesting
   that both physical and human geographers should rethink their notions of
   'science' and space–time.
2 Do postmodern views of diversity conflict with theories of social justice?
   Derek Gregory (1994: 203–205) poses a similar question. McDowell (2002)
   discusses the implications of understanding diversity as a problem of/for
   theory. Both are key readings. Rather different solutions to the apparent
   conflict are offered by Harvey (1996: Introduction and chapter 12) and Howitt
   and Suchet-Pearson (2003). Harvey approaches diversity and social justice
   from a Marxist point of view that emphasizes class relations, whereas Howitt
   and Suchet-Pearson explore the idea of 'situated engagement' from the stance
   of postcolonial cultural geography. Note the way in which answers to this
   question are embedded within wider theoretical understandings. David Smith

(2000: Chapter 10) considers the 'postmodern dilemma' within a broader discussion of a geographically sensitive ethics.

NOTES

1 This response, though not indefensible, is unlikely to find favour among geographers, especially in the light of the close alliance between theory and explanation/understanding and the current enthusiasm for theorizing in some areas of human geography.
2 Physical geography may also be seen as dealing with open systems, raising similar questions about how theories can be 'tested'.
3 In Kuhn's view, paradigm shifts are rare occurrences. A paradigm is much more than a local theory. Newtonian physics is a paradigm, according to Kuhn, because it provided a broad picture of the world. However, Kuhn has been criticized for not offering a precise definition of the term.
4 The quotation from Hubbard et al. (2002) above demonstrates how difficult it is to embrace postmodernism wholeheartedly since the notion of a 'distorted' representation requires some external referent against which a representation can be compared.

REFERENCES

Barnes, T. and Duncan, J. (eds) (1992) *Writing Worlds: Discourse, Text and Metaphor in the Representation of Landscape.* Routledge, London.

Barnes, T. and Gregory, D. (1997) Grand Theory and geographical practice. In Barnes, T. and Gregory, G. (eds) *Reading Human Geography: The Poetics and Politics of Inquiry.* Arnold, London, pp. 85–91.

Bauer, B., Veblen, T. and Winkler, J. (1999) Old methodological sneakers: fashion and function in a cross-training era. *Annals of the Association of American Geographers* **89**, 679–687.

Castree, N. (2003) Geographies of nature in the making. In Anderson, K., Domosh, M., Pile, S. and Thrift, N. (eds) *Handbook of Cultural Geography.* Sage, London, pp. 168–183.

Castree, N. and Braun, B. (eds) (2001) *Social Nature.* Blackwell, Oxford.

Chouinard, V., Fincher, R. and Webber. M. (1984) Empirical research in scientific human geography. *Progress in Human Geography* **8**, 347–380.

Duncan, J. and Ley, D. (1982) Structural Marxism and human geography: a critical assessment. *Annals of the Association of American Geographers* **72**, 30–59.

Graham, E. (2000) What kind of theory for what kind of population geography? *International Journal of Population Geography* **6**, 257–272.

Gregory, D. (1994) *Geographical Imaginations.* Blackwell, Oxford.

Gregory, K.J. (2000) *The Changing Nature of Physical Geography.* Arnold, London.

Hall, K., Thorn, C., Matsuoka, N. and Prick, A. (2002) Weathering in cold regions: some thoughts and perspectives. *Progress in Physical Geography* **26**, 577–603.

Haraway, D. (1991) *Simians, Cyborgs, and Women: The Reinvention of Nature.* Routledge, New York.

Harvey, D. (1996) *Justice, Nature and the Geography of Difference.* Blackwell, Oxford.

Hirschboeck, K. (1999) A room with a view: geographic perspectives on dilettantism, cross-training, and scale in hydrology. *Annals of the Association of American Geographers* **89**, 696–706.

Hollis, M. (1994) *The Philosophy of Social Science.* Cambridge University Press, Cambridge.

Howitt, R. and Suchet-Pearson, S. (2003) Ontological pluralism in contested cultural landscapes. In Anderson, K., Domosh, M., Pile, S. and Thrift, N. (eds) *Handbook of Cultural Geography.* Sage, London, pp. 557–569.

Hubbard, P., Kitchen, R., Bartley, B. and Fuller, D. (2002) *Thinking Geographically: Space, Theory and Contemporary Human Geography.* Continuum, London.

Jay, M. (1998) *Cultural Semantics: Keywords of Our Time.* University of Massachusetts Press, Amherst.

Kortelainen, J. (1999) The river as an actor-network: the Finnish forest industry utilization of lake and river systems. *Geoforum* **30**, 235–247.

Kuhn, T. (1962) *The Structure of Scientific Revolutions.* University of Chicago Press, Chicago.

Ladyman, J. (2002) *Understanding Philosophy of Science.* Routledge, London.

Litva, A. and Eyles, J. (1995) Coming out: exposing social theory in medical geography. *Health and Place* **1**, 5–14.

Massey, D. (1991) Flexible sexism. *Environment and Planning D: Society and Space* **9**, 31–57.

Massey, D. (1999) Space–time, 'science' and the relationship between physical and human geography. *Transactions of the Institute of British Geographers* **24**, 261–276.

McDowell, L. (2002) Understanding diversity: the problem of/for 'Theory'. In Johnston, R., Taylor, P. and Watts, M. (eds) *Geographies of Global Change*, 2nd edn. Blackwell, Oxford, pp. 296–309.

Meadows, M. (2001) Biogeography: does theory meet practice? *Progress in Physical Geography* **25**, 134–142.

Peet, R. (1991) *Global Capitalism.* Routledge, New York.

Philo, C. (2000) Foucault's geography. In Crang, M. and Thrift, N. (eds) *Thinking Space.* Routledge, London, pp. 205–238.

Popper, K. (1945) *The Open Society and its Enemies.* Routledge and Kegan Paul, London.

Popper, K. (1960) *The Poverty of Historicism.* Routledge and Kegan Paul, London.

Sayer, A. (1984) *Method in Social Science: A Realist Approach.* Hutchinson, London.

Smith, D.M. (2000) *Moral Geographies: Ethics in a World of Difference.* Edinburgh University Press, Edinburgh.

Somers, M. (1998) 'We're no angels': realism, rational choice, and relationality in social science. *American Journal of Sociology* **104**, 722–784.

Spedding, N. (1997) On growth and form in geomorphology. *Earth Surface Processes and Landforms* **22**, 261–265.

Stoddart, D. (1966) Darwin's impact on geography. *Annals of the Association of American Geographers* **56**, 683–698.

The Uses of Geography

A Policy-Relevant Geography for Society?

Alisdair Rogers

There can be few disciplines more useful and relevant to society than Geography. It has a long-standing reputation for problem-solving research, coupled with a tradition of fieldwork and a suite of practical skills and technologies. Geographers focus on issues of everyday concern, but also often take a long historical view of such things as land-use and climate change. In fact, one of the most commonly cited reasons given by young people wanting to study geography as a degree is that it addresses the burning issues of the day in an unpretentious fashion, producing rational insights and solutions.

But if all this is true, why can one find such widespread complaint and self-doubt about Geography's policy relevance in the discipline's books and journals? In recent years there have been several high-profile debates and contributions that have chided geographers for their poor contribution to policy and problem-solving (Hoggart, 1996; Peck, 1999; Martin, 2001; Dorling and Shaw, 2002). Jamie Peck (1999: 131) comments that 'the relationship between geographical research and the policy process remains a fraught one', noting that 'human geographers have on the whole been conspicuous by their absence from substantive policy debate'. In broad agreement, Ron Martin (2001: 191) claims that the impact of geography on the realm of public policy has been 'disappointingly limited'. 'All washed up and nowhere to go', laments Hoggart (1996). Are such opinions simply a matter of academic self-laceration or do they conceal a more serious set of problems in the relationship between geographical research and matters of social concern and public policy?

The aim of this chapter is to examine the relationship between geography and public policy. This interface has an important history, one that puts current anxieties into perspective. The chapter starts by outlining this history, including the so-called 'relevance' debate in human geography and the supposed lack of contact between physical geography and environmentalism in the 1970s. It then considers what geographers do that does shape and inform public policy, focusing in particular on environmental issues. This section sets out the discipline's strengths and its potential. It is followed by a discussion of why things are not as straightforward as they might appear, which reveals the obstacles separating geographers and the policy realm. I suggest that not all the problems lie on the side of geographers. Finally, the chapter concludes by asking what we mean by being relevant. Perhaps the discussion is too narrow, seeing geography's contribution purely in terms of providing information and ideas to governments and other powerful bodies. What other ways of being relevant and useful are there, and to whom?

A Short History of Geography and Policy

The apparent paradox of a potentially useful discipline that does not actually deliver was also noted three decades ago by Coppock (1974). In his presidential address to the Institute of British Geographers, he observed that geographers' contribution to problem-solving had been growing steadily for 25 years, but that government did not seem aware of this. He was worried that unless the discipline was more active in putting forward good research-based solutions to society's problems, other disciplines would step into the breach instead. In a remark that indicates how far university geography has changed, Coppock expressed concern that geographers had historically concentrated too much on teaching and not enough on research. But he did not think that these were insurmountable problems, and he was bullish about geographers' potential to serve society. Anyone reading his address 30 years later might be struck by how little has changed.

Coppock's views were part of a wider development that took place in the early 1970s that has come to be known as the 'relevance debate' (Johnston, 1997; see also Pacione, 1999). There had been several years of social upheaval and political unrest in the West, including urban riots, anti-war protests, the feminist movement and student revolts. Against this background, a number of (largely human) geographers attacked what they saw as the discipline's conservative and narrow-minded condition, calling for greater attention to such 'relevant' issues as poverty, inequality, Third World development and racism. With hindsight, it is clear that these issues had been relatively neglected. Nor was the failing confined to human geographers. Despite the upsurge in public concern for the environment, starting in the 1960s and including the first Earth Day in 1971, there was little interaction between physical geographers and environmentalism (Simmons, 1990). Simmons suggests that ecologists were quicker to respond to environmental anxieties than geographers, who may have been deterred by the aura of pseudo-science surrounding much early interest in this area. Others argued that physical geography was too preoccupied with mechanistic and reductionist explanations of processes and landscapes to tap the more holistic and historical sensibility of environmental science (Newson, 1992; see Chapter 5 in this volume by Harrison). Newson also speculates that physical geographers were too interested in apparently pristine environments, free from human influence, to fully engage with the ecological crisis.

William L. Graf (1992) illustrates the complicated history of the changing relationship between science and public policy with regard to the rivers of the Western USA. He describes the period 1900–30 as one of 'policy without science', where hydraulic engineering projects were undertaken without fully understanding their consequences for the landscape. Starting with the New Deal, between 1930 and 1950 Graf describes a 'science for environmental control', when there was a close relationship between hydrology, geomorphology and public policy. This led to more rational river management. The high point of geographical (and geological) involvement in river policy came between 1950 and 1970, when large-scale experiments were conducted on catchments, involving Arthur Strahler, Luna Leopold, Stanley Schumm and others. Even then, however, the US Geological Survey tried to ignore research that did not fit their preconceived ideas. Since 1970 Graf has identified an era of 'science for impact assessment', during which the critical mass of geomorphologists and hydrologists was broken up, and research fragmented among different universities and centres. Research funding shifted to issues such as water quality rather than more basic processes. The proliferation of agencies with responsibility for water management and land-use issues has made the relationship between science and policy much more complicated. Economic issues loom larger. Graf concludes that researchers and decision-makers are now 'uneasy partners' (1992: 17), suggesting that this relationship came under pressure from changes on both sides, not just from scientists alone.

Set against the standards of the early 1970s, there is no doubt that Geography's involvement with major social and environmental issues is now very much greater, and more based on research rather than just education. Modern-day critics may have forgotten this earlier history. But the relationship between what geographers do and what society might ask of them has never been straightforward. As Graf's study of US rivers shows, there is no progression from an irrelevant past to a relevant present, nor the reverse, a decline from a useful past to a useless present. Moreover, the relationship involves two parties, the scientific community of geographers and the policy community, both of which are subject to changing pressures and priorities.

Geography for Public Policy

Geography has undoubted strengths as a policy-relevant discipline, with a track record of applied research and practical solutions. But what exactly is it that geographers do that distinguishes it from related sciences such as engineering, ecology, sociology, or economics? Many authors have tried to spell out this distinctive contribution (see, for example, Cooke, 1992; Pacione, 1999; Massey, 2001). Although there is unlikely to be complete unanimity, there are at least six features of Geography that enable geographers to have positive effects on public policy. I have chosen the features outlined below because they can be found in both Physical and Human Geography.

In an era of Big Science, there is much focus on global processes and systems, including the atmosphere and oceans, their interaction, geo-chemical cycles, and biodiversity. Such research often involves incredibly large spatial and temporal data sets, and increasingly turns to the potential of e-Science, defined by UK's Department of Trade and Industry as: 'Science increasingly performed through distributed global collaborations enabled by the Internet, using very large data collections, terascale computing resources and high performance visualizations.'[1] Among such projects is one called climateprediction.net, which in 2004 ran the world's largest climate prediction experiment using thousands of home computers. Geographers are involved in this project, and others in climatology and climate prediction, usually alongside scientists from other disciplines (Liverman, 1999). But Geography's particular strength lies more in understanding the regional consequences and making regional predictions of such global models, for example producing river and coastal flooding scenarios (Bray et al., 1997). In temporal terms, Cooke (1992) advocates an 'historical imperative' for Geography. This is a focus not on the immediate present or on very long timescales, but on the neglected domain of the recent past, where human and physical systems interact, and where, for example, geomorphological or hydrological data can be supplemented by historical records. At the scale of regions and centuries, human and physical factors interact to complicate the pictures provided by more mathematical models. It is a scale where geographical research provides much-needed perspective to policy-making.

The second feature of Geography that informs policy-making is an insistence on the relevance of context. Geographers are generally aware that universal explanations or policy prescriptions don't work well – one size does not fit all. Theories, explanations, models and plans that work in one part of the world do not necessarily travel to another. Peck (1999) distinguishes between 'shallow' policy researchers who aim to smooth the transfer of policy solutions from one place to another, and 'deep' researchers who are more aware of locally embedded solutions. Economists are typical of the former, geographers of the latter. Trudgill and Richards (1997) contrast the policy world's preference for generalization with environmental scientists' sensitivity to context. Furthermore, they caution that policies devised for the large scale need not be successful at smaller scales. The liming of northern Swedish lakes in an attempt to redress the supposed damage caused by acid deposition is a good example of a flawed policy (Bishop, 1997). The action failed to recognize that there were regional variations in background acidity. Urban or inner city policies that fail to appreciate that the particular mix of disadvantage and decline varies from one city to the next are likely to fail. Human and physical geographers have shown a consistent appreciation of context-dependence, and this provides an essential corrective to the over-generalization of policy.

Third, Geography combines insights and methods from both the social and natural sciences, and provides an integrated approach to environmental problems. Although this point has been repeated so often it is in danger of becoming a hollow cliché, it nonetheless bears repeating (see Chapter 2 in this volume by Viles). Cooke calls this the 'institutional imperative', identifying a potential weakness between environmental advice and managerial decision-making: 'Too often, scientists fail to understand the complex and restricting institutional contexts of their research, and managers fail to appreciate the complexity and limitations of environmental data' (1992: 138).

The proximity of social and natural scientists in departments of Geography, and their routine interaction, diffuse a greater awareness of both sides of this equation. Human and Physical geographers share a sense of complexity, feedback, context-dependence and non-reductionist understandings, elements that are vital to policy science in environmental issues.

Geography has a long tradition of fieldwork, a practical and personal involvement with the objects of study – whether wetlands or neighbourhoods. Collecting cores and samples oneself or speaking to workers and residents first-hand are essential aspects of any investigation. Ronald Cooke (1992) terms this 'the landscape imperative', the deployment of field-based skills to observe, explore, and monitor real places. The landscape provides clues to geographers about how processes are inter-related and why contexts matter. Cooke, for example, describes how close observation of desert stone pavements revealed that they were sites of deposition as well as wind erosion. This undermined the assumption that they were intrinsically infertile features, and alerted geographers to how easily they might be disrupted, for example, by tracked vehicles during the First Gulf War. Contact with the human subjects of policy-research is often a necessary corrective to the kind of depersonalized and abstract models of human behaviour that can be generated from the office computer. The increasing popularity of various forms of participatory research not only allows a better understanding of people's lives from the inside, but enables researchers to involve the subjects of inquiry in the policy process itself (see the contributions to Limb and Dwyer, 2001). Although there is now an overdue critical analysis of the politics and practices of fieldwork, revealing its power relations and ethical considerations, it remains a valued skill within the discipline.

Fieldwork is closely related to a range of other skills, techniques and methodologies that constitute the geographers' tool-kit. Long-established skills such as surveying and cartography have been transformed and expanded by a range of technological innovations. These include digital information, remote sensing, Geographical Information Systems, automated cartography, and spatial modelling. Now often described under the headings of geocomputation or GIScience, the capabilities to analyse, represent and communicate geographical data have become extraordinarily powerful (McDonnell, 2003). Orford et al. (2003) outline the exciting possibilities that scientific visualization holds for the traditional geographical concern with cartography. One of the problems of connecting science and policy is communication, and the new generation of interactive mapping promises to enable geographers to convey their findings and insights more effectively.

The sixth and final feature of Geography that makes it useful is more nebulous and easily overlooked. The discipline was founded in nineteenth-century European universities to promote geographical education and awareness among the population. This was not confined to the

Visual Analysis - Crux,

university lecture hall or schoolroom, but often involved the lecture theatres of the national geographical societies and the meeting places of church groups, provincial societies and working-class clubs. The role of disseminating geographical knowledge is now more likely to be performed by magazines, television and websites (how many other disciplines can claim their own TV channel, National Geographic?). Although such media are usually scorned by professional geographers for being shallow and popularizing, they also communicate scientific ideas about environmental issues in an accessible way to the general public. Henderson-Sellers (1998) argues that the ethical communication of science, is 'very difficult'. Using the science of climate change as an example, she shows how poor reporting in the media creates uncertainty and ignorance. Here she finds a 'valuable role for geographers' to engage in more effective dissemination of scientific findings and their related implications. An informed citizenry is indispensable to adequate policy formation.

This is a select list of the things that geographers are already doing that contribute to public policy. Expertise in spatio-temporal scale and context, an understanding of the integration between human and physical geography, a skills base of fieldwork, cartography, remote sensing and spatial modelling, and a long-standing concern for effective communication, form a significant armoury. What is there to worry about therefore? In the next section I will examine why things are not as straightforward as they might appear, by focusing on the obstacles between Geography and policy.

What Divides Geography and Policy?

To the extent to which there is a problematic relationship between Geography and policy, it can be discussed under two headings. First, there are internal features of the discipline, widely shared with other sciences, that inhibit the involvement of geographers in relevant work. Second, there are obstacles in the relationship between the two communities. I will say less about the policy realm itself, although its limitations will be evident from the discussion.

There are many hierarchies in the world of knowledge, although they are not necessarily defensible or logical. In one hierarchy, physical and natural sciences are elevated above the social sciences and humanities. In another, formal and abstract disciplines that rely upon quantifiable statements are deemed more important than knowledges based upon interpretation, understanding or qualitative judgements. A third hier-archy places pure or basic science above applied knowledge, and this is found as much in Geography as elsewhere: '[t]here is still a widespread view that policy study is somehow intellectually inferior to the "higher" pursuit of "theorizing" ' (Martin, 2001: 198).

In fact, K.J. Gregory outlines a range of different kinds of research distinguished by their level of direct involvement and immediate applic-ability. Pure or 'blue skies' research is 'not specifically related to envir-onmental problems and not profitable in the current state of knowledge or technological development' (2000: 199). It might involve speculation or exploration about matters with no obvious utility and is usually justified on the grounds that it may eventually prove useful. If applicable, Gregory describes this as 'grey skies' research. This can be distinguished from applied research, defined by Pacione (1999: 3) as 'the application of geographical knowledge and skills to the resolution of social, economic and environmental problems'. A simple contrast can be made between pure research which aims to develop theory and concepts, and applied research which uses existing theories to work on practical problems. Gregory also suggests that geographers engage in planning, management and sustainability activities, which are more hands-on and less concerned with research itself.

One might think that applied and problem-solving research would be highly valued, but in the realm of science and universities this is not always the case. This is for a number of reasons. First, it is often assumed that applied research, for example, consultancy, is less intellectually demanding or rewarding than more theoretical studies. Second, there is a concern that research undertaken on behalf of clients compromises the independence or autonomy of the researcher. In the standard model of science, research is supposed to be as uncontaminated as possible by outside influences as a guarantor of its objectivity. The ideal of university science is to publish findings and make them as accessible to as many people as possible. Work that appears in widely cited international jour-nals enhances the reputation of the geographer. But research undertaken for a client may be constrained in terms of publication. With reference to his consultancy work in environmental geomorphology, Coates (1990) admits that there are constraints in terms of lack of flexibility, short timeframes and confined research sites. In his view, these are balanced by the satisfaction of working on real problems and the potential to earn financial rewards, although the latter is still regarded with suspicion among the academic community. Finally, practical work for outside agencies is not a secure source of funding. It is known as 'soft money'.

Even in the top US universities, earned income from patents and consultancies is not usually enough to cover departmental costs.

There is a growing trend for university departments of Geography to set up separate and sometimes inter-disciplinary research units to carry out consultancy or policy-relevant work. GMAP, created by academics from Leeds School of Geography to supply services to retailing companies in 1983, proved so successful that it was acquired by the Skipton Building Society Group. A good example of a multi-disciplinary venture is Environmental Scientific Services, founded in 1986 at University College London. It conducts environmental monitoring for UK clients.[2]

The higher status accorded to pure over applied science has been reinforced in the UK by the Research Assessment Exercise (RAE). This periodic audit of all university research is used to rank departments and universities and then allocate public funding to research. The principle of allocation is that top-ranked departments receive most funding. Although there are several criteria involved in the assessment, the gold standard is regarded as research published in international peer-reviewed journals such as *Nature* or *Journal of Climate*. The findings of applied research, sometimes described as 'grey literature', are not so highly regarded (Peck, 1999). Therefore, there are strong career pressures not to engage in policy-relevant research that does not result in journal publications.

In many ways the distinction between pure and applied research is artificial. The insights of one can be readily transferred to the other. New techniques and instruments can be devised for applied research that inform basic science. Leopold's uniqueness method for landscape quality came out of his research for the Federal Power Commission on applications to build an HEP dam on the Snake River, Idaho, for example (Gregory, 2000). Applied studies can also test theories. But, as Peck observes, the distinction is also buried deep within the core values of western science, which rank detachment above involvement, clean work above dirty, mental labour above manual and pure motives above financial ones. It is therefore one of the most inhibiting factors in translating the potential of Geography into policy relevance.

The difference between pure and applied science also enters the relationship between the two realms or communities of geographers and policy-makers. Trudgill and Richards (1997) describe how this interaction can be initiated by one side or the other, giving rise to two contrasting models of environmental science and management. In the 'science-led view', the sequence begins with an understanding of the basic environmental processes and devised policies based on it. In the 'policy-led view', the process starts from an identification of social ideologies and processes and then devises policies, taking into account social constraints. Only when these are implemented are physical geographical constraints considered. Put this way, one can see that there are two different balances of power. In the first, geographers are trusted to follow their own lines of inquiry. In the other view, geographers must fit their work into pre-existing priorities over which they have less sway. But it is the policy-led view that is increasingly advocated, with consequences for fundamental research.

If Geography is only found at the downstream end of the relationship, then it can do little more than record or evaluate outcomes. A more critical kind of Geography would question 'the parameters, presumptions and promises of policies, rather than just their outcomes' (Peck, 1999: 133). Doreen Massey (2000; 2001), among others, has forcefully argued that government's power to set the agenda prevents the discipline's full involvement. She is particularly critical of the UK's thinking on regional policy, which appears to ignore Geography's substantial contribution. But her solution is not for geographers to sulk, but to engage more by making connections with the network of policy-makers, opinion-formers and politicians. In other words, geographers should be less timid in their relations with the policy realm and more confident about shaping the upstream end of the policy–science sequence.

Any desire to be relevant may be confounded by the increasing proliferation of public bodies and agencies which constitute a bewildering policy context. This includes international and regional organizations, such as the European Commission, as well as national and local government agencies and non-governmental organizations of various types. A hallmark of the neo-liberal state is the distribution of governmental roles and services across a range of often *ad hoc* institutions, blurring the lines of responsibility and accountability. At the same time, as Banks and Mackian (2000) emphasize, the emergence of multi-level governance does create new openings for policy-relevant work. Based on their own involvement in UK Health Action Zones, they advocate a closer involvement with local policy contexts.

In addition to these institutional obstructions, there are differences between geographers and policy-makers that might well be thought of as cultural. Here we might include the different timescales with which each community operates. Policy-makers often require clear answers delivered to tight deadlines, while scientists are more used to a longer perspective. The language and terminology used by geographers may be unintelligible to politicians, lay persons or civil servants. This is not simply a matter of jargon, but also what Martin (2001) dismisses as fuzzy notions, supposedly analytical concepts that have no real meaning. He singles out 'embeddedness' and 'flexible specialization' for rebuke. From their perspective, geographers often despair that policy-makers want dumbed-down analyses. It is often believed that if you want anyone to take your research seriously, it must be expressed in no more than eight bullet points on one side of a piece of paper. The complexities of most geographical systems cannot be represented this way. One should also not underestimate the problems policy-makers face. They are also members of large bureaucracies, the priorities and practices of which are subject to change, not least in association with the political cycle of elections. Immigration is a prime example of this: both Canada and Australia have pursued different objectives as the federal government has changed after elections. Time and resources are constraints, meaning that government has a limited capacity to receive information. Different departments of national and local governments may be in conflict with one another.

The relative lack of individuals who move between universities and the policy environment (although this is less marked in the USA), contributes to this mutual incomprehension. There are initiatives to bring the two communities together. The International Metropolis Project, for example, was founded by the Canadian federal government's Citizenship and Immigration Department and the Carnegie Endowment for International Peace specifically to bring together scholars, policy-makers, elected politicians and NGOs on the issue of immigration and cities. Established in 1995, it has devoted considerable effort and resources to enable public policy and academia to jointly address problems. Many Canadian geographers are active in Metropolis, contributing important research. But those involved would probably agree that bringing all the parties together has been a time-consuming effort.[3]

The relationship between what geographers do and what society, in the form of policy-makers, wants is therefore not as straightforward as one might imagine. The higher status accorded to pure research, although probably not as marked as it once was, may inhibit geographers from doing relevant research. There are institutional conflicts and obstacles, over where the initiative and funding comes from, who controls the final research and at what point in the policy process geographers can intervene. Finally, there are cultural differences between the two communities. Although these are obstacles, the proliferation of different kinds of policy body, including trades unions, charities, local authorities, and regional governments, is creating new openings. To some extent, the variety of options enables individual geographers to avoid compromising their political values. This is important, because lurking behind the reluctance of many geographers to engage with public policy is a distrust of government. This raises the final question considered in this chapter: to whom should Geography be relevant?

Who is Geography For?

In a blistering contribution to the 'relevance debate' of the 1970s, David Harvey (1974) asked, 'What kind of geography for what kind of public policy?' Rather than assume that Geography should be relevant by serving the state, he called on geographers to challenge what he termed 'the proto-fascist corporate state'. Inspired by Marxism, Harvey assaulted the state for its militarism, its obsession with rationality and efficiency, and the way it placed economic growth above social redistribution. What Harvey identified most clearly is that there was more than one way to be 'relevant', and that 'subservience' to the government of the day was not the only option. His intervention revealed a schism within those geographers seeking to be relevant, between those willing to work within the limits of public policy formation and those intent on confronting the state. This division still persists (Martin, 2001).

What options are available to geographers who choose radicalism over reform? To critics, such as Martin, radicals are frequently guilty of being impractical or inactive. Theoretical sophistication becomes an excuse for not doing anything relevant, he argues. Castree (1999) also notes, more sympathetically, that left-wing geographers have not made much practical contribution to making a better world. In a thoughtful essay on the relationships between activism and the academy, Nick Blomley (1994) captures further dimensions of this anxiety. Progressive or radical academics are often faced with the choice of doing work for politically marginal groups or trying to advance their own career by publishing in the 'right' journals. Even when actively involved in challenging government on behalf of tenants, road protestors or trade unions, for example, they may be reluctant to be seen to co-opt or speak on behalf of supposedly weaker parties. Paul Routledge's reflections on his involvement with Earth First! in its campaign against road-building in Glasgow reveal the same anxiety (Routledge, 1996). Trying to combine roles both inside and outside the university confronts activist-academics with difficult choices: do they try to lead or do they stay silent?; how committed are they to the cause, when they have a safe job to protect them?; can one be both a committed supporter of a cause and an objective researcher or witness? is writing about their experiences on the front line just a way of exploiting the efforts of others for their own careers?

There are many instances of geographers who are active outside the formal policy process and who do try to carry their political principles into their work (see the special issue of *Area* 1999, edited by Kitchin and Hubbard, and Fuller and Kitchin 2004). They protest against road-building, support community housing schemes, fight for homeless rights in courts, and any number of other causes. From physical geography, Martin Haigh (2002) describes how his personal commitment to Deep Ecology was manifested in a campaign for land reclamation in the Himalayas. Because information is now so critical to policy issues, geographers are well placed to contribute. Information politics usually involves finding, representing and disseminating alternative facts to official sources, something that geographers are well equipped to provide. But activism can also involve organizing skills, public relations, and networking, bolstered by access to resources such as libraries, computers, and photocopiers. Sometimes it means doing the donkey work, at other times it consists of providing expertise in court cases and public inquiries. Much of this work does not appear in print, and it is easy to think that activist geographers are few and far between. But the upsurge of anti-globalization protests since the 1990s, together with the continuing struggles of the feminist movement, the conflicts over conservation and land-use across the world, the fight for disability rights and a host of other causes are creating new openings for relevant Geography. As Kitchin and Hubbard (1999: 195) observe, however, 'the extent to which academically motivated research should seek to be (and can be) empowering and emancipatory' is still an open question. What is more certain is that there are many ways in which geographers can be useful to society, which can accommodate physical and human geographers, radicals and reformers, activists and academics.

Conclusion

Geography has a long history of usefulness, in times of peace and war, in contexts of imperialism and development. Looking back, not all would agree that these interventions have been to the obvious betterment of humanity. Harvey (1974) suggests that a legacy of racism, imperialism, and ethnocentrism leaves Geography with more to be ashamed of than proud of. The involvement of geographers with public policy has not, however, been either constant or uncomplicated, as Graf's account of

American river management shows (Graf, 1992). The paradox of an obviously useful discipline that has delivered policy-relevant research only inconsistently was observed 30 years ago and is still raised today. The discipline most certainly does have a range of theories, skills and insights that are particularly suited to conducting socially useful research, in human, environmental and physical geography. Concepts such as spatial and temporal scale, context-dependence, and the integration of human and physical systems are complemented by a good track record of practical field-based research, cartography, modelling and GIScience. The often overlooked roles of education and public information, bridging the communities of scientists, citizens and policy-makers, have a prominent position in the discipline. Most geographers would acknowledge the importance of teaching students as their major contribution to changing society (see Chapter 17 in this volume by Castree).

The explanation of this paradox lies partly in the range of obstacles or problems that separate geographers and the policy realm. The higher status accorded to pure science over applied work, something buried deep in Western science and ironically reinforced by government policies towards academia, remains one significant problem. Other institutional obstacles include the proliferation of levels of government and the concentration of geographers on downstream outcomes. There are also 'cultural' differences between academics and policy-makers that can only be bridged through persistent hard work. But beneath this is a more profound question. To what extent should geographers not only set the agenda of research, but choose to whom their work is relevant? One the one hand, there is research that assists the management of society and the environment, clearing up their messes without necessarily addressing the cause of the problem. A recent example is a collection of short essays by US geographers called *The Geographical Dimensions of Terrorism* (Cutter et al., 2002). Expertise in hazards, understanding risk, vulnerability and emergency planning, spatial analysis and the geopolitics of terrorism are brought together in a timely volume. Its lead editor wrote:

> As I watched the September 11th events unfold on television, it was obvious that the discipline could assist in the disaster response and recovery efforts, but more importantly, that it *should* take a lead role in guiding public policy in understanding what made people and places vulnerable to these and other environmental threats. (Cutter, 2003: 5)

For some, however, the more relevant questions will lie in what responsibility the USA has had for fomenting terrorism and instability, or why western societies have provoked such violent opposition (see the special issue of *Arab World Geographer* 2001). These geographers may use their talents in peace campaigns, protest marches and educating citizens to the unpleasant realities of the twenty-first century. For all the internal wrangling it generates, that the discipline accommodates both responses is one of its strengths.

ESSAY QUESTIONS AND FURTHER REFERENCES

1   Do you agree that the relationship between Geography and public policy is necessarily a fraught one? This is the main theme of this chapter, and most of the references listed below are relevant. But you could start with Peck (1999), Coppock (1974) and Massey (2001) who set out the main issues. A more critical perspective concerning human geography is given by Martin (2001) and Dorling and Shaw (2002), but do not feel that you have to agree with everything they write. Graf's (1992) discussion of US river policy and Liverman's (1999) account of climate change are more positive. You may have your own examples from other parts of the course you have done.

2. Is it possible for a geographer to be both a scholar and an activist? Nick Blomley (1994) asks whether one can be true to the values of academia, which might include detachment and objectivity, and at the same time be an activist or an advocate for a cause. There are political, ethical and personal issues at stake here. Start with the series of short articles in *Area* 1999 (see Kitchin and Hubbard, 1999) and the free on-line 'e-book' called *Radical Theory/ Critical Praxis* edited by Duncan Fuller and Rob Kitchin (2004), noting the different views taken by Don Mitchell in his chapter and most of the other contributors. For a rare discussion from a physical geographer, see Haigh (2002).

NOTES

1   The definition of e-Science can be found at http://www.e-science.ox.ac.uk/ and details of climateprediction.net are at: http://www.climateprediction.net/index.php

2   Details of GMAP can be found at: http://www.gmap.com. Environmental Scientific Services has a website at http://www.geog.ucl.ac.uk/ecrc/ensis.stm.

3   See http://international.metropolis.net/frameset_e.html. The Canadian regional centres of excellence in Vancouver, Toronto and elsewhere can be accessed from this site and feature examples of ongoing geographical research on migration and cities. I have benefited from Dan Heibert's reflections on Metropolis.

REFERENCES

Arab World Geographer (2001) Forum on September 11. *Arab World Geographer* **4**, 77–99.

Banks, M. and Mackian, S. (2000) Jump in! The water's warm: a comment on Peck's 'grey geography'. *Transactions of the Institute of British Geographers* NS **25**, 249–254.

Bishop, K.H. (1997) Liming of acid surface waters in northern Sweden: questions of geographical variation and the precautionary principle. *Transactions of the Institute of British Geographers* NS **22**, 49–60.

Blomley, N.K. (1994) Editorial: activism and the academy. *Environment and Planning D: Society and Space* **12**, 383–385.

Bray, M., Hooke, J. and Carter, D. (1997) Planning for sea-level on the south coast of England: advising the decision-makers. *Transactions of the Institute of British Geographers* NS **22**, 13–30.

Castree, N. (1999) 'Out there'? 'In here'? Domesticating critical geography. *Area* **31**, 81–86.

Coates, D.R. (1990) Environmental geomorphology. *Zeitschrift für Geomorphologie* Suppl-Bd **79**, 83–117.

Cooke, R.U. (1992) Common ground, shared inheritance: research imperatives for environmental geography. *Transactions of the Institute of British Geographers* NS **17**, 131–151.

Coppock, J.T. (1974) Geography and public policy: challenges, opportunities and implications. *Transactions of the Institute of British Geographers* **63**, 1–16.

Cutter, S.L. (2003) The vulnerability of science and the science of vulnerability. *Annals of the Association of American Geographers* **93**, 1–12.

Cutter, S.L., Mitchell, J.T. and Wilbanks, T.J. (2002) *The Geographical Dimensions of Terrorism*. Association of American Geographers, Washington DC.

Dorling, D. and Shaw, M. (2002) Geographies of the agenda: public policy, the discipline and its (re)turns. *Progress in Human Geography* **26**, 629–646.

Fuller, D. and Kitchin, R. (2004) *Radical Theory/Critical Praxis: Academic Geography Beyond the Academy?* Praxis (e)Press, Vernon and Victoria, BC (available online at http://www. praxis-epress.org).

Graf, W.L. (1992) Science, public policy, and western American rivers. *Transactions of the Institute of British Geographers* NS **17**, 5–19.

Gregory, K. (2000) *The Changing Nature of Physical Geography*. Arnold, London.

Haigh, M.J. (2002) Land reclamation and Deep Ecology: in search of a more meaningful physical geography. *Area* **34**, 242–252.

Harvey, D. (1974) What kind of geography for what kind of public policy? *Transactions of the Institute of British Geographers* **63**, 18–24.

Henderson-Sellers, A. (1998) Communicating science ethically: Is the 'balance' achievable? *Annals of the Association of American Geographers* **88**, 301–307.

Hoggart, K. (1996) All washed up and nowhere to go? Public policy and geographical research. *Progress in Human Geography* **20**, 110–122.

Johnston, R.J. (1997) *Geography and Geographers: Anglo-American Geography Since 1945*, 4th edn. Arnold, London.

Kitchin, R.M. and Hubbard, P.J. (1999) Research, action and 'critical' geographies. *Area* **31**, 195–198.

Limb, M. and Dwyer, C. (eds) (2001) *Qualitative Methodologies for Geographers*. Arnold, London.

Liverman, D. (1999) Geography and the global environment. *Annals of the Association of American Geographers* **89**, 107–120.

Martin, R. (2001) Geography and public policy: the case of the missing agenda. *Progress in Human Geography* **25**, 189–210.

Massey, D. (2000) Practising political relevance. *Transactions of the Institute of British Geographers* NS **25**, 131–134.

Massey, D. (2001) Geography on the agenda. *Progress in Human Geography* **25**, 5–17.

McDonnell, R.A. (2003) GISystems, GIScience and remote sensing. In Rogers, A. and Viles, H. (eds) *The Student's Companion to Geography*. Blackwell, Oxford, pp. 167–172.

Newson, M. (1992) Twenty years of systematic physical geography: issues for a 'New Environmental Age'. *Progress in Physical Geography* **16**, 209–221.

Orford, S., Dorling, D. and Harris, R. (2003) Cartography and visualization. In Rogers, A. and Viles, H. (eds) *The Student's Companion to Geography*. Blackwell, Oxford, pp. 151–156.

Pacione, M. (1999) In pursuit of useful knowledge: the principles and practice of applied geography. In Pacione, M. (ed.) *Applied Geography*. Routledge, London, pp. 3–18.

Peck, J. (1999) Grey geography? *Transactions of the Institute of British Geographers* NS **24**, 131–135.

Routledge, P. (1996) The third space as critical engagement. *Antipode* **28**, 399–419.

Simmons, I. (1990) No rush to grow green. *Area* **22**, 384–387.

Trudgill, S. and Richards, K. (1997) Environmental science and policy: generalization and context. *Transactions of the Institute of British Geographers* NS **22**, 5–12.

Whose Geography?
Education as Politics

Noel Castree

If you're reading these words you're almost certainly a student studying degree-level geography in an English-speaking country. This chapter is probably on a reading list for a course you're taking on the nature of contemporary geography. Whether you're an undergraduate or a Master's student, the course is doubtless a compulsory part of your degree. You may not like this fact. Unless you're intending to go on to become a university geographer yourself, you may well think that the course is both boring and rather pointless. After all, who, you might ask (apart from people like me and your professors), really cares about such questions as 'Is geography a divided discipline?' or 'Is geography a science?' (the focus of Chapters 4 and 6 in this volume). Surely there are more interesting and relevant things you could be learning about – the kinds of things, in fact, dealt with in your other geography degree modules (such as why famines still occur in a world of food surpluses, why the Antarctic ice sheet is apparently collapsing or how to perform a Chi square test).

In this chapter I hope to persuade you that you'd be wrong to think in this way. Specifically, my aims are threefold. First, I want to make you reflect critically on the kind of geographical education you are receiving as a university student. If you stand back from all the different modules you're taking (including those compulsory ones you may not like!), what is your degree as a whole designed to achieve? By personalizing the question in this way, my second aim is to make you appreciate just how relevant the issues dealt with in a book like this one can be. For what could be more 'practical' than your education? And what could be more 'useful' than you spending some time reflecting on what the wider aims of that education are? Education is not just about the inculcation of knowledge (or at least it shouldn't be). Rather, education is part of the process through which we become the kind of people we are: it shapes our very *identities* as thinking and acting beings. This is, I shall argue, a deeply political affair. Indeed, it seems to me that education is politics by other means: it is anything but neutral. When I use the term 'politics' here I am not referring to the affairs of governments but, rather, to the fact that many social practices entail value judgements. These practices are not given in nature but, instead, reflect the values of those who engage in them. Accordingly, the third aim of this chapter is to give you the tools to understand the non-neutrality of your university (and, indeed, pre-university) education. *Choices* are made on your behalf about what you are taught and how you are taught. Likewise, whether you realize it or not, *you* make choices about what you expect from your university education. Yet how often do you think about them? Infrequently or never is, I suspect, the answer that applies to most readers of this chapter. Yet these choices determine the entire character of your geography education. Are they good choices? What values underpin them? And what are the aims of the education you receive on the basis of these choices?

These several questions explain the title I've chosen for this chapter – a title that, hopefully, has already piqued your interest. It's designed to suggest that the discipline of geography is a *contested* one at the level of both research and teaching. Professional geographers (like me) have struggled among themselves and with non-academic stakeholders over what geography is (or should be) about. This may surprise you. After all, academic disciplines are sometimes seen as rather civilized (even dull) places where research and teaching are quietly pursued – a far cry from the rough-and-tumble of, say, the public debates over whether and when the allied forces should withdraw from Iraq forthwith (debates which were headline news when this chapter was written). But nothing could be further from the truth. At the research level, human geography illustrates this well. In recent years, an array of new approaches – feminist, anti-racist, gay and lesbian and disabled, to name but a few – have called into question not only what human geographers choose to study but also how they conduct research. For instance, in her uncompromising book *Feminism and Geography*, Gillian Rose (1993) argued that human geographers (who, even today, are mostly men) have tended to ignore issues of direct relevance to women. More contentiously, she argued that the discipline's researchers tended to conduct research in a distinctively masculinist way: that is, they tended to value 'objectivity' and 'reason' over other (more feminine?) ways of knowing the world. In short, Rose was asking whether geography is a discipline about men, by men and for men.

Though these struggles over geographical research clearly impinge upon geography teaching, few in the discipline have considered how in any systematic way. Thus, if one looks at the discipline's main journal devoted to teaching issues – the *Journal of Geography in Higher Education* – one rarely finds any sustained discussions of the politics of teaching. Instead, one typically encounters essays on the nuts-and-bolts of pedagogy (like how to run a problem-based field-class). Rarer still are interventions like this chapter: that is, ones that challenge university students themselves (rather than those of us who teach them) to reflect upon the means and ends of their education. It's difficult to know why this is the case. In writing this chapter I hope, in some small way, to compensate for this relative inattention to a profoundly important issue: the issue of whose interests – yours or someone else's? – a geographical education should serve. Instead of just being passive consumers of higher education, I want to incite you to become active participants in determining the shape of your learning experience.

Education as Politics

In a book called *Teaching to Transgress*, the cultural critic Gloria Watkins (otherwise known as bell hooks) bemoaned 'the overwhelming boredom, uninterest and apathy that so often characterises the way professors and students feel about teaching and learning' (hooks, 1994: 10). In her view, both partners in the education process frequently forget what is at stake in their encounter (be it in the lecture theatre, the seminar room or, as in the present case, in the pages of a book). Misconstruing education as the simple transmission of information from one party (teachers) to another (students), these partners can fail to see the true importance of pedagogy. For Watkins, education is always life-changing for students – whether they realize it or not. This has three dimensions. *What* students learn decisively influences their post-university life-chances (for instance, if you can speak Chinese, then you have a head-start in getting a job with, say, a Western multinational firm seeking to expand its Far East operations). *How* students learn is also vital. For instance, the student who looks for a single, ostensibly 'correct' answer to everything is very different from one who is able to accept the world's complexities, ambiguities and paradoxes. Finally, education is life-changing because it is part of a wider set of experiences that, over time, constitute students' very identities. I made this point in my introduction, but let me now expand upon it. There's a well-known saying that goes like this: 'as the twig is bent, so the branch grows'. Along with a few other key things – such as the family and television – the education system has a major role to play in bending the twig that is a child, and in shaping the growing branch that is a teenager and a young adult. After all, by the age of 21 or 22 (the typical age of graduation from a first degree), most students in Western countries have spent some 80 per cent of their lives in full-time education. During this time, the knowledge that students assimilate is not simply 'added on' to fully formed characters – like icing on a cake or an extension to a house. Rather, that knowledge helps to mould students into certain kinds of people. Formal education cannot, in short, fail to shape the character of those who experience it.

In these three ways education is always political and always consequential. A sober recognition of this inescapable fact is, in my view, liberating for both teachers and students at all levels of the educational system. It means, in theory at least, that the what, the how and the why of teaching are always up for grabs. There is no one 'correct' set of things that students should know; there is no one 'proper' way of learning; there are no 'self-evident' goals of education. Instead, there are only ever *choices* about what to teach, how to teach and to what ends. This said, when these choices are made and accepted by a sufficient number of teachers, then they tend to become 'common sense'. In reality, then, the content, the manner and the aims of teaching tend to become 'fixed' for long periods of time in societies like our own. Watkins' book is an attempt to remind teachers (and their students) that things could be otherwise: that together we have an 'awesome responsibility' (hooks, 1994: 206) to reflect critically and frequently on what university (and pre-university) teaching is about.

I can bring these rather abstract observations to bear on geography in a particularly graphic way. In early 2003, one of the more respected British newspapers – *The Independent* – published a provocative article entitled 'Is geography brainwashing?' (6 February 2003). It focused on high-school rather than university geography, but is useful for my argument nonetheless. It claimed that geography teaching has become overly 'biased' in recent years in the UK. Instead of teaching useful skills (like map-reading) or basic knowledge (like the names of major cities and rivers), the article feared that geography teaching had become left-wing propaganda. To quote: 'Are geography classrooms places where students are now taught to bow before the altar of environmentalism, while learning that multinationals and Western governments are the devil incarnate?' Clearly believing that the answer is 'yes', the article goes on to imply that we need to get back to a form of geography teaching that is somehow objective and value-free.

Whether or not British high-school geographers are fed left-wing nostrums I shall let others decide. My more immediate concern is the article's belief that it is possible to disentangle 'political' from 'non-political teaching'. For isn't one person's propaganda actually another's truth? And aren't dualisms like fact versus fiction, reality versus rhetoric, truth versus bias often used to hide the fact that those who claim only to speak about the first side of these binaries are doing so to hide *their own* meddling in the fabrication and dissemination of knowledge? If some readers of this chapter are answering these questions with a confident 'no', then I'd point out to you that even 'facts', 'reality' and 'truth' are not always what they seem. This is true even in physical geography, which is often seen as more objective and scientific than human geography. A fascinating case in point is research done by David Demeritt (2001). Demeritt asks: What are the facts about major environmental problems of our time? This is, clearly, an important question because a plethora of countries worldwide are spending a lot of time and energy trying to mitigate these problems. Taking global warming as his focus, Demeritt argues that the facts about atmospheric temperature increase by no means speak for themselves. If they did, then the role of scientific researchers (like physical geographers) would simply be to carefully record these facts and then let the politicians decide what, if anything, to do about global warming. But there is, Demeritt insists, much more going on than this. Treating research scientists almost as an anthropologist would treat a foreign tribe, Demeritt examines the habits, the unwritten assumptions and the technical apparatuses that, together, determine how these scientists generate knowledge about something as big, complex and dynamic as the global atmosphere. His conclusion is startling: these scientists, he argues, must make so many simplifications, qualifications and short-cuts in both their temperature measurements and the computer models they use that it's ultimately unclear whether their 'facts' are fictions – ones that in no way constitute an objective reflection of what's really going on in the atmosphere – or whether their fictions are posing as facts. Accordingly, the 'scientific truth' about global atmospheric temperature trends cannot be (or *should* not be) reported in policy circles, classrooms or anywhere else in an uncritical way. This is emphatically *not* to suggest that scientists simply make things up as they please. But it *is* to say that scientific knowledge is more than simply a 'mirror' held up to nature.

The point is, I hope, clear enough: because *all* knowledge is at some level political, then *all* geography teaching is at some level political, *even when* it involves communicating supposedly non-political 'factual knowledge'.

Teaching always involves value judgements about what to teach and what not to teach; about what is worth knowing and what is not; about how to think and how not to think; about which skills are 'relevant' and which are not. I could go on, but you get the idea. There is no such thing as 'apolitical' knowledge, and your teachers always actively sift and sort the geographical knowledge they present you with. These teachers are, in effect, 'gate-keepers' who sanction and censure what you can know in the classroom or lecture hall or on a field-class.

If you accept what I'm saying, then two things follows. First, people like me have a responsibility to reflect upon the values written into our teaching practices. But, second, university students like you also have a responsibility to question the content, manner and aims of your higher education. Since, in my view, the second responsibility tends to be honoured in the breach, let me now suggest some useful tools for you to think critically about your own learning experience.

The Aims of a Geographical Education

It's no surprise if you rarely pause to reflect deeply on your educational experience. After all, you were compelled (by law) to enter full-time education from a very early age. For most of your life education has been part of 'the normal run of things'. What's more, your teachers are the ones who seem to have all the power: *they're* the people who decide what you will and will not learn once you've decided to study their subject. Speaking for myself, I entered university (and was the first in my family to do so) simply because (a) most of my friends did so; and (b) because I thought it would help me get a good job. I chose geography over other subjects because I'd excelled at it at high school and because I enjoyed it (and, let us not forget, there's *pleasure* to be had from learning). Finally, I chose my specific university (Oxford) because of its reputation. In fact, I was so in thrall to its prestige that I didn't look too closely at the content of the geography programme I'd be taking if I were fortunate enough to gain access to the university. In short, to the extent that I reflected on my university education at all, it was in a highly superficial way. I'm sure many readers of this chapter can relate to what I'm saying. So let us now try to reflect in a non-superficial way upon the kind of education you are getting as geography degree students.

I want to focus on degree-level geography not just because most of my readers are university students. More than this, degree studies are different to pre-university ones in a significant respect. The onus is typically placed on *you* to manage your own learning. There is (in theory at least) less spoon-feeding at universities. Lectures, lab classes, readings lists, etc. are designed to offer you a framework to, in effect, educate yourselves. This is why it's all the more surprising – and regrettable – that some students (and some university teachers) still implicitly adopt what Watkins (hooks, 1994: 5) calls 'the banking system of education'. Here, both academics and their students assume that the principal purpose of education is *training*. Like empty vessels, the latter expect the former to fill their heads with knowledge. Dutifully assimilated, the student's mastery of this knowledge is then 'tested' by their teachers in term-papers and examinations. But surely one of the reasons for being at university is to *think*: that is, to exercise judgement about the world, *including* judgements about whether what you're doing at university is worthwhile.

So what are you doing as a 'geographer'? At first sight, this is a difficult question to answer for two reasons. To start with, you're all in different geography departments worldwide with rather different syllabi. Second, geography as a whole is remarkably diverse: one can learn about statistics, glaciology, uneven development and drought to name but a few. So there's no 'essence' to geography, no timeless set of things that are researched and taught about (see Chapter 2 in this volume by Viles). Yet there are arguably some signals in the noise. Almost three decades ago, the German critical theorist Jürgen Habermas (1978) argued that Western societies were characterized by three knowledge types. The first of these was 'instrumental-technical' knowledge. This was 'useful' knowledge that allowed people to master their social and physical environments. In Habermas's view, it was threatening to displace two other important forms of knowledge: namely, 'interpretive-hermeneutic' and 'critical-emancipatory' knowledges. The former was geared to understanding the world not explaining it, to values not techniques, to empathy not logic, to means rather than ends. The latter was geared to questioning the world rather than taking it at face value, to assisting oppressed groups rather than regarding their oppression as 'just the way things are'. All three knowledges, Habermas argued, are promoted in a variety of places (for instance, in the family, in businesses, and in civil society). But the education system, he insisted, is one important site where they are formally delivered. Crudely, Habermas argued, the first form of knowledge is taught primarily in the physical sciences, computer studies and business schools, while the latter two are to be found more in the arts/humanities (as in, say, English literature) and in the social sciences (as in, say, Marxist sociology).

I mention Habermas's work because as geography students you are arguably exposed to *all three* of these knowledge types in your studies. As a Bachelor's or Master's student you can, for example, learn how to control floods *and* why you should care for the distant strangers to whom you're connected through trade relationships; or you can learn how to interpret satellite imagery *and* why poor single women are 'spatially entrapped' in inner-city neighbourhoods. A geography degree offers you a remarkable mixture of technical, moral, aesthetic and critical knowledges. What's more, you get a say in the relative balance of these knowledges. The modular nature of most modern degrees means that university students can pick-and-mix course units as they see fit (so long as they do those compulsory modules that make you read a chapter like this one!).

Each of you will have a preference for the kind of knowledge mentioned above you most value in your degree studies. To my mind, the fact that the discipline combines these three knowledge domains is a good thing. But lest it sound like I'm arguing that you and I (as geographers) inhabit the best of all possible educational worlds, I want to sound a more critical note. I argued earlier that all teaching (and all research and knowledge) is political. I further argued that if you, as students, remain unconscious of this fact, then you risk being the objects, rather than the subjects, of your education. But even if you're aware of the political nature of your education (as you hopefully now are after having read this chapter), forces much larger than you threaten to channel your new-found sensibilities in a particular direction. In the next (and penultimate) part of this chapter, I want to say something about these forces and how they might impinge on how you value the mixture of knowledge types you experience during your geography studies.

The Degree Business: Geography as a Commodity?

Academic disciplines have never been insulated from wider governmental, economic or cultural forces. As David Harvey (1996: 95) famously put it, geography 'cannot be understood independently of the . . . societies in which [it is] embedded'. The 'nature' of geography is thus determined not only by internal struggles within the discipline – like those between the aforementioned Gillian Rose and her antagonists – but also by external influences. The geographer Allen Scott (1982) was among the first to analyse these influences. He argued that, though students don't realize it,

their geography education (like all education) has a twin societal function. First, it is designed to make the existing order of things seem
'normal' (a *legitimation* function). Societies, Scott maintained, cannot remain stable if their citizens are constantly questioning and challenging
the social order. Education, in his view, creates more-or-less conformist
people and thus acts as an important glue to hold society together.
Second, Scott also observed that education has an *accumulation* function.
That is, it helps to produce people who will go on to become 'good
workers' with the necessary intellectual and practical skills to expand
their national economy.

Though this may sound like a rather crude argument, Scott was not
suggesting that education is *only* about social control and economic
reproduction. Universities in particular, he argued, have a 'relative autonomy': that is, they are partly independent of governments, businesses
and the wider public. Indeed, it's that very independence that has
allowed many human geographers to develop and teach Habermas's
second and third knowledge types since Scott wrote his essay. But it's
here that I want to make you reflect not just on what you're taught in
your degree but how you value it. For this is not determined by you
alone. Instead, it's partly determined for you by wider societal forces.

Let me explain. Recently, a central government minister in Britain
decried the proliferation of what she called 'Mickey Mouse degrees',
while another was dismissive of what he called 'ornamental subjects'.
The implication was there were 'proper degrees' that all university students should be taking. But what is a 'proper degree'? The answer,
clearly, depends upon what you think the goals of a university education
are. For the ministers in question, it was obvious that 'proper' meant
vocational degrees (like management studies and nursing) or else academic degrees (like geography and physics). Their preference for these
over 'Mickey Mouse degrees' (like soccer studies) rested on the convic-
tion that degrees should equip people to be effective workers for the
future. 'Ah ha!', you might say, 'but there the ministers have got
geography all wrong.' Yes, geography is by and large an 'academic'
discipline (when compared with, say, urban planning). And, yes, geography students tend to be fed enough 'instrumental-technical' knowledge
so that they possess the core transferable skills to be cogs in the machine
that is capitalism. But what the ministers have forgotten, you might be
thinking, is that geography is one of several academic disciplines that
teaches lots of 'non-useful', 'non-utilitarian' knowledge. So geography,
it follows, can allow students to be the kind of people they want to be –
compliant citizens or subversives, depending on the case!

So far so good. But I'd suggest that the counter-view is equally plausible: that the ministers are actually correct. First, it is arguable that universities are a very good place for Habermas's second and third knowledge types to be expressed. Take critical-emancipatory knowledges like feminism, anti-racism and environmentalism. These are definitely *not* the kind of knowledges that satisfy the legitimation and accumulation functions that, in Scott's view, education is made to serve. But by allowing them to be expressed in universities, they are arguably neutered. Students can be 'fed' these knowledges in the 'banking' approach to learning that Watkins bemoans without any visible threat to the societies those knowledges call into question! These students still come out of universities being the kind of people that the ministers so obviously desire. Second, even if this is not true, when geography professors teach about the machinations of the World Trade Organization or why animals have rights, this is not *qualitatively* different from teaching about spatial autocorrelation. To be sure, the *topics* are varied. But, equally, in all three cases students are acquiring transferable, analytical skills that can help them to be accountants as much as anti-road protestors.

Third (and here I turn to those wider forces I promised to talk about above), the way you internalize what you learn as a geography student is structured by your *expectations* of your degree. And your expectations are, in part, socially conditioned – they do not emerge from you alone, fully-formed, as if you existed as a sovereign individual. In a book entitled *Academic Capitalism*, the educational sociologist Sheila Slaughter (1997) has argued that Western universities are losing some of that relative autonomy I mentioned earlier. For her, they are becoming more like businesses whose principal commodities are degrees and whose main market is students. In the UK, for example, government funding for universities has declined, while degree students have, for the first time, been made to pay for their own education. Heavily reliant on student funding to survive, British universities have doubled their intake in little over a decade. Meanwhile, many students are understandably keen to ensure that their money is well spent. For Slaughter, higher education has become a commodity for sale, while graduates have become higher education's commodities.

We can examine Slaughter's thesis with reference to the ideas of the famous nineteenth-century economist Karl Marx. According to him, all commodities – be they shoes or degrees – have a use-value and an exchange-value. The former is a thing's practical utility (what you can do with it), whereas the latter is its monetary worth (how much it can be sold for). The use-value of a degree is thus what you can do with the knowledge that's been accumulated over x number of years, while its exchange-value is how much that knowledge is worth to others (like an employer). In capitalist societies, Marx argued, most people must ultimately sell themselves to others (as labourers) for the bulk of their lives if they are to survive. *Ipso facto*, a university degree clearly contributes to a person's employability. In the 1970s, a French theorist (Jean Baudrillard) added a twist to Marx's analysis of commodities and thereby to this perspective on degrees. He argued that commodities also have a sign-value. This is the symbolic worth of any commodity within a given society. Thus a degree from Harvard clearly has a higher sign-value than one from, say, the University of Nebraska (no offence intended to students of the latter institution!). If we add Marx and Baudrillard together, we can see what Slaughter is getting at: in Western societies, exchange-value and sign-value are given such importance by people that they deeply affect the kind of use-values they look for in commodities. To simplify, in the case of higher education, Slaughter implies that students are now more likely to demand 'relevant' degree programmes (especially from prestigious universities) because this will maximize their employability. And the more that students pay for their own higher education, the more they need to be able to land a well-paid job in the first place. It's a vicious cycle.

Though you may think this argument is overstated, it at least has the virtue of challenging you to reflect on how your attitude to your higher education is, in part, structured for you. Do you view your degree as a means to build your CV or résumé and become properly 'credentialized'? Or do you expect something else (more?) from it? Don't get me wrong, at some level your education *should* help you to secure gainful employment. You *necessarily* have to be concerned with the way the use-, exchange- and sign-value of your degree can combine to launch you into a career. But this doesn't mean that your degree is *simply* a means to the end of employment. And, even if you choose to see it that way, you can also make decisions about what bundle of skills and knowledges to take away from your university studies.

These choices and decisions matter an awful lot – for you, for society and for the discipline of geography in the future. They matter for you for the reasons already mentioned: because they shape the person you become (are becoming) as well as your future (work and non-work) opportunities. They matter for society because society consists, ultimately, of lots of people like you and me: individual agents whose actions, together, constitute, reproduce and sometimes transform the institutions, relationships and rules that structure those actions in the first place. In the parlance of sociologists, agents make societies but societies, in turn, condition what agents can realistically think and do. Though Scott was right that education is often remarkably conformist in its legitimation and accumulation functions, it is also potentially productive of people who are prepared to question the existing social order. What kind of person has your geographical education helped you become and what kind of society will your future actions promote? Finally, your expectations of your degree influence the future of geography as a discipline because they affect us – the people who teach you. As university students you can vote with your feet. If you don't like what we want to teach you, then, ultimately, we won't teach it. David Harvey (2000) provides a graphic example, recounting how few students now take his annual graduate seminar on the work of Karl Marx compared to its popularity in the 1970s – the reason being that most contemporary students regard Marx as either a curiosity or just an out-dated Victorian theorist. If Harvey's experiences were to be repeated in geography departments worldwide, then Marxist geography might, in a few short years, cease to be taught at degree level in any meaningful way. The same is true, in principle, for any aspect of a university geography curriculum: its survival is, in significant part, contingent on students' judgements as to its value.

Conclusion: A Student Manifesto

This chapter, as befits its title, has asked some fundamental questions about who and what geography is for. It has done so at the teaching level because this is a vital, yet under-examined, element of the role the discipline plays in the wider society. The chapter has been written in the active voice because I've wanted to make you reflect on the two sides of the education coin, namely, what you're taught and what you choose to make of that teaching. My argument has been that since all geography teaching is political, it is vital for both university teachers and students to make well-justified choices as to the content and aims of a geographical education. By way of a conclusion, let me offer student readers a mani-festo of sorts to guide your future reflections – and mine – on your undergraduate or postgraduate experience. The manifesto consists of a set of recommendations, as follows:

1   *Never* take what you're taught at face value; *always* scrutinize the choices your professors make in the content and manner of their teaching. This does not mean you should constantly challenge your

professors! But it does mean that you should ask yourself what underlies the syllabus decisions made on your behalf by your teachers.

2   *Routinely* ask yourself what your higher education in general and your geography degree in particular are for. Aim to think clearly about the 'point' of the particular education you're getting, especially when you're invited to make choices about what kinds of course units to take (as opposed to those non-elective units that you must take).

3   *Always* remember that nothing is set in stone: the content of geography teaching is up for grabs when seen in the long term and you, as much as your teachers, have a responsibility to take it in directions that you feel are valuable ones. Though you can do little to alter things during your degree, your comments on course evaluations or those of your student representatives on faculty–student committees can make a difference in the longer term. The trick is to ensure these are considered comments about the substance of your education rather than more trivial things.

Tiring and difficult though it seems at first sight, following these recommendations might just enable you to become an active player in your education and in geography's evolution, rather than an unthinking buyer in the marketplace for degrees.

ESSAY QUESTIONS AND FURTHER READING

1   What is the point of a geographical education? To answer this question, consult Castree (2000), Harvey (1996), Gould (1985), Pepper (1987), Pickles (1986), Powell (1985) and Scott (1982). As you compose your answer, reflect upon the balance of knowledges you've *chosen* to study and *had* to study during your degree – using Habermas's tripartite distinction. Has this balance been a good one for you and, if so, why?

2   What, in your view, are the prime purposes of higher education? The writings listed below by Gitlin, Graham, Harman, Hitchens, hooks, Illich and Slaughter are full of interesting ideas in relation to this question.

REFERENCES

Castree, N. (2000) What kind of geography for what kind of politics? *Environment and Planning A* **32**, 2091–2095.

Demeritt, D. (2001) The construction of global warming and the politics of science. *Annals of the Association of American Geographers* **91**, 307–337.

Gitlin, T. (1995) *The Twilight of Common Dreams: Why America is Wracked by Culture Wars*. Owl Books, San Francisco.

Gould, P. (1985) Will geographic self-reflection make you blind? In Johnston, R.J. (ed.) *The Future of Geography*. Methuen, London, pp. 276–290.

Graham, G. (2003) *Universities: The Recovery of an Idea*. Imprint Academic, Thorverton.

Habermas, J. (1978) *Knowledge and Human Interests*. Polity, Cambridge.

Harman, J. (2003) Whither geography? *Professional Geographer* **55**, 415–421.

Harvey, D. (1996) On the history and present condition of geography. In Agnew, J., Livingstone, D. and Rogers, A. (eds) *Human Geography: An Essential Anthology*. Blackwell, Oxford, pp. 95–107.

Harvey, D. (2000) *Spaces of Capital*. Edinburgh University Press, Edinburgh.

Hitchens, C. (2002) *Letters to a Young Contrarian*. Basic Books, New York.

hooks, b. (1994) *Teaching to Transgress*. Routledge, London.

Illich, I. (1971) *De-Schooling Society*. Calder and Boyers, London.

Pepper, D. (1987) Physical and human integration: an educational perspective from British higher education. *Progress in Human Geography* **11**, 379–404.

Pickles, J. (1986) Geographic theory and education for democracy. *Antipode* **18**, 136–154.

Powell, J.M. (1985) Geography, culture and liberal education. In Johnston, R.J. (ed.) *The Future of Geography*. Methuen, London, pp. 307–325.

Rose, G. (1993) *Feminism and Geography*. Polity, Cambridge.

Scott, A. (1982) The meaning and social origins of discourse on the spatial foundations of society. In Gould, P. and Olsson, G. (eds) *A Search for Common Ground*. Pion, London, pp. 141–156.

Slaughter, S. (1997) *Academic Capitalism*. Johns Hopkins University Press, Baltimore, MD.

Index

Academic Tribes and Territories 27, 30–1, 37
activism 45, 288–9
  epistemological activism 155–7
actor-network theory (ANT) 153–5
Agassiz, Louis 83
Ackerman, Edward 61
ANT (actor-network theory) 153–5
anthropology 129, 177, 189
anti-essentialism 156
anti-globalization 45, 251, 289
Association of American Geographers, The 97

Barnes, Trevor 97, 101, 155, 217, 267–8
Baudrillard, Jean 304
Becher, Tony 27, 30, 31, 35
Berry, Brian J.L. 168–70, 175
Best, Beverley 156
Bhaskar, Roy 73
biogeography 34, 82–3, 172
body 9, 40, 44, 45, 46–9, 52, 158
  embodiment 48, 267
  see also performance
Bunge, William 57, 62, 69–70, 173, 217, 222

Butler, Judith 48, 158
Buttimer, Anne 62, 174

capitalism 44–5, 143, 155
  and education 301–5
Cartesian dualism 33, 145
cartography 33, 181, 189–205, 283, 290
  cartographic visualization 189, 205
  see also maps
causation 29, 83
  cause and effect 83–6
Castree, Noel 152, 154–5, 269, 288
census data 241, 252–4
Chalmers, Alan 59
chaos theory 75, 258
  complexity 75, 80, 83, 86–91
  non-linear dynamics 89–91, 215
Chorley, Richard J. 62, 65, 133, 137, 207–8, 233
Clifford, James 177–9
Clifford, Nick 30
climate change 206–7, 283, 291
  greenhouse effect 209–10
climatology 263
colonialism 43, 45, 49
  and geography 43, 59, 226
communities 39, 45, 50–3
  language communities 268

research communities 9–25, 27, 39, 285–8
Comte, Auguste 66, 69, 70–1 *see also* positivism
complexity 75, 80, 83, 86–91
emergence 86–91
see also chaos theory
computing 18, 189, 194, 280
advances in computing 85, 125, 189, 194, 213
Internet 199–200, 242, 280
Cooke, Ron 280–2
Coppock, J.T. 278, 291
critical human geography 39–52, 153, 158, 160, 291
critical rationalism 68–9, 219, 222 *see also* Popper, Sir K.
critical realism 73–5, 77, 153, 214, 219–20, 265–6 *see also* Sayer, A.
critical theory 300–1
cultural geography 17, 237–8
the cultural turn 267
Cutter, Susan 20, 290
cycle of erosion 123–6, 132–4, 136, 262 *see also* Davis, W.M.

Darwin, Charles 84, 259, 262–3
influence on geography of 84
Davis, W.M. 84, 123–6, 132–4, 136–7, 262 *see also* cycle of erosion
de Blij, H. and Murphy, A.B. 169–71
deduction 69–70, 88, 92, 133
deductive-deterministic modelling 214–15
deductive method 81, 92, 123–4, 135
deductive-nomological method 67–70, 81
Deep Ecology 289
Delaney, David 43
Demeritt, David 221, 298
development studies 105–9
difference 39–54, 143–4
and identity 44–5

and place 44, 47
social construction of 40
discourse 98, 103–5
Doel, Marcus 160–1
Dorling, Danny 197, 201, 244, 248, 256, 291
Driver, Felix 43, 105
dualism 47–9, 145, 154–5, 158, 160–1, 298
mind–body 47–8
mind-matter 141, 145–6
nature–culture 47–8
see also Cartesian dualism

ecology 82–3
economic geography 170–2
education 1–2, 10, 106–9, 162–4, 280, 282–3, 294–307
degree courses 31
purposes of 294–307
Egypt 106–8
emancipatory knowledges 39–52, 300–1, 305–6
emergence 86–91 *see also* chaos
empiricism 59, 67, 70–2, 118, 122, 133, 135, 139, 140–1, 218–19, 238, 260, 263, 266
empirical statistical models 210–14
logical empiricism 133, 140
environmental determinism 104, 119, 134
environmental geomorphology 284
environmentalism 278–9, 303
environmental management 32, 72
human–environment relations 11, 13, 29, 32–6, 57, 60, 119, 134–5
epistemology 17, 84, 101–4, 139, 151, 155–7, 158, 259
and ontology 17, 139–40, 151, 259
equifinality 89–90
e-Science 280
Escobar, Arturo 108–9, 111
essentialism 156, 157, 160
anti-essentialism 156

ethnography 226–39 *see also*
fieldwork
evolution 64–5, 262–3 *see also* Darwin
exceptionalism 119
Hartshorne–Schafer debate 64–5,
72, 100–1, 119, 174
exclusion 39–53
and space 42, 145–6, 200–1
see also power

falsification 68–9, 82, 92, 179, 219, 265
see also critical rationalism,
Popper, Sir K.
feminism 40, 42, 45, 266, 267, 278, 295,
303
feminist epistemology 43, 48
feminist geography 48, 51, 99, 102,
143–4, 266
feminist theory 102–4
see also gender
Ferguson, Rob 30
fieldwork 33, 128, 226–39, 282
in physical geography 33, 128, 232–5
see also ethnography
finitude of scope 161
Foucault, Michel 96, 104, 112, 230–2

Geertz, Clifford 13, 178, 180, 238
gender 40–5, 48, 102, 156, 159, 266
geography and 42–3
gender and knowledge 48, 103
see also body, feminism, masculinism
geocomputation 18, 20, 211, 222, 282
GIS 17, 20, 33, 220, 282
geographical knowledge 167–72,
200–2, 283, 298
Geographical Information Systems
(GIS) 17, 20, 33, 220, 283
geography
arts and sciences in 26–7, 300
definitions of 57, 83, 96, 168–72, 216
degree courses in 31, 294–306
emergence as a discipline 10, 59–60
fragmentation of 9–23

future of 22–3, 36, 50–1, 146, 202–3
history of 42–3, 59–64, 83–6, 125–6,
132–44
as human–environment
relations 11, 13, 29, 332–6, 57, 60,
119, 134–5
in Australia 19, 31
in the United Kingdom 19–20,
297–303
in the United States 106, 132–5
institutionalization of 19, 27, 60
organization of 31
and policy 206–7, 220, 277–92
relations of physical and human
geography 12, 16, 26–37, 63, 127,
145, 262
relations to other disciplines 13, 26
geomorphology 82–91, 124–6, 132–3,
136–40, 216, 232–5
cycle of erosion 84, 123–6, 132–4,
136, 262
environmental geomorphology 284
evolutionary approaches to 262–3
hillslope processes 122, 125–6
history of 125–6, 132–4, 136–40
process-based studies in 21, 65,
85–8, 124–6, 136–40
Gilbert, Grove Karl 84, 137
Gilmore, Ruth Wilson 44
Glissant, Eduoard 48–9
globalization 45, 109, 164
anti-globalization 251, 289
and inequality 251
Golledge, Reginald 97, 217
Graf, William L. 279–80
Gramsci, Antonio 237
Gray, J. 26
Gregory, Derek 70–2, 77, 102, 104,
144, 160, 270
Gregory, Kenneth 31, 32, 270, 284–5
Guelke, Leonard 70–2, 77, 141

Habermas, Jurgen 66, 183, 300–1, 303,
306

Haggett, Peter   62, 65, 69, 122, 207, 222
Haigh, Martin   289
Hannah, Matthew   161
Haraway, Donna   42, 43–4, 103, 111, 267
  situated knowledge   43–4, 51, 103, 267
Harley, J. Brian   164, 181, 200
Hartshorne, Richard   65, 101, 119, 135–6, 173, 174
  Hartshorne–Schaefer debate   64–5, 72, 100–1, 119, 174
Harvey, David   47, 50–1, 62, 68, 69, 73, 140, 142–3, 173, 174, 200–1, 254, 264, 288, 289, 301, 305
Herbertson, Andrew J. 60
Hesse, Mary   208–9
hillslope processes   122, 125–6
Hirschboeck, K.   261, 270
historical materialism   142, 264–5 see also Marxism
history of geography   42–3, 59–64, 83–6, 125–6, 132–44
  and colonialism   43, 45, 49
  quantitative revolution   61–2, 69–70, 85, 140, 168, 207, 215, 220, 226
historical geography   134–5
Holt-Jensen, Arild   71
hooks, bell   296
Horton, R.E.   85, 136
human–environment relations   11, 13, 29, 32–6, 57, 60, 119, 134–5
human geography   39–52, 96–111, 140–4, 258
  divisions within   9–23
  and relations to physical geography   12, 16, 26–37, 63, 127, 145, 262
humanistic geography   62–3, 72–3, 127, 141–2, 174–5, 217, 222
hydrology   122, 136, 261, 279
  streamflow modelling   212–13

hypothesis-testing   67–9, 70–1, 81–2, 178, 190–3, 261

idiographic discipline   64–5, 118–20, 126–8 see also Hartshorne–Schafer debate, nomothetic
imperialism   10, 41–2, 45
induction and inductive method   92, 120–2, 217–20
inequality   105–10, 251
Institute of British Geographers   16, 278
interdisciplinary research   73
interpretation in geography   96–112, 136, 154, 238, 267–8

Johnston, Ron   30, 31, 127, 141
journals in geography   14–16, 30, 172, 284–5, 288

Kant, Immanuel   118–19, 146
Kirkby, Michael J. 125–6, 222
Kuhn, Thomas   189, 266–7, 271 see also paradigms

landscape   21–3, 28, 42, 48–9, 83–5, 86–7, 88–92, 131–5, 137, 141, 222, 226, 232–5, 282
  cultural landscape   134–5
  landscape change   21–3, 83–5, 86, 132–4, 137, 232–5, 237
  landscape imperative   282
landsystems   90
Latour, Bruno   153–5
laws   29, 65–9, 70–1, 73–5, 118–19, 138–9, 154, 207, 209–10, 214, 216, 226, 260, 265–6
  scientific laws   29, 65–9, 154, 209–10, 260
  laws in Geography   65–9, 70–1, 73–5, 118–19, 138–9, 214, 216, 226, 265–6
Lawson, Victoria   105–9
Ley, David   62
Lyotard, Francois   178–9

MacEachren, A.M.   194–7, 200
Mackinder, Sir Halford J. 28, 57, 60
maps   18, 30, 60, 151, 164, 175, 181,
    189–205, 236, 254
  cartography   33, 181, 189–205, 283,
    290
  definitions of   189
  history of   190–3, 194
Marshall, J. 118, 120, 128
Martin, Ron   277, 284, 287–8
Marx, Karl   303–4, 305
Marxism   142–4, 145, 176, 264–5, 266,
    269, 288, 303–4
  Marxism and Darwinism   259, 269
  and geography   142–4, 176, 264–5,
    288, 303
  historical materialism   142, 264–5
masculinism   42 see also gender
Massey, Doreen   33, 40, 270, 286
McDowell, Linda   269–70
meta-narrative   167–83
meta-theory   167–83
Mink, Louis   182–3
Mitchell, Timothy   106–9
modelling   33, 85, 128, 138–9, 206–23
  analogues   208
  computer modelling   85
  deterministic modelling   214–15
  mathematical modelling   210–15,
    221–2
  stochastic modelling   212
  types of modelling   207
  validation of   217–20

natural hazards   32
natural science   20, 34, 60–4, 76, 80, 97,
    133–4, 142, 153, 176, 265, 281, 283
  and social science   20, 64, 97, 142,
    281, 283
nature   33, 40, 47–8, 60, 75, 81, 153–4,
    178, 269
  nature–culture   40, 47–8, 269
  nature–society   153–4
  social construction of   76, 153–4

nomothetic discipline   65, 118–20 see
    also Hartshorne–Schaefer debate,
    laws
non-linear systems   82, 88–91, 215 see
    also chaos
non-representational theory   158–60

objectivity   42, 59, 76, 80, 98, 101, 107,
    135, 152, 284, 295
observation   17, 60, 65–8, 81–2, 117,
    263, 265–6, 269–70
  and theory   84–5, 92, 117, 120–2,
    133, 139, 173, 210, 216, 260–1,
    268
ontology   17, 101, 139, 146, 151, 259 see
    also epistemology
overpopulation   106–9

paradigm   266–7, 271 see also Kuhn
Peck, Jamie   277
performance and
    performativity   158–60 see also
    body, non-representational theory
philosophy   181–2, 259, 264–6 see also
    epistemology, ontology
physical geography   14–16, 26–37,
    63–4, 124–6, 132–4, 136–40, 176–7,
    232–5, 279
  fieldwork in   33, 128, 232–5
  history of   125–6, 132–4, 136–40
  process-studies in   21, 65, 85–8,
    124–6, 136–40
  and relations to human
    geography   12, 16, 26–37, 63, 127,
    145, 262
  and science   27, 80–92, 139
Pile, Steve   157, 160
place   39–41, 44–6, 50–1, 119, 127, 141,
    175, 227, 238
  and difference   39–41, 44–6
policy   104, 210, 220–1, 245
  geography and policy   106, 210,
    220–1, 277–91
politics of education   294–306

Popper, Sir Karl 67, 68, 82, 85, 123, 222, 264
population 106–9, 140, 189, 241–56
 census enumeration 241–56
 overpopulation 106–9
positionality 103, 143
positivism 62, 64, 81–2, 262, 266
 logical positivism 66–7
 Vienna Circle 66–9
post-colonialism
postmodernism 111–12, 143–6, 177–84, 157–8, 268–9, 270
post-structuralism 27, 99, 111–12, 152–7, 160–1
 and geography 99, 160–1
power 40–1, 43–6, 50, 96, 102–4, 107, 163–4, 178, 230–2, 237–8, 299
 and cartography 181, 190–3, 200–2
 and knowledge 43–6, 99, 178, 200–2
 and representation 162–3
prediction 67–9, 88, 117, 121–3, 141, 210–11, 217–18, 260, 265
process 131–47
 process studies in physical geography 21, 65, 85–8, 124–6, 136–40

quantification 69, 84, 140, 241–56
quantitative revolution 61–2, 69–70, 140

race 40–9, 241–9
 racial segregation 242–4
Radical Statistics Group, The 250
realism 151–2, 265 see also critical realism
reductionism 86–8, 139, 173, 211
 in physical geography 86–8
regression 120–2
reflexivity 100–5, 111
region 10–11, 18, 22, 45, 51, 60, 122, 134–5, 168, 175, 280
regional geography 10–11, 65, 119, 134–5, 144, 168–9, 173–5, 216

relativism 151–2
'relevance debate' 278
remote sensing 85
representation 105–6, 151–64, 181
 cartography and 189
 crisis of 268–9
Research Assessment Exercise 14, 24, 285
Rhoads, Bruce 33, 233
Richards, Keith 33, 57, 281, 285
Robinson, A. 196
Rose, Gillian 295
Routledge, Paul 288
Royal Statistical Society, The 251

Said, Edward. W. 235–6
Sauer, Carl O. 32, 134
Savigear, R.A. 125
Sayer, Andrew 73, 214, 265
scale 33, 40, 44–6, 50, 71, 87, 168–9, 208, 214, 218, 263–4, 280
 and difference 44–6, 50
 in physical geography 33, 83–6, 90–1, 122, 138
 timescale 85, 87, 135, 262–3
Schaefer, Frederick K. 64–5, 100–1, 119, 140 see also exceptionalism
sexuality 41, 43, 48, 159
 science 57–77, 80–92, 96–111, 118, 128, 139, 153, 260, 264
 critiques of 70–6, 96–111
 definitions and nature of 57–8, 81
 e-Science 280
 methods of explanation in 66–9, 118, 123
 pure and applied 284
 scientific method 66–9
 sociology of 75, 97, 153–4, 180
 see also spatial science
Science and Technology Studies (STS) 153
'Science Wars' 26, 33, 34, 75
Scott, Allen J. 143, 301–3
self 42, 48

Semple, Ellen C.   84, 104, 134
Shresthsa, Nanda   109
situated knowledge   43–4, 51, 103, 267
Slaughter, Sheila   303–4
Smith, Neil   50–1, 264
Snow, C.P.   26–7
Snow, Dr John   190–3
social constructionism   154, 159, 267
social theory   264–6
Soja, Edward W.   143, 157, 160
Somerville, Mary   28
space   41, 43–6, 74, 101, 142–3, 145,
    157–8, 168, 229–32, 260–1
  space and time   125, 260–1, 263
  spatiality   51
spatial science   61–4, 98–9, 100–1, 140
specialisms in geography   9–23, 29,
    221
Spivak, Gayatri   156
statistics   241–56
Statistics Commission, The   250–1
Strahler, A.N.   61, 85, 136, 138, 140,
    216, 279
structuration   143
subdisciplines in geography   9–23, 39,
    221
systematic geography   11
systems theory   85

theory   67, 82, 120, 123, 125–6, 139,
    140, 144–6, 158, 208, 227–9, 232–3,
    258–70
  definition of   120, 259–61
  meta-theory   167–83

theory and observation   84–5, 92,
    117, 120–2, 133, 139, 173, 210, 216,
    260–1, 268
thirdspace   157
Thrift, Nigel   158–60
Tickell, Adam   9, 22
time   33, 86–90, 119, 124–6, 132–4,
    211–12, 215, 261–2
  evolutionary theories   262–4
  time-dependent processes   86,
    137–8
  time and space   125, 260–1, 263
Trowler, Paul   27, 30, 31, 35
Trudgill, Steve   281, 285
Tuan, Yi-Fu   62, 141
Turner, Billie Lee II   29, 96

Universal Soil Loss Equation   211–12

validation   217–20
verification   67, 217 see also
    falsification
Vienna Circle   66–9 see also
    positivism
virtual reality   199–200

Weber, Max   119, 175, 230–2
White, Hayden   177–9
Woods, Clyde   50
Wooldridge, Stanley   136, 216, 217
World Bank   105, 107
Worsley, Peter   33–4

Zanzibar   235–8